Food and Globalization

Consumption, Markets and Politics in the Modern World

Edited by
Alexander Nützenadel and Frank Trentmann

Oxford • New York

English edition
First published in 2008 by
Berg
Editorial offices:
First Floor, Angel Court, 81 St Clements Street, Oxford OX4 1AW, UK
175 Fifth Avenue, New York, NY 10010, USA

Berg is the imprint of Oxford International Publishers Ltd.

This book has been produced with the support of the Volkswagen Foundation.

Library of Congress Cataloging-in-Publication Data

Food and globalization : consumption, markets, and politics in the modern
world / edited by Alexander Nützenadel and Frank Trentmann.—English ed.
    p. cm.—(Cultures of consumption series)
    Includes bibliographical references and index.
    ISBN-13: 978-1-84520-678-9 (cloth)
    ISBN-10: 1-84520-678-9 (cloth)
    ISBN-13: 978-1-84520-679-6 (pbk.)
    ISBN-10: 1-84520-679-7 (pbk.)
    1. Food industry and trade. 2. Food supply—Political
aspects. 3. Consumption (Economics)—Social aspects. 4. Food habits—
Cross-cultural studies. 5. Globalization—Economic aspects. I. Nützenadel,
Alexander. II. Trentmann, Frank.

    HD9000.5.F584 2008
    382'.41—dc22
                                                        2008005169

British Library Cataloguing-in-Publication Data

A catalogue record for this book is available from the British Library.

ISBN 978 1 84520 678 9 (Cloth)
      978 1 84520 679 6 (Paper)

Typeset by JS Typesetting Ltd, Porthcawl, Mid Glamorgan
Printed in the United Kingdom by Biddles Ltd, King's Lynn

www.bergpublishers.com

Food and Globalization

Cultures of Consumption Series

Series Editor: Frank Trentmann

ISSN 1744-5876

Previously Published Titles

The Making of the Consumer
Knowledge, Power and Identity in the Modern World
Edited by Frank Trentmann

Consuming Cultures, Global Perspectives
Historical Trajectories, Transnational Exchanges
Edited by John Brewer and Frank Trentmann

Fashion's World Cities
Edited by Christopher Breward and David Gilbert

The Khat Controversy
Stimulating the Debate on Drugs
David Anderson, Susan Beckerleg, Degol Hailu and Axel Klein

The Design of Everyday Life
Elizabeth Shove, Matthew Watson, Jack Ingram and Martin Hand

Forthcoming Titles

Governing Consumption
New Spaces of Consumer Politics
Clive Barnett, Nick Clarke, Paul Cloke and Alice Malpass

Alternative Food Networks
Reconnecting Producers, Consumers and Food?
Moya Kneafsey, Lewis Holloway, Laura Venn, Rosie Cox, Elizabeth Dowler and Helena Tuomainen

Contents

List of Tables

List of Illustrations

Acknowledgements

This book would not have been possible without the help and assistance of a number of people and institutions. We are especially grateful to the three foundations that have generously supported research and conferences: the Volkswagen Foundation, the Economic and Social Research Council, and the Arts and Humanities Research Council. In May 2005, the Netherlands Institute for Advanced Study in the Humanities and Social Sciences (Wassenaar) kindly hosted a first meeting to discuss food and globalization. A year later a meeting at Trinity Hall, Cambridge, gave us an opportunity to deepen our discussions. We should like to thank these institutions and their staff for their help and hospitality. As a collective intellectual product, this book also owes a good deal to the many experts who contributed to these workshops: Sunil Amrith, Katarzyna Cwiertka, Victoria de Grazia, Penny van Esterik, Jack Goody, Raymond Grew, Jonathan Morris, Eric Vanhaute, Cormac O'Grada, Anneke van Otterloo, Hans Bass, Boris Loheide, and Laura Rischbieter. Finally, we should like to thank Stefanie Nixon for her help with preparing the final manuscript, Laura Bevir for the index, and everyone at Berg.

Alexander Nützenadel and Frank Trentmann

List of Contributors

William Gervase Clarence-Smith is Professor of the Economic History of Asia and Africa at the School of Oriental and African Studies, University of London. He has published *Cocoa and Chocolate, 1765–1914* (London, 2000), *The Global Coffee Economy in Africa, Asia and Latin America, 1500–1989* (Cambridge, 2003, co-edited with Steven Topik), and *Cocoa Pioneer Fronts since 1800: The Role of Smallholders, Planters and Merchants* (London, 1996, edited). He is currently chief editor of the *Journal of Global History*.

Susanne Freidberg is Associate Professor of Geography at Dartmouth College. She is the author of *French Beans and Food Scares: Culture and Commerce in an Anxious Age* (Oxford, 2004) and the forthcoming *Fresh: A Perishable History* (Cambridge, MA).

Christian Gerlach is Assistant Professor of History at the University of Pittsburgh. Major publications include: *Kalkulierte Morde: Die deutsche Wirtschafts- und Vernichtungspolitik in Weißrußland 1941–1944* ['Calculated Murder: The German Economic and Extermination Policy in Byelorussia'] (Hamburg, 3rd edn, 2000) and *Krieg, Ernährung, Völkermord: Forschungen zur deutschen Vernichtungspolitik im Zweiten Weltkrieg* [War, Food, Genocide: Studies on the German Extermination Policies in the Second World War] (Zurich and Munich, 2nd edn, 2001).

Peter Jackson is Professor of Human Geography at the University of Sheffield. He is currently directing an inter-disciplinary research programme on 'Changing Families, Changing Food', funded by The Leverhulme Trust (http://www.sheffield.ac.uk/familiesandfood). His recent publications include *Commercial Cultures: Economies, Practices, Spaces* (Oxford and New York, 2002, co-editor) and *Transnational Spaces* (London, 2004, co-editor).

Paul H. Kratoska is Managing Director of NUS Press at the National University of Singapore. Publications include *Food Supplies and the Japanese Occupation in Southeast Asia* (London, 1998), *The Japanese Occupation of Malaya: A Social and Economic History* (London, 1998; Japanese translation Tokyo, 2005), and *Asian Labor in the Wartime Japanese Empire* (Armonk, NY, 2005).

Michelle Craig McDonald is Assistant Professor of Atlantic History at Stockton College and was the Harvard-Newcomen Postdoctoral Fellow in Business History at the Harvard Business School in 2005–6. Her publications include: 'The Real Juan Valdez: Opportunities and Impoverishment in Global Coffee,' Harvard Business School (2005) and 'The Chance of the Moment: Coffee and the New West Indies Commodities Trade,' *William and Mary Quarterly* (2005). She is currently writing a book about the importance of West Indian coffee to early American economic development.

Sidney Mintz is Research Professor at Johns Hopkins University in Baltimore. He has written extensively on the social history of the Caribbean region, as well as on the anthropology of food, especially the roles of sugar and soya beans in the global food system. His publications include *Sweetness and Power: The Place of Sugar in Modern History* (New York, 1985) and *Tasting Food, Tasting Freedom: Excursions into Eating, Culture, and the Past* (Boston, 1996). He has co-edited a collection of essays on soya foods, *The World of Soy,* which is now in press; and is at work on a book on the Caribbean region, to be entitled *Three Ancient Colonies.*

Maren Möhring is Lecturer in Modern and Contemporary History at the University of Cologne and Feodor-Lynen-Fellow (2007/08) at the Institute for Social and Economic History at the University of Zurich. Her publications include *Marmorleiber: Körperbildung in der deutschen Nacktkultur (1890–1930)* (Cologne, 2004). She is currently writing a book about foreign cuisine in postwar Germany.

Marina Moskowitz is Reader in History and American Studies at the University of Glasgow. Publications include *Standard of Living: The Measure of the Middle Class in Modern America* (Baltimore, MD, 2004) and *Cultures of Commerce: Representation and American Business Culture* (New York, 2006, co-editor).

Alexander Nützenadel is Professor of European Economic and Social History at the University of Frankfurt (Oder). He is Director of an Interdisciplinary Research Group on the History of Globalization, funded by the Volkswagen Foundation (2004–9). Publications include *Stunde der Ökonomen: Wissenschaft, Expertenkultur und Politik in der Bundesrepublik, 1949–74* (Göttingen, 2005) and *Landwirtschaft, Staat und Autarkie: Agrarpolitik im faschistischen Italien* (Tübingen, 1997).

Dana Simmons is Assistant Professor in the Department of History at the University of California, Riverside. Publications include 'Waste Not, Want Not: Excrement and Economy in Nineteenth-century France' in *Representations* 96 (Fall 2006) and *Bare Minimum: Science, Scarcity and Standards of Living in Modern France* (forthcoming).

Steven Topik is Professor of History at the University of California, Irvine. Recent publications include *The World that Trade Created: Society, Culture, and the World Economy, 1400 to Present* (with Ken Pomeranz) (Armonk, NY, 2nd edn, 2006) and *From Silver to Cocaine, How Latin American Commodity Chains Made the Modern World (1500–2000)* (Durham, NC, 2006).

Frank Trentmann is Professor of History at Birkbeck College, University of London. His recent publications include the volumes of essays *Consuming Cultures, Global Perspectives: Historical Trajectories, Transnational Exchanges* (Oxford, 2006, with John Brewer) and *The Making of the Consumer: Knowledge, Power and Identity in the Modern World* (Oxford, 2006). He is the author of *Free Trade Nation: Commerce, Consumption and Civil Society in Modern Britain* (Oxford, 2008).

Neil Ward is Professor of Rural and Regional Development and Director of the Centre for Rural Economy at Newcastle University. Recent publications include *The Differentiated Countryside* (Routledge, 2003, with Jonathan Murdoch and colleagues) and *Rural Development and the Economies of Rural Areas* (Institute for Public Policy Research, 2006).

Richard Wilk is Professor of Anthropology at Indiana University. Recent publications include *Fast Food/ Slow Food: The Cultural Economy of the Global Food System* (Walnut Creek, CA, 2006) and *Home Cooking in the Global Village: Caribbean Food from Buccaneers to Ecotourists* (Oxford and New York, 2006).

–1–

Introduction

Mapping Food and Globalization

Alexander Nützenadel and *Frank Trentmann*

Food and globalization are inseparable. Since ancient times long-distance trade has involved staple foods and luxury products such as wine, tea, coffee, rice, spices and dried fish. Securing greater access to food was a driving force behind colonial expansion and imperial power. Food markets were the first to become globally integrated, linking distant areas and cultures of the world. In no other area have the interactions between global exchange and local practices been as discernible as in changing food cultures. Food consumption plays a crucial role in the construction of local and national identities and in the changing self-understanding of social groups, migrants and ethnic communities. But food consumption and distribution have also been major arenas of political contention and social protest, ranging from demands for food entitlements and social citizenship to distributional conflicts between producers and consumers, from movements for 'free trade' to those championing 'fair trade'. Yet in much of the literature on 'globalization' food has played little more than a Cinderella role, marginalized and subordinated to the leading cast of financial markets, migration, communication and transnational political cooperation.

Food has played a distinctive role in the course of globalization, arguably at least as important as those of finance, transport, and industry, which tend to dominate writing on the subject. Human societies can manage without money, telegraph cables, or cotton goods. They cannot go without food. Food is a necessity of human existence. It concerns culture as well as calories. In the 1960s Lévi-Strauss singled out food as a way of decoding the unconscious attitudes of a society.[1] Since then, anthropologists have moved away from a structuralist reading of food, stressing instead processes of internal differentiation as well as the influence of external factors like political economy.[2] Food helps to order and classify social norms and relations – dogmeat on a plate may be a sign of impurity and barbarism in some cultures, a tasty delicatessen in another. These orders are unstable, with room for change over time, as well as subject to internal differentiation. Still, it is possible to highlight certain properties and mechanisms that make food such a central and contested medium in the history of globalization. Most existentially, food is about survival. Unlike any other commodity traded through global networks, food becomes part of our human body and selves. 'You cannot eat money' – nor can you eat the electrodes of global communication networks. Food, by contrast, is ingested and digested, its nutrients being broken up and absorbed by our bodies, our organs and tissues. Food becomes part of us. It should therefore not be surprising that food is an important source of personal identity and public anxieties. 'You are what you eat.' In addition to its nutritional qualities, food involves processes of sociability and communication. Food is not just swallowed but prepared, arranged, and displayed. It requires additional receptacles, cooking utensils, and spaces for storage, cooking, and consuming. Eating is a social process that shapes family and communal relations through its changing routines and rituals – the evolution of breakfast, the Thanksgiving Dinner, and so forth. A fast-food restaurant like McDonald's can be a social meeting-place, a space for teenagers to hang out after school, as well as a counter for take-away food.[3] Food, too, involves taste and taste formation. It is a marker of social distinction – hence Michelin stars and celebrity restaurants, and the practice of eating out.[4] It is also a marker of national identity and civilization – the 'white loaf' that in the eighteenth and nineteenth centuries came to symbolize civilization and liberty versus the 'dark bread' of barbarism and dependence. As Felipe Fernández-Armesto has neatly put it, food 'is what matters most to most people for most of the time'.[5]

It is therefore not surprising that food has been at the forefront in the current battle over globalization, with French activist farmers smashing their way into a McDonald's and international social movements agitating against genetically modified crops. Food serves as a lightning-rod for all sorts of anxieties and disquiet about the human condition in late modernity, about the speed of life (fast food/slow food), the dominance of science ('Frankenfoods'), a loss of 'authenticity' and diminishing connection with nature (industrial versus organic foods), the invasion of the local by the global (McDonaldization), and physiological and mental stress and disease (obesity and bulimia). There are arguments to be had about the ways in which public debate about these subjects has become polarized, sometimes at the expense of scientific truth and critical reflection; biotechnology, for example, is not just the result of capitalist monopoly imposed by international corporations but has been promoted by peasants (often illegally) and the governments of India and China – nor are fears of a 'terminator' technology based on fact.[6] But it is equally important to place such current debates in their long-term historical context, to understand the pathways and traditions out of which contemporary concerns and developments arise, and to recognize the multiple and often contradictory dynamics of the pairing of food and globalization in the past.

This volume offers a series of entry points into these dynamics and tensions, with chapters exploring the relationships between empire and markets, migration and identities, global and local actors, and food and ethics. Ironically, the very centrality of food in human history has tended to make our understanding of these global dynamics more, not less, fractured. The study of food is marked by fragmentation, broken up into specialist inquiries into nutrition or status, environment or political economy, food chains or cultural symbolism.[7] This volume tries to move in the opposite direction, creating points of contact between scholars from history, geography, anthropology, and science studies. One genre that has offered a synthetic perspective in recent years has been that of the 'commodity biography'. We now have case studies of sugar, cod, the pineapple and many more which trace the production, diffusion, consumption and representation of a single foodstuff to illuminate the worlds of labour, power, and material culture that helped to circulate it.[8] In this volume, we also include particular foodstuffs, like coffee and rice, but we are equally keen to explore the local and international settings, the political traditions and social and ethnic groups that shaped the way in which food has been produced, traded, consumed, and connected to moralities and identities.

Conversely, a focus on food also helps to provide a more historical perspective on globalization. Globalization has been described as 'a process which embodies a transformation in the spatial organization of social relations and transactions – assessed in terms of their extensity, intensity, velocity and impact – generating transcontinental or interregional networks of activity, interaction, and the exercise of power'.[9] For historians, the critical term in such a definition is 'process'. Instead of invoking an abstract concept or formal model, as often the case in the social sciences, we pursue a more historical understanding of globalization, exploring change over time. Instead of a unique condition or a distinct state of the world, globalization is better conceived as an evolving process.

Globalization is not irreversible, nor does it follow the logic of a simple linear development. Rather, it is historically contingent in several ways. There have been periods of both global integration *and* disintegration in modern history. Even in periods of accelerated global integration, not all parts of society follow the same pattern, nor do all regions and nations of the world. Globalization is uneven and incomplete. It refers to a complex process of inclusion and exclusion, of changing cultural, social and economic hierarchies, which constantly redefine the boundaries between groups, states, and nations.[10]

Nor is globalization a 'natural' or self-sustained process. It depends on the ideas, perceptions and interests of individual and collective actors. And globalization has always faced strong resistance from those who feared negative consequences.[11] Political and social conflicts have been inherent in globalization. We therefore cannot fully understand this phenomenon merely by analysing structural changes and developments such as migration, capital flows or trade. We also must include cultural perceptions, political debates and social practices that shape globalization. As in all historical circumstances, chance, contingency and agency play a major role.

To question a deterministic and teleological reading of globalization also means to accept that this process has not simply been a diffusion of Western hegemony and values. Recent studies by historians and social scientists tend to see globalization as a fragmented and multi-centred process, rather than homogeneous and linear.[12] To speak of 'multiple globalizations' is to recognize the non-Western roots of global trade and the intersections among a diverse set of global circuits. Globalization of food production and consumption has not exclusively been linked to the rise of industrial economies and modern trade institutions in the Atlantic World. There was an Asian path to global food markets too. It is problematic to presume that globalization produces 'a single world market', as classic trade models suggest. Instead, different regional markets emerged that were interconnected but not fully integrated. The development of different trade areas in the contemporary world (the European Union, the North American Free Trade Area, the Association of South East Asian Nations) is evidence of the 'regionalist', multi-centred logic of globalization.

Deciding when to date globalization from is highly controversial. Some authors view the last two decades as a distinct, radically new era marked by the rise of the global economy, the emergence of institutions of global governance, and the global diffusion and hybridization of cultures. From this point of view, contemporary globalization represents a wholly novel condition, which has been linked to the idea of a 'second modernity.'[13] Other scholars have been more prepared to stretch the phenomenon back in time, but want to reserve it to the era of industrial modernity. In this view, the decades before the First World War witnessed a first era of globalization that radically set it aside from earlier economic periods.[14] True, it was only when industrial production, steamships, and telegraphs compressed time and space in the nineteenth century that world markets become integrated, in the sense that a fully shared common market emerged, with converging commodity prices and factor incomes. The years between 1870 and 1914 saw the breakthrough of an integrated global food and trade system. Prices tell the story. In 1870 the price of wheat in Liverpool was still 58 per cent higher than that in Chicago. By 1913 the difference had fallen to a mere 13 per cent. If in the late 1860s it still cost 4*s*. 7½*d*. to ship a quarter of wheat from New York to Liverpool, the price had fallen to 11½*d*. by 1902.[15] To emphasize the very recent history of globalization might be valid in a strictly quantitative sense concerned with market integration and converging prices; it is equally important, though, to recognize that even today the scope and reach of globalization remains uneven, with over a billion people living in abject poverty, excluded from the technological, financial, and consumption networks that connect the better-off populations on this planet. A focus on converging price data can distract unduly from the quantitative as well as the qualitative significance of global cultural and material exchanges in earlier periods. Even in the eighteenth century, global flows of food were not limited to luxury consumption. They involved growing numbers of plebeian European consumers and producers; teapots were a widespread accessory in the lodging-houses frequented by the poor in eighteenth-century London.[16] Nor was trade in food limited to the Atlantic economy or to inter-Asian trade.

Another group of scholars approaches globalization from the very opposite end of human history. Here globalization is a phenomenon as old as humanity itself. Arguably the birth of globalization lies some 60,000 years back when the first humans migrated from Africa. Standardized food production began about 10,000 years before the first McDonald's opened, when wild rye and wheat were brought under cultivation and Asian jungle fowl became the chicken of European consumers.[17]

The focus of this volume is to recover the material, political, and moral dynamics of food, connecting early modern to contemporary processes of globalization. This is not to deny the significance of much older transformations, such as the domestication of animals, when hunters became farmers, the invention of cooking, or the ways in which food became ritualized in the world religions. But the period from the fifteenth to the twentieth centuries saw a qualitative change of a different order, marked by the Columbian exchange, the expansion of transatlantic and Asian commercial and imperial networks, the spread of new technologies and knowledge, and the push of industrialization – it was a time when transport and communication systems bridged spatial distance and when world-wide mass migration changed societies and cultures, fostering a world of unprecedented global exchange of goods, services and people.

The trade in spices, sugar, and later wheat expanded by leaps and bounds, tying together distant regions in new networks of production, trade, and consumption. Trade in pepper and other spices between Asia and Europe increased in the sixteenth century, when direct maritime contacts were established between the two continents. In 1500, the amount of spices imported was roughly 2,400 tons. By 1700 it had risen to 8,500 tons.[18] Even more important for European consumers were sugar imports, which in the same period increased from a few tons to about 80,000 tons. By 1700, sugar imports (measured in terms of volume) represented about 75 per cent of all agricultural imports from the tropical and semi-tropical regions. Initially a drug and a luxury product, sugar spread to all social groups in the seventeenth century. In the course of the nineteenth century, exports of crops from the southern hemisphere to Europe increased rapidly. While in 1790 their overall quantity amounted to roughly 400,000 tons, exports from the 'Third World' had reached 18.5 million tons on the eve of the First World War.[19] Most of this expansion took place after 1850, when European demand for staple food rose dramatically and declining transportation costs made intercontinental trade more profitable. Between 1850 and 1913, world trade in agricultural products grew at a faster pace then ever before, at an average annual rate of 3.44 per cent. In 1913, food accounted for 27 per cent of world exports.[20]

Numbers, however, only tell part of the story of what was a new phase in globalization. The trade in new foods went hand in hand with processes of imperial expansion and migration, new systems of production, distribution and consumption, tensions between cultural imperialism, on the one hand, and hybridization and resistance on the other, the rise of new organized producer and consumer agencies, battles between free trade and protectionism, emerging new knowledge regimes in nutrition and science, and a reshaping of social and ethnic identities. It was the moral geography of food that was transformed in this period, as much as the price on the world market.

Empire, Markets and Power

Current political battles over food and globalization are nothing new. From the outset, global food exchanges have been embedded in imperial and economic power structures. The discovery of the New World, the expansion of Europe and the emergence of modern colonial systems in the late fifteenth century created intensive networks of food and trade between the Americas, the Caribbean and the metropoles of Europe. The Atlantic World was the centre-stage of an integrated system of food chains linking the plantation economy of the Caribbean, Brazil and Peru with European consumers – the 'first planetary empires', in Sidney Mintz's apt phrase.[21] In Southeast Asia, the Islamic World and parts of Oceania, European commercial organizations like the Dutch and the English East India Companies organized many aspects of colonial trade and governance long before formal colonial governments were established. As William Clarence Smith shows in his contribution, trade with spices, tea, coffee beans or cacao were at the core of a rapidly growing commercial space that stretched from China across Vietnam and Arabia to Europe and the New World. Europe played an important role in these trade networks with rapidly expanding consumer markets, but it was not the only player. Other regions mattered too.

The recent debate about the cause of the 'great divergence' between the West and the East – that is, why the European and North American economies began to pull ahead in the course of the nineteenth century – has focused fresh attention on the relationship between the wealth of nations and colonial exploitation.[22] This debate, of course, has a long history, stretching back three centuries to the controversy between mercantilists and the advocates of a new science of political economy, most famously Adam Smith in his *Wealth of Nations* (1776), which emphasized the gains from trade and the costs of territorial empire. More recent revisionist writers like Ken Pomeranz have emphasized the role of a slaved-based system of extraction in the colonies in the economic growth of the imperial core.[23] How much slavery and imperial exploitation explain the growth of European as opposed to Asian economies is a subject of ongoing debate.[24] Still, there can be little doubt that consumer societies in Britain, France or the Netherlands would have developed quite differently without colonies. In his contribution, Mintz links the rise and transformation of colonial regimes to the emergence of a 'global food system', a process that evolved in several stages over the past five hundred years. Colonialism bequeathed a long and profound legacy to international food regimes. In the nineteenth century, mass migration led to the reorganization of agriculture in the Old and the New World. In the third quarter of the nineteenth century, the spread of free trade in Europe, starting with the repeal of the corn laws in Britain (1846) and then spreading to continental Europe and beyond, opened the expanding consumer markets of the industrial nations to the rest of the world.[25] At the same time, the more open liberal commercial order eliminated the preferential access of British West Indian sugar planters, who faced growing competition from the expanding beet sugar industry in Europe.

This was only one facet of a dramatic change in the relationships between European metropoles and their colonies. The 'colonial settler regime' began to supplant the older colonial system of exotic goods and spices. In the second half of the nineteenth century overseas production of wheat and meat rapidly expanded within a global trade network. This expansion was not located in the tropics or subtropical zones but took place in temperate climates in the former colonies of the European settlement in the United States, Argentina and Chile, and in the remaining white-settler colonies of the British Empire, like Canada, Australia, and New Zealand. At no stage in the late nineteenth century was this global economy of food ever fully liberal or open; Canada and Australia as well as the United States retained important tariffs and trade barriers. Still, technological advances in shipping and refrigeration facilitated a thickening of commercial ties between the New and the Old Worlds. And, after the 'great depression' in the late nineteenth century, the decade before the First World War witnessed intensified global flows of finance and services.

This era of 'liberal' expansion came to an abrupt end with the implosion of global markets during the First World War, the world depression (1929–31) and the Second World War. A new food system now emerged, marked by three distinctive characteristics. First, state regulation assumed a more decisive role, aimed at protecting domestic producers, but also trying to regulate international flows of food. Second, there was a new awareness of global imbalances between food production and human needs, together with growing attention to the problem of distribution between uneven regional demand and supply. And finally, the food sector was evolving into a highly commercialized industrial system, a significant stepping-stone towards what in recent years has become a 'life sciences integrated' system.

These global processes had very different outcomes in different regional systems and cultural settings. This is the main theme of Rick Wilk's chapter on the cultural and economic significance of European food exports to Belize.[26] Unlike other colonies of the Caribbean, Belize was not part of the regional plantation economy. Traditionally it was an exporter of timber. Since the first European settlements, Belize was therefore highly dependent on food imports from Europe and later from the United States. Even though food trade, as well as the banking system, was almost entirely in the hands of foreigners and multinational food processing companies, Wilk rejects the traditional narratives of globalization such as 'McDonaldization'. These often presume an 'authentic' local cuisine was submerged and displaced by foreign or 'global' cultural and culinary trends. According to Wilk, the increasing influence of European products (and often, re-imported 'colonial' goods) was not necessarily an expression of colonization and foreign dominance. Rather it reflected a complex setting of ethnicity, social status and rank which classified both people and their cuisines. Consuming foreign products was thus a common practice of those social and ethnic groups who were keen to acquire higher status. At the same time, European tastes and technologies were regarded as markers of progress and civilization that determined the position of each colony in the political geography of empire. The role of 'distinction' and conspicuous consumption in cementing status orders has been well known to social scientists since Thorstein Veblen and Pierre Bourdieu.[27] There is no reason to limit this analysis to classes within a national society. We may extend it to an imperial economy of distinction. Here was one reason why efforts of the imperial metropolis to render agriculture in the colony more self-sufficient and prosperous failed. These imperial dynamics continue to cast a shadow over colonial food cultures long after political independence. Wilk identifies a destructive cycle that continues to the present, as Belizean supermarkets sell large quantities of foreign food, while local producers are unable to compete with highly subsidized farmers from the North.

The formation of global food markets was rooted in regional dynamics and market integration. Trade stretched well beyond imperial or colonial settings. The emergence of rice production and trade in Southeast Asia was an exercise in economic regionalization, as Paul Kratoska shows in his contribution to this volume.[28] Already in the early twentieth century, the economic zone extended from southern China to India, with territories under British, Dutch, French, American, Thai and Chinese rule, accounting for more than 80 per cent of global rice exports. This expansion was fuelled by a rising demand for rice in Asia, Europe and North America. Massive investments in irrigation and infrastructure, fostered by French and British colonial offices, as well as the immigration of Chinese labour, made rice plantations highly productive. Even though tariffs and other market barriers existed, free trade advanced thanks to the support of most regional powers and colonial administrations. As in the West, the Great Depression of the 1930s brought to an end a relatively peaceful era of commercial exchange and economic development in Southeast Asia. Together, aggressive Japanese imperialism and new nation-building hampered a swift reconstruction of the Southeast Asian trade zone. The relation between colonialism and globalization was ambivalent and contradictory. In some cases, imperial rule was a driving force in expanding markets and integration, while in others it destabilized long-established economic relations and trade institutions.

A good example of how decolonization could lead to the internationalization of commodity markets is provided by Steven Topik's and Michelle Craig McDonald's chapter on 'Americanizing Coffee: The Refashioning of a Consumer Culture'.[29] With the War of Independence, coffee rapidly supplanted tea in the newly independent United States of America, and became a symbol of national autonomy and anti-colonialism against the British Empire. Coffee-drinking was regarded as an act of patriotism and freedom. Colonial embargoes and commercial policies redirected

American coffee importers from the Caribbean to Brazil. Economic relations between the United States and Brazil deepened once American merchants and shippers supplanted the British in the Atlantic slave trade, integrating Brazil and Africa into a United States-based triangular trade after Brazilian independence in 1822. Ironically, a plant which for generations had stood for slavery and exploitation now became the national symbol of economic independence and political freedom. At the end of the nineteenth century, the United States imported more than one-third of global coffee production, compared to a mere 1 per cent in 1800. The assimilation of coffee into the daily life of Americans was further reinforced by the arrival of immigrants from continental Europe, where coffee played an important part in consumption.

Migration and Diffusion

Even though colonial empires were a driving force behind globalized markets, transnational food chains often evolved along different pathways. Spatial diffusion was not always driven by imperial power, trade or market regulation. Migrants have always been important agents in the transnational circulation of food. Travellers, merchants and migrant labour brought with them new products and cuisines, and changed local food habits and consumption patterns. In addition to the growing variety of supplies and consumer choices, 'food migration' played a fundamental role in redefining ethnic relations, cultural identities and national representations. Maren Möhring's case study is West Germany, where ethnic food was almost unknown until the 1960s.[30] The rising demand for labour during the economic boom of the 1950s and 1960s brought millions of migrants from Southern and Southeast Europe to the Federal Republic. Many former 'guest workers' opened restaurants and snack bars. Within a few years, the culinary landscape in West Germany was transformed, as 'exotic' foodstuffs and foreign 'national' cuisines sprang up. Möhring points to the ambivalences in the 'ethnicization' of food. On the one hand, after years of being relatively sheltered from more global food cultures, West German society was opening up to foreign cuisines and lifestyles. For many migrants, establishing an ethnic restaurant brought new opportunities for income and upward social mobility. However, Möhring cautions us against seeing here simply a happy story of peaceful multiculturalism and cultural hybridization. Commodifying and consuming 'the other' has often been a source of exploitation and racial stereotyping. Dining out in an ethnic restaurant produced specific forms of class, ethnic and gender differences. Like Topik and Craig McDonald for the early United States, Möhring argues that the emergence of distinct national or regional cuisines is an intrinsic effect of globalization.

In her analysis of the seed trade in nineteenth-century America, Marina Moskowitz rearranges several other pieces of the conventional picture of globalization.[31] They concern scale. Globalization is often equated with the rise of large, corporate, highly integrated sectors of mass production and retailing. True, agriculture in the United States was highly integrated in the global trade networks of the late nineteenth century. American farmers exported an increasing share of staple foods like meat, maize and wheat to European markets. Standardized large-scale agriculture and high vertical integration of food and transportation industries developed in this period, giving American farmers a lead over European producers. On the other hand, this period also witnessed a rapid expansion of market gardening and of the local production of fresh produce in the United States. The trade in seeds and local horticulture increased rapidly thanks to the growing demand of private households and small-scale farmers who looked for greater variety. While the seed trade extended the food chain, it also fostered a new awareness of local quality and freshness. Instead of resulting in global concentration and convergence, therefore, the provision of fresh produce showed the ways in which global dynamics were balanced by local forces. Transcontinental and transnational exchange lengthened the season for which certain commodities were available, and provided exotic options that might not be grown in particular local environments. The case of fresh produce provision in post-bellum America demonstrates the parallel evolution of local and global scales of provisioning. It also reveals the limited abilities of the global to reorder the local, and the specifically local natural and cultural factors that contain and condition global influences.

Global Actors

What sets the decades after 1880 apart from earlier periods was a much greater level of global institutionalization.[32] National governments began to regulate the production, trade and consumption of food more systematically. This was in part to protect national producers against foreign competition. After the mid-Victorian era of greater free trade and open markets, many countries – including the United States and most of continental Europe – raised their import duties and introduced other non-tariff barriers. Food regulation now included veterinary and food controls in order to contain the spread of epizootics and plant diseases. However, as Alexander Nützenadel shows in this volume, national protectionism and international cooperation were sometimes two sides of the same coin.[33] As in other fields of political activism, rural producers and their political spokesmen set up their own international organizations in order to create and shape international rules and market regulations. This did not automatically mean that domestic producers were just looking for new modes of protectionism. Alongside domestic protectionist politics, agrarian producers also pursued an international strategy for stabilizing food markets. Here the enemy was not the consumer, but industrial and financial cartels. The International Institute in Rome, founded in 1905, for example, looked towards a fair system of global trade by eliminating the market power of international banks and industrial trusts.

This vision of a global trade system was harshly disrupted by the First World War. The Great War is often considered to mark the end of the 'first globalization', since it destroyed the international networks of trade, finance and governance that had expanded during the nineteenth century. But this is only one part of the story. The war also made Europeans painfully aware of how much they were dependent on food imports from overseas. Food supply was a decisive factor in the war. After more than half a century of relative abundance, mass starvation returned to Europe. For the first time in generations, industrialized countries faced food shortages and famines. Enormous bureaucratic organizations and rationing systems were established to handle the growing problems of supply and distribution of staple foods. Decreased production in the European theatre of war and the loss of Russia as an exporter of grains created a large demand for agricultural exports from overseas. Against the backdrop of war, a 'new internationalism' began to emerge that, instead of free trade and the free flow of goods, looked towards international mechanisms of coordinating food, of eliminating cycles, and of stabilizing markets. Here was a shift towards a 'visible hand' that it was hoped would align the interests of European consumers and overseas producers in a new era of global governance that would continue to influence social movements, thinkers, and politicians in the new global era of the United Nations after the Second World War.[34]

Nutrition was a crucial component in this 'new international' view of the global. As Dana Simmons shows in her chapter, war and genocide created the conditions for nutrition to become a science of social hygiene.[35] While, during the nineteenth century, a chemical understanding of nutrition had dominated scientific debates, malnutrition was now studied as a medical pathology. Nutrition scientists turned away from chemical equations in favour of aetiologies. Medical doctors, not chemists, shaped this new field. Doctors in European cities, ghettos, and internment and concentration camps sought to identify and track the physiological and moral symptoms of a newly classified disease: malnutrition. Nutritional science, however, was not a self-contained European invention. Its formation was closely linked to colonial practices and experiences in countries that Europeans would come to label the 'Third World'. Colonial methods entered Europe precisely at the moment when mass starvation struck the heart of the European empires.

Simmons' discussion offers further evidence that the era of the World Wars was not – as is often suggested – a period of mere de-globalization and isolation. True, aggressive nationalisms and autarky characterized agrarian policy, food regimes and trade organization during the inter-war years. However, self-sufficiency was never fully achieved, trade and exchange remained vital and knowledge about nutrition and starvation circulated among social experts and medical scientists. Moreover, the experience of hunger and deprivation created new forms of international solidarity that shaped discussions on international food aid during and after the Second World War.

With the foundation of the Food and Agriculture Organization (FAO) at the end of the Second World War, international food aid was institutionalized. During the 1950s and 1960s, however, the fight against hunger in the 'Third World' was supplanted by a broader approach of development policy, based on industrial technology, capital transfer and production-oriented concepts of a 'green revolution'. As the limits of large-scale production became evident (especially in Africa), the FAO and other Non-Governmental Organizations launched a new programme that aimed to help the rural poor become independent producers. Up to 100 million small subsistence producers – one-fifth of the planet's population – were to be integrated in a market economy, not only by selling their products but also by modernizing their production with high-yielding seeds, fertilizers, machinery, pesticides and irrigation. This moment of attempted economic 'globalization' seemed an ideal opportunity for the providers of such input packages – industrial and often transnational companies – to expand their markets. According to Gerlach, however, the FAO's Industry-Cooperative Programme (1966–78) was ultimately an exercise in the limits of global governance.[36] But the experience of recent decades shows that ambitious goals for increasing staple food production in Africa and reducing world hunger are difficult to achieve.

Food Chains and Moral Geographies

The topics of world hunger and the science of starvation are a reminder that, in modern and contemporary history, food and globalization are about ethics as much as about taste and identity. This ethical dimension has played itself out as a tension between two developments. One, that ties in well with the role of FAO and a global action plan to overcome world hunger, is that of a new-found sense of global responsibility towards distant others. Just as globalization has bridged earlier spatial and temporal distances and the food chain has become longer and longer, so the ethical chain of caring has become more extensive. This ethical stretching concerns both metrics – a concern for the welfare of distant producers by Fair Trade supporters – and a contraction of the distance between humans and the animal kingdom and the environment as a whole – as in the widening of the circle of responsibilities towards animals amongst vegetarians or a concern with sustainability amongst environmentally conscious consumers. Enlightenment thinkers like Adam Smith were already pondering the effect of a commercializing world on moral awareness and obligations towards distant others.[37] But this was always only one side of the ethical dynamics of food in globalization. For global integration also sparked anxieties about vulnerability and dependence. To open one's doors to cheap food from distant sources, in this view, might bring short-term benefits but be a road to disaster and famine in the long run. Global opening could thus appear as a denial of the responsibility towards one's compatriots. It was no coincidence that the period of intense global integration before the First World War was followed by one of blockade and hunger in which the control of food became a weapon of total war. In modern history, the relationship between food and globalization is an ebb and flow between these two ethical impulses, between opening out and caring for distant others, on the one hand, and focusing on the nearest and dearest closest to home, on the other.

In the last twenty years, the 'food chain' has developed into one of the most successful ways of thinking and talking about food, both in the social sciences and in public discussion and policy more broadly. The 'food chain' took off from the idea of the 'commodity chain'.[38] Its main attraction was to provide a way of following food from farm to fork. Instead of dividing up the study of food into sectors – one concerned with farmers, another with retailers, yet another with customers – the 'food chain' captured spatial continuity, and with it what happened to food at which point of the chain, when and where value was added, and when and where profit was extracted.

The question is to what degree food can be usefully understood in terms of a more generic commodity chain. As we have already stressed, food is a highly peculiar commodity, or to be precise it is a bundle of quite different foodstuffs with highly specific values, associations, and identities attached to them. Food carries moral geographies that set it apart from most other goods that circulated through networks of trade. Of course, there are industrial goods like cars to which many people attach a strong sense of national pride; in many European countries, customers tend to buy a national make. Still, few customers would be especially interested in, say, where the rubber in the tyres came from. Foodstuffs, by contrast, raise sensitive questions of authenticity: is it 'genuine' German beer, or not; are these 'real' English strawberries or not; is it 'authentic' Italian coffee or not. Of course, many of these claims to authenticity are products of what Hobsbawm and Ranger in a different context called 'invented traditions'.[39] Significantly, these authentication regimes arose in the same period as nations invented their own traditions, in the second half of the nineteenth century. Nonetheless, the concern with authenticity registers profound concerns about risk and trust.

Where our food comes from and whether our position in the global food economy is secure is an anxiety that has distant historical precursors. They take us back to the ambivalent relationship between empire and globalization. Peter Jackson and Neil Ward use the case of sugar to flesh out the moral geographies of a food with a mixed identity.[40] Sugar comes in two forms: cane sugar, mainly grown in the Caribbean and parts of Latin America, and beet sugar, mainly grown in Europe. Instead of following a mechanistic food chain approach, Jackson and Ward are interested in the meanings that are created in and through sugar by consumers and producers – and the historical meanings that are suppressed or redefined. More than most foodstuffs, sugar raises profound questions about responsibility and care – both about the current plight of farmers and about historical responsibilities towards a food regime with the blood of slavery on its hands. In recording how beet sugar farmers talk about their place in the subsidized sugar regime of the European Union, they reveal the moral geography of the food chain, with its assumptions about entitlements, what are fair or unfair practices, and the very restricted sense of personal responsibility towards the fate of distant, disadvantaged cane sugar producers. These moral geographies show the danger of thinking about 'space' as a separate category from 'place'. What emerges instead is a more relational view of space, where local and global scales and responsibilities mutually condition each other. Far from being the victim of the 'global', the 'local' helps to give the global its particular meaning.

Suzanne Friedberg unravels further the multiple and connected histories of transnational food trade.[41] Applying a cultural economy approach to the export of vegetables from sub-Saharan Africa to Europe, she moves our understanding away from a crude model of a North–South divide. Friedberg reveals the importance of particular local factors and settings, including the particularities of the vegetables themselves; in Burkina Faso, exporters stayed in the trade in part because it raised them to the high status of patrons of the peasantry. But she also highlights the particular local demands and management regimes that British supermarkets (buying vegetables from Zambia) bring to bear on farmers compared to their French counterparts in Burkina Faso. British retailers have applied to local farmers standards of transparency and social responsibility that require them to pay for raising their standards to 'best practice'. There is an irony here that shows the dialectics at work between ethics and globalization. Global integration has raised awareness amongst consumers in the North about social, ethical, and environmental standards of production. At the same time, these same standards have become the management tools used by supermarkets and retailers to enhance their profit margin *vis-à-vis* local producers in the South.

This moral story has many twists and turns that run through the history of food and globalization. A good deal of the contemporary excitement and engagement about 'reconnecting' consumers in the North with producers in the South rests on a dubious view of history. One popular view is that movements like Fair Trade are an opportunity to 'remoralize' the world economy, to tap into the caring concerns of good consumers to attain a better deal for distant producers exploited by ruthless, unaccountable corporations. In the concluding chapter to this volume, Frank Trentmann follows the different kinds of 'moral economies' through which consumers and producers have been connected in the modern period.[42] 'Moral economy', in the singular, became a popular category in the 1960s, as much an ideological weapon as a scholarly term of analysis. It conjured up a lost world of mutual obligations and communal solidarity that were supposedly ripped apart by modern capitalism and replaced by a de-moralized science of liberal economics that would underpin the global world economy. However, to view modern history as a watershed between a moral era and a demoralized era where only capital and profit matter is deeply problematic. 'Traditional' societies are not necessarily free of commercial and profit relations, nor are 'modern' societies just material vessels drained of ethics and reciprocity. Trentmann follows the different moral visions guiding consumers in the modern world. One hundred years ago, at the crest of an earlier wave of globalization, millions of organized consumers in Britain rallied to Free Trade (not Fair Trade) as the highroad of citizenship, human solidarity, and universal peace. Cheap food in a globally integrated market would create strong and peaceful relations between consumers in the metropole and distant producers. Ironically, it was the popular imperialism of Conservative women in the inter-war years that replaced this liberal culture with a new moral universe that, in parts, anticipated the outlook of the Fair Trade that is familiar today. Consumers, Conservative housewives preached, had the purchasing power, indeed the duty, to buy from their cousins and distant producers in the colonies. This brand of ethical consumerism was coloured by race and imperialism, but it equally looked towards 'reconnecting' consumers and producers, seeking to channel ethics and moral obligations into a direct relationship between consumers and producers, instead of a more diffused network of market relations.

Food provides useful insights in the complex genealogy of globalization. This book is an effort to bring together perspectives from a variety of disciplines that have recently been engaged in this debate: history and anthropology, geography and culture studies, economics and sociology. By drawing on case studies from different historical epochs and geographic areas, this volume sheds light on how the process of historical change is spelt out in economic, cultural and political perspectives. It reconsiders the traditional division between eras of globalization and de-globalization by exploring the persistence of food markets and the rescaling of consumer cultures in past and present. The global transformations of food exchanges often followed different trajectories from those of other commodity markets, since they were embedded in complex settings of colonial expansion, national sovereignties and competing moral geographies. It is therefore essential to explore the different levels of global enmeshment in each domain. This volume is far from giving a final answer to this ambitious research agenda. It aims, however, to deliver a more systematic understanding of the nature and legacies of global food transformations in the modern world.

Notes

1. C. Lévi-Strauss, *The Raw and the Cooked* (New York, 1970).
2. J. Goody, *Cooking, Cuisine and Class* (Cambridge, 1982).
3. J. L. Watson (ed.), *Golden Arches East: McDonald's in East Asia* (Stanford, CA, 1997).

4. The literature on food, status and taste, and on the practice of eating out is vast. A good starting point is A. Warde, *Consumption, Food and Taste: Culinary Antinomies and Commodity Culture* (London, 1997). See also the anthropological perspectives in P. Caplan (ed.), *Food, Health and Identity* (London, 1997); P. Weissner and W. Schiefenhovel (eds), *Food and the Status Quest: An Interdisciplinary Perspective* (Providence, RI, 1996).

5. F. Fernández-Armesto, *Food: A History* (London, 2002), p. xiii. Additional overviews can be found in K. F. Kiple, *A Movable Feast: Ten Millennia of Food Globalization* (Cambridge, 2007); M. Montanari, *The Culture of Food* (Oxford, 1994); R. Tannahill, *Food in History* (London, 1973).

6. See R. J. Herring, 'Why did "Operation Cremate Monsanto" Fail? Science and Class in India's Great Terminator-Technology Hoax', *Critical Asian Studies*, 38(4) (2006): 467–93.

7. As a rare example of interdisciplinary cooperation see R. Grew (ed.), *Food in Global History* (Boulder, CO, 1999).

8. Sidney W. Mintz, *Sweetness and Power: The Place of Sugar in Modern History* (New York, 1985); M. Kurlansky, *Cod: A Biography of the Fish that Changed the World* (London, 1998); M. Kurlansky, *Salt: A World History* (New York, 2002); F. Beauman, *The Pineapple: King of Fruits* (London, 2005); M. Redclift, *Chewing Gum: The Fortunes of Taste* (London, 2004).

9. D. Held, D. Goldblatt, A. McGrew and J. Perraton, *Global Transformations: Politics, Economics and Culture* (Stanford, CA, 1999), p. 16.

10. M. H. Geyer and J. Paulmann, 'Introduction: The Mechanics of Internationalism', in M. H. Geyer and J. Paulmann (eds), *The Mechanics of Internationalism: Culture, Society, and Politics from the 1840s to the First World War* (Oxford, 2001), p. 6.

11. See A. Hurrel and N. Woods (eds), *Inequality, Globalization and World Politics* (Oxford, 1999); E. Rieger and S. Leibfried, 'Welfare State Limits to Globalization', *Politics & Society* 26 (1998): 363–90; J. Brewer and F. Trentmann (eds), *Consuming Cultures, Global Perspectives: Historical Trajectories, Transnational Exchanges* (Oxford and New York, 2006).

12. A. Appadurai, *Modernity at Large* (Minneapolis, 1996); A. Amin and N. Thrift, *Globalization, Institutions and Regional Development in Europe* (Oxford, 1994); J. A. Guidry, M. D. Kennedy and M. N. Zald (eds), *Globalizations and Social Movements: Culture, Power, and the Transnational Public Sphere* (Ann Arbor, MI, 2000).

13. U. Beck, *What is Globalization?* (Cambridge, 1999).

14. M. Geyer and C. Bright, 'World History in a Global Age', *American Historical Review* 100 (1995): 1034–60; K. H. O'Rourke and J. G. Williamson, 'When did Globalisation Begin?', *European Review of Economic History* 6 (2002): 23–50.

15. W. W. Rostow, *The World Economy* (London, 1978), pp. 161ff. For the importance of shipping, see K. O'Rourke and J. G. Williamson, *Globalization and History: The Evolution of a Nineteenth-Century Atlantic Economy* (Cambridge, MA, 1999).

16. J. Styles, *The Dress of the People: Everyday Fashion in Eighteenth-century England* (New Haven, CT, 2007).

17. See, most recently, K. F. Kiple, *A Movable Feast: Ten Millennia of Food Globalization* (Cambridge, 2007).

18. C. H. Wake, 'The Changing Pattern of European Pepper and Spice Imports, 1400–1700', *Journal of European Economic History*, 8 (1979): 361–403.

19. P. Bairoch, *Economics and World History* (Chicago, 1995), p. 93.

20. W. A. Lewis, 'The Rate of Growth of World Trade 1870–1913', in S. Grassman and Erik Lundberg (eds), *The World Economic Order: Past and Prospects* (London, 1981); see also: G. Federico, *Feeding the World: An Economic History of Agriculture, 1800–2000* (Princeton, NJ, 2005); O'Rourke and Williamson, *Globalization*.

21. Sidney Mintz in this volume.

22. See P. Bairoch, *Economics and World History: Myths and Paradoxes* (Chicago, 1995), pp. 57–98; P. O'Brien, *Colonies in a Globalizing Economy, 1815–1948*, Working Papers of the Global Economic History Network (GEHN), 08/04, 2004.

23. K. Pomeranz, *The Great Divergence: China, Europe, and the Making of the Modern World Economy* (Princeton, NJ, 2000).

24. P. C. C. Huang, 'Development or Involution in Eighteenth-Century Britain and China? A Review of Keith Pomeranz's "The Great Divergence: China, Europe, and the Making of the Modern World Economy"', *The Journal of Asian Studies*, 61(2) (2002): 501–38; P. Parthasarthi, 'The Great Divergence', *Past and Present* 176(1) (2002): 275–93.

25. P. Bairoch, 'European Trade Policy, 1815–1914,' in P. Mathias and S. Pollard (eds), *Cambridge Economic History of Europe*, VIII (Cambridge, 1989), pp. 1–160. For the European free trade moment and the collapse of the Cobden–Chevalier treaty network, see P. Marsh, *Bargaining on Europe: Britain and the First Common Market, 1860–92* (New Haven, CT). Just how much material difference the most-favoured-nation-treatment in these treaties made for international trade is a subject of debate. For a revisionist view, assigning it at best a marginal role, see O. Accominotti and M. Flandreau, 'Does Bilateralism Promote Trade? Nineteenth Century Liberalization Revisited', Centre for Economic Policy Research Discussion Paper no. 5423 (January 2006).

26. Rick Wilk in this volume.

27. T. Veblen, *The Theory of the Leisure Class: An Economic Study of Institutions* (New York, 1953; 1st edn, 1899); P. Bourdieu, *Distinction: A Social Critique of the Judgment of Taste* (Cambridge, MA, 1984).

28. Paul Kratoska in this volume.
29. Steven Topic and Michelle Craig McDonald in this volume.
30. Maren Moehring in this volume.
31. Marina Moskowitz in this volume.
32. See A. Iriye, *Global Community: The Role of International Organizations in the Making of the Contemporary World* (Berkeley, CA, London, 2002).
33. Alexander Nützenadel in this volume.
34. For this shift, see Trentmann, *Free Trade Nation* (Oxford, 2008). For the pressure of war and different food regimes, see A. Offer, *The Agricultural Origins of the First World War* (Oxford, 1991); F. Trentmann and F. Just (eds), *Food and Conflict in Europe in the Age of the Two World Wars* (Basingstoke, 2006); Christoph Nonn in H. Berghoff (ed.), *Konsumpolitik: Die Regulierung des Privaten Verbrauchs im 20. Jahrhundert* (Göttingen, 1999).
35. Dana Simmons in her chapter. See also now N. Cullather, 'The Foreign Policy of the Calorie', *The American Historical Review*, 112(2) (2007).
36. Gerlach in this volume.
37. P. Singer, *Animal Liberation: A New Ethics for Our Treatment of Animals* (New York, 1975); P. Singer, 'Famine, Affluence, and Morality', *Philosophy and Public Affairs*, 1 (1974): 229–43; J. C. Tronto, *Moral Boundaries: A Political Argument for an Ethic of Care* (New York, 1994).
38. D. Leslie and S. Reimer, 'Spatializing Commodity Chains', *Progress in Human Geography* 23 (1999): 401–20.
39. E. Hobsbawm and T. Ranger (eds), *The Invention of Tradition* (Cambridge, 1983).
40. Peter Jackson and Neil Ward in this volume.
41. Susanne Freidberg in this volume.
42. Frank Trentmann in this volume.

Part I
Evolution and Diversity

–2–

Food, Culture and Energy
Sidney W. Mintz

I wish to consider here some of the ways that the globalization process throws into relief the role of culture, and that of energy, in the shaping of food systems. Food in society is a culturally inflected vehicle of symbolic meaning. So prosaic and everyday, and yet so vital, food is among the most powerful of all social indices of difference and identity. Certainly true for the societies that preceded the rise of a global food economy, this is still true today. Hence the ongoing standardization and mass production of foods world-wide, and the aggregate pressures to disseminate those foods to all corners of the globe in impersonal, routinized ways, can easily be read as a dangerous attack, intended or not, upon local and cultural distinctiveness.

Because foods must be produced, processed and distributed, energy also enters into any conception of globalization. Energy use is a coefficient of technological level; it is at the same time an expression of the economic and cultural values of producers and consumers. Dramatic changes in food production and transport have sensitized students of food systems to the paramount role of energy. We are told, for example, that the average mileage travelled by today's food from producer to consumer continues to rise. Pop sociology or not, such figures lay bare important trends. In the United States it is claimed that the *average* distance that such food travels within the society – omitting from this figure all foreign food imports – is now about 1,500 miles. Energy, and particularly fossil fuels as energy sources, enters into these calculations of food travel – and equally or more so, into the energy costs of producing food. A declining fraction of the world's population now accounts for a larger and larger fraction of total global food production, in part because of the substitution of alternative energy for human effort. Whenever fossil fuels supplant human and animal input, culture and energy are intersecting.

It is with history that any dialogue about food globalization should begin. I welcome the opportunity to write it down without having to justify myself – not always the case when dealing with my anthropological colleagues. The processes that underlay the growth of food globalization over time were multiplex and intersecting. Viewed globally, each era in that history did not so much succeed what had preceded it as become added to or grafted upon it. The accumulation and then spread of various features of food systems was irregular, but it went on almost continuously. Even during times of war and instability, changes in food systems kept unfolding;

and what continued to happen was always built to some degree upon what had happened already.

There are many tentative outlines of how food-related periods took on their characteristic shape during the globalizing process. My own outline is short, built around what I think of as several decisive episodes – for lack of a better word – in food history. Each, it seems to me, stands for a period, in some cases for a period of several parts. But rather than starting with the domestication of plants and animals or even far earlier with the control of fire, I want to begin here with the discovery of the New World and its long-term global consequences.

The Columbian exchange was surely the single most important food globalization event in world history.[1] While the broader significance of the Columbian exchange is surely familiar to you all, and though I will refer to it again later, I want to note here some of its more important consequences.

There is an understandable desire, when talking about the Columbian exchange, to chronicle the dramatic significance of the spread, acceptance and culinary reinterpretation or 'indigenization' of potatoes, maize, tomatoes, peanuts, cassava; a vast array of fruits such as the pineapple or papaya; vegetables such as capsicums, both sweet and hot; and beans, including the lima, the string, and the *frijol* or red bean, across the surface of the globe. It surely is an exciting saga. But at least of equal moment was the early implantation in the New World of Old World swine, cattle and poultry. Over time, what the national anthem of the United States calls 'amber waves of grain' became seas of soya beans instead. Early in *that* saga, Brazil and Argentina joined the United States – to the great annoyance of the North American producers – in shipping vast quantities of these Asian beans to Asia, exploiting New World land and water reserves to satisfy Asia's growing desires for soya-fed pork and chicken. Of course these are *recent* events; but they began with the arrival in the New World of Old World food animals, and the later conversion of an ancient Asian source of vegetable protein for humans into the major feed of those same animals. The Columbian exchange thus underlay what followed upon it; its original character lies beneath the major changes of subsequent centuries.

The next episode after the Columbian exchange was the initiation of the plantation sectors of the tropical Americas, beginning no later than the first decades of the sixteenth century. Sugar won from Old World sugarcane grown on Hispaniola (today's Dominican Republic and Haiti) was probably shipped to Cádiz for the first time in 1516. From those beginnings, a vast plantation economy grew thereafter on the Caribbean islands, and on the neighbouring mainland littoral, and flourished unevenly for centuries. In its widest extent it stretched from Pacific coastal Peru and Atlantic coastal Brazil to as far north as Louisiana. Confined at first to sugar, those plantations were an important early consequence of the shaping of the first planetary – that is to say, *transoceanic* – empires. These empires were marked by the first global division of labour and the first basic provisioning of the white world by labour that was nearly all non-white. The consequences were both complex and long-lasting. I have contended that the major demographic lever for world slavery was the New World sugar plantations. New World slavery lasted nearly four centuries and involved at least 11 million slaves, not counting their descendants. If I were to try seriously to write here about a plantation *episode* and to describe its scale and eventual crop repertory, I would have time to mention nothing else.

In my view, another such episode, having as much to do with the economic and political signals it sent as with food itself, would come in the mid-nineteenth century. Centuries after the start of the plantations, this episode unfolded in the United Kingdom. It was when the Corn Laws that protected British homeland agriculture were being repealed there (1846), at the same time that the British West Indian planters were being stripped of their preferential access to British consumers of sugar, molasses and rum. The world of trade was changing, and because of it, the loci of the plantations proliferated, turning up now across Asia and the Indian Ocean. This was also approximately at the same time that beet sugar became commercially profitable. Note that beet sugar and cane sugar are, both chemically and in the view of the consumer, just the same. A temperate-zone agricultural product literally identical to its tropical predecessor had been produced for the first time. This was the start of an irrevocable change in relationships between the metropoles and their colonies.

That same nineteenth century, of course, witnessed many other such episodes, some far larger than food, and some connected to food. It was a century of world-wide migration. Between 1800 and 1900, an estimated 100 million people, about half of them white and the other half non-white, crossed the oceans to labour in other lands. Their international destinations differed almost entirely. (Some substantial fraction of the African slave trade was involved: slavery did not end until 1865 in the United States, 1886 in Cuba, and 1888 in Brazil.) The destinations of that enormous immigrant population in the nineteenth century, of which the enslaved were part, were foretold, so to speak, by their complexions; the larger implications of that divided stream of labour have yet to be fully analysed.

From the last quarter of the nineteenth century, and continuing unevenly until the onset of the World Depression (1929–40), there began the creation of what Friedmann and McMichael have described as the 'settler-colonial regime' (I use their terminology here).[2] This first regime meant the organization of an enormous overseas expansion of the production of wheat (and to a lesser extent, though also importantly, of meat) within a global network of interdependence. This time production took place not in the tropics or subtropics, as in the case of the plantations, but mostly in temperate countries and ex-colonies of European settlement outside Europe itself – what Crosby dubbed the 'neo-Europes' – such as Argentina, Australia, New Zealand, Canada, Chile and even the United States. In every locale where that regime grew, it confiscated local lands, timber, water and other resources (usually labelled 'idle resources' at the time) belonging to native peoples and imposed itself upon collapsing indigenous economies, destroying indigenous cultures. Some of the consumers of these vast quantities of wheat and meat lived in the producing countries; over time, and to an increasing extent, they would be found in other colonial regions; but mostly they lived in the European lands that had initiated that overseas production. Something we hear about today was said to be happening during those 75 years or so: it was said to be an era of free-market activity, in which the playing-fields were being made level, and profits for the metropoles were growing. But it was an era that ended in war, soon followed by depression.

That Depression was followed by a second global conflict from which, among the industrial capitalist countries, the United States emerged the most intact and the strongest. The postwar economy it then developed, making use of its wealth in human and material resources, led to the growth of what Friedmann has called its second food regime, following upon its first, settler-colonial regime.[3] This regime is hard to characterize in a few words, but following Friedmann, I mention three major features. The state became deeply involved in the regulation of domestic food production undertaken for export; it organized that production through trade restrictions that were solidly protectionist and mercantilist nationally; and those steps in turn made it possible for the United States to become a global postwar food exporter. Thus the United States moved quite easily from F.D.R.'s original measures to support the rural American economy when it was still in the grip of the Depression, first, to large-scale foreign aid, initially to the postwar European states, and then to an effective and profitable system for disposing of enormous subsidized agricultural surpluses. The agrarian sectors of many lands were vulnerable to United States food exports at the time because those exports were subsidized, and could undercut local food production. Friedmann writes that this was a time when 'transnational integration of agrofood sectors' was proceeding apace:

> Agriculture became industrialized and agricultural products changed from final consumer goods to industrial raw materials for the manufacture of highly processed, value added foods... When this happened, each agricultural product became in principle substitutable, not only by products of farmers in other places, but also by other products entirely. There was a shift from a world market in which Europe imported traditional dietary staples of wheat, meat, and dairy products, to a transnational agrofood sector in which corporations increasingly sought raw materials and markets globally.[4]

This food regime was built upon the rich resources in land, water and fossil fuels that the United States possessed, and upon the production of cheap – because mass-produced and subsidized – foods for both Americans and foreign consumers.

It is this second regime that is currently expanding and changing, and under a variety of pressures. Lang and Heasman call it the 'productionist paradigm', with particular reference to 'the industrialization of food over the last 200 years and its concomitant advances in chemical, transport and agricultural technologies'.[5] The authors suggest that this 'paradigm' has outlived its usefulness to today's America, and prophesy that it will be supplanted in the course of the next half century by one of two other such paradigms. They call these the 'life sciences integrated' paradigm and the 'ecologically integrated' paradigm. It does violence to their discussion of these alternatives to say simply that in their view, one is health-oriented, to the individual and to the environment, entailing wider public participation in the food policy decision-making process by governments and by private citizens, while the other relies more upon scientific policy decisions by corporations, and is more slanted toward market-defined efficiency in production and distribution than toward any weighing of the social outcomes of such efficiency, and hence less aimed at environmental and preventive individual health concerns. The authors then ask whether the next half-century will be devoted to open struggle between these rivalrous alternatives, rather than to the victory of either – leaving no doubt as to why their book is entitled *Food Wars*.

In these comments, I have labelled 'episodes' a few points of my own, while giving ground to the terminology of others for points that they are making. My aim was to enumerate here a few junctures in the past when an ensemble of forces – technological, economic, political, or military – could effectuate large-scale changes in the ways that the world's food was being provided: where, by whom, under what arrangements, and at what costs. I did not tarry to think long about what nouns to label them by.

Globalization, then, is a longitudinal process, one best grasped historically at first, and beginning at least 500 years ago – some might argue far earlier – and still very much in flux. From what I understand of it so far, the globalization of food has been an uneven and asymmetrical process. It is not irreversible; and it has surely not been – whether from environmental, health, or social perspectives – beneficial for everyone.

History may not repeat itself; but historical process can reveal continuities, sometimes even delineating how the same economic and political forces were able to structure different events in homologous ways. I have suggested in recent work, for example, that despite the differences in time, place and food substance, important similarities are to be found in the histories of tea in the United Kingdom and Coca Cola in the American South.[6] The United Kingdom in the mid-nineteenth century, and the United States' South in the first decades of the twentieth, underwent some similar changes in the relationships between agriculture and industry. In both cases, drunkenness emerged as a threat to successful industrialization. In both cases – though almost a century apart – temperance campaigns in favour of tea and of Coca Cola were waged by divines; and both these drinks, heavily laced with sugar and caffeine, successfully delivered factory proletarians to their machines, sober as judges, every Monday morning. Soft-drug temperance beverages by no means solved the problem of alcoholism; but they surely helped. Needless to add, they also made a very great deal of money for the Quakers on the one hand, and the Baptists on the other, who peddled them. I offer this scant *précis* simply to exemplify the larger point I mean to make.

History can help us to discern such parallels, and leads at least some of us to wonder whether there are like causal factors at work. The two parts of my miniature example unfolded at different times, but seemed to share marked processual features, so I call my comparison between them 'same-stage' (systadial), rather than synchronic. I believe it useful, when possible, to make systematic comparisons and to seek large-scale historical patterns of change, when these may be detected in the world history of food.

Surely one of the abiding impressions one carries away from any serious reading of food history is of powerful forces for change, some natural or environmental, but many others of an economic or political kind, wearing away at old and massive food habits. The dietary consequences of the Columbian exchange, as foods such as potatoes or peppers reached Europe, and as wheat, the vine, the olive, and Old World farm animals reached the Americas; the long-term effects on world habits of plantation production of such commodities as sugar, molasses, rum, chocolate and coffee; the wider availability of wheat and meat after the establishment of the settler-colonial regime; the later rise of global trade in such items as tinned corned beef, oleomargarine and condensed milk, to be followed later by the mass production of value-added foods in the second regime – these pulsations of an ever more widespread world food system have led some to think that the name for what was happening was progress, perhaps even irreversible progress. Certainly what one is seeing is change, and very often directed change; but though it has been powerful and persuasive, it has been by no means inevitable, nor was it guaranteed to be benign.

I would like to turn now to culture; I confess that I feel more at home writing about it. In preparing these comments, I was led to ask myself what issue, in my own learning about food, was that which most preoccupied me. I realized that I have often been attracted by a common occurrence in food history: when one food replaces or comes to supplement another. Such occurrences are interesting, among other things, because they almost always play themselves out against a context of marked food conservatism. I have suggested elsewhere that this is a weighty conundrum for students of food: how can the same people cling fiercely to certain features of their diet, even while forsaking, swiftly and often even happily, other features?

It is a serious question. I think that the grandparents of young working-class Americans – youths who can, these days, distinguish raw tuna from raw salmon by their taste and texture – would probably have become ill at the idea of their grandchildren putting pieces of raw fish in their mouths. I have witnessed that change, the before and the after, in the second half of my lifetime. I clearly remember my fellow soldiers in the Second World War averring that the Japanese must be subhuman because they ate raw fish. When I would point out that we Americans matter-of-factly ate raw clams and oysters, I was simply told that *that* was 'different'.

The spread of the capsicums, the hot peppers, to India, Sichuan and West and North Africa provide other cases of rapid change. One of the most arresting examples of the attractiveness of hot peppers is the United States itself where, and only a few decades ago, eating chilli was considered a sure sign of foreignness and probably of lower-class status – even if Tabasco Sauce was considered a forgivable regional weakness in some circles. In all these cases, as in the spread of sucrose, tea, coffee, chocolate and even distilled alcohol in much earlier times, it is worth keeping in mind that while such changes are clearly tied to the subjective pleasures or benefits that a new food can provide the individual, these new foods take on their initial momentum because truly powerful socioeconomic and political forces are at work behind them.

Changes in food and in taste are changes in culture, and I want to examine that concept in a bit more detail. Culture is a term that anthropologists in the United States once treated as their own; anthropological studies of foods and food systems are very old. As an anthropologist, when I talk about culture I am also anxious to underline its own diachronic aspect. In the words of A. L. Kroeber, 'a cultural fact is always a historical fact; and its most immediate understanding, and usually the fullest understanding of it to which we can attain, is a historical one'.[7] In groups of our own human species, over time, every cultural system, including the food subsystem, has been a historical, human-made product.

Even before a professional anthropology existed, anthropologists were contributing significantly to the study of the relationships between food and ritual or food and social structure. They made studies of fishing, hunting and gleaning, of horticulture, and of pastoralism, particularly in societies of the sort once called 'primitive'. Most of the societies they studied were small, in numbers and in area, and their economies mostly (though not altogether) self-contained, and largely explicable in terms of themselves.

Hence when anthropologists first studied food production, distribution and consumption, they saw these as integral parts of the economic and political order of small whole systems – Firth's *Primitive Polynesian Economy*, on the people of Tikopia, would be one example.[8] From the outset, anthropologists studied the diversity of foods and the organization of their production, just as they did the specific character of each such food system. Food – like dress, say, body grooming, or language – marked dramatically the differences among human groups. We know that members of different groups took such differences very seriously. The readiness of people to die rather than to eat or be polluted by tabooed food substances – as in the Spain of the Inquisition or in the Sepoy Rebellion – is legendary.

Yet there is also plentiful evidence that people can change their foods, and even the economic organization that had produced them. A striking example is provided by those North American Indian peoples of the prairies and woodlands who became bison-hunting equestrians. They abandoned agriculture and settled village life for a life of mobility, carnivorousness and combat on the Great Plains, punctuated by the vainglories of coup-counting by mounted warriors, the sun dance and the vision quest. Their houses were now of leather, rather than earth and wood; their hunting bows became shorter, and lances were added as armament; ceramics faltered, then disappeared; and gender relations were transformed for the worse. The whole food system was remade for those Plains peoples: maize, beans and squash were almost entirely supplanted by bison meat, fresh and cured, and farming by hunting.

Less extreme but more common, many cultures can be shown to have radically changed *some* parts of their food-related behaviour, while faithfully retaining much of the rest. This twinning of cultural conservatism and openness to change in a really intimate sphere of life is a cultural question – one that I believe we anthropologists have still not adequately answered, though we may have made some contributions to its understanding. It is also the kind of question that becomes more pressing as the globalization of food advances.

Many hints of the specific forces at work appear in early contributions to the study of food and social change, such as Richards' pioneering *Land, Labour and Diet in Northern Rhodesia.*[9] More recent work – Weismantel's *Food, Gender and Poverty in the Ecuadorian Andes*[10] or Ray's *The Migrant's Table*[11] or, from a different vantage point, Freidberg's *French Beans and Food Scares* – tell us more.[12] Papers in Carola Lentz's edited collection, *Changing Food Habits*,[13] and in Helen Macbeth's edited *Food Preferences and Taste* are exemplary for their sensitivity to relevant factors in selective change.[14]

The complexity of change is captured by McDanaugh's description of the innovation of buffalo-eating among the Tharu of Nepal, for example.[15] Once tabooed along caste lines, buffalo meat is now becoming a regular part of Tharu diet, though not quite yet in public. As young males get to taste buffalo meat while working outside their communities; as Tharu economic security increases; and as the power of regional caste hierarchy declines, the prohibition has begun to lose its power. Tharu still carefully guard in public the social distinctions that set them symbolically above lower castes, and in relation to higher castes. But buffalo meat is food for the castes below them, so eating it makes it a provocative case. For the Tharu, eating buffalo is to appear downwardly mobile. Moving up – so-called 'sanskritization' – by the Tharu would involve eating less meat, not more. At the same time, the Tharu continue to find the eating of *beef* totally out of the question, such that the ongoing change we do see is neither random nor wholesale. Instead, Tharu food behaviour is changing in accord with wider social and economic changes, to which they are subjected as a caste (or 'ethnic') community.

A different case is provided by Mary Weismantel's study of the Ecuadorian highland Indians of Zumbagua. In the post-Conquest period, barley and fava beans were adopted by these Andean people, supplementing their traditional potatoes, and barley porridge became one of their most important foods – indeed, a food by which they identified themselves. In the modern era, particularly as their subsistence agriculture has declined, the Zumbagueños have been managing their food preferences in ways dictated primarily but not solely by economic considerations. Weismantel points out that the guinea pig, *cuy*, is an important native food: the typical feast food for one's *compadre*, or ceremonial co-parent. Weismantel quotes the local saying 'Why do we have *cuyes*? Because we have *compadres*.' Nowadays, however, wealthy white townspeople can be more valuable as *compadres* than dependable fellow Indian neighbours. But white *compadres* cannot be served barley and *cuy*; they should get chicken and rice, both of which must be purchased. As Weismantel puts it, '...because agriculture changes, the definition of a desirable *compadre* changes. The new relations with white *compadres* ... make subsistence activities even less important.' And as subsistence production declines and men travel more to the cities in search of work, more and more food is bought, and less and less produced locally.[16]

These cases privilege the significance of economic forces, which are often prime movers in the transformation of food habits – because they first remake the conditions of food production. But it is cultural factors that inform and modify the ways that economic factors work themselves out. In what manner constraint and cultural feedback operate to produce particular results in a changing society is a basic problem for an anthropology of food.

Economic conditions, religious proscription, time available for food preparation, gender differences, advertising, emulation, peer pressure – the factors that enter into the decisions that we simply label 'food choice' seem endless, and we still do not fully understand them. Yet what these studies suggest to me is that analyses of dietary change are enriched when careful account is taken of those stable features of the food system, such as the system of land tenure and the traditional sexual division of labour, that provide its background. It is common now to stress the fluid character of modern life, and to be sure, change is everywhere. Sociologically, it is important that a big piece of China's population – 100 million people, and so, more than the entire US labour force – is now urban and migratory, moving from city to city in search of work. By any measure, that is a hell of a lot of transients, who eat when, what and where they can. Yet, in understanding China's food system and food habits, it must be at least equally important that well over 1.2 billion in that country – give or take another 100 million or so – still live rural, mostly agrarian, lives. If we mean to judge the consequences of, say, McDonald's for China, then to notice how many people are mostly staying put for now lets us look more calmly at the behaviours of those who are moving. I would say much the same for India – probably even more so, in fact, since the decentring of rural sectors in China so far has surpassed the Indian situation.

And so, change, yes – and on a global scale. But has this meant the end of culture, or of the behavioural determinants that word was once meant to describe? I doubt it. The fluidity of culture does not alter, for example, the fact that, no matter how fast the world changes, acquisition of language by the young remains a long process to be undertaken individually, by each and every one of the world's infants. Most of the world's children still grow up in families and learn their languages in communities – this, in spite of all of the world's distress, as well as in spite of its globalization. We humans do not emerge like insects full-grown from our chrysalises. Culture adheres to human beings because they live socially, in groups; those groups make and validate culture. People still do live in groups, and socialize their children in them.

I turn finally to the subject of energy. I have long been bewitched by that moment in the history of science when the calorie was given a new concreteness as a measure of heat – both in the form produced, say, by human effort in manual labour, and in the form of food, in terms of its caloric content. When Lavoisier proclaimed that 'La vie est une fonction chimique' he opened the door to a wholly remade sense of how the world ticked. What had been simply approximate in the relations between people who worked, and the food they ate or could afford, had been made far more precise. Putting it that way, of course, leaves out a lot of things about food, such as vitamins, the institutionalization of foods in society over time, and the role of taste in diet. Yet it lays bare the ways that, through science, equivalencies emerge from seemingly incommensurable categories of information, and those equivalencies help us to see better what happens in food systems. For instance, if we are told that an acre of sugarcane yields us 8 million calories, but that it takes 135 acres to achieve the same caloric total with beef cattle, this is a datum that, if it does nothing else, makes us think. It enables us to grasp more firmly the significance of also knowing that it takes 40 calories' worth of fossil fuel to produce one calorie of beef protein.

There is no useful way to talk about the global food market without talking about energy. Globalization of food so far, at least from the pioneer Caribbean sugar plantations of the sixteenth century to the very present, has rested in large measure on a prodigal use and systematic undervaluation of land, water, forest, minerals, and fossil fuels, resources most of which lay largely outside Europe, in regions that have been successively integrated within the global network over the last five centuries.

But I did not realize when I first wrote down these remarks how timely they would soon become, especially with respect to fuels. Of course people have been talking about the end of fossil fuels, just as they have about, say, overpopulation, for a long time. But now there seems to be considerably less time left for us to make jokes about it.

Amid the figures and data that experts cite in regard to the supply of fuel, one calculation more than any other stands out in my mind. It is the work of the geologist M. King Hubbert, who was chief of research for Shell Oil, and it is referred to as Hubbert's Curve.[17] Way back in 1949, Hubbert came up with a prediction about the US crude oil supply, and patched it on to a bell curve. He was interested in the peak year, after which production would presumably never again match what it had been. He thought that for the United States it would happen around 1970. Then it did; but nobody paid much attention until the OPEC crisis in 1973. By then, the United States was importing one-third of its fossil fuel, and United States production could no longer affect the world price of oil in any way – *at least, not through the market.* There have been several predictions since Hubbert's death about the world's crude oil supply, carrying his calculations forward. Some say the global supply will soon peak; others say it already has. In fact, it does not make much difference. Those of us who shrink from seeing any relationship between the American adventure in the Middle East and oil can continue to make fun of conspiracy theorists. But there's no conspiracy at all about the shrinkage of the world fossil fuel supply.

Accordingly, it seemed to me appropriate to think about at least some of the consequences of a lengthy period during which the costs of fossil fuel will rise, sharply at first. Some people may expect the price of fossil fuel to decline again. I do not. If it does not, then we may soon be witness to the grudging abandonment of some of the most quixotic features of food globalism. Radicchio produced in the Salinas Valley of California will turn up less frequently on the salad plates in the Hilton hotel restaurants in places like Thailand, I suppose. But the long-term effect on the world food system of a declining global fossil fuel supply will be enormous, even if knowing what features of that system will disappear first is not easy to guess.

In their splendid little energy primer, Pimentel and Pimentel show just how important it is for us students of food to understand energy, because it has to do not only with what food the world produces, and at what costs in energy, but also with what foods the world has been invited, persuaded, coaxed, bribed and constrained to consume – again, at costs in energy that are usually left unspecified.[18] Being reminded of the rather depressing fact that humans cannot produce energy, only convert it, and then plotting its use in the production of our sustenance is eye-opening. The significance of photosynthesis for the human food repertory is the place to begin. The Pimentels point out that only 0.01 per cent of available solar energy is actually captured by the earth's plants and converted into biomass. Of that tiny fraction, only a similarly tiny fraction ends up as edible plant food; and of that edible plant food, as you all know, a substantial fraction is regularly fed to animals today, so that we humans can then eat the animals.

It was in this manner that Asia's main protein source was transformed miraculously by the wonders of modern biotechnology into the world's best animal feed. An hour in a supermarket, reading the contents of packaged food, tells us just how important the wonder bean has become – though hardly at all in the ways that we might have expected, knowing its past history. To reap the benefits of its nutraceutical promise, lecithin, oil, and above all animal feed, great swaths of the Brazilian tropical rain forest as well as of the American Midwest have been put to the plough. Now the bean itself has been reborn as some sort of new green Godzilla, an ancient Asian crop sprung from a mating of Western science and Western food habits. In this case, cultural and economic pressures have been merged to missionize for the West's carnivorous orientation and then to peddle that orientation worldwide. I think that at least some of the implications for energy use of this grand undertaking are quite clear. An assiduous long-term project to convert Asia to a high animal-protein diet similar to that in the West will prove disastrous for the global environment and for global health. But that project is advancing, aided by the soya bean's generally excellent reputation as a health food and an answer to famine. I do not think that the fact that many Asians may seek a diet like ours, even without any encouragement from the West, justifies our trying so hard to sell them on it.

Here in the United States Pimentel and his colleagues, having predicted vast changes over the next half century, count among those changes a sharp shift away from meat-eating and toward vegetable protein consumption. I have reservations about their optimism in this regard, but cannot rule it out. Looked at coldly, while I find it difficult to believe people in the United States will one day be cheerfully downing as many calories in bean curd as they now down in hamburger, I am given pause by what has happened with sushi, hot peppers, yogurt, and a good many other foods in the United States during the last half century. And though it is not proclaimed in our newspapers, I recognize that the hamburgers in the United States armed services and in our school lunch programmes these days contain up to 40 per cent soya protein. I continue to think that massive change away from meat in the United States is unlikely, though recognizing at the same time that economic pressures caused by rapidly declining agricultural land, water, forest and fossil fuel resources, certainly may bring substantial change in their wake, and some of those changes may be for the good.

James Kunstler argues quite chillingly that *nothing* will kick in to replace fossil fuels in the near future, if ever – hence his title.[19] Though his book is highly imaginative, his views on the historical role of fossil fuels in creating the modern world, its food and its present population, strike me as convincing. If he is right, we can anticipate a struggle from those who feel that they *have* to keep what they have got. I think that the more powerful national states will not accept cutting their standards of living – measured, among other things, by hamburgers – by choice. In such a case, the global food economy will probably contract grudgingly and imperfectly, and here are a few guesses about the shape of the contraction.

The first cut will be as between food and non-food, and non-food will win. People are going to live without strawberries out of season. The second cut, within foods, will be between non-perishables and perishables, and non-perishables will win. People will be obliged to give up fresh strawberries before they have to give up dried apricots. The third cut will be between staples such as cereals and legumes, and other less basic foods, and staples will win. Less basic foods, including ethnic exotica, will give ground to dried beans and barley (unless these latter only *are* ethnic exotica). These are big sloppy categories; but I think my guesses are obvious enough at least to be thought-provoking. Food prices will rise; *all* food prices will rise. (Of course all food prices *have* been rising; but, as they used to say when I was a boy, 'You ain't seen nothin' yet.') While there will be no headlong rush toward bean curd and carrot juice, I do think that, even in the developed countries, the consumption of legumes will rise, and the consumption of animal protein, especially fish and red meat, will fall. But needless to add, such hardships will not be borne equally.

I suspect that in some class segments in both Europe and America, there will be some doubling up in family homes – even more grandparents and grandchildren in the equivalent of the North American two-family houses of the 1930s. Kunstler, by the way, thinks that the long-term fuel crisis will finish off the North American suburb, which he sees as becoming our future slums.[20] But in any event, heat and cold are going to take on new – or rather, old – meanings, with reference to who lives with whom, how we define privacy, and within what space the young will learn to be adults. It follows that who cooks regularly, and for whom, and who eat together regularly may also change, quite possibly in a 'more traditional' direction.

As for the rivalry that Lang and Heasman envisage between two alternatives for the United States food system,[21] one better attuned to environmental and energy considerations and the other shaped more by corporate intent, if Kunstler is right, the jury may be out for much less time than the authors think. If, as I believe, world capitalism has staked its future on the gradual absorption of the labour power available in China, India and Russia (and, to a lesser extent, Africa and Latin America) as industrial proletariats – as both producers and consumers within a global economy – then the world will get a lot warmer, a lot faster. But neither Kunstler nor anyone else is able to tell us now whether the growing scarcity of fossil fuels will cut into current food production and distribution systems in one year, five or ten.[22]

If changes of the kind Kunstler envisions do indeed come to pass, I think there is certain to be more cooking at home. High-end restaurants will be in for a rough time; high-energy innovations, such as microwave cookers and convection ovens, will lose ground to less exotic devices. Many of us easily remember when part of our summer food, at least, was grown in the back yard, and those days may soon be back. In all this 'futurism' there is of course much room for discussing family-based, non fossil-fuel-based, sustainable agriculture. The unimaginably difficult task of getting from here to there, which Kunstler dwells upon, makes the emergency look like a very long one indeed.[23]

I think there is something to be thought about, when these not wholly zany prognostications are considered seriously. Occupying less space, even growing some of our own food, using less fossil fuel, investing more manual effort, and cooking more ourselves, will of course be described as a lowering of our standards of living. 'The American way of life', Vice-President Cheney famously remarked, 'is not negotiable.' And I hasten to point out, before someone points it out to me, that I have yet to plant my first radish in this brave new world that I am imagining. But then, unlike our President and Vice-President, I have also to profit from my first oil well.

My feeble attempts at humour are not meant to suggest that this scenario – if there is anything to it at all – will be a happy one. If anything, the struggle between those who consider themselves realists and those they call either idealists or fools will become fiercer. The policy of keeping the prices of such things as water and oil artificially low has had many benefits, including improved nutrition for countless millions. But it has also produced institutional changes, particularly economic changes, that have not all been good and that will be extremely difficult to modify, above all because there are now such powerful interests vested in them. While atomic

energy may lessen the shock of the end of fossil fuel – people threatened with the
end of automobiles, air conditioning and television will be much more favourably
disposed to nuclear plants than they are now – the unimpeded year-round flow of
giant tasteless strawberries, once it falters, may never be restored. More worrisome,
it will clearly take more than one or two little wars to keep the oil flowing, and there
are still lots of people who are prepared to defend a fossil-fuel-based way of life that
way.

But I have taken up too much of the reader's time already. What may be worse, I
have done so as if I had opinions on these matters. I hope that you will at least find
some provocation in these remarks.[24]

Notes

1. A. Crosby, *The Columbian Exchange* (Westport, CT, 1972).
2. H. Friedmann and P. McMichael, 'Agriculture and the State System', *Sociologia Ruralis*, XXIX (2) (1989): 93–117.
3. H. Friedmann, 'After Midas's Feast: Alternative Food Regimes for the Future', in P. Allen (ed.), *Food for the Future* (1993), pp. 213–33.
4. Friedmann, 'After Midas's Feast'.
5. T. Lang and M. Heasman, *Food Wars* (London, 2004), p. 19.
6. S. Mintz, 'Quenching Homologous Thirsts', in William Merrill and Ives Goddard (eds), *Anthropology, History, and American Indians: Essays in Honor of William Curtis Sturtevant*, Smithsonian Contributions to Anthropology No. 44. (Washington, 2002): 349–57.
7. A. Kroeber, *Anthropology* (New York, 1948), p. 255.
8. R. Firth, *Primitive Polynesian Economy* (New York, 1950 [1939]).
9. A. Richards, *Land, Labour and Diet in Northern Rhodesia* (Oxford, 1939).
10. M. Weismantel, *Food, Gender and Poverty in the Ecuadorian Andes* (Philadelphia, 1988).
11. K. Ray, *The Migrant's Table* (Philadelphia, 2004).
12. S. Freidberg, *French Beans and Food Scares* (Oxford, 2004).
13. C. Lentz (ed.), *Changing Food Habits* (Amsterdam, 1999).
14. H. Macbeth (ed.), *Food Preferences and Taste* (Providence, RI, 1997).
15. C. McDanaugh, 'Breaking the Rules: Changes in Food Acceptability among the Tharu of Nepal', in Macbeth, *Food Preferences and Taste,* pp.155–66.
16. M. Weismantel, *Food, Gender and Poverty in the Ecuadorian Andes* (Philadelphia, 1988).
17. J. Kunstler, *The Long Emergency* (New York, 2005).

18. D. Pimentel and M. Pimentel, *Food, Energy and Society* (London, 1979).
19. Kunstler, *The Long Emergency*.
20. Kunstler, *The Long Emergency*.
21. T. Lang and M. Heasman, *Food Wars* (London, 2004).
22. Kunstler, *The Long Emergency*.
23. Kunstler, *The Long Emergency*.
24. Readers should be advised, should some of the content of the present chapter now appear a little dated, that its original core grew out of a talk delivered at Wassenaar as long ago as 19 May 2005, and may therefore now perhaps lay claim to a certain historical interest on that account.

–3–

The Global Consumption of Hot Beverages, c.1500 to c.1900

William G. Clarence-Smith

Europeans exploring the world from the fifteenth century discovered a new universe of hot beverages. They brought chocolate home from the Americas, and tea, coffee and salep from the Old World, while simultaneously helping to diffuse the consumption of these and other beverages outside Europe. They also transferred seeds and seedlings around the globe, transforming patterns of production. By the 1880s, it was roughly estimated that 500 million people preferred tea, compared to 200 million people opting for coffee, and 50 million for chocolate.[1]

There was no single cause for evolving patterns of consumption, as Brian Cowan rightly indicates for Britain.[2] Coffee was not unambiguously part of the rise of an urban, secular and 'modern' Western bourgeoisie, as Wolfgang Schivelbusch and Jean-Maurice Bizière would have it. Schivelbusch also exaggerates the aristocratic and feminine aura of chocolate in the West.[3] Taxes affected consumption, but Simon Smith falls into the trap of trying to explain everything in these terms.[4] In reality, there was a subtle interplay between factors, and a global approach serves to question dominant Eurocentric narratives.

The addictive properties of psychoactive alkaloids remain hotly debated. Some plants, whether ingested by humans as beverages or in other ways, produce bitter substances as insecticides or herbicides. If habit-forming for humans, as seems likely, these alkaloids may have led people to cling tenaciously to their accustomed product. In other cases, however, the same addictive properties may have provoked a rapid shift in consumption, as whole societies became 'hooked on a new drug'. However, although alkaloids vary in their properties, it is hard to correlate these variations with particular social choices.[5]

Forming a barrier to the spread of hot beverages, especially in tropical Africa and Asia, were alkaloids obtained from products that were chewed, smoked or inhaled as a powder. All three methods furnished nicotine from tobacco, a New-World plant that Europeans disseminated around the globe, while opium and cannabis were mainly smoked. To the extent that these were smoked, they might complement hot beverages, whereas masticatories were more direct competitors. Made up of betel-leaf (*Piper betle*), areca nut (*Areca catechu*), and lime paste, the betel quid originated in Southeast Asia, and was enthusiastically chewed from Madagascar to South China. South Arabians and East Africans chewed fresh *qat* leaf (*Catha edulis*). Nutritious kola nuts (*Cola nitida* and *acuminata*), containing caffeine and theobromine, were tropical Africa's masticatories of choice, penetrating into North Africa and the American tropics. Finally, fresh coca leaves (*Erythroxylum coca*) yielded cocaine on chewing, a habit that spread along the Andes.[6]

The Early Modern Spread of Hot Beverages

By 1500, millions of East Asians already drank tea, containing caffeine, in ways that were still evolving. *Camellia sinensis*, grown on smallholdings from central Vietnam to central Japan, yielded the precious leaves. East Asians typically drank 'green tea,' made with leaves dried unfermented, and with nothing added. Under China's Ming dynasty (1368–1644), cake and powdered tea concoctions gave way to infusions of leaves. Semi-fermented 'oolong' teas, developed in Fujian and Taiwan in Ming times, were suited to mixing with jasmine petals. The Manchu, China's Inner Asian governing class from 1644 to 1911, preferred 'black tea', fully fermented prior to drying, as it went well with their beloved mare's milk. Powdered green tea remained important in Japan, while Korea largely turned away from tea under the Yi dynasty (1392–1910). Tea bushes even went wild in southern Korea, and a late eighteenth-century revival was almost imperceptible.[7]

Inner Asia was China's main initial export market. While settled Muslim elites sipped green leaf tea, pastoralists ingested immense quantities of cheap 'brick tea'. These compressed blocks, or tablets, were made with tea dust, coarse leaves, and even twigs. Bricks came to be classed as green or black, although they were often at various stages of fermentation. Pastoralists shredded bricks into a kind of soup, made with butter, milk, salt and flour. Tea provided essential inputs for diets that were almost entirely deficient in vegetables.[8]

The rest of East Asia's 'near abroad' consumed considerably less Chinese tea. Some green tea went to Southeast Asia to meet the needs of the Chinese community there, but the indigenous peoples generally stuck to the ancient custom of betel chewing.[9] From the seventeenth century, if not earlier, South Asians consumed small quantities of black tea, as milk was a crucial ingredient in their traditional diets. However, betel was again a considerable barrier.[10]

From the seventeenth century, Chinese tea exports expanded to encompass the Middle East and the West, with green tea initially predominant.[11] This remained the principal choice of Portugal and its colonies.[12] Flavoured with mint, green tea also became the chief hot beverage of Morocco and neighbouring Saharan regions.[13] In contrast, Britain, Ireland, and North America came to consume mostly black tea, better suited to mixing with milk, and easier to preserve in good condition during the long sea journey.[14] Russia imported increasing quantities of brick tea from the late eighteenth century, together with black and green leaf tea for wealthier customers, coming overland or by sea.[15] By the nineteenth century, Iran (Persia) had also largely opted for a mixture of black and green teas, both leaf and brick.[16]

Growing tea beyond East Asia only developed from the early nineteenth century, mainly on large European-owned plantations in northeastern and southwestern India, Sri Lanka (Ceylon), Java and Sumatra. The indigenous Assam variety of northeastern India, little suited to making green tea, was increasingly prominent, and planters sought to develop a local market for it.[17] Portuguese and Brazilian officials had less success in stimulating tea cultivation at this time, whether in the Azores or in the states of Rio de Janeiro and São Paulo.[18] From the late nineteenth century, Russian, Iranian and Turkish governments adopted somewhat more effective import-substituting policies, in the mountains above the Black Sea and the Caspian Sea.[19]

The Middle East's established hot beverage was salep, already known to the Ancient Greeks. It was made with young orchid tubers, notably *Orchis morio*, collected from the wild in lime-rich mountains extending from the Balkans to northwestern India. The tubers were dried, roasted and powdered, and then mixed with hot milk or water. The species used for salep apparently contained no alkaloid, however, unlike the *Dendrobium nobile* employed to make a medicinal tonic in East Asia. From at least the seventeenth century Levantine salep arrived in the West, and the beverage reached as far as North America.[20]

Coffee consumption spread from southern Arabia from the fifteenth century. Made with the roasted and ground beans of *Coffea arabica*, growing wild in the southwestern Ethiopian highlands, coffee gave the name caffeine to the alkaloid that it contained. Served black and increasingly sweetened, it conquered much of the Middle East within two centuries, stimulating cultivation in Yemen from around the 1540s.[21] Cultivation also accompanied patchy consumption around the Indian Ocean from the seventeenth century, and later spread into the South Pacific.[22] In 1734, Armenians were selling coffee in northwestern China, where many Hui Muslims lived, but in general China's 'tea barrier [was] unbreakable till the twentieth century'.[23]

Once the West began to imbibe coffee from the seventeenth century, north-central Europeans became ardent consumers. The poor frequently adulterated their coffee with the roasted and ground root of chicory, *Cichorium intybus*, which contained no alkaloid. Europeans transferred the coffee tree to their Indian Ocean and Caribbean colonies, and planting boomed in Latin America in the nineteenth century, notably in Brazil.[24]

In Mesoamerica, the Spaniards discovered chocolate, or cocoa, containing the alkaloid theobromine. The botanical origins of *Theobroma cacao* lay in the Upper Amazon, but only Mesoamericans cultivated the tree at the time. They roasted and ground the beans, and drank a bitter, spiced, and often cold concoction. The Spaniards popularized a hot sweet version of chocolate around the Caribbean Basin, in southern Europe, and in the Philippines. North Europeans and North Americans were lesser consumers, usually preparing the drink with milk. As for chocolate confectionery, it only became significant in the late nineteenth century.[25] East Asians and Muslims learned about chocolate, but consumption was very restricted, limited to areas such as Morocco, influenced by Iberia, and southeastern China, the original home of a large Chinese expatriate community in the Philippines.[26]

Many people in the Americas preferred to obtain caffeine from plants of the *Ilex* family. Harvested from the wild in eastern Paraguay and neighbouring parts of Brazil, the parched and roughly broken leaves of *Ilex paraguayensis* were infused to make *mate*, to which Europeans added sugar. Jesuit missionaries eventually managed to establish plantations in their Paraguayan 'reductions', and mules carried 'Jesuit tea' to the *gauchos* of the Pampas, across the Andes to Chile, up the Andes to Ecuador, and, above all, to the great silver mines of Peru and Bolivia. In the northern Andes and to the east, some people substituted the leaves of *Ilex guayusa*, derived from Amazonian forests. From Virginia to Mexico, 'black tea' (*yaupon* or *upton*) was prepared from leaves and buds of *Ilex cassina*, growing in sandy coastal soils. None of these beverages made significant headway in Europe, where leaves of the common holly, *Ilex aquifolium*, were sometimes infused, as in Germany's Black Forest region.[27]

New World caffeine was also derived from plants of the *Paullinia* genus. *Guaraná* was the standard beverage of the Amazon and Orinoco basins, until it was challenged by coffee in the late nineteenth century. It was made from the crushed seeds of *Paullinia cupana* or *sorbilis*, cultivated in the middle Amazon, which were mixed with cassava (manioc) and water to form a paste. Shaped into cylinders and dried rock-hard, *guaraná* lasted for years, and could be grated at will into hot or cold water. Lowland Amerindians from southern Colombia to Peru preferred *yoco*, prepared from the bark of *Paullinia yoco*, growing wild in Amazonian forests.[28]

Taxation

The relative cost of commodities is the standard economist's explanation for consumer choice between commodities, and taxation has historically loomed particularly large in determining the prices of hot beverages. Thus, the final collapse of the state monopoly on tea sales in Ming China, together with light or non-existent excise duties, favoured consumption. In contrast, heavy Korean taxes on tea may partly explain the commodity's poor performance there.[29]

Low import duties were the Islamic norm, as a sultan's overriding duty was to cheapen his subjects' cost of living. Ottoman sultans thus failed to protect Yemeni peasants from an inflow of Caribbean-grown coffee, and even halved the duty on foreign imports in 1738. However, the increasingly autonomous Mamluk authorities in Egypt heeded the protests of Cairo traders dealing in Yemeni beans. They banned imports of coffee coming via Europe in 1760, and Muhammad 'Ali renewed this prohibition in 1830. As for Moroccan and Mauritanian reformers, they advocated moral persuasion to reduce ballooning tea imports, thought to be threatening economic and political independence. A monarch might also encourage import-substituting cultivation, as the Shahs did with tea in northern Iran.[30]

Mercantilist Western rulers mercilessly taxed imported colonial 'luxuries', which had to be shipped in national bottoms, and restricted imports if they lacked tropical dependencies. Frederick the Great of Prussia went so far as to ban coffee imports in 1768, assiduously propagating the virtues of German beer, and licensing the first factory to powder roasted chicory roots in 1770. Faced with massive smuggling, Frederick shifted to issuing coffee-roasting licenses in 1781, although even this measure was abandoned after his death in 1787. Austria, equally bereft of tropical possessions, adopted milder measures to restrict imports in 1770. Sweden and Denmark, with only small tropical colonies, expressed similar anxieties.[31]

Mercantilist fiscal constraints slowly faded, favouring growth in consumption. A famous case was the slashing of British tea duties in 1784, from 119 per cent to 12.5 per cent *ad valorem*, to counter smuggling from the Continent. This led to a surge of legal imports from China, and helped to make tea an item of mass consumption among labourers. Similarly, Spanish tariff reforms, following defeat in the Seven Years War in 1763, brought the cost of cocoa beans down sharply, on both the metropolitan and the colonial markets.[32]

Not only did taxes shoot up again during the French Wars from 1793, but blockades were also introduced. Deprived Continental consumers turned to locally grown chicory, spreading to France at this time. Habsburg subjects mainly resorted to roasted barley, but also to a bewildering variety of other products, such as other cereals, acorns, beechmast, figs, turnips, beans and lupins. Similarly, disruptions in salep imports from the Levant probably led the English to a greater reliance on Oxfordshire's wild orchids.[33]

Simon Smith makes import duties the sole determinant of the waltz between coffee and tea imports in post-1815 Britain. Tariffs were initially skewed to protect coffee planters in the Caribbean and Sri Lanka, and later changed in response to pleas from tea planters in India. However, the British Caribbean's cocoa planters received similar initial tax advantages, without witnessing a corresponding surge in metropolitan imports. Low and equal British import duties for all beverages from around 1850 coincided with a recovery of tea and a decline of coffee, and yet there was also a marked rise of cocoa from the 1870s. Moreover, Russia was the sole country in Continental Europe where falling and converging import duties benefited tea. Elsewhere, coffee was the victor, except in Spain, which clung to chocolate.[34]

Nevertheless, fiscal decisions certainly mattered. Late eighteenth-century commercial liberalization in the Iberian empires led to a promising growth in tea imports, which was only choked off when independent Latin American states adopted tariffs to protect locally grown coffee and cocoa.[35] Russian imports of tea per head rose rapidly as trade with China was liberalized, and Russia later enjoyed some success in developing tea cultivation under tariff protection in its Caucasus colonies.[36] Portugal ceased to be a mainly tea-drinking nation after duties favoured coffee from African colonies, while discriminating against tea imported from Macau from 1870, because it was not actually grown there.[37]

The virtual abolition of import duties, together with a phenomenal reduction in transport costs, turned hot beverages into items of mass consumption in Western countries by 1900, but different drinks prevailed, according to local tastes. Relative costs cannot by themselves explain the differential uptake of specific beverages, even if discrimination in taxation influenced consumer choices.[38]

Medicine and Temperance

In the initial phase of adoption, hot beverages were frequently taken as medicine, and theories of 'humours' exercised great influence well into the nineteenth century. However, the humoural claims and counter-claims put forward for each drink are hard to follow. Contemporaries contradicted one another with great abandon, while making the most extreme and fanciful health claims, both positive and negative. Medical opinions may thus have exercised little overall influence on consumer choice before the late nineteenth century, even if they were important to individuals. Among the most common claims, at least partly backed by later scientific research, were that tea and coffee kept people awake, coffee reduced sex-drive, and chocolate and salep increased it.[39]

In hygienic terms, heating liquids was long recommended, on the basis of trial and error. The founding Chinese text praised tea for this reason, while boiling milk was recommended in India. Western medical authors also favoured hot beverages for hygienic reasons, till the adoption of innovations such as chlorination, pasteurization, and refrigeration. 'Bitters' and 'sodas' then became popular. Coca-Cola, initially made with coca leaves and kola nuts, was launched in 1886 as a temperance drink and a 'brain tonic'.[40]

Reformers more widely championed beverages that were healthy alternatives to the 'demon alcohol'. The Chinese founding text stressed that tea did not intoxicate, a virtue that was constantly repeated in East Asian writings. Similarly, some Muslims saw tea and coffee as beneficial alternatives to prohibited alcohol and opium. Temperance became significant in the West from the Reformation, with Martin Luther himself campaigning against inebriation. For nineteenth-century reformers, hot beverages had the further advantages of warming the badly dressed and the ill-housed, and filling nutritional deficiencies. Chocolate and salep were nourishing in their own right, while coffee and tea were often drunk with milk and sugar.[41]

Religion

Religious beliefs were yet another influence on the consumption of beverages, with tea usually acting as a kind of bridge between the co-existing East Asian faiths of

Confucianism, Buddhism and Daoism (or Shinto in Japan). Buddhists valued tea for its stimulating properties, ideal for meditation, while Daoists prized it as the 'elixir of life'. Japan's tea ceremony, originally inspired by Zen Buddhism, became a quasi-religious liturgy in its own right from the sixteenth century. In Korea, however, Buddhist monks were left as the main consumers of tea, suffering from bouts of Neo-Confucian persecution from the fifteenth to the nineteenth century.[42]

Coffee divided Muslims from an early date, as some *ulama* thought that it might belong to the same category as alcohol, prohibited by the Qur'an. In addition, the rise of coffee was associated with the rivals of the *ulama*, the Sufi mystics, who engaged in morally questionable meditation and trances. As for the coffee house, it stood accused of hosting an infinity of vices, while keeping the faithful away from the mosque. From 1511 onwards, many pious Muslims thus supported attempts to close coffee houses, and even to prohibit coffee altogether.[43]

Tea seemingly became a concern for Islam at a later date. Influenced by Wahhabi puritanism in Arabia, Somalia's Sayyid Muhammad b. 'Abdallah Hasan, known as the 'Mad Mullah' to his European foes, placed tea on a list of banned substances around 1900. Mauritanian scholars only appear to have begun debating the religious legitimacy of drinking tea in the 1920s. A pious preference for green tea developed, at an unknown date, for fear that black and oolong teas might breach injunctions against fermented substances.[44]

Other faiths used beverages to signal external or internal barriers. Ethiopians turned coffee into a marker of religious difference and superiority. The Ethiopian Orthodox ('Coptic') Church banned the 'vile' Muslim habits of drinking coffee, smoking tobacco, and chewing *qat*. These prohibitions began to break down in the eighteenth century, but coffee drinking was still a mainly Muslim custom around 1900.[45] Some 'orthodox' Hindus, notably Brahmins, opposed the consumption of tea, possibly more worried about the caste of those brewing the drink than about the 'purity' of the tea.[46]

Divisions created by the Christian Reformation allegedly influenced choices of beverages. Protestant Europe was depicted as the domain of coffee, associated with a sober, pious and industrious lifestyle, while chocolate was linked to corrupt and decadent Baroque Catholicism. Thus the persecution of the Jesuits, culminating in the order's dissolution in 1773, harmed global chocolate consumption. Italy, partly under Spanish rule, was the land where 'the precious chocolate' was taken for breakfast and the evening *rinfreschi*. Clerics in Rome were among the drink's best customers, and it was even rumoured that Pope Clement XIV died by imbibing poisoned chocolate in 1774. Charles Dickens reflected established stereotypes when he portrayed a French *monseigneur* as an inveterate chocolate drinker.[47]

This is an oversimplification, with tea posing particular problems. Far from merely being an Anglophone Protestant alternative to coffee, tea straddled the main divisions in Christianity. It was the preferred beverage of Catholic Portuguese-speaking elites until the mid-nineteenth century, and spread from Siberia and the

Volga Basin to encompass all of Orthodox Russia. Moreover, fault-lines between Protestants and Catholics were at times expressed in terms of tea against coffee in the Low Countries. In addition, tea, coffee and chocolate were all three associated with reformed sobriety in the Protestant bastions of England and the Netherlands, while eclectic Protestant Virginians across the ocean imbibed not only black tea, but also green tea, coffee, chocolate and salep.[48]

Gender

The privileged association of certain beverages with men or women has often been affirmed, but stereotypes were only partially applicable. East Asian tea houses were in theory reserved for men, but this was not strictly enforced, particularly as time progressed. Some tea houses harboured courtesans or prostitutes, and others were apparently open to families.[49]

In Islamic countries, coffee was widely drunk in the intimacy of the home, but coffee houses evolved as a male preserve. Once female singers had been ejected from these establishments, some became centres of cross-dressing and male homosexuality. In seventeenth century Iran, they were described as 'veritable houses of sodomy', where Caucasian dancing boys sported effeminate clothes and hairstyles.[50]

Coffee had male associations in Britain, whereas tea was relegated to female domesticity. Coffee houses were technically out of bounds for women, even if some presided over such establishments or served in them. Others, of 'loose morals', slipped in occasionally, and the presence of 'effeminate pretty fellows' was at times noted.[51] Although tea was often served in coffee houses, it was the mistress of the bourgeois household who 'presided in the drawing-room, making the tea from her tea-caddy, arranging social contacts for her guests, and organizing diversions.' Rituals associated with tea were controlled by women, with ladies giving afternoon tea to each other in a kind of rota. Moreover, ladies could quite properly buy tea in grocers' shops.[52]

As coffee houses were barred to them, respectable British and American ladies turned to rural tea gardens. These were open to both sexes, but patronized mainly by women in the eighteenth century. Open from May to September, they were situated in fashionable areas close to large towns. There were arbours or 'genteel boxes', in which to rest, whisper and take refreshment, and they were lit up at night. Tea gardens were swallowed up by nineteenth-century metropolitan sprawl, but they were replaced by teashops from the 1880s, again with a strong feminine ethos.[53]

Salep appears to have been a largely female drink in Islam, traditionally reputed as a 'fattener' for young brides, and in the eighteenth-century West it retained something of this aura, being drunk 'out of china cups, like chocolate'. However, in London, salep was chiefly sold from street stalls to men and boys engaged in strenuous physical activity outdoors. It also became part of British sailors' rations.[54]

Chocolate was a drink frequently linked to women. It was introduced to France and Austria by Spanish queens, and a popular motif for Rococo painters was the breakfast scene. A woman in her *boudoir*, revealing much ample flesh, languidly took her morning chocolate, sometimes in the company of a priest. Assorted male relatives might be present, but in the background. In 1857, Gustave Flaubert still represented chocolate as a lady's breakfast drink.[55]

In reality, the Western gendering of exotic beverages was nothing like as clear as these examples might suggest. It was coffee that Austrian women were said to treasure, and 'women's coffee circles' throve in nineteenth-century German-speaking lands. Coffee rapidly became integrated into the British domestic sphere, and Scandinavian women seemed equally fond of tea and coffee. Arthur Young complained in 1767 of humble British men 'making tea an article of their food almost as much as women', and the beverage conquered the gentleman's club in the nineteenth century.[56]

Class

Social elites usually determined which exotic drinks were initially embraced, and beverages could function as stark markers of status. Planters in the Portuguese African island of Príncipe purchased tea at exorbitant prices from passing ships in 1836, when they were surrounded by abundant coffee and cocoa trees tended by their slaves. Conversely, tea could become an indicator of cross-class solidarity, epitomized by the British 'cuppa' of the Second World War.[57]

Elements of social levelling were found early in East and Inner Asia, although there were contrary trends. In twelfth-century urban China, tea was already an item that 'even the poor cannot do without', even in northern areas where it did not grow. Japanese tea became truly popular from the fourteenth century. Inner Asian pastoralists were so addicted to brick tea that they bartered vast numbers of horses for it, militarily strengthening their Chinese enemies. That said, who drank what kind of tea carried numerous social connotations. Beverages also acted as a social marker in Korea from the fifteenth century, for tea was left to Buddhist monks, while the secular elite drank alcohol, and the common people made do with concoctions based on roasted barley or scorched rice.[58]

It is often claimed that East Asian tea houses were idyllic cross-class public spaces, where class barriers were temporarily suspended. However, there was great variation across China and Japan. In particular, there was a marked polarity between the 'refined' tea houses patronized by the literati, and establishments that existed to relieve the thirst of commoners.[59]

Islamic coffee houses had a 'middle class' reputation, and coffee houses probably did tend to act as a refuge for the middling sort. That said, there existed a great range of such establishments, from the grandest of buildings to the most humble of facilities. All classes might drink coffee at home, or buy it from urban street vendors, whereas poor people were those more likely to patronize taverns, serving prohibited alcohol.[60]

The gradual and partial displacement of coffee by tea in the Middle East has been linked, tentatively, to colonial and semi-colonial influences on elites, which then 'trickled down' the social hierarchy. Russian and British cultural norms may thus have nudged the majority of consumption from coffee to tea in Iran and Anatolia. Egypt, an area where tea had gained much ground by the 1920s, was perhaps influenced by the British occupation after 1882. The transition from coffee to tea in Hadhramaut (East Yemen) was well advanced by the 1930s, prior to the establishment of a loose British protectorate, and was attributed to migration to Southeast Asia. Coffee never seems to have caught on in Morocco, where tea ceased to be a luxury in the mid-nineteenth century, becoming 'a staple of Moroccans' diet and a vital part of their social life'.[61]

Class factors may help to explain the divergent fates of New-World beverages. Europeans associated most American products with poor and culturally marginal people. Drunk by slaves, Amerindians and mixed-race peons, beverages such as *mate* and *guaraná* seemed uncouth to Spaniards and Portuguese. Even determined Jesuit efforts to market the output of their Paraguayan *mate* plantations in Europe proved vain. Similarly, elites in the southern United States dismissed *yaupon* as fit only for the poor.[62] Chocolate was the great exception, because so many tales were told of its place in the sumptuous banquets of Aztec emperors. The drink thus acquired strong connotations of royalty and aristocracy.[63]

Once adopted in the West and by settlers, chocolate diffused down the social scale, notably in Spain and its empire. By the seventeenth century, urban Spaniards of the middling sort commonly partook of a thick chocolate beverage at breakfast, into which they dipped little cakes or biscuits. This habit spread to some of the common people of Madrid, which was seen as a 'regrettable extravagance', especially when servants drank chocolate to ape their social superiors. It was alleged that to be without chocolate in Spain was like lacking bread in France, and prisoners were punished by being denied chocolate. As for the colonies, chocolate in eighteenth-century New Spain was drunk by valets, cobblers, muleteers, coachmen, and even slaves.[64]

In the non-Hispanic Western world, chocolate slowly penetrated down the social scale. Britain's Royal Navy issued slabs of chocolate to seamen from 1780, replaced breakfast gruel with an ounce of chocolate in 1824, and halved the rum ration a year later. The urban poor of the Low Countries made do with cocoa shells, boiled with milk and flavoured with sugar and cinnamon to make 'small coffee'. From the 1870s, new industrially-processed low-fat chocolate beverages began to spread through the industrial working class.[65]

Schivelbusch boldly declares that coffee was 'the beverage of the modern bour-geois age', incarnating the new values of the rising European middle class.[66] The beverage allegedly represented 'sobriety, serious purpose, trustworthiness and respectability', contrasting with the 'outmoded extravagance and immorality' of the decadent aristocracy. It was thus associated with intellectuals, scientists and businessmen. Beer and wine vanished from bourgeois Habsburg breakfast tables from the mid-eighteenth century, with coffee as the main agent 'civilizing' the middle class. At the same time, there was something 'bohemian' about coffee, relished by Venetian artists for its radical chic, as well as its relative cheapness.[67]

Nineteenth-century French writers certainly did much to popularize coffee's reputation, and none more so than Honoré de Balzac. In novels praised by Karl Marx among others, Balzac vaunted the virtues of coffee from the 1830s, while airily denouncing chocolate for contributing to the fall of Spain, by encouraging sensuality, laziness and greed. Indeed, Balzac promoted his image as one of the most excessive coffee-drinkers in history. Jules Michelet also praised coffee's stimulating effects, writing in 1863 that coffee was 'the sober drink, the mighty nourishment of the brain'.[68]

In reality, coffee was never merely confined to the middle classes. It initially moved up in Britain, and temporarily made great inroads in the working classes after 1815. Russia's Peter the Great ordered his nobles to drink coffee as a sign of Europeanization, and Queen Marie-Antoinette of France, the epitome of the frivolous noblewoman, loved coffee for her breakfast. Going the other way, coffee was cherished by Habsburg artisans by 1800, and indispensable for German workers by the 1840s. Labourers dipped their bread into a coffee soup, frequently adulterated and mixed with milk, making coffee a major item in Central European diets, together with potatoes, bread and cheap brandy.[69]

Labelling tea a bourgeois beverage is equally problematic. In Britain, it initially took root at court, promoted by Charles II's Portuguese queen, before moving on to the middle classes. By the 1790s it had shifted further, to become a staple of labourers in southern England, where 'white bread, tea and sugar, formerly the luxuries of the rich, became mainstays of a poverty diet'. Challenged by coffee after the Napoleonic wars, tea soon regained its hold over British workers. Conversely, tea in Russia began as a beverage of Asian ethnic minorities and rough miners and fur-trappers in Siberia.[70]

Salep also ranged across classes. Istanbul's street vendors served it in winter on a brazier, which also warmed customers, whereas the inhabitants of palaces were more likely to ingest it in ornate desserts. The beverage had a middle-class following in eighteenth-century England, and yet was better known as a drink of porters, coal-heavers, and sailors. Charles Lamb, who investigated salep in the 1820s, declared it to be an ideal breakfast for chimney-sweeps, taken with a slice of bread and butter.[71]

Politics

Rulers often suspected that public establishments serving hot beverages were centres of dissidence, and yet Chinese and Japanese tea houses, ubiquitous and popular from the fifteenth century, stirred surprisingly few fears about public order. One European traveller in the mid-nineteenth century, a disturbed time for China, simply noted that peace reigned in these numerous establishments, despite the fact that they were 'crowded with hundreds of natives'. Secret societies sometimes met there, without seeming to worry the Chinese authorities unduly. At worst, frustrated modernizers lambasted tea houses as centres of idleness, unruliness and vice from the late eighteenth century, criticism that grew after the Republican Revolution of 1911.[72]

Muslim monarchs were much less relaxed. They frequently closed down coffee houses, enlisting the *ulama*'s support by appealing to claims about immorality and religious laxity. An alternative strategy, probably politically more effective, was to place informers in these dens of political opposition, to report back on the feelings of patrons.[73]

In the West, not only coffee houses but also coffee itself acquired subversive connotations. Coffee houses spawned radical newspapers, clubs, and pamphlets, and were seen as hothouses of sedition. Even Spain and its colonies were affected by such ferment in the late eighteenth century. The Restoration monarchy in Britain briefly prohibited both coffee houses and the retailing of coffee and similar beverages. Some claim that the French Revolution took shape in the coffee cups of the *philosophes*, although Voltaire, the high priest of these intellectuals, actually preferred chocolate.[74]

The momentous switch of the United States away from tea bolstered the reputation of coffee as a 'revolutionary beverage'. The rights of the East India Company to sell tea directly in North America, together with the duties imposed on the commodity, came to symbolize the iniquities of British rule, leading to the 'Boston Tea Party' of 1773, similar events elsewhere, and a patriotic boycott of tea. Coffee consumption pulled well ahead in the course of the nineteenth century, whereas Loyalist Canada imported over three times as much tea per head as the United States in 1886.[75]

However, this story requires considerable qualification. Thomas Jefferson actually encouraged switching to chocolate, in solidarity with the new country's southern neighbour. Moreover, Americans did not simply reject tea. With a large and dynamic merchant fleet, they sought produce from all over the world, and tea flooded in together with coffee and cocoa. Indeed, the United States remained a major global consumer of tea, and American demand did much to stimulate nineteenth-century exports of oolong tea from Taiwan, and green tea from Japan. It was probably heavy Central European immigration that tipped the cultural balance in favour of coffee.[76]

As for Latin Americans and Filipinos, they long wavered. Chocolate, *mate* and *guaraná* were esteemed beverages, and were of New World origin. Elites adopted coffee and tea on the European model, local coffee production increased spectacularly, and yet popular habits remained tenacious. Chocolate and *mate* were particularly resistant to the rise of coffee, if only in places.[77] It was in Cuba, remaining under Spanish rule till 1898, that coffee was most precociously flaunted as the 'national drink', in opposition to the chocolate of the increasingly unpopular Spaniards.[78]

Conclusion

Changes in the consumption of hot beverages were rarely, if ever, monocausal. Thus, the 'invented tradition' of black tea as the quintessentially British beverage has obscured disconcerting historical shifts, which cannot easily be accounted for by any one phenomenon. Simplistic associations of beverages with addiction, health, religion, gender, class or politics are all equally suspect. Repeatedly, a drink has been marked in certain ways on adoption, but then has followed a twisting trajectory through society. Beverages have often been claimed to represent specific identities, but such representations have been repeatedly contested, eroded and outflanked.

To better understand why hot beverages were accepted or rejected, and by whom and when, there is a need to progress beyond evidence concerning Western elites. Their dietary habits and ideas are now well known, but they were not representative. It is harder to investigate how humble social groups in the West consumed and regarded different products. Even more striking is how much more is known about the West, including the New World and other 'Neo-Europes', than about Muslims and East Asians, the two other main protagonists in the global story of hot beverages up to 1900.

Three specific problems relating to non-Western consumption patterns stand out from this account, requiring further probing by scholars with the requisite skills. In the first place, the seemingly harmonious and long-lasting East Asian consensus around tea and tea houses, broken only by Korea, needs to be interrogated. Secondly, Islam's principled rejection of alcohol makes it surprising that many Muslims have been antagonistic to hot beverages. Thirdly, the long resistance of tropical Africa and Asia to adopting hot beverages may only in part be explained by established alternatives, notably various kinds of masticatories.

Acknowledgements

Parts of this chapter have been previously published in William G. Clarence-Smith, *Cocoa and chocolate 1765–1914, London: Routledge, 2000, Chapters 2–3.* Reproduced here by permission of the publisher.

Notes

1. P. L. Simmonds, *The Popular Beverages of Various Countries* (London, 1888), p. 179.
2. B. Cowan, *The Social Life of Coffee: The Emergence of the British Coffeehouse* (New Haven, CT, 2005), pp. 257–63.
3. W. Schivelbusch, *Tastes of Paradise, A Social History of Spices, Stimulants and Intoxicants* (New York, 1992); J.-M. Bizière, 'Hot Beverages and the Enterprising Spirit in Eighteenth-century Europe', *Journal of Psychohistory*, VII(2) (1979): 135–45.
4. S. D. Smith, 'Accounting for Taste: British Coffee Consumption in Historical Perspective', *Journal of Interdisciplinary History*, XXVII(2) (1996): 183–214.
5. S. D. and M. D. Coe, *The True History of Chocolate* (London, 1996), pp. 31–4; A. Barr, *Drink: A Social History* (London, 1998), p. 276.
6. K. F. Kiple and K. Conèe Ornelas (eds), *The Cambridge World History of Food* (Cambridge, 2000); A. F. Hill, *Economic Botany* (New York, 1952); H. F. Macmillan, *Tropical Gardening and Planting, with Special Reference to Ceylon* (Colombo, 1925).
7. P. Butel, *Histoire du thé* (Paris, 1989), pp. 13–41; J. C. Evans, *Tea in China: The History of China's National Drink* (New York, 1992), pp. 74–102; A. and I. Macfarlane, *Green Gold: The Empire of Tea* (London, 2003), Ch. 3; C. Robequain, *The Economic Development of French Indochina* (London, 1944), pp. 198–9; Anthony (Brother of Taizé), 'A Short History of Tea', *Transactions of the Korea Branch of the Royal Asiatic Society*, LXXII (1997): 5–6.
8. L. J. Newby, *The Empire and the Khanate: A Political History of Qing Relations with Khoqand, c.1760–1860* (Leiden, 2005), pp. 133–5; M. I. Sladkovsky, *The Long Road: Sino-Russian Economic Contacts from Ancient Times to 1917* (Moscow 1981), pp. 147, 228; A. Ibbetson, *Tea, from Grower to Consumer* (London, c.1925), pp. 56–7; Evans, *Tea*, pp. 74, 83, 94–5; Macfarlane and Macfarlane, *Green Gold*, pp. 149–52.
9. L. Wang, *Chinese Tea Culture* (Beijing, 2000), p. 150; A. Reid, *Southeast Asia in the Age of Commerce, 1450–1680, Volume 1, the Lands below the Winds* (New Haven, CT, 1988), pp. 36–45; C. S. Wilson, 'Southeast Asia', in K. F. Kiple and K. Conèe Ornelas (eds), *The Cambridge World History of Food* (Cambridge, 2000), Vol. II, p. 1163.
10. P. J. Griffiths, *The History of the Indian Tea Industry* (London, 1967), pp. 11–13; Evans, *Tea*, p. 96; D. F. Rooney, *Betel Chewing Traditions in South-East Asia* (Kuala Lumpur, 1993), pp. 2, 13–14.
11. Aleíjos, *T'u ch'uan: grüne Wunderdroge Tee: Schicksal einer Heilpflanze in fünf Jahrtausenden* (Vienna, 1977), Ch. 4; Evans, *Tea*, pp. 96–7.
12. T. Linhares, *Historia econômica do mate* (Rio de Janeiro, 1969), pp. 74, 224; J. Caldeira, *Apontamentos d'uma viagem de Lisboa á China e da China a Lisboa* (Lisbon, 1852–3), Vol. II, p. 107.

13. O. Carlier, 'Le café maure; sociabilité masculine et effervescence citoyenne (Algérie XVIIe–XXe siècles)', *Annales, Économies, Sociétés, Civilisations*, XLV(4) (1990): 976–7; G. Lydon, 'On Trans-Saharan Trails: Trading Networks and Cross-cultural Exchanges in Western Africa, 1840s–1930s', PhD Thesis, Michigan State University (2000), pp. 324–6.

14. Butel, *Histoire*, pp. 49–59, 68–9.

15. Sladkovsky, *The Long Road*, pp. 130–1, 142, 146, 182, 225–6, 228, 233–6.

16. R. Matthee, *The Pursuit of Pleasure: Drugs and Stimulants in Iranian History, 1500–1900* (Princeton, NJ, 2005), Ch. 9.

17. Butel, *Histoire*, pp. 129–64, 148, 185–9; D. M. Etherington, 'The Indonesian Tea Industry', *Bulletin of Indonesian Economic Studies*, X(2) (1974): 84–5; J. J. B. Deuss, *De theecultuur* (Haarlem, 1913), pp. 1–5.

18. G. Clarence-Smith, *The Third Portuguese Empire, 1825–1975, a Study in Economic Imperialism* (Manchester, 1985), p. 66; D. P. Kidder, *Sketches of Residence and Travel in Brazil* (London, 1845) Vol. I, pp. 251–2.

19. Matthee, *The Pursuit*, pp. 257, 261, 264, 287–8; C. M. Hann, *Tea and the Domestication of the Turkish State* (Huntingdon, 1990).

20. M. Grieve, *A Modern Herbal* (Harmondsworth, 1980), 3rd edn, pp. 603–5; D. Hartley, *Food in England* (London, 1954), pp. 576–7; L. S. Fitchett, *Beverages and Sauces of Colonial Virginia, 1607–1907* (New York, 1906), p. 64; L. Fortner, 'A Noble Winter Orchid' (2001) http://www.orchidlady.com/pages/orchidGarden/denNobile.htm.

21. M. Tuchscherer, 'Coffee in the Red Sea Area from the Sixteenth to the Nineteenth Century', in W. G. Clarence-Smith and S. Topik (eds), *The Global Coffee Economy in Africa, Asia and Latin America, 1500–1989* (Cambridge, 2003), pp. 50–66; Matthee, *The Pursuit*, Ch. 6.

22. W. G. Clarence-Smith, 'The Spread of Coffee Cultivation in Asia, from the Seventeenth to the Early Nineteenth Century', in M. Tuchscherer (ed.), *Le commerce du café avant l'ère des plantations coloniales* (Cairo, 2001), pp. 371–84; F. Mauro, *Histoire du café* (Paris, 1991), Chs 11 and 14.

23. S. A. M. Adshead, *Material Culture in Europe and China, 1400–1800: The Rise of Consumerism* (Basingstoke, 1997), p. 64.

24. S. Topik, 'The Integration of the World Coffee Market', in W. G. Clarence-Smith and S. Topik (eds), *The Global Coffee Economy in Africa, Asia and Latin America, 1500–1989* (Cambridge 2003), pp. 27–36; Grieve, *A Modern Herbal*, pp. 197–9.

25. W. G. Clarence-Smith, *Cocoa and Chocolate, 1765–1914* (London, 2000) Ch. 2; N. Harwich, *Histoire du chocolat* (Paris, 1992), Chs 1–4.

26. E. and A. Pelletier, *Le thé et le chocolat dans l'alimentation publique* (Paris, 1861), p. 123; N. Matar, *In the Lands of the Christians: Arabic Travel Writing in the Seventeenth Century* (London, 2003), pp. 64, 173; *Der Gordian, Zeitschrift für die Kakao- Schokoladen- und Zuckerwarenindustrie*, XVIII (1912–13): 5,842.

27. J. C. Garavaglia, *Mercado interno y economía colonial* (Mexico City, 1983), pp. 37–62, 83–96, 245–54; Linhares, *Historia*, pp. 23–9, 48–58, 70–80; Ibbetson, *Tea*, pp. 57–9; Grieve, *A Modern Herbal*, p. 407.

28. Hill, *Economic Botany*, pp. 480–3; J. Orton, *The Andes and the Amazon* (New York, 1876), pp. 290, 524–5; Simmonds, *The Popular Beverages*, pp. 81, 213–14.

29. R. Gardella, *Harvesting Mountains: Fujian and the China Tea Trade, 1757–1937* (Berkeley, CA, 1994), pp. 28–9; Evans, *Tea*, p. 95; Butel, *Histoire*, p. 32.

30. Tuchscherer, 'Coffee', pp. 56–7; C. R. Pennell, *Morocco since 1830: A History* (London, 2000), pp. 76, 89, 106; Lydon, 'On Trans-Saharan Trails', pp. 324–5; Matthee, *The Pursuit*, pp. 287–8.

31. J. Schneider, 'Die neuen Getränke: Schokolade, Kaffee und Tee, 16.–18. Jahrhundert', in S. Cavaciocchi (ed.), *Prodotti e tecniche d'oltremare nelle economie europee, secc. XIII–XVIII* (Florence, 1998), p. 563; R. Sandgruber, *Bittersüsse Genüsse: Kulturgeschichte der Genussmittel* (Vienna, 1986), p. 80; Barr, *Drink*, pp. 212–14; Schivelbusch, *Tastes*, pp. 73–9; Bizière, 'Hot Beverages', pp. 137, 139.

32. J. Burnett, *Liquid Pleasures, a Social History of Drinks in Modern Britain* (London, 1999), pp. 52–6; Clarence-Smith, *Cocoa*, pp. 38–40.

33. Burnett, *Liquid Pleasures*, p. 84; Barr, *Drink*, p. 214; Sandgruber, *Bittersüsse Genüsse*, pp. 79-80; Grieve, *A Modern Herbal*, p. 603.

34. Smith, 'Accounting for Taste'; Clarence-Smith, *Cocoa*, pp. 46–56; F. B. Thurber, *Coffee, from Plantation to Cup, a Brief History of Coffee Production and Consumption* (New York, 1881), pp. 215–16, 243; J. Othick, 'The Cocoa and Chocolate Industry in the Nineteenth Century', in D. Oddy and D. Miller (eds), *The Making of the Modern British Diet* (London, 1976), pp. 78, 86–7.

35. Clarence-Smith, *Cocoa*, pp. 38–53.

36. Sladkovsky, *The Long Road*, pp. 127, 194, 221–6; Matthee, *The Pursuit*, pp. 261, 264.

37. Clarence-Smith, *The Third Portuguese Empire*, p. 66; C. A. Montalto de Jesus, *Historic Macao* (Hong Kong, 1902), p. 345.

38. Clarence-Smith, *Cocoa*, Ch. 3.

39. Coe and Coe, *The True History*, pp. 121–9, 154, 175–6; Barr, *Drink*, pp. 273–5; Macfarlane and Macfarlane, *Green Gold*, pp. 44–9; Matthee, *The Pursuit*, pp. 159–60; R. S. Hattox, *Coffee and Coffeehouses: The Origins of a Social Beverage in the Medieval Near East* (Seattle, 1985), pp. 64–71.

40. Macfarlane and Macfarlane, *Green Gold*, p. 39; S. P. Sangar, *Food and Drinks in Mughal India* (New Delhi, 1999), p. 90; Burnett, *Liquid Pleasures*, pp. 23–4, 33–5, 103; Coe and Coe, *The True History*, p. 126.

41. Macfarlane and Macfarlane, *Green Gold*, p. 39; Evans, *Tea*, p. 33; Matthee, *The Pursuit*, p. 165; Schivelbusch, *Tastes*, pp. 22, 31; Barr, *Drink*, pp. 291–3; Grieve, *A Modern Herbal*, p. 603.

42. Butel, *Histoire*, pp. 16–23, 32–8; Macfarlane and Macfarlane, *Green Gold*, pp. 44, 55–63; Wang, *Chinese Tea Culture*, pp. 52–68; Morgan Pitelka (ed.), *Japanese Tea Culture: Art, History and Practice* (London, 2003), pp. 7–9; Anthony, 'A Short History', pp. 5–6.

43. Farid Khiari, *Licite, illicite, qui dit le droit en Islam: l'arrivée du café dans le monde arabe, une affaire d'état en 1511* (Aix-en-Provence, 2005); Hattox, *Coffee*, pp. 30–61; Matthee, *The Pursuit*, p. 171; E. W. Lane, *An Account of the Manners and Customs of the Modern Egyptians* (London, 1986, reprint of 1896 edn), p. 346; A. Ubicini, *La Turquie actuelle* (Paris, 1855), pp. 277–8.

44. A. S. Bemath, 'The Sayyid and Saalihiya Tariga; Reformist Anticolonial Hero in Somalia', in S. S. Samatar (ed.), *In the Shadow of Conquest: Islam in Colonial Northeast Africa* (Trenton, NJ, 1992), pp. 40–1; Lydon, 'On Trans-Saharan Trails', p. 328; Butel, *Histoire*, p. 232.

45. C. G. H. Schaefer, 'Coffee Unobserved: Consumption and Commoditization of Coffee in Ethiopia before the Eighteenth Century', in M. Tuchscherer (ed.), *Le commerce du café avant l'ère des plantations coloniales* (Cairo, 2001), pp. 26–7; A. B. Wylde, *Modern Abyssinia* (London, 1901), pp. 266–7.

46. Butel, *Histoire*, p. 189; Griffiths, *The History*, p. 618.

47. Schivelbusch, *Tastes*, pp. 85–92; Coe and Coe, *The True History*, Ch. 5; M. Vaussard, *Daily Life in Eighteenth Century Italy* (London, 1962), p. 194; Burnett, *Liquid Pleasures*, pp. 71–3.

48. Linhares, pp. 74, 224; Sladkovsky, *The Long Road*, pp. 142–7; Matthee, *The Pursuit*, pp. 237–8, 254; Barr, *Drink*, p. 211; Cowan, *The Social Life*, p. 161; Butel, *Histoire*, p. 95; H. J. Slijper, *Technologie en warenkennis, tweede deel, organische producten en eenige ook voor Ned.-Indië belangrijke cultures* (Purmerend, 1927), pp. 140–1; Fitchett, *Beverages*, pp. 60–7.

49. I. Kramer, 'Tea Drinking and its Culture', in Ding-bo Wu and Patrick D. Murphy (eds), *Handbook of Chinese Popular Culture* (London, 1994), pp. 60–2; Shao, Q., 'Tempest over Teapots: the Vilification of Teahouse Culture in Early Republican China', *Journal of Asian Studies*, LVII(4) (1998): 1012–14; Evans, *Tea*, pp. 60–5; Butel, *Histoire*, pp. 123–5.

50. Hattox, *Coffee*, pp. 73, 107–9; Matthee, *The Pursuit, pp. 169–72.*

51. Cowan, The Social Life, pp. 231–2, 242.

52. *Burnett, Liquid Pleasures, pp. 50–2.*

53. J. M. Scott, *The Tea Story* (London, 1964), pp. 152–4; Macfarlane and Macfarlane, *Green Gold*, pp. 80–2.

54. *Encyclopaedia Britannica* (1929) Vol. XIX, p. 876; Grieve, *A Modern Herbal*, p. 603; Hartley, *Food*, pp. 576–7.

55. Schivelbusch, *Tastes*, pp. 85–92; Coe and Coe, *The True History*, p. 226; E. Stols, 'Le cacao: le sang voluptueux du nouveau monde', in E. Collet (ed.), *Chocolat, de la boisson élitaire au bâton populaire* (Brussels, 1996), p. 52; J.-C. Bologne, 'Le chocolat et la littérature française et européenne des XIXe et XXe siècles', in Collet (ed.), *Chocolat*, p. 228.

56. Burnett, *Liquid Pleasures*, pp. 51, 56, 79; Butel, *Histoire*, p. 169; Sandgruber *Bittersüsse Genüsse*, p. 77; Bizière 'Hot Beverages', p. 140.
57. T. Omboni, *Viaggi nell'Africa occidentale* (Milan, 1846), pp. 243–4; Burnett, *Liquid Pleasures*, p. 66.
58. Butel, *Histoire*, pp. 32–3; Gardella, *Harvesting Mountains*, pp. 24–5; Macfarlane and Macfarlane, *Green Gold*, pp. 54–5; Evans, *Tea*, pp. 74, 83; Bak, S., 'From Strange Bitter Concoction to Romantic Necessity: The Social History of Coffee Drinking in South Korea', *Korea Journal*, XLV(2) (2005): 43–4.
59. Macfarlane and Macfarlane, *Green Gold*, p. 63; Kramer, 'Tea Drinking', pp. 61–2; Shao, 'Tempest', pp. 1012–14.
60. Hattox, *Coffee*, pp. 73, 77–128; Matthee, *The Pursuit*, pp. 162–4; Lane, *An Account*, pp. 346–7; Carlier, 'Le café', p. 983; L. Valensi, *Le Maghreb avant la prise d'Alger, 1790–1830* (Paris, 1969), pp. 46, 66; P. Boyer, *La vie quotidienne à Alger à la veille de l'intervention française* (Paris, 1963), pp. 212–14; H. Ingrams, *Arabia and the Isles* (London, 1942), pp. 42, 44–5.
61. Butel, *Histoire*, pp. 217, 225–6, 231–3; Matthee, *The Pursuit*, pp. 237–8, 264–6; Ibbetson, *Tea*, p. 47; Ingrams, *Arabia*, p. 152; Pennell, *Morocco*, p. 76.
62. Garavaglia, *Mercado*, pp. 54–62, 92–3; Ibbetson, *Tea*, p. 59; Scott, *The Tea Story*, p. 109.
63. Harwich, *Histoire*, Chs. 1–2; Coe and Coe, *The True History*, Chs 3–4.
64. C. E. Kany, *Life and Manners in Madrid, 1750–1800* (Berkeley, CA, 1932), pp. 149–52, 271, 329, 419; Schneider, 'Die neuen Getränke', p. 550; Simmonds, *The Popular Beverages*, p. 212; Stols, 'Le cacao', pp. 44–5, 50–1; E. Arcila Farías, *Comercio entre Venezuela y México en los siglos XVII y XVIII* (Mexico City 1950), pp. 40–1, 273.
65. G. Wagner, *The Chocolate Conscience* (London, 1987), pp. 16–17; Barr, *Drink*, p. 254; A. W. Knapp, *Cocoa and Chocolate, their History from Plantation to Consumer* (London, 1920), p. 15; M. Libert, 'La consommation du chocolat dans les Pays-Bas Autrichiens', in Collet (ed.), *Chocolat*, p. 78; Othick, 'The Cocoa and Chocolate Industry', pp. 77–82.
66. Schivelbusch, *Tastes*, p. 38.
67. Burnett, *Liquid Pleasures*, pp. 50, 71–3; Sandgruber, *Bittersüsse Genüsse*, pp. 75–6; Coe and Coe, *The True History*, pp. 215–16.
68. Schivelbusch, *Tastes*, pp. 35, 92–3; Bologne, 'Le chocolat', pp. 224–9.
69. Burnett, *Liquid Pleasures*, pp. 58, 74–5, 79, 81–4; *The New Encyclopaedia Britannica* (Chicago, 1993), Vol. XXVI, p. 973; Coe and Coe, *The True History*, p. 223; Schneider, 'Die neuen Getränke', pp. 558–63; Sandgruber, *Bittersüsse Genüsse*, pp. 76–7, 80–1.
70. Burnett, *Liquid Pleasures*, pp. 31–2, 52–6, 81–4; Sladkovsky, *The Long Road*, pp. 116, 147.
71. Cankan, 'Beverages: Beyond Turkish Coffee and Ayran' (2001) http://www.cankan.com/gturkishcuisine/47c-beverages.htm; Hartley, *Food*, pp. 576–7; Barr, *Drink*, p. 252; Grieve, *A Modern Herbal*, p. 603.

72. Evans, *Tea*, pp. 140–2; Wang, *Chinese Tea*, p. 71; Shao, 'Tempest', pp. 1021–30; Kramer, 'Tea Drinking', p. 62.
73. Hattox, *Coffee*, pp. 30–61; Matthee, *The Pursuit*, pp. 167–72.
74. Cowan, *The Social Life*, Ch. 7; Schneider, 'Die neuen Getränke', pp. 575–6; Bizière 'Hot Beverages', p. 136; Coe and Coe, *The True History*, pp. 205, 225–6; Kany, *Life*, pp. 149–51; Biblioteca Nacional del Perú, *Mercurio Peruano* (Lima, 1964 reprint), Vol. I, p. 110, and Vol. XI, p. 168.
75. Butel, *Histoire*, pp. 99–100; Scott, *The Tea Story*, pp. 101–8; Barr, *Drink*, pp. 207–8; Simmonds, *The Popular Beverages*, pp. 188–9; Thurber, *Coffee*, p. 207.
76. A. M. Young, *The Chocolate Tree, a Natural History of Cocoa* (Washington, 1994), p. 36; J. D. Phillips, *Salem and the Indies* (Boston, 1947), p. 347; Gardella, *Harvesting Mountains*, pp. 60–3, 110–11; Scott, *The Tea Story*, pp. 108–9.
77. Clarence-Smith, *Cocoa*, Chs. 2–3; C. Fuentes, *The Buried Mirror: Reflections on Spain and the New World* (London, 1992), p. 279; Linhares, *Historia*, pp. 76–99.
78. F. Pérez de la Riva, *El café, historia de su cultivo y explotación en Cuba* (Havana, 1944), pp. 175, 177.

−4−

The Limits of Globalization?

The Horticultural Trades in Postbellum America
Marina Moskowitz

It was the first Saturday after I moved to Alexandria, VA, in the summer of 1991. I walked out of my apartment toward the Market Square surrounding City Hall and was struck by the sight of flowers – vibrant flowers in the arms, bags, and baskets of virtually everyone I passed on the street. Although the flowers initially caught my eye, I quickly realized that these were only the crowning purchase in a very different type of 'weekly shop' than I had experienced before. The bags and baskets also held baked goods, pantry items like jams and honey, and especially produce. The seasons dictated what appeared in the market basket: summer's trinity of corn, tomatoes, and peaches would soon be replaced by apples, pears, and root vegetables, and so on throughout the year.

Like so many of my new neighbours, I became a regular shopper at the Saturday Farmers' Market in Old Town Alexandria. Over time we all developed allegiances to specific vendors; we saw them week after week and chatted as acquaintances do, but in this case the topics of idle conversation – the weather, how work was that week – might have a profound effect on what I ate that week. My own fledgling market relationships with a fisherman from the Chesapeake Bay and fruit growers from Shippensburg, PA spanned not only the boundaries of Market Square, but also the rough geographic parameters from which this urban market drew its commodities. In the intervening years, farmers' markets have flourished in the United States, growing in number and scale as consumers have coalesced around a nexus of environmentalism, health concerns, scepticism of corporate provision, and fascination with food.[1] For growers and other small-scale food producers, these settings can provide a financial boon, shoring up both the balance sheet of a specific business and a traditional sector of the American economy: Mark Toigo, one of the Shippensburg orchardmen, says that selling directly to consumers at farmers' market 'is the only way traditional family farms will survive'.[2] Above all, these markets seem to be celebrations of the local.

But was this always the case? In Alexandria, the city proudly, and repeatedly, stakes a claim for the oldest market continually operating in the same location. If generations of Alexandria residents and area growers have gone to the same square to pursue this same act of buying and selling food, has this act always held the same meaning for them? How have the contexts in which they engaged in the market changed? The changing historical contexts might well change that frame of 'local' in which the current generation slots the experience of participating, whether as buyer or seller, at a farmers' market.[3] Even today, in the very celebration of the local that farmers' markets appear to represent, there is a tacit acknowledgement that the extra-local is the norm for food provision in the United States. The scale of what that experiential frame encompasses changes – 'local' has different boundaries at different times. For example, the Fresh Farm markets in and around Washington, DC, require their vendors to be resident and produce their commodities within a 150-mile radius of the city.[4] But this present-day extent of the local – a manageable drive before the ring of the cowbell that signals the opening of the market – would have seemed vast in an era reliant on horsepower for personal transport of people and goods. This is not to say that such movement of goods did not happen in, say, the middle of the nineteenth century, but that the definitions and perceptions of local, regional, and global exchange are dynamic. Not only do these perceptions change over time, but practices of food provision may be interpreted even within a specific era in different ways depending on how those practices are framed.

In the provision of produce – fruit and vegetables purchased by the consumer in what nineteenth-century growers referred to as their 'green' state (as opposed to canned, frozen, dried, pickled or otherwise preserved) – this issue of the locale of food takes on special significance.[5] In the purveying of produce, there is strong impetus to provide both the most 'fresh' food and the most readily available, even, or especially, when it would be 'out of season' for a specific geographic market. These market aims are often contradictory, and can pull both producers and consumers in opposite directions. The horticultural trades, broadly defined to include both those growing produce for market and those supplying such producers with seeds and other plant stock, test both the influence and the limits of globalization in food production.

Examining these tensions reminds us that globalization is not, and historically has not been, a linear process. Taking a longer view of the provision of produce in the United States, for example, shows impulses towards both expansion and retrenchment of exchange, even occurring simultaneously, expressed in different ways, but often in the service of building a national economy. From its founding, the United States was embedded in global food systems, as is discussed by other authors in this volume, such as Sidney Mintz, and Steven Topik and Michelle Craig McDonald. But for a consideration of fresh fruit and vegetables, it is instructive to look at the historical contexts of the nineteenth century, when the growth of American horticultural endeavour provided a link between the domestic economy of individual growers and the political economy of the nation, particularly in the period following the Civil War when the trades sought to use their commercial potential to knit the national landscape and economy back together.[6]

Even when embedded in global food *systems*, many American consumers were nonetheless still at the end of relatively short food *chains*; the distinction I draw here is that between large-scale movement of commodities on a collective, often national, scale, and the more precise movement of specific foodstuffs from producer through processors and distributors to consumers. The trade in fresh produce was influenced by both of these trajectories; the broader food systems might exert global economic and culinary influence even when the specific supply was local. In order for gardeners to sell their wares, they needed a market, in the broadest sense of the word – potential consumers who wanted, or could be guided to want, their produce. So the trade of market gardeners was influenced not just by the conditions of planting and the logistics of transport, but also by cuisine. Culinary practices, whether traditions of family, region, nationality, or ethnic group or innovations encouraged by neighbours or advice literature, informed the market for produce. Local practices were developed in tandem with generations, if not centuries, of cultural exchange, which provided the horticultural, culinary, technological, and economic contexts for food provision.

The Provision of Produce

The nineteenth century witnessed massive changes in the demographics of the United States, with seemingly contradictory dispersal and concentration occurring in juxtaposition. One marker of the start of the century was the Louisiana Purchase of 1803, doubling the landmass of the country, and over the course of the century a series of federal land acts facilitated ownership claims on this land and land farther west. A trend toward cheaper land values and smaller available parcels of land culminated in the Homestead Act of 1862, which exchanged land claims for a pledge of improvement and nominal filing charges. These measures allowed the distribution of population across the North American continent, but at the same time, certain areas held concentrations of people unimaginable from generation to generation. It was the 1920 census that established the United States as an urban nation, with a majority of the population living in cities; but the move toward urbanization, in demography as well as landscape development, occurred over the course of the nineteenth century. Although the designation of city was given to a huge spectrum of places – from the overwhelming population leader of New York to concentrations of 2,500 people that most people today barely would consider a town – it was the new density of population (especially away from the eastern seaboard) as much as the scale of these cities that was remarkable to those witnessing the changes.[7]

These dizzying demographic shifts called for new considerations in food provision: on the one hand, how could cities like New York or Chicago be supplied with enough food for their growing population, and on the other, how could isolated farmers enter into exchanges, whether for cash or other goods? These questions would be answered through a myriad of means, from transportation technology to developments in food preservation to new markets and forms of exchange. Still, to a large degree, the questions were answered by the horticultural trades that flourished over the course of the nineteenth century. Those supplying fresh food were not only farmers but also gardeners. In the nineteenth century, the distinction between farming and gardening was not drawn solely as we might draw it today, between economic and leisure-time activities, or between productive and ornamental plantings, but rather between types of produce. Farmers grew grains, and other staple crops (as well as raising livestock), and gardeners grew vegetables and fruits.[8]

One such market gardener, or 'trucker', as such commercial growers were also called, Edward Mitchell, explained in his account of trade the pull of the New York markets for both producers and consumers:

> A visit to some of our famous markets, such as Washington Market, of New York City, cannot fail to produce a correct impression of the great demands of life, and how they are supplied, as well as the great position of him who grows the supplies. ... For a moment consider the statistics of the increase of population in New York City for the last ten years, all of which are consumers, and compare it with the increase of producers, and you will find the former nearly double in ratio that of the latter every year. Increase of inhabitants, both by natural birth and by foreign emigration [*sic*], all of whom cling fondly to the city and all its enchantments, go to swell the ranks of consumers. These things are inevitable, and must be prepared for, and so long as these facts remain unchanged, there will be no glut in the market, and prices of all products will hold good and amply repay the producer. What is true of New York City is only too true of every other.[9]

These gardeners grew more than they needed for family sustenance, but on a more modest, and often regional, scale than their agricultural counterparts. Prescriptive literature for market gardeners often included sample plans for an economically productive landscape; these sources indicate that market gardening was viable on a few acres of land, and often included plans for garden plots as small as half an acre.[10] At a time when, by virtue of the Homestead Act, the 'standard' American family farm was generally thought of as forty acres, there was a clear distinction in these pursuits. The considerably smaller scale of the garden was twinned with a much greater intensity of production, although advice to gardeners varied in the number and breadth of crops that they recommended planting.

As individuals, market gardeners were usually the proprietors of small businesses, but collectively, their sector grew considerably, especially over the latter half of the nineteenth century. A special bulletin on market gardening written in conjunction with the last census of the nineteenth century, taken in 1890, recorded a labour force of about 250,000 involved in the trade, with annual produce valued at US$75 million.[11] While gardeners raised crops for a broad sector of the US marketplace, from elites looking for novelty or out-of-season fruits and vegetables (as indeed had European elites for generations) to the burgeoning institutional consumers such as restaurants, hotels, and railroad companies, much of the contemporary literature about the trade suggests that the market most frequently envisioned was working families in urban, and often industrializing, locations. Even within this generalized sector, there was socioeconomic variety, ranging from labourers exchanging part of their earnings in a company-owned store to middle-class clerks shopping at local greengrocers.

What all of these consumers shared was that they no longer fit the Jeffersonian vision of interlocking but largely self-sufficient farming families considered typical of late eighteenth- and early nineteenth-century America. Of course, whether that vision ever fully described American food provision might be questioned, as periodic seasons of abundance led some farm families to enter the marketplace, if irregularly. Also, there were always community-based artisans and professionals, but their families may still have maintained kitchen gardens, or exchanged their services for goods within the local community.[12] One may well ask what the small-scale raising of produce, distributed on a regional scale, for a largely domestic market, has to do with the global trends that we find in food production and supply today. But I think it is important to think about these first steps away from a reliance on home production of food as precursors, in structure if not scale, to the worldwide food industries upon which some of the other authors in this volume comment.

The difference that emerged over the course of the nineteenth century was therefore not only selling and buying food for the family table, but selling to consumers and buying from producers one did not otherwise know, and might not encounter within one's own community. This shift to a more impersonal or even anonymous food chain based solely on commercial, rather than any other type of communal, links, and increasingly mediated by wholesalers, agents, or grocers, seems to me a necessary precursor to the widespread sourcing of food that became common in the twentieth century.[13] But it is also a reminder of the different frames placed on the practices of food provision; the very act that provides a sense of connection to twenty-first-century participants in farmers' markets may also have been a first foray into an abstract commercial world for our nineteenth-century counterparts.

Increasingly over the nineteenth century, however, the transport and import of food, even fresh produce, did occur in the US marketplace. The geographic scale of the United States supplied ground for experimenting in the technological and horticultural realms that would underpin a widening market for fresh food. Market gardeners of course relied on good transport links to take their produce to market; broadening the geographic radius of delivery meant not just a wider market but also the ability to specialize in fewer crops, without fear of saturating the market. Although reliable refrigerated trucks did not emerge until the second quarter of the twentieth century, market gardeners did make use of the railroads (and the sometimes overlooked canals) to penetrate distant markets, while ships brought imported goods, especially from the Caribbean in the case of fresh produce.

Part of the trade of the gardener was reading the market accurately; although the practice of horticulture did not allow for quick changes in the production cycle, it did allow for a variety of distribution channels.[14] Other innovations had to do with packing methods, which could mean the difference between success and failure, regardless of the quality of one's crops. At the same time, growers experimented with the timing of harvesting, and bred crops that they hoped would withstand longer journeys. Of course, even within the realm of fresh produce there was a wide spectrum of the success with which goods could be packed and shipped – cabbages were heartier than tomatoes, apples more resilient than peaches. Thus, the trade built upon a variety of types of knowledge, and also investment. In the words of one adviser to the trade, Burnet Landreth, writing in 1893:

> The market gardener, filling a multiform position as a cultivator of the soil to an intense degree, as a careful packer of products in such a manner as to make his goods attractive and saleable, as a shipper and a close reader of market intelligence, must have the best agricultural appliances and commercial aids, none of which can be produced without money, consequently the subject of capital is one of considerable importance.[15]

The practice of reading the market – in both deciding what to grow and deciding where, when, and how to sell – led nineteenth-century gardeners, and by extension, their wholesalers, agents, and consumers, to consider directly the geography of food provision. As a very crude rule, it can be said that growers at greater distances to specific markets found their advantage in seasonal timing, particularly in the ability to provide produce to a specific place earlier in the year than it could be grown there (though sometimes late crops were as highly valued in the opposite trajectory), while local growers had the advantage of freshness, where goods could go literally from farm to market on the same day. But the calculus of value behind these generalizations was highly complex, and often revealed no clear 'best way' for either farmers or consumers, when quality mattered as well as quantity, and quality was, of course, a subjective judgement.

The gardener Mitchell gave much thought to these issues of value in his 1870 text; considering how best to market his tomatoes, he offered an assessment of the changing supply to the New York markets, as he was situated just outside of the city. He noted that as early as the middle of May, tomatoes appeared in Washington Market (the primary produce market in New York City), arriving from growers in Bermuda at the high price of 50 cents a quart. These stocks were replaced as rapidly as possible with tomatoes from Virginia, and the price on the Bermuda tomatoes dropped off, as the 'distance which the [Bermuda tomatoes] had to be transported necessarily detracted from their value when compared with the more fresh article received from Norfolk'. Finally, the local growers from New Jersey and Long Island began supplying New York consumers, because 'a home article had a good market awaiting it'. As he weighed his options for how to make the best profit from his own tomatoes, Mitchell summed up the situation around New York:

The Southern facilities for raising produce for an early market are superior to ours, and for a short time they reap a liberal profit; but the distance they have to travel, and the rough handling they receive, necessarily decrease their value when put in competition with our home fruit; yet these shipments have their effect in bringing our home produce into market at a lower rate than it otherwise would without this competition.[16]

In the end, Mitchell sold his tomatoes locally, but in a variety of markets: some through agents at the wholesale market, some to greengrocers, and some to canners, who would come and pick their own tomatoes, saving him labour costs.

The example of Edward Mitchell's tomatoes shows that there was indeed trans-national exchange, as well as regional trade, at play in the delivery of fresh produce as early as the late 1860s, immediately following the Civil War. Though the technical and logistical limits of global trade in produce were overcome over time, many American horticulturalists still saw their economic sector as ripe for further development on a regional and national level. Since the early republic, horticulture was put forward by some as a hybrid of agrarian and mercantile interests. In the aftermath of the Civil War, those in the trade saw still more potential for their endeavours. Horticulture could build, or revive, local economies. Southern planters were encouraged to turn from monocrop agriculture to more varied gardening, to supply both their own region and the population centres of the North. Easterners were advised to supply the needs of urban dwellers through market gardening rather than compete with farmers in the Midwest, who, with access to cheaper land, could supply the core grain needs for much of the country. For the temperate climates of the West Coast, particularly California, horticulturalists advocated investment in fruit growing; the state that entered the Union as a result of the population boom of the Gold Rush might find a more reliable economic base supplying the rest of the country with produce. If these regional activities were balanced, a self-sufficient national food system, and economy, would be the result. As the seed grower W. Atlee Burpee wrote, 'Our large cities afford good markets for nearly all fruits and vegetables and the supply frequently does not equal the demand.'[17] Horticulturalists encouraged a balanced system of growing to meet this demand, in order also to underpin expanding industrialization, with its attendant demographic concentrations; a form of economic nationalism, a concept also discussed by Paul Kratoska in the Asian rice trade elsewhere in this volume, emerged. Of course, a long-term vision did see the United States engaged in global trade – especially as exporters – but the need to firm up a domestic market system in the vastly changed landscape following the Civil War placed some limits on this development. Still, it is important to remember the impact of the sheer size of the United States when framing a discussion of the local and global in food provision. The attempts of horticulturalists to link their domestic economies of specific families and firms to the larger project of the American political economy were on a geographic scale that elsewhere would almost certainly have encompassed transnational exchange. Fruit from California might seem no less foreign to a consumer at Washington Market than tomatoes from Bermuda did. In this way, nineteenth-century food provision in the United States might be seen as a microcosm of the types of global exchange of fresh food that would become increasingly possible over the course of the twentieth century, with new transport technology and new hybrids of fruits and vegetables, an example of which we find in Susanne Freidberg's chapter in this volume.

As Edward Mitchell's experiences, as well as those recounted by many of his peers, show, even in the nineteenth century the commercial exchange of produce had several layers. Though Mitchell's stated concerns were with finding a market that paid best for his produce in least competition with other regional, national, or transnational growers, Mitchell and the many market gardeners like him were also consumers. The burgeoning trade of small-scale market gardeners themselves constituted a market for purveyors of plant material, especially seeds. Even with their expansion of food provision, in both geographic and sometimes economic terms, market gardeners can also be thought of as 'middlemen' (or women, as indeed the trade encompassed both genders). Although they raised the crops that served as food for their market, they often bought in, among other things, the seed and young plants to grow this food. The same United States Census report mentioned above charting the trade's output, also traced its input, including $1.4 million worth of seed purchased in 1890.[18] The seed trade recognized this receptive sector of their market and catered to them with specific catalogues, advice pamphlets, and special prices for multiple purchases; catalogues such as Johnson and Stokes' *Money Growers Manual* emphasized the return on the small investment necessary to buy seeds.[19] The seed trade envisioned a particularly attentive audience, because market gardeners were also sometimes relative novices to horticulture. Although a demographic profile of market gardeners is beyond the scope of this chapter (and perhaps beyond the scope of extant historical records), the nineteenth-century literature – everything from advice manuals to memoirs of successful trade to fiction – on the subject does suggest a profile of new and largely book-taught horticulturalists.

With this new market, the seed trade, also expanding broadly over the nineteenth century, were able to position themselves as purveyors of food, or at least the means to grow food, among the other commodities they supplied. Although participants in the seed trade sold a broad array of products that encompassed both food stock and other elements of the landscape, such as ornamental flowers and lawn grass, many sellers recognized their potential contribution to the provision of food. As the seedsman John Auer wrote in his trade catalogue:

> Those who plant our seed can rely upon having choice vegetables. Nothing is a greater comfort or more profitable to a family than a good vegetable garden. It is drawn upon every day of the year for healthful and delicious food. ... There is nothing like the pure article fresh from the garden. Try them, and always bear in mind that it is as easy to raise good vegetables as poor ones.[20]

Francis Brill, a seed grower and horticultural author, concurred that seeds were an important part of the agrarian economy. He wrote:

> The growing of seeds has become an important branch of farm industry, and the increasing demand for all leading seeds, owing to the constant growth of our country, and the accompanyingly increased interest in horticulture, render this business worthy the attention of those having land suitable for the purpose ... This business is an extended branch of vegetable-growing.[21]

Extending the food chain in this way expands the frame placed around the market exchange of food.

The Provision of Plants

In 1866, B. K. Bliss and Son, purveyors of seeds based in Springfield, Massachusetts, printed in their annual catalogue a testimonial letter from the Reverend Henry Ward Beecher that read, simply, 'Your seeds are capital.' Whether the pun on the word capital was intentional or not (though scholars of Beecher might suspect that it was), the compliment suggests how the growing seed trade underpinned the agrarian economy of the United States.[22] For a relatively modest investment, consumers of seeds acquired a stock of 'accumulated goods devoted to the production of other goods', or capital toward the production of grain and vegetable produce.[23] Through the copious seed catalogues of the nineteenth century, consumers were encouraged to try new kinds of produce and new varieties of old favourites. The benefits of vegetable seeds to appetite, health, and the family purse were detailed, along with horticultural and sometimes culinary advice. For example, the seed seller James Gregory published 'a little treatise' entitled *How to Cook Vegetables*, which offered advice 'on the cooking of every species of vegetable advertised in my Catalogue', giving 'simple, neat, and direct methods'.[24] Growing food was presented as both morally and financially rewarding, no matter on what scale it was carried out; urban artisans and labourers might sow just a few plants on spare ground or in boxes or pots, while farmers were taught the value of the kitchen garden, even at the expense of a proportion of their market crops.

The products grown from seed might directly constitute food, or by extension, supply animal feed, enabling the rearing of livestock, which would in turn contribute food, or a power source for further production. Animal and vegetable by-products could be used to restore nutrients to the soil, enabling further generations of planting and food production. Of course, these agrarian cycles were not new to the nineteenth century; but what was new to the era was the widespread distribution and massive diversity of seeds available for purchase. Many farmers and gardeners could, if they desired, skip one step of the cycle of sowing, growing, and harvesting; designating a certain proportion of any crop to go to seed might still be desired by some growers, but was not as necessary as it might have been in the Colonial and early Federal eras.

Seeds became one more item in the agrarian budget. How much consumers were willing to spend on these commodities was based on individual assessments of their worth, especially in relation to the value of the produce that could be raised from them, and could be consumed rather than saved for seed. These assessments reveal the ways in which the assignment of value was often linked to nutritive worth, whether manifested in soil improvement, animal feed, or human food.[25] The Rawson family were market gardeners and seed growers; the son kept in print advice originally offered by his father: 'Better to pay twice the market price for an article that is first-class in every respect than have poor trash, even if it is to be had as a gift ... I have always made it a practice when purchasing seed for my own use (of such varieties as I do not raise, and so have been obliged to buy), to secure the best, regardless of cost, and have always found this to pay. Quality, not price, is the chief point to look to in purchasing seed.'[26]

Because supplying one's own table and buying at market were not mutually exclusive – many families combined both practices – the seed companies could target both of these markets simultaneously. The two sectors in fact complemented one another, as the firms used the professional standing of market gardeners to advertise the benefits of certain varieties that they tended to buy (often those that were particularly early or prolific), while popularity for the home table might convince market gardeners of the worth of trying a particular crop. Still, even if the seed companies successfully advocated for trying particular types and varieties of produce, they needed to ensure repeat consumption in order to have a viable business. By the end of the nineteenth century the seed trade in the United States spanned over 800 firms, underpinned by a broader international trade, and used aggressive advertising and marketing campaigns to convince farmers and gardeners to buy from firms rather than harvest their own seeds.[27] In the light of these conscious attempts at marketing, what was attractive to consumers about buying seeds, and vegetable seeds in particular?

One set of considerations was rooted in the seemingly simple issue of space. Growers had to decide whether it was more advantageous to use every foot of available land for usable produce (whether consumed at home or in the market) and buy seeds afresh, or allow part of their land to go to seed. Purchasing new seeds every year was especially attractive to market gardeners; if you were farming forty acres of grain, letting a small portion of one field go to seed to save it for the next year's crop was not an issue, but if you were intensively gardening a half-acre plot, seed saving was not so viable. Seed growers insisted that seeds should be selected from the best specimen of whatever species was grown in the garden; but those growing for produce would necessarily want the best of the crop for market.[28]

In determining the value of seeds in relation to crops, however, growers needed to consider their worth in a broad sense: they needed to evaluate quality as well as quantity. The naked eye and the personal palate are much more assured judges of produce than of seeds. Although horticultural manuals offered some suggestions as to how to gauge the freshness of seeds – noting whether they floated or sank in water was a common test – ultimately, most consumers had to trust their producers, whether themselves or others, and the circumstances in which seeds were grown. As Brill wrote, 'In the business of seed-growing, a reputation for strict integrity and intelligent care forms an important portion of the capital required. The name of the grower adds a money value to the product.'[29] It appears from the agricultural and horticultural literature that farmers were more trusting of themselves, while amateur growers and market gardeners (and even farm families when choosing for their kitchen gardens) favoured professional seed dealers more frequently.[30] There is of course a botanical basis for such a distinction, again stemming from the space available for growing. On large expanses of land with higher concentrations of fewer crops, particular types of plants were more likely to remain in relative isolation from one another, producing fairly pure seed. In a small-scale vegetable garden, this isolation was virtually impossible; the cross-pollination of plants by wind, birds, and insects could result in significant changes to future generations of plants. As Gregory explained his own seed farm:

On my four farms I have grown this season over seventy acres of seed and seed stock, embracing over one hundred varieties. Some may infer that in growing so many varieties there is danger of admixture; but this is a matter I specifically guard against by completely isolating every variety of the same kind. My farms are located somewhat like the angles of a right-angled triangle, and are about one mile distant from each other; in addition to this the different lots of three of them are very much scattered. Of all these advantages I avail myself to the utmost to produce complete isolation.[31]

For growers who preferred particular attributes of specific varieties, or even relied on them for market purposes, the calculation of the worth of seeds and their produce incorporated this idea of botanical risk. While the commercial seed trade rarely offered guarantees for its products, hundreds of thousands of consumers nonetheless favoured their products over those they might raise themselves.

While the unintentional mixing of plants might be a liability, the planned breeding of plants was another advantage for the seed firms, in the eyes of many of their consumers. Any noteworthy characteristic of a plant might be highlighted or combined with other attributes through crossing or hybridization. For plants productive of food, particular attention was paid to the length of time to bearing; hardiness, especially for particular climates; how prolific the plant was, especially in relation to its size; the size and shape of the produce it bore; and, of course, flavour. Seed companies vied with one another to create, or purchase from their creators, particular strains and varieties of vegetables that they believed would be attractive to growers; the new names for varieties often reflected the firm or breeder who developed them, so that even when sold by other companies, the seeds would provide advertising for a competitor. Although the botanical point continues to be debated, there is no question that in the nineteenth century the received wisdom taught that the seeds of hybrid plants were not productive of further generations of plants, or at least not of any reliably true to the original. In developing hybrids that were perceived as attractive options for both home and professional gardeners in terms of both taste and economics, seed companies were also encouraging repeat customers.[32]

Through these varied means and responses, the commercial seed trade proved increasingly appealing to many growers, especially of vegetable produce, as a first venture in each planting season. Seeds were at the heart of the global food systems that had started as early as the Columbian Exchange, but they can also be considered to be at the start of the specific food chains from which Americans bought produce. The transatlantic exchange of seeds had occurred for centuries, and greatly affected the flora, both ornamental and economic, of the young United States. This cultural dissemination of the past was recalled by seed companies in their marketing literature, in which geography lessons were sometimes the by-product of their commitment to horticultural education. The seed firm Bagg and Batchelder, of Springfield, MA, began each catalogue description with the native locale of the plant in question, for example: 'The Beet is a biennial plant and is a native of the sea coast of the south of Europe... The Cucumber is a tender annual, a native of the East Indies... The Tomato is a tender annual, a native of South America.'[33] For gardeners, understanding where a plant originated gave the opportunity to try to replicate the growing conditions of that place, even if by artificial means such as hothouses or irrigation systems, in order to raise the best crop possible. This knowledge might also make potential consumers more appreciative of particular crosses or hybrids that were bred to withstand climactic conditions different from their native ones. While the seed firms led customers through these horticultural lessons, they were also explaining the origins of certain common, and occasionally not so common, foods, and showing the ways in which global exchanges were embedded in even the home production and consumption of vegetables.

The horticultural advice stemming from plant origins also suggested that, while compensation could be made for growing plants in other climactic and soil conditions, the best results, and thus the most fertile seeds, might be obtained in areas with similar growing environments. Other advice, by contrast, indicated that it was exactly when plants were 'tested' – for example by growing them in a more northern climate than their native one – and survived that they proved their mettle as productive of a next generation; many companies touted northern-grown seeds as the hardiest. Botanical knowledge and folk wisdom blended in the pages of catalogues and advertisements; for example, one seed seller tempted Southern gardeners with his Northern-grown cabbage seeds by writing, 'Every gardener of experience knows when earliness is sought for, the farther north the seed he plants is grown, the better.'[34] However contradictory the advice given and the marketing methods employed, seed companies made one thing clear: there was no advantage to planting seeds that had been grown locally, and firms would try to source the best samples possible for any given crop.

Most firms that sold seeds were themselves consumers of them, and worked with growers across the United States, and often throughout Europe (and to a lesser extent other locations) as well. No attempt was made to mask these origins: indeed catalogue descriptions frequently mentioned the country, or region, of origin of the seeds; and in some instances, even specific growers, if they were recognized for particular hybrids, were mentioned by name. In a simple statement, echoed by numerous other firms, B. K. Bliss and Sons, of New York City, wrote in their catalogue, 'Aware of the importance to the Farmer and Gardener of having such seeds as can be relied upon, every effort has been made to select such only as will give perfect satisfaction. A large proportion of our seeds are of American growth. Those which cannot be successfully grown in our country are annually imported from the most reliable European growers.'[35]

Of course, in some instances the sourcing of seeds by firms had less to do with horticultural merit than with logistics and economics: in any given season, where might seeds be purchased most reliably and cheaply? Much as small-scale growers developed 'favourites' among the seed companies, even for particular crops, so too did firms develop particular relationships with growers. However, in a trade that operated to a certain extent at the mercy of nature, last-minute changes in provisioning were sometimes necessary, as one grower's seed crop might be rained out and another's might be unexpectedly prolific. Flexibility in the supply of seeds was crucial to the trade; again the influences of the local and the extra-local were balanced in the selling of seeds for vegetable crops. Though sourcing seeds from far-flung locales, many in the trade were consciously trying to tip the balance of exchange in their favour. Brill explained the benefits of the American seed trade:

> The business of seed-growing is rapidly extending in this country, and is attended by a corresponding falling off of importations... A large share of our garden-vegetables are natives of subtropical or even tropical countries, and these in our warm soils and under our clear bright skies, attain a perfection unknown in Europe. They mature more thoroughly and produce larger and better seed than it is possible to raise abroad. As a consequence the former prejudice of our gardeners against American seeds has well-nigh disappeared; and at present not only are they preferred at home, but the quantities exported annually increase.[36]

The US market gardeners of the nineteenth century grew produce that was transported long distances for their own day, but were still often limited to regions of the North American continent. However, those gardeners used seeds that might have been imported from other regions of the country, or abroad. So if we take the longer horticultural view of food provision, the globalization of food may be said to occur even at times and in places where there is not an obvious transport of food.

The horticultural trades operated in at least three ways that brought issues of extra-local exchange in food provision to the fore, though always in balance with local forces. First, in marketing seeds, the trade offered horticultural description that often included the native setting of particular plants, so that even those growing for the most local of consumers, the home table, might have an awareness of the broader origins of their food. Second, even when produce was distributed and consumed locally, the seeds from which the vegetables were grown might have been imported from elsewhere – in the case of the US seed trade, usually from Europe. And finally, the rise of market gardening brought gardeners into direct competition with growers from other regions of the United States, and even other countries. Through this market competition, both growers and consumers considered the different qualities of vegetable produce that could be grown at home and away, and assigned monetary value to such elusive qualities as freshness and taste.

While the last of these telescoping perspectives encompasses the first two, the three together show the different scales of exchange through which ideas about the 'locale' of food are developed – from broad cultural exchange, to the exchange of 'capital' (in this case, the stock of seeds), to the exchange of food itself. Although the horticultural trades participated in these broad exchanges in numerous ways, the provision of fresh produce also exhibits the ways in which global forces were always balanced by local endeavours. The advantages of transcontinental and transnational exchange were seen primarily in the lengthening of the season for which certain commodities were available, or the provision of exotic options that might not be grown in particular locales. Many consumers, however, in both Edward Mitchell's day and our own, see a virtue to local growth and the minimal transport of fresh produce that they may not apply to other types of food. The case of fresh produce provision in postbellum America shows both the influences and the limits of the relationship of food and globalization.

Notes

1. In a recent lecture, the US food writer Joan Nathan cited statistics showing an increase from about 300 farmers' markets across the country in 1970 to 4,000 today. J. Nathan, 'The New American Cooking,' lecture, Library of Congress, Washington, DC, 6 November 2006.
2. Mark Toigo, quoted by Judith Weinraub, 'Buy Fruit, Save a Farm: Increasingly Farmers Markets Keep Growers Going', *Washington Post*, 3 August 2005, p. F1

(accessed at http://www.washingtonpost.com/wp-dyn/content/article/
2005/08/02/AR2005080200478.html).

3. H. Tangires, *Public Markets and Civic Culture in Nineteenth-Century America* (Baltimore, MD, 2003).

4. C. Kettlewell, 'Harvest Home', *Washington Post*, 27 June 2003, p. WE30 (accessed at http://www.washingtonpost.com/ac2/wp-dyn?pagename= article&node=&contentId=A35665-2003Jun26&notFound=true). See also, the Fresh Farm market regulations listed at http://www.freshfarmmarket.org/forms/ farmerapp_2006.pdf.

5. F. Brill, *Farm-Gardening and Seed-Growing* (New York, 1884), p. 7.

6. Margaret Schabas examines the ways in which the concept of 'an economy' grew into an entity distinct from the natural world, particularly over the course of the eighteenth century. Though drawing primarily on European theorists in natural philosophy and economic discourse, the coincident timing to the birth and growth of the American republic makes her text extremely useful for the understanding of economic nationalism in the first century of US history, and especially the connection between domestic and political economies, as seen clearly in the realm of horticulture (M. Schabas, *The Natural Origins of Economics* (Chicago, 2005)).

7. See, for example, H. Chudacoff and J. Smith, *The Evolution of American Urban Society* (New York, 2004); P. Gates *et al.*, *The Jeffersonian Dream: Studies in the History of American Land Policy and Development* (Albuquerque, NM, 1996); P. Kastor, *The Nation's Crucible: The Louisiana Purchase and the Creation of America* (New Haven, CT, 2004); S. Levinson and B. Sparrow, *The Louisiana Purchase and American Expansion, 1803–1898* (New York, 2005); R. Mohl (ed.), *The Making of Urban America* (New York, 1997).

8. F. Brill, *Farm-Gardening and Seed-Growing* (New York, 1884), pp. 7–8.

9. E. Mitchell, *Five Thousand a Year; and How I Made It* (Boston, 1870), pp 124–5.

10. See, for example, H. Rawson, *Success in Market Gardening* (New York, 1910), p. 93. (An earlier edition of this text was written by W.W. Rawson, and published in 1892.)

11. B. Landreth, *Market Gardening and Farm Notes* (New York, 1893), p. 1.

12. A. Kulikoff, *The Agrarian Origins of American Capitalism* (Charlottesville, VA, 1992); M. Bruegel, *Farm, Shop, Landing: The Rise of a Market Society in the Hudson Valley 1780–1860* (Durham, NC, 2002).

13. It is interesting to note that the late twentieth and early twenty-first centuries appear to be witnessing a reaction against this anonymity, with new attention paid to the economic and health benefits of local production and consumer attachment. The ESRC/AHRC Cultures of Consumption projects on Alternative Food Networks and Food Commodity Chains are addressing these newer trends.

14. Landreth, *Market Gardening*, pp. 4–11.
15. Landreth, *Market Gardening*, p. 5.
16. Mitchell, *Five Thousand a Year*, pp. 36–7.
17. W. Atlee Burpee and Co., *How to Grow Melons for Market* (Philadelphia, 1895), p. viii. For postbellum regional horticultural advice, see, for example, Allison & Addison, *Handbook of the Garden* (Richmond, VA, 1868); Brill, *Farm-Gardening and Seed-Growing,* p. 3, 8; J. Gregory, *Annual Circular and Retail Catalogue* (Marblehead, MA, 1874), inside front cover; Charles Shinn, *Pacific Rural Handbook* (San Francisco, 1879).
18. Landreth, *Market Gardening*, p. 1.
19. Johnson and Stokes, *Money Growers' Manual* (Philadelphia, 1893).
20. John Auer and Co., *Annual Catalogue* (Schnectady, NY, n.d.), p. 19.
21. Brill, *Farm-Gardening and Seed-Growing,* pp. 3, 10
22. B. K. Bliss and Son, *Spring Catalogue and Amateur's Guide for 1866* (Springfield, MA, 1866), inside front cover. See also, H. Beecher, *Plain and Pleasant Talk about Fruits, Flowers, and Farming* (New York, 1859); D. Applegate, *The Most Famous Man in America: The Biography of Henry Ward Beecher* (New York, 2006).
23. Quotation taken from the definition of 'capital', Merriam-Webster On-Line Dictionary, www.merriam-webster.com.
24. J. Gregory, *Annual Seed Circular* (Marblehead, MA, 1872), p. 37.
25. I would like to thank Emily Pawley for her helpful comments on the relationship between economic and nutritive value; her doctoral research, 'Accounting with Money and Materials in Early American Agriculture,' promises to be a significant contribution to the understanding of value in agrarian economies.
26. Rawson, *Success in Market Gardening*, pp. 69, 77.
27. D. Tucker, *Kitchen Gardening in America: A History* (Ames, IA, 1993), p. 84.
28. See for example, Gregory, *Annual Circular and Retail Catalogue*, p. 4.
29. Brill, *Farm-Gardening and Seed-Growing*, p. 3
30. Throughout the nineteenth century, a healthy scepticism toward purchased seeds was evident, especially in agricultural (as opposed to horticultural) sectors; the debate over seed saving vs. seed buying was played out in the agricultural press. See for example *American Farmer*, 1 August 1892, and *American Gardener*, May 1886. I do not mean to imply that all Americans in the nineteenth century had equal access – whether economic, geographic, or social – to store-bought or mail-order seeds. However, over the course of the century the reach of the seed trade was vast and greatly democratized; economic and social relief programmes such as the distribution of seeds by the United States government only provided a one-step remove from the commercial realm, as the government contracts for seeds distributed at no or low cost were highly sought-after within the trade.
31. Gregory, *Annual Circular and Retail Catalogue*, p. 3; see also, Brill, *Farm-Gardening and Seed-Growing*, pp. 10–11.

32. In recent generations, and especially in relation to genetically modified and 'terminator' seeds, the manipulation of seeds, especially for perceived commercial benefit for seed producers (as opposed to the benefit that might accrue to consumers of seeds) has come under increasing public scrutiny. To date, my research in nineteenth-century American agricultural and horticultural texts has not discovered a parallel scepticism towards the earlier practices of hybridization.

33. Bagg and Batchelder, *Illustrated Catalogue of Flower and Vegetable Seeds* (Springfield, MA, 1875), pp. 52, 59, 68.

34. Gregory, *Annual Circular and Retail Catalogue*, inside front cover.

35. B. K. Bliss and Sons, *Spring Catalogue and Amateurs' Guide* (New York, 1868), p. 73. For similar examples, see also Rawson, *Success in Market Gardening*, p. 75; Gregory, *Annual Circular and Retail Catalogue*, p. 3; H. Sibley and Co., *Seed Catalogue* (Rochester, NY, 1883), p. 1; Hovey and Co., *Hovey's Illustrated Catalogue and Guide* (Boston, 1869), p. 103.

36. Brill, *Farm-Gardening and Seed-Growing*, pp. 3–4.

–5–

Commercial Rice Cultivation and the Regional Economy of Southeastern Asia, 1850–1950
Paul H. Kratoska

Trading and settlement patterns across Asia owe much to the availability of rice in particular locations. In the early nineteenth century, the majority of those who ate rice also grew it, but a century later a large and growing number of people depended on specialized producing areas, particularly in mainland Southeast Asia, for their supplies of rice. By the early twentieth century, commercial rice production in Southeast Asia accounted for more than 80 per cent of the rice entering the world export market. It also defined a regional economy that extended from southern China to India and included territories under British, Dutch, French, American, Thai and Chinese administrative control. The availability of inexpensive rice within this zone made possible the movement of several hundred thousand workers from southern China, India and Java to sparsely populated regions in the Malay Peninsula, Sumatra and Ceylon where emerging plantation economies required substantial imported labour. It also freed growing numbers of people from the burden of producing their own food, and by the 1920s rural areas across the region were becoming dependent on imported rice as people abandoned rice planting in favour of other economic activities.

The regional rice economy flourished during a period of trade liberalization, when there were few barriers to the movement of goods and people within the region and a peaceful trading environment. In the 1930s the Depression brought tighter controls over the economy and policies that encouraged self-sufficiency. The war brought a near-total breakdown of regional trade, and the postwar years were dominated by an economic nationalism built on economic planning and import substitution, a very different set of principles from those that had supported the Southeast Asian rice industry and the regional economy it served

From Subsistence to Commercial Rice Cultivation

Subsistence Rice Cultivation

Rice is generally thought of as the staple food of Southeast Asia, and by 1900 this was largely the case; but in some areas it was a fairly recent development. In Java, for example, a rice-based diet only displaced an earlier consumption pattern based on root crops, maize and a wide range of leafy vegetables during the nineteenth century, and dried cassava roots (*gaplek*) and maize remain important in the central and eastern parts of the island.[1] Rural diets in Southeast Asia also included fresh or salted fish and condiments made from chilli peppers and fish sauce or prawn paste, which were a significant source of nutrition, but people ate very little meat.

Rice cultivation is a laborious process with uncertain outcomes. The plants are vulnerable to damage from excess flooding, drought or disease, while rats and birds consume a significant proportion of any crop. Southeast Asia had a large number of rice varieties. British officials found between 300 and 400 in Malaya, the Americans recorded names for 1,300 in the Philippines, the French listed nearly 2,000 varieties and sub-varieties in Vietnam, and the Ministry of Lands and Agriculture in Siam identified 4,764.[2] Farmers grouped rice into three major categories: early or short-term, medium-term, and late or long-term.[3] Fields generally contained a mixture of plants from all three categories, and this had a number of benefits for subsistence farmers. Short- and medium-term varieties provided food in the latter part of the growing season, when rice stocks sometimes ran low, while long-term varieties gave larger yields and supplied the grain that farmers stored to sustain them for the rest of the year. Because different varieties ripened at different times, reaping the grain was done plant by plant, using small blades that cut individual heads of grain. While this process was labour-intensive, it spread harvest work out over time. Moreover, a mix of seeds provided insurance against crop failure, because plant diseases or an irregular water supply were likely to affect some varieties more than others.

Commercial Rice Production

While rice was an important food across much of southeastern Asia, it was often grown in places where conditions were less than optimal. Farmers planted rice on individual smallholdings for personal use as part of a pattern of mixed cultivation that included root crops and fruit, and fished or hunted to supplement their basic diet. They stored rice in household or village granaries and prepared it for consumption on a daily basis by pounding the grain in mortars to remove the husks. Most communities had little or no surplus labour, and no interest in growing rice as a cash crop.

Large-scale commercial rice cultivation did not develop in older-established agricultural communities, but on newly opened lands. Farmers moved from established settlement areas into extensive marshy plains in Lower Burma, central Siam and southern Vietnam (Cochinchina), where they cleared plots of land that were larger than was the norm for subsistence and planted rice for export. Rice remained a crop grown by smallholders, but producing a surplus for sale required extra manpower during the planting and harvest seasons, a need that was met in various ways but was a consistent feature of market-oriented rice cultivation. It also required construction of waterways for transport and a degree of flood control that was beyond the capacity of individual farmers to supply.

In the 1860s the British administration in Lower Burma began to construct embankments along major waterways, mounds of earth that were normally 12 feet (3.6 metres) wide at the base and between 6 and 9 feet (1.8 and 2.7 metres) high, to limit flooding on existing or potential rice lands. By the early 1930s embankments protected a cultivated area in excess of 485,000 hectares and secured the livelihood of many hundreds of thousands of people. They were also responsible for heavy silting of delta waterways and contributed to the spread of water hyacinth, which choked many rivers and creeks. British administrators eventually concluded that the policy of building embankments had been a mistake, but the process could not be reversed because vast areas of agricultural land would have been lost if the embankments were not maintained.[4]

In Cochinchina, the French administration dug some 1,300 kilometres of canals to control flooding in the trans-Bassac area between 1893, when the process began, and 1930. Added to existing rivers and canals, this effort produced a network containing approximately 2,000 kilometres of navigable waterways. Padi (rice in the husk) was carried to mills on small boats, and as of the 1930s the government had registered around 2,660 inland vessels. The canals were intended for irrigation as well as transport, but water control remained rudimentary, and farmers depended on inundation rather than controlled irrigation to bring water onto their lands.[5] Conditions were less extreme in the central plains of Siam, and the Rangsit Irrigation scheme provided a higher degree of control over water supplied to rice fields than was found in Burma or Cochinchina.[6]

Commercial rice cultivation had very different requirements from subsistence farming. Rice mills could not handle mixtures of varieties because hullers had to be set to a specific spacing, and if a batch of padi was not uniform in size some grains passed through with husks intact and others were crushed. Accordingly there was pressure in commercial growing areas for farmers to use seed that would produce crops with grain of a uniform size, which entailed a process of seed selection. The quality of the rice exported from Cochinchina was notoriously poor precisely because the grain supplied to the mills did not meet this standard, and both Burma and Siam struggled to maintain an acceptable standard for exports, because middlemen and traders often mixed grain of different qualities.[7]

The classification of rice varieties on the basis of their maturation period was a growers' system. Millers categorized rice on the basis of the size, shape and milling qualities of the grain, while wholesale and retail traders used another set of terms based on appearance and the proportion of broken grains. For example, after milling, rice in Siam was divided into three broad categories: White Rice, White Broken Rice, and Meal. White Rice was divided into five grades based on the proportion of broken grains, with the best export quality limited to less than 5 per cent. Rice consumed in the country might have as much as 50 per cent broken grains.[8]

The Rice Export Industry

Commercial rice cultivation developed in Luzon and in Java in the second half of the eighteenth century, stimulated by the planting of crops such as coffee, tobacco, hemp, and sugar for export. Trade liberalization in the Philippines led to commercial planting of sugar in Pampanga, a province just north of Manila. As sugar growing expanded there, rice cultivation declined. Farmers from Ilocos, in northwest Luzon, responded by moving onto empty lands in Pangasinan, Nueva Ecija and Tarlac to plant rice, which supplied Pampanga and Manila.[9] In Java export cultivation followed a shift in the trade of the Dutch East India Company away from spices and toward commodities such as sugar, coffee and indigo. There, too, specialized rice-growing districts met the needs of people engaged in the production of non-food crops.[10]

In the nineteenth century this pattern was replicated on a much larger scale. The availability of inexpensive rice from mainland Southeast Asia made possible the plantation economies of Ceylon (tea), the west coast of the Malay Peninsula (rubber and oil palm), and the east coast of Sumatra (tobacco, rubber and oil palm), each of which became a food deficit area importing between 50 and 70 per cent of the rice consumed. It also lay behind the development of smallholding economies across the region planting rubber and other crops.

While cheap rice was a prerequisite for the development of the plantation economies, the stimulus for commercial rice cultivation lay elsewhere. The rice export industry in mainland Southeast Asia began in Burma and was a response to demand in Europe. In 1870, when the plantation economy in Sumatra was just beginning to take shape, Burmese ports exported 440,000 tons of rice annually, with 80 per cent of this grain going to European destinations. As Sumatran plantations brought in increasing numbers of labourers, they purchased Burmese rice to feed this workforce. By the 1890s, when plantations began to develop in Malaya, Burma was exporting 1 million tons of rice annually, with roughly the same proportion of this total still going to European markets as in 1870, which left some 200,000 tons available for sale in the region.[11]

Outside of Southeast Asia, rice from Burma sold in three markets – Europe and other areas of the West, Ceylon and India, and the Far East, with each sector controlled by a different set of traders. Demand in Europe was met by European-owned firms, in South Asia by Indian companies, and in Southeast and East Asia by Chinese merchants, although Indian and European traders dominated the trade with Netherlands India and handled as much as 25 per cent of Burma's trade with the Straits Settlements. The highest-quality grain generally went to the European market, along with very low-grade rice used for industrial starch. Rice sold for local consumption in Malaya was just below the European standard, and Malayan buyers also purchased parboiled rice for sale to Indian estate labourers.

Siam and Cochinchina began export production slightly later, and their crops sold mainly in Asia. For poorer grades there was little difference between rice produced in different countries, and the market was extremely price-sensitive. However, Chinese consumers in Malaya preferred Siamese rice and were willing to pay a premium price for the better qualities: in 1930 First Class Siamese rice cost about 12 per cent more than the best Saigon rice. Burma's share of the Malayan market, at one point around 50 per cent, fell during the 1920s, and by the time the Depression struck, Burma accounted for just 24 per cent of Malaya's rice imports; 75 per cent came from Siam.[12] At the Ottawa Conference in 1932 the Government of India pressed the Straits Settlements to give preference to empire rice (effectively, Burmese rice) over non-empire rice, but the Straits government refused on grounds that the government did not wish to impose any duty on rice, which would hurt the country's plantation and mining interests, and had no other way of controlling rice imports.

Approximately three-quarters of Siam's rice exports were sold through Singapore or Hong Kong, both to meet local demand and for re-export. Ocean-going freighters could not cross the bar at the mouth of the Chao Phraya River, and loaded and unloaded at a place called Kohsichang, some 30 kilometres outside the bar. These vessels typically carried around 7,000 tons of rice, but loading them from lighters that ranged in capacity from 150 to 600 tons was both expensive and time-consuming, requiring 4–5 days to complete. Rice exported to Singapore was carried in coastal vessels that were small enough to clear the bar and could load grain directly at the mills, minimizing waiting time and lighterage charges.

This system suited the needs of Chinese rice traders in Singapore, where rice was unloaded in the outer harbour and either transferred directly to ocean-going freighters or brought by lighters to warehouses along the Singapore River. The arrangement kept the need to store rice to a minimum, an important issue because storage space was limited and expensive. Traders also preferred to receive small quantities of grain at frequent intervals for immediate distribution, because large shipments tied up capital and caused prices to fall. Moreover, while milled rice deteriorated rapidly in storage, unmilled rice could be held for more than a year and the general practice was for producing countries to store grain as padi and gradually mill it for export throughout the year.[13] For all these reasons the tendency in the rice trade was to adopt 'quick turnover' methods, and minimize stocks of grain held in Singapore.[14]

Some territories purchased rice as an industrial product, some imported it to supplement local food supplies or to make up occasional shortfalls in the domestic crop, and some bought rice to meet the subsistence needs of a significant part of their population. Purchases for Europe, which amounted to around 1.3 million tons a year shortly before the Second World War, fell into the first category. In Europe rice was used in brewing and as a commercial starch, and rice flour was mixed with wheat flour for baking. The second category included rice sold to India and China, where imports from Southeast Asia were a marginal addition to the vast quantities of foodgrains produced domestically. During the 1930s India produced 25–29 million tons of rice annually and generally imported between 1 and 1.5 million tons, some of it inexpensive rice from Burma that went to feed farmers growing higher-quality Indian varieties for export. Production levels in China are unclear, with different sources for the late 1930s showing figures ranging from 25 to 38 million tons of milled rice. China imported around 1 million tons annually until 1936, when political unrest disrupted the trade. China's rice imports amounted to less than 3 per cent of domestic consumption, and India's to less than 6 per cent. In years when Southeast Asian rice production was large and prices low, China and India purchased more rice; when crops were smaller and prices high, they purchased less. The two countries thus acted as reservoirs that absorbed surplus rice but did not depend on it. Until the early 1920s Japanese buyers in some years purchased large amounts of Southeast Asian rice on speculation and in others bought little or none, depending on local crop conditions and the availability of food from alternative sources. It then became national policy to confine rice purchases as much as possible to Japan and Japan's colonial territories. Rice sent to Japan subsequently was largely for industrial use rather than for food.[15]

The third category consisted of exports to food-deficit areas (places such as Singapore, Hong Kong and North Borneo, in addition to Malaya, Ceylon, and the East Coast Residency of Sumatra) that had large immigrant workforces and would have found it difficult to meet subsistence requirements in any other way. Malaya and Ceylon together imported around 1.1 million tons of Southeast Asian rice each year.[16] Without imported rice, the plantation economies of these territories, and the urban economies that handled the output of the plantations, could not have existed. However, demand within the region was far from sufficient to sustain the rice industries of mainland Southeast Asia. As Table 5.1 indicates, the proportion of rice exports that found a market in the region was 30 per cent in 1914–15 and had declined

Table 5.1 Rice Exports from Mainland Southeast Asia, by Destination

Years	Total Rice Exports	Exports to China and India		Exports to Southeast Asia		Exports to Other Destinations	
		Quantity (000 tons)	Per cent	Quantity (000 tons)	Per cent	Quantity (000 tons)	Per cent
1914–15	4,341	1,921	44	1,314	30	1,106	25
1924–25	5,866	1,829	31	1,377	23	2,660	45
1934–35	7,318	4,443	61	1,525	21	1,350	18

Sources: Annuaire Statistique de l'Indochine, 1943–1946; Reports on the Maritime Trade and Customs Administration of Burma, various years, India Office Records V/17; Statistical Year Book of Siam, various years, and 'Report of the Export and Import (8 Sept. 1916–25 Nov. 1931)', National Archives of Thailand R7 Communications 7/1.

to 21 per cent two decades later. The table also clearly shows the extent to which Southeast Asian producers depended on sales to China and India.

The Regional Rice Economy at its Apogee and the Impact of the Depression

From 1910 through to 1935, 50–60 per cent of the rice crop in Burma, 40–50 per cent of that in Siam, and 25–35 per cent of the crop in Cochinchina was exported. At the start of this period around 6.5 million tons of rice was entering the world export market annually, and almost 90 per cent of this grain (5.7 million tons) originated from these sources.[17] Burma accounted for about half of the rice exported from Southeast Asia, with the rest more or less equally divided between Indochina and Siam.[18]

The rice economy was based on a set of favourable conditions: reliable supplies of rice from producing areas and reliable markets, peaceful conditions, a free trade environment, a legal and administrative framework that supported commercial activity, efficient business networks that extended across the region and infrastructure that could handle the milling, transport and storage of rice. For rice-deficit areas there were a number of considerations that weighed in favour of the policy of importing food. Prices for rice purchased from mainland Southeast Asia were low, and the cost of importing rice was small relative to the returns from other forms of export production. Plantations were established in forested areas where the population density was low, and rice cultivation in the immediate vicinity of the plantation zones was inadequate to supply the needs of the plantation workforces. Moreover, farmers in these regions could earn better incomes from other economic activities, such as planting rubber or coconuts or fruit trees on smallholdings, or obtaining casual work on estates and in urban areas, than they could from growing rice.

There were objections to this level of dependence on imported food. Although rice was relatively inexpensive, deficit areas exported significant amounts of capital each year to pay for it, and were vulnerable because domestic production could not possibly have met local requirements if external supplies were cut off. Three sets of circumstances had the potential to cause a breakdown in the regional rice-based economy. The first was a failure of the rice crop through flooding, drought or plant disease. The second was a collapse of the export market for plantation crops, which might make it impossible for importing territories to pay for rice. The third was a disruption to regional trade arising from political or military disturbances. Early in the twentieth century these risks seemed unimportant. With rice grown on a large scale for export in three major river deltas, a complete failure of the rice crop across the region was unlikely. The plantation economy sold a wide range of crops to markets throughout the world, and the likelihood of a complete breakdown of this system was remote. Finally, the colonial powers that dominated the rice producing and consuming areas maintained peaceful conditions internally, and seemed sufficiently powerful to fend off any external threat.

By the 1940s all three of these contingencies had come to pass. In 1919–20 a poor rice crop in Siam caused the government there to ban exports for the year, and while there was sufficient rice to meet the needs of the deficit areas in Burma and Cochinchina, prices climbed to extremely high levels and importing areas had to pay heavily to secure supplies.[19] The Depression caused dramatic falls in the demand for commodities exported from Southeast Asia and sharp declines in prices. And finally, in late 1941 the Japanese invasion and the occupation brought regional trade to a standstill, resulting in serious food shortages in deficit regions.

The output of rice rose in commercial rice-growing areas of Southeast Asia during the 1930s, but demand outside Asia – in Europe, Africa and the Caribbean – declined. Great Britain and France sought to deal both with the economic downturn and with a perceived strategic threat arising from Japan's aggressive economic penetration of the region by containing their trade as much as possible within their own empires. France increased purchases of rice from Vietnam, but the British Empire offered little support to Burma, which struggled to find new markets. Siam, with no empire behind it, sent trade missions to rice-producing and rice-consuming territories across Asia to gather information on the rice trade and promote the sale of Thai rice, particularly in East Asia; but these initiatives yielded few results.[20] When poor crops in northeast Asia toward the end of the decade forced Japan to resume purchases of Southeast Asian rice, Britain's Foreign Office wanted to use the situation to try to contain Japan's expansionist programme, but both Burma and Siam rushed into this newly opened market.

Individual colonial administrations responded to the Depression by attempting to reduce their dependence on external sources of supply for basic necessities and become more self-sufficient. With demand for exports low and prices falling, the outlay for imported rice was less acceptable than before. The administrators responsible for rice-deficit regions had two tools at their disposal to stimulate domestic rice production. The first was the use of taxes or quotas to limit imports of foreign rice, and this method was adopted in the Netherlands Indies, where rice from mainland Southeast Asia could be replaced by grain produced within the colony. The Dutch administration completely stopped imports from sources outside the Netherlands Indies into South and East Borneo and the Moluccas and restricted imports to Menado in order to force these territories to buy rice produced in Bali, Lombok and the Celebes. For Bangka, West Borneo, Djambi, Riau, Palembang and Aceh, quotas rather than an outright prohibition were used to shift consumers away from imported grain. The East Coast of Sumatra, situated far from rice-exporting areas in the archipelago and needing inexpensive food to sustain its plantation industries, was allowed to continue importing rice from Burma.[21]

Elsewhere in the region, taxes or quotas on imported rice would have driven food prices higher because there were no existing domestic sources of supply.

Administrations needed to avoid sharp rises in rice prices because plantations, which were their major source of export earnings, depended on cheap food to hold costs down and remain competitive. Malaya and Ceylon attempted to stimulate local production of rice by raising farm incomes through increased yields, constructing irrigation works and using scientific and technical research to improve seeds and cultivation methods.

The impact of the Depression went beyond a fall in demand and a corresponding decline in prices for rice exports. Buyers working on behalf of rice mills often gave advances or loans to cultivators as a way of ensuring that they could purchase grain on favourable terms. This practice created an enormous mass of debt, and foreclosures dispossessed substantial numbers of farmers, particularly in Burma. By this time, too, population growth and the subdivision of inherited landholdings among multiple heirs had reduced the size of the plots of land held by many farmers to subsistence levels. In Siam, for example, more than a quarter of the residents of seven of the country's main rice-producing districts farmed the minimum area needed to feed an ordinary-sized family (0.8 hectare) or less.[22] The combination of poverty, rural indebtedness, and a shortage of land left regions such as Lower Burma, the Mekong Delta, and north central Luzon ripe for political agitation, and all would become centres of unrest. Along with direct responses to the economic downturn, these changes contributed greatly to the deterioration of the regional economy

By the mid-1930s the economic situation in the region had substantially improved and there was less economic pressure to reduce rice imports, but efforts to increase local production continued because of the growing threat to regional trade posed by Japan. However, the measures introduced – such as construction of irrigation works and associated infrastructure – were costly, and progress was slow. When Japanese forces invaded at the end of 1941, the plantation zones remained heavily dependent on imported rice, and the occupation years brought great hardship to the people living there.

The War and its Aftermath

Japan's invasion of Southeast Asia brought all three of the major rice-exporting regions into the enlarged Japanese empire – Thailand and French Indochina through alliances with Japan, and Burma by conquest. The rice produced in these territories was more than sufficient to meet food requirements in Southeast Asia, but the Japanese could no longer move grain to the places where it was needed. Farmers were unable to sell their surplus rice and responded by planting less. Production in many rice-exporting areas fell to levels that only met farmers' own needs, and people in deficit areas survived by eating locally produced root crops and vegetables[23] (see Tables 5.2 and 5.3).

Burma was particularly exposed to Allied raids from aircraft based in India, and small boats used to move rice within the country became targets for attacks. By the

Table 5.2 Rice Production (000 tons)

Years	Burma	Thailand	Indochina	Total
1940–41	8,037	4,923	6,867	19,827
1945–46	2,845	3,699	4,491	11,035

Source: Food and Agriculture Organization of the United Nations. *The World Rice Economy in Figures, 1909–1963.* Commodity Reference Series No. 3. Rome: FAO, 1965, Table 4, p. 15.

Table 5.3 Area planted with Rice (000 acres)

Years	Burma	Thailand	Indochina
1940–41	12,900	9,923	13,700
1945–46	7,000	9,855	9,800

Source: Food and Agriculture Organization of the United Nations. *The World Rice Economy in Figures, 1909–1963.* Commodity Reference Series No. 3 (Rome: FAO, 1965), Table 4, p. 15; *Annuaire Statistique de l'Indochine, 1943–1946;* TNA Ministry of Finance 0301.1.38 B/38; and Statistical Year Books for Thailand.

end of the conflict, parts of the country that had depended on rice shipped from the Irrawaddy Delta were facing food shortages. In Cochinchina, the rice-producing region of Vietnam, the cost of living increased nearly fivefold, but the controlled price for padi rose only slightly. The black market paid slightly more; but even black market trading lagged behind the cost of living, and it involved substantial risks. The Japanese military offered high wages for coolie labour (as much as 8 piastres per day by July 1945), and many rice planters in the Mekong Delta abandoned agriculture to work on military construction projects. In 1944 the northern part of Vietnam experienced severe food shortages and a very large number of people died of starvation or hunger-related illness. The French authorities estimated that 700,000 people died, while Vietnamese estimates range as high as 1.5–2 million.[24]

Thailand experienced a smaller decline in production than its neighbours. In October 1942 record flooding caused serious damage to the Thai rice crop, and killed many draught animals. The surplus for the year amounted to about 550,000 tons, and this grain was shipped out of the country. In 1943 farmers in Vietnam and Burma reduced the amount of rice they planted, but because of the flood farmers in Thailand had not felt the consequences of a fall in exports and planted a normal crop. In 1944 Thai farmers also experienced problems selling their surpluses, and by 1945 they were planting less grain as well. The 1945 harvest was poor, causing demand for rice to shoot up, and prices to increase accordingly – a situation that further stimulated postwar production.[25]

The war and occupation caused serious damage to the rice export industry, with Burma the worst affected. By the time the conflict ended, large numbers of draught animals had perished, tools were in very short supply, canals had deteriorated, the machinery in rice mills was old and in a state of disrepair, and transport had been severely damaged. The damage to the transport network was a particular problem, and would require several years to remedy. Much of the rice exported from mainland Southeast Asia was moved by water, and there had been heavy losses of inland vessels as well as damage to docks and harbour facilities. Railways and road transport had also been badly damaged by air raids, and a lack of maintenance and spare parts affected rolling stock and motor vehicles.[26]

Independence and Economic Nationalism

Immediately after the war the allocation of surplus food on a world-wide basis was controlled by a wartime body known as the Combined Food Board, reconstituted in June 1946 as the International Emergency Food Council. Its functions were later taken over by the Food and Agriculture Organization of the United Nations. The Council's Rice Committee met in Washington, but in October 1946 a sub-committee was set up in Singapore to arrange shipping programmes for rice and to handle distribution within the region. The Combined Food Board/IEFC made allocations on the basis of information supplied by participating countries, which agreed to draw food only from sources selected to supply them. The Singapore sub-committee was empowered to pool supplies allocated to the region and then readjust the distribution agreed in Washington.[27]

On the basis of estimates of the quantities of grain available in Burma, Siam and southern Vietnam for the period 1 October to 31 December 1945, the Combined Food Board allocated almost 470,000 tons of rice to a list of twelve recipients.[28] However, the estimates far exceeded the amounts that actually became available, and by mid-November the figure had been revised downward to 216,000 tons.[29] For the next three years rice supplies remained inadequate, and grain distributed under international allocation procedures was far below the needs of the region.

The demand for rice was strong during this period, and the mechanisms of international food control held prices at levels far below those that would have prevailed in a free market. There were many reasons for this policy, including the risk that the high prices rice would have commanded in a free market would have fuelled inflation and impeded economic recovery, and that poorer countries might have found it impossible to buy any rice at all in a free market. Siam was doubly handicapped, in that British policy aimed at punishing the country for cooperating with Japan during the war, and for a time prices paid for Thai rice were substantially lower than those paid in Burma. Thai dealers responded by selling poor-quality grain through official channels, and smuggling as much as possible of the better grades of rice out of the country to be sold in lucrative black markets in Malaya and elsewhere. Rice-buying nations were supposed to control smuggling and black market trading, and faced possible cuts to their allocations if their efforts were ineffective; but supplies received through the international system were insufficient, and governments unofficially condoned black market activity. In the words of Britain's Special Commissioner for Southeast Asia in 1947:

> If there is a little of the Nelson touch, a certain turning of the blind eye on the part of the authorities (which *unofficially* they are inclined to admit) to some of this smuggling it must be remembered that much of the smuggled rice is bought up by the planters and estate owners for their labourers and that the more rice for these people means less unrest throughout the country and less fertile soil for agitators to work on.[30]

Nationalist ideology emphasized the need for nation-states to be economically self-sufficient, and wartime shortages reinforced the idea that an interdependent regional economy left food-deficit territories dangerously vulnerable. Moreover, the fact that this economy was to a considerable extent in the hands of 'foreign' elements – Chinese, Indians, Arabs and Westerners – made it a threat to national sovereignty and an unacceptable drain on domestic resources. Postwar leaders pursued economic policies that were often inefficient and overrode considerations of comparative advantage, but promised self-sufficiency and placed economic power in local hands.

When international controls were lifted in 1949, governments introduced control measures that forestalled a return to pre-war trading arrangements. Development initiatives in the 1950s called for import substitution to achieve self-sufficiency, particularly in essential items such as rice, and unrest in rice-producing areas made such policies both economically desirable and politically prudent. Moreover, rice was a major source of foreign exchange for Burma and Thailand, and political leaders took steps to prevent Chinese or Indian or European traders from regaining the dominance over the rice trade that they had possessed before the war. Moreover, changes in regulations governing the movement of goods and of funds, and an attenuation of the personal ties that had once drawn the Chinese community across Southeast Asia together, made regional trading activities more difficult than before.

Support for domestic rice production served another purpose as well. With the introduction of parliamentary bodies and electoral politics, the large numbers of rice farmers across the region became an important source of votes, and steps to improve their welfare had a potential political pay-off. It was also vital to avoid a large-scale exodus of farmers to the cities. Their contribution to food supplies was of great importance, but even more significant was the fact that people who abandoned farming were likely to face unemployment and poverty, and this could lead to social unrest.

The need to improve the lives of farmers was counterbalanced by strong pressures to keep food prices low. While high prices for rice would benefit farmers, they were potentially disastrous, because export agriculture, the small but growing industrial sector, and the rapidly expanding cities all depended on inexpensive rice. The solution appeared to lie in improved productivity, and by the 1970s high-yielding varieties of rice resulting from hybridization were increasing crop yields, and because many of the new varieties had short growing seasons, double cropping became the norm in much of the region. As a result of these developments, the number of varieties of rice cultivated in Southeast Asia diminished significantly. High-yielding rice required better water control, and more use of fertilizer and insecticides than traditional varieties. With improved transport, imported fruits and vegetables became widely available, and the consumption of animal protein and fish from the sea increased. However, older sources of protein, such as freshwater fish caught in rice fields and irrigation canals, largely disappeared from local diets owing to the deleterious effects of chemical fertilizer and insecticides.

Conclusion

Because many studies of Asian economic history adopt a national or country-by-country approach, the operation of a regional economy in Southeast Asia has been obscured. This regional economy depended on Chinese, Indian and local trading networks that carried goods throughout southeastern Asia, and was based to a considerable extent on an interaction between rice-surplus and rice-deficit territories. The Depression and the Japanese Occupation disrupted the regional economy, and the nationalist leadership of the states that won independence after the war created nationally-based alternatives. The regional trading economy survived in a limited fashion, but even major ports such as Hong Kong, Singapore and Penang could no longer survive on trade, and from the 1930s found it necessary to augment their earlier economic activities by creating an industrial sector.

The regional rice industry met the demand for inexpensive rice before the war and might have done so again; but ethnic conflict halted Burma's postwar recovery and Vietnam's protracted military struggle against France and then the United States prevented rehabilitation of the rice industry there. Arguments in favour of policies promoting rice cultivation in food-deficit areas were compelling in the absence of effective alternatives based on comparative advantage.

The rice industry in southeastern Asia followed a pattern familiar in other parts of the world. The creation of plantations and large-scale migrations of labour triggered social and economic changes, including increased production of food for commercial distribution. The expansion of agricultural production took place on what the British termed 'waste' land, lands not under cultivation or used for other purposes. The free trade regime that took shape in the nineteenth century and persisted into the 1920s supported these arrangements, but the economic crisis of the 1930s and the anticipation of military conflict in the region led to increased government controls, and post-war nationalism brought a shift to national economies based on autarky rather than comparative advantage.

Notes

1. A. M. P. Scheltema, *The Food Consumption of the Native Inhabitants of Java and Madura*, trans. A. H. Hamilton (Batavia, 1936), pp. 9, 24.
2. H. W. Jack, 'Rice in Malaya', *Malayan Agricultural Journal*, XI(5–6) (1923): 52; P. Huard and M. Durand, *Connaissance du Viet-Nam* (Paris, 1954), p. 123; 'Report on Agricultural Science & Seed Selection, Introductory Note, in National Archives of Thailand (henceforth NAT), Ministry of Agriculture 15.2/23 (Part II); Imperial Institute, *Indian Trade Enquiry: Reports on Rice* (London, 1920), p. 124. See also A. Coquerel, *Paddy et Riz de Cochinchine* (Lyon, 1911), pp. 3–15.
3. For Siam see 'Note on the Classification of Paddy', *The Record*, No. 13 (July 1924), p. 24; for Cochinchina, Coquerel, *Paddy et Riz de Cochinchine*, p. 3; for Burma, Department of Agriculture, Burma, *Rice*, Markets Section Survey No. 9 (Rangoon, 1936), p. 12.
4. Report on the Administration of Burma, 1931–32, pp. 99–100; *Report of the Water Hyacinth Committee, Bengal*, pp. xviii, 59. See also the correspondence in Burma, National Archives Department (henceforth NAD) Series 1/15(E), Accession no. 4312 (1922–3), and B. O. Binns, *Agricultural Economy in Burma* (Rangoon, 1948), pp. 65–6.
5. C. Robequain, *The Economic Development of French Indo-China* (London, 1944), pp. 110–12.
6. D. Johnston, 'Rural Society and the Rice Economy in Thailand, 1880–1930' (Ph.D. dissertation, Yale University, 1975), Ch. 2.
7. See, for example, the discussions of the Siamese Board of Commercial Development's Subcommittee for Investigation into Internal Conditions of Rice Industry in 1931, in NAT, Ministry of Commerce and Communications (7th Reign) 7/14, and comment by The Borneo Co. and Couper-Johnston & Co., in 'Resolutions passed by the Sub-committee regarding Exporters' Recommendations', in NAT, Ministry of Agriculture 15.2/22.
8. Abstract of Commercial Directory for Siam, 1929, Third Edition, p. 38, in NAT, Ministry of Agriculture 15.2/19 (Part I). Information on this point for Vietnam is found in H. Russier and H. Brennier, *L'Indochine française* (Paris, 1911), pp. 221–2; see also Coquerel, *Paddy et Riz de Cochinchine*, p. 118.
9. M. S. McLennan, *The Central Luzon Plain: Land and Society on the Inland Frontier* (Quezon City, 1980).
10. R. E. Elson, *Cultivation System and 'Agricultural Involution'* (Melbourne, 1978).
11. Cheng Siok-hwa, *The Rice Industry of Burma, 1852–1940* (Kuala Lumpur, 1968), pp. 237–8.
12. Unsigned 'Note regarding the rice situation in Singapore', 11 September 1930, in NAT Ministry of Commerce (7th Reign) 8.1/1; Govt. of Burma. Ministry of Forests, *Report of the Rice Export-Trade Enquiry Committee* (Rangoon, 1937).

13. 'Report of the 1924 Food Supply Committee', p. 8. The Anglo-Thai Corporation and The Borneo Company, 'Memorandum on the possibilities of obtaining in Bangkok, Siam, and moving to Malaya, large quantities of rice during a post-hostilities emergency period', 6 September 1943, Great Britain, The National Archives (UK): Public Record Office; henceforth TNA: PRO, CO 852/510/19. The length of time that milled rice could be stored without deterioration depended on whether it had been milled from new padi or old. Rice from new padi could be kept for six weeks at best, while that from older padi could be stored for as long as four months: 'Report of the 1924 Food Supply Committee', p. 5.

14. R. J. Wilkinson to Gov SS, 14 June 1912, Arkib Negara Malaysia (Malaysian National Archives, henceforth ANM) High Commissioner's Office 31/1912.

15. R. B. Stevens, Office of the Adviser in Foreign Affairs, 'Memorandum on the Japanese Rice Control Law', 4 February 1935, NAT, Ministry of Foreign Affairs 67.10/31.

16. This paragraph draws on 'Memorandum on Rice Supplies', The National Archives (UK), TNA: PRO, UE404/43/71, FO371/69093 (1948), V. D. Wickizer and M. K. Bennett, *The Rice Economy of Monsoon Asia* (Stanford, CA, 1941), and B. Rose, 'Appendix' to *The Rice Economy of Asia* (Washington, DC, 1985).

17. See Department of Agriculture, Burma, *Rice*, pp. 3–4.

18. Imperial Institute, *Reports on Rice*, p. 72.

19. P. H. Kratoska, 'The British Empire and the Southeast Asian Rice Crisis of 1919–1921', *Modern Asian Studies* 24(1) (1990): 115–46.

20. Prince Purachatra, the Minister of Commerce and Communications, travelled to Singapore, Hong Kong, China, Japan, Korea and the Philippines in late 1930 and early 1931. These efforts are discussed in NAT, Foreign Ministry 67/10/26 and 67.10/31, and Ministry of Commerce and Communications 7/14. See also Dormer to Henderson, 21 October 1930, TNA: PRO F5880/5880/40, FO371/15531 (1930), and Snow to Henderson, 8 January 1931, TNA: PRO F886/408/40, FO371/15531 (1931).

21. Information on the Netherlands Indies is taken from an address by the Director of Economic Affairs to the *Volksraad* during 1934. The copy in my possession is a translation found in NAT, Ministry of Foreign Affairs 67.10/43), and does not indicate the date of the meeting. See also H. W. Dick, 'Interisland Trade, Economic Integration, and the Emergence of the National Economy', in A. Booth, W. J. O'Malley and A. Weidemann (eds), *Indonesian Economic History in the Dutch Colonial Era* (New Haven, CT, 1990), pp. 296–321. Restrictions were first introduced in 1933, a year when the commercial rice-producing territories all had exceptionally good crops, and rice production in Java was increasing as a result of restrictions on sugar cultivation. M. J. van Schreven, Netherlands Chargé d'Affaires, Bangkok, to Phya Srivisar Vacha, State Councillor for Foreign Affairs, 7 April 1933, NAT, Ministry of Foreign Affairs 67.10/23.

22. Phya Indra Montri (F. H. Giles), 'Note on Paddy and Rice', NAT, The Ministry of Commerce and Communication (7th Reign) 8.1/1 (Part I).

23. Various sources of figures for rice production during the war differ somewhat, but the trends indicated in the tables are reported consistently.

24. Nguyên Thê Anh, 'Japanese Food Policies and the 1945 Great Famine in Indochina', and M. Furuta, 'A Survey of Village Conditions during the 1945 Famine in Vietnam', in P. H. Kratoska (ed.), *Food Supplies and the Japanese Occupation in South-East Asia* (Houndmills, 1998), pp. 208–26, 227–37.

25. 'Changes in Siamese Economy Arising from the War', enclosed in 'War Cabinet. Far Eastern Sub-Committee. Changes in Siamese Economy. Memorandum by the Economic Advisory Branch, Foreign Office and Ministry of Economic Warfare', F.E.(E)(44)4, 21 December 1944, TNA: PRO FO 371/41857; Baker, 'The Siamese Rice Trade with Malaya', TNA: PRO CO 852/568/12.

26. 'Memorandum on Rice Supplies', TNA: PRO UE404/43/71, FO 371/69093.

27. K. C. Tours, Chairman, Joint Supply Board, 'Memorandum on the Rice Position in Malaya', in 12 November 1946, ANM RC Sel 1102/46. See also TNA: PRO CO 537/1401. A history of the activities of the Rice Division of the IEFC is found in ANM MAF 75/72.

28. Secretary of State for War for the Overseas Reconstruction Committee, Memorandum on 'Rice Allocations for Far Eastern Liberated Territories', 22 November 1945, TNA: PRO CO 852/568/12.

29. Secretary of State for War, Memorandum on 'Rice Allocations for Far Eastern Liberated Territories', 10 December 1945, Cabinet, Overseas Reconstruction Committee, O.R.C. (45)51, TNA: PRO CO 852/568/13. See also 'Rice Allocations for Far Eastern Liberated Territories', Memorandum by the Secretary of State for War, 22 November 1945, Cabinet, Overseas Reconstruction Committee, O.R.C. (45)46, TNA: PRO FO 371/46302.

30. Killearn to Bevin, 18 August 1947, Cabinet. Official Committee of Food Supplies from South East Asia, 'Report on the Activities of the Office of the Special Commissioner in South East Asia during the Second Quarter of 1947', S.E.A.F. 47(40). Burma Economic 3701/47, The British Library: India Office Records M/4/761. Emphasis in the original.

Part II
Diffusion and Identities

–6–

A Taste of Home

The Cultural and Economic Significance of European Food Exports to the Colonies

Richard Wilk

The great European colonial empires of the recent past were complex constructions. While their economic and political histories have been written for centuries, the role that culture, particularly material culture, played in the creation, maintenance and collapse of colonial empires has only received attention recently.[1] Warwick Anderson has drawn our attention to the intense scrutiny of excretion by colonial authorities, and has thereby shown how the colonial discourse about health and sanitation was deeply concerned with cultural order, social boundaries, ideals of civilization and control of subject populations.[2] We should likewise expect that food and cuisine played an equally complex and important role; yet with a few notable exceptions the food culture of colonialism has been little studied or understood.[3]

This chapter is drawn from research done for a book on the history of food and globalization from the standpoint of the Caribbean/Latin American country of Belize. The book's main subject is the continuing entanglement of local food and cuisine with the global food trade and international gastronomy. I have set out to undercut the now-traditional stories of authentic local food and cuisine either valiantly resisting, or being tragically displaced by foreign or global culture. I am also sceptical of more recent happier tales of creolization, hybridity and local appropriation (what I have called the 'Golden Arches East' story, after the book of the same name).[4] Instead I depict local and global as mutually dependent, each requiring and constituting the other; far from being opposites, local specificity and global homogeneity are two products of the same process.[5] It is therefore impossible to understand the uniqueness of Belize without also seeing just how typical it was – and vice versa.

The book traces the dynamics of this mutual interdependence as it changed over time; but in every period the polarity between local and foreign food was renewed. In this chapter I concentrate on the century from the abolition of slavery in 1834 through the depth of the Great Depression in 1935, a period when food played a particularly important role in the complex relations of ethnicity, status, nationality and rank in the British Empire, of which Belize (then British Honduras) was then a tiny part. My goal is to show that food was a very important means through which local people were ordered into groups, and the position of the colony within the empire was both expressed and confirmed. I do not assume that these classifications were imposed by the upper class or the centre of the Empire in a dictatorial system of cultural order; rather I follow Bourdieu in positing that classifications and boundaries, and their political and economic meanings, were both contested and accepted in complex ways that changed over time. While parts of the order of cuisine in Belize may have looked like a slavish copy or mimicry of British practices in the homeland, their meanings always had an important local dimension, and they played a part in a local contest for power and status that was far different from their original context. In a familiar paradox of Empire, then, food and cuisine extended the cultural and political goals of the colonial power in ways that were quite alien to, and often not understood by, the agents of the colonial power. Familiar everyday objects and foods were used in quite unfamiliar ways, and vice versa.

The Setting

Belize is a particularly interesting setting because, unlike larger colonies with exist-ing agrarian economies, the area has been highly dependent on food imports from the time of first European settlements to the present day. The depredations of early explorers and Buccaneers along the Caribbean coastline, along with the resettlement policies of Spanish missionaries in the interior, combined to eliminate most of the indigenous Mayan-speaking people by the end of the seventeenth century, leaving what was essentially an unclaimed and empty forest full of valuable timber and exotic tropical products.[6] Ragtag and disorganized groups of logwood and fustic cutters, turtle hunters, and fugitives, and their African and Indian slaves gradually settled along the coast and offshore islands. While they undoubtedly grew and hunted some of their own food, because they were engaged in the extraction of very valuable dyestuffs their labour was valuable, and it was actually cheaper for them to buy imported foodstuffs, particularly the preserved rations that served throughout the Atlantic world as naval stores: salt meat and fish, biscuit, peas, flour, coffee, sugar and liquor. This dependence on imported food has continued through all the twists and turns of economic history, and today Belize still spends a very unusually large portion of its GDP importing food. This means the country has always been very sensitive to both the economic costs and the cultural values of food in the colonial and international systems.

By the time slavery ended in 1834, Belize was still a protectorate under the name of the 'Honduras Settlement', ruled mostly by a local council and magistrates, and the economy had shifted from logwood to mahogany and cedar, which were used in furnishing Victorian homes and vehicles (particularly steamships and railway carriages). The port also became an entry for European consumer goods traded to neighbouring Hispanic republics. While foreign banks and companies gained increasingly concentrated control of the timber trade, Belize City merchants were locally dominant, and one of their major sources of profit was selling imported workers' rations, other staples, and luxury foods and drinks.

The population grew rapidly in the nineteenth century, with an influx of Mayan and Mestizo refugees from the War of the Castes in neighbouring Yucatan and ex-Confederates from the American Civil War, the arrival of Garifuna (Black Carib) exiles from the island of St Vincent, and the importation of Chinese and East Indian labourers. Owing to its increasing size, and its economic and diplomatic role in the American Civil War, the protectorate became a colony in 1862 and a Crown Colony in 1871, acquiring the name British Honduras, which it kept until 1973, when it was renamed Belize.

Despite many attempts to establish plantation agriculture of export crops, or some other viable economic base, logging remained the only substantial industry until well into the twentieth century. Compared to the situation in the neighbouring Hispanic republics, in British Honduras labour was expensive, and there was little internal trade, so agricultural production for the local market was always limited and costly. Even during the First World War, when food and fuel was scarce and expensive throughout the British Empire, British Honduras' food imports continued to grow. Over the century from 1835 to 1935, the balance of trade shifted sharply to the negative in the 1880s, and was never positive again after 1919.[7]

The economics of this food-dependent import economy were complex, and in some respects specific to small colonies that were dependent on a single export commodity. But the pattern of dependency on imported food and an increasing trade imbalance was common to most of the other British Caribbean islands, as well as many Pacific dependencies. While in the large economic scheme of the empire the amount of food exported from the UK to the colonies may have been fairly small, it was extremely important to the colonies that depended on it, and even in colonies that produced much of their own food, home-country foods were culturally significant. The social and cultural dynamics of this demand are worth exploring in more detail. To be sure, some of the demand for foods from home was the result of the established tastes of exiles and expatriates from the home country, who found it difficult or had no desire to adapt to exotic diets in countries where they were no more than sojourners.[8] Nostalgia and longing for the foods of childhood and home no doubt also played a role. Ideas about the relationship between diet and health must have also had a major effect, and most Europeans in overseas colonies received stern warnings about eating only familiar foods that were prepared under European supervision and to European sanitary standards, though in practice the dietary advice given to expatriates varied widely over time and space, and from expert to expert.[9] But the scale of food imports into the colonies went far beyond the demand of expatriates and sojourners; home country-foods played an important role in the colonial system of class, race and status within each colony, and they were consumed in many different contexts.

The detailed history of food exports from Europe has yet to be written. It is difficult to assess just how much prepared and processed food a single country like England (and later Great Britain) exported through history, and how important it was to the development of the British economy. The quantities of food imports that were re-exported in processed, mixed and repackaged forms were never accurately measured, and most economic historians have tended to view them as relatively unimportant compared with cloth and other manufactured goods. On the other hand, a recent reappraisal by the economic historian Anne McCants suggests that: '...luxury trades of the early modern period were in fact transformative of the European economy... New evidence will show that global groceries, long thought to be merely exotic, were actually in wide use by the early decades of the eighteenth century.'[10]

We do know that export food-processing industries had an early start in England. As early as the late sixteenth century, quantities of processed fish and beer were exported from British ports to the Continent. As large-scale imports of exotic food and drug products began in the following century, the re-export trade grew accordingly. At the end of the seventeenth century, two-thirds of the tobacco, 90 per cent of the spices and 80 per cent of the textiles imported to England were re-exported.[11] However, we do not know how much of this was processed and packaged in England, and how much was simply sold in the same bulk packages in which it was imported. We do know that, even in the seventeenth century, large numbers of English glass and pottery retail packages are already showing up in the trash heaps of colonial towns and cities in the New World, as well as in smaller numbers in Asia and Africa. By the early eighteenth century England was the centre of a world trade in retail-packaged food and beverages.[12] Almost any construction in Belize City today unearths large quantities of English and continental liquor, beer and wine bottles dating from the seventeenth century onwards, as well as large numbers of clay pipes, medicine bottles and other durable containers.

Specific Products

In the early nineteenth century most food imported into British Honduras consisted of wheat flour and salted meat or fish shipped in barrels; and other wooden bulk containers containing beer, wine, liquor and other beverages. Salted pork was cheaper and more common than beef, and, by contrast with other Caribbean colonies, salt fish was never as popular there as preserved meat. While prepared ship's biscuits and pilot bread were common in the eighteenth century, wheat flour had largely replaced them by the middle of the nineteenth century. The sources for the staples shifted gradually through the nineteenth century from Europe to the United States; but even late in the century many North American goods were still transshipped through British ports, especially Bristol and London.

Luxury foods made up a surprisingly large part of the food trade to Belize, including everything from anchovies to *cornichon*, tongues to tripe, and olive oil to curry powder. These were also shipped through British ports, which had developed sophisticated physical and social infrastructure and technologies for the complex task of breaking bulk packages, grading, sorting, processing, mixing and repackaging spices, raw foods, stimulants and beverages. The ports imported huge quantities of heterogeneous raw food ingredients from around the world in a huge variety of qualities and weights and measures, and exported standardized and reliably graded processed foods in increasingly sophisticated and durable packages that ensured their quality and longevity. The food- processing industry also promoted the growth of new technologies, and a large number of ancillary industries.

As the century progressed, bulky staved wooden barrels, pipes, kegs and hogsheads were used for only the cheapest and lowest-quality foods and raw ingredients, and processed foods and drinks were shipped more often in bottles, crocks, pots, cans, firkins, tins, kits and boxes, which were in turn carefully packaged in standard cartons, cases, crates, chests and casks. Large-scale industries manufacturing glass, wood, ceramics, and metal for packaging developed around the port of London, along with firms that developed new materials like pasteboard and cardboard, and techniques for printing elaborate labels, seals, and advertisements. The multiplex of heterogeneous colonial spices and edible ingredients flowing into the port of London were processed primarily for the home market; but the export trade for these processed foods and condiments developed right along with the domestic. As early as the seventeenth century, for example, tobacco was imported from the New World, dried and blended in London and Bristol, and then reshipped back to New World colonies as snuff or smoking mixture. Even sugar-producing colonies imported refined white sugar from England; other goods following a circular route include spices, liquors, and patent medicines.

Processing and mixing of products in British ports often had the effect of obscuring the origins of the original raw materials. Many times the British merchant did not even know the exact origins of lots of spices, sugar, and other products, because these were only identified by the name of the ports they were shipped from. So they might know only that a cask of fish oil was from shipped from New York, not where it was actually rendered. In addition, some goods, like black and white pepper, coffee, and tobacco, were loaded loose in bulk, either filling a ship's hold or as dunnage and packing material to stabilize other cargo, so that they could come from a number of ports. The result was a substitution of identity: exotic products from around the world became culturally British and were capable of signifying both home and the global power of Empire.

Branding

The century from 1834 to 1935 also saw the rise of branding as an essential technology in the colonial flow of food, a trend that parallels the increase in packaging and processing. Branding began in antiquity as a means of assuring quality, by citing the geographical origin of a commodity, as in Irish beef, Port wine or a Yorkshire ham. But the power of such location-branding was gradually lost as commodity chains grew in size and complexity. Yorkshire ham became a generic term for a particular style of curing, a fate of many local products as diverse as Cheddar cheese and Tequila. As the incidence and danger of food adulteration increased in the mid-nineteenth century, individual and company names became the agents of trust. Food processors and packagers thereby inserted themselves into the commodity chains and superseded the actual producers of foodstuffs in the minds of consumers. The Quaker John Horniman first packaged teas in Britain, and he passed the power of his personal reputation to his descendants, a pattern repeated in many family food-processing companies.

Gradually the agent of quality appropriated the role of the producer, a process that was easily furthered if the agent was responsible for mixing, processing and packaging. This can easily be seen in the coffee business, where unblended beans retained their nationality (Kenyan, Colombian, etc.), while blends took the name or brand of the processor or roaster. Many of the early individual merchants and partnerships were absorbed, towards the end of the nineteenth century, by early multinational food-processing companies, who created *nationality* brands like Anglo-Swiss and Franco-American, and various kinds of Empire branding. In the context of the global food trade, nations became sorts of 'super-brands' that evoked complex forms of loyalty and emotion.

Branding also provided opportunities to manipulate the meaning and identity of foods in new ways, and there was a steady increase in the volume of newspaper food advertising in places like Belize. Initially this came from local merchants, whose major claims were quality, freshness and novelty, beginning most of their advertisements with 'Just Arrived', 'Landed This Week', or 'Just Imported'. Later advertising began to present more complex themes beyond quality, taste and purity. Before 1850 local merchants were independent dealers who sold the assortments of goods sent by their purchasing and shipping agents. In the 1860s Belize merchants competed with one another to sign contracts as 'sole agents' for British and American producers, and by the late 1870s, in a practice begun with soap and patent medicines, they imported food and drink advertisements to reprint in local newspapers. Retail trade in branded pre-packaged products became dominant, and only a few lower-priced imported foodstuffs like salt pork and flour were still sold in bulk. By the end of the century manufacturers had a much stronger hand in directly selling their products overseas, with their own promotions and travelling commission agents. By advancing credit and signing restrictive agreements, European and American companies gained indirect control over local merchants and eliminated competition between merchants, to the detriment of local consumers, who faced fixed prices and an increasingly limited selection of brands.

Culinary Diglossia

Most evidence shows that marketing responded to, rather than creating, demand for imports. This begs the question of why metropolitan goods were so desirable, when local products were usually fresher and sometimes cheaper. It is easy to assume that demand for home-country products was somehow 'natural' amongst a colonial population that retained cultural identification with the home country.[13] But some colonies were largely self-sufficient in food and developed their own hybrid colonial/local cuisine, and in countries like China, European food had a very limited appeal and distribution outside the European enclaves. Belize, however, was like other Caribbean islands in lacking an indigenous agricultural base and a strong pre-colonial culinary tradition. Instead of a blended cuisine, or an enclave of European food, Belize developed a kind of dietary *diglossia*, with distinct European and local cuisines that were like distinct but related languages.[14] As in linguistic diglossia, urban and educated people used the high-ranking register, and avoided the 'local tongue' as much as possible.

Upward mobility required acquiring taste and competence for the European standard, and distancing oneself from the taint of local produce and cooking. Rural people and the poor depended on local produce by necessity, and used a variety of cuisines and cooking styles that the Colonial officials saw as qualities of 'race'. Along with dress, language, and skin colour, food was a key element of the system through which the diverse population was divided into categories and groups, each of which was restricted to locations, institutions, and occupations to which they were supposedly biologically suited. Colonial officials argued that each 'race' preferred its own staples and spices, as if dietary preferences were fixed by nature; unfortunately, the categories proved woefully unstable and the populace unwilling to stay in place.

European food was itself an unstable and contestable category. While officially British, the elite of the colony including substantial numbers of Germans, North Americans and other Europeans, and many of the original British migrants traced their ancestry to Scotland rather than England. At a distance from Europe, with limited ingredients and few trained cooks, different European and North American food traditions were 'compressed' into a generic bundle of dishes, distinguished as much by the mode of serving and the grammar of meals as by ingredients and flavours. The 'upper register' of meals required full table settings of china and silverware, servants to bring the dishes to table, a set sequence of dishes beginning with soup and ending with a sweet, and the familiar grammar of starch, meat and green vegetable.[15] Loyalty to England itself was more likely to be expressed through preferences for particular brands, or emblematic dishes such as Christmas pudding, than in daily routines.

The lower register of culinary diglossia is much harder to reconstruct, because the meals of the working and rural classes were rarely recorded or described, and they also varied considerably by season, location, and the ethnic background and origins of the diners. Among the urban poor of mixed origin who formed the majority of the population the midday meal, rather than the evening dinner, was the main meal of the day. Breakfast and evening 'tea' were light meals dominated by home-made breads and leftovers from the main meal. Single-pot stews based on starchy tubers or plantains were the most common dishes; in most of the nineteenth century the staple for the working poor was 'saltfish and plantains', a thick soup flavoured with coconut milk, served along with fiery hot Habañero peppers either fresh or pickled with vinegar, onions and carrots.

Dietary diglossia created basic cultural and economic contradictions. On the one hand the home country and the government of the colony desperately wanted to make the colony more self-sufficient and prosperous. The timber industry was never sustainable, and went through a long series of boom and bust cycles, with a long-term trend towards mechanization and concentration that reduced employment and government revenue. The colonial period saw a continuous parade of agricultural commissions and reform programmes trying to figure out how to get a country with thousands of fertile acres and unemployed workers to feed itself. But despite government's efforts at building an agricultural college, assessing high import duties, providing free land to immigrants and even subsidizing local food production, imports stubbornly kept rising both in quantity and cost.[16] The local government was itself caught in a conflict of interest; although sound policy required greater self-sufficiency, import duties were the major source of government revenue.

In the face of official disapproval, the local preference for imported food was, by a strange inversion, a form of resistance to colonial pressure. The high price of imported foods actually gave them an added tinge of value and status.[17] Attempts to get local people to eat local food, even at the 1918 peak of wartime austerity, were actively resisted, and farming of anything but export crops was thought demeaning. Dietary diglossia equated civilization with European-style food and service, and much of the cultural effort of the respectable classes was devoted to public displays of proper consumption that were meant to be 'uplifting' for the populace at large: public cake-walks, tea-parties, and ice-cream socials were held by most churches, schools, clubs and Masonic lodges both to raise funds and to 'provide a good example' to the poor. At the same time the institutions and instruments of social exclusion, the schools, the clubs, and the legal system, made sure that few local people ever moved beyond their 'station' to learn and practice elite culture. These complex contradictions between the colonial 'civilizing mission' and the rigidity of racism and cultural chauvinism are a common theme in the history and anthropology of colonialism.

In practice the social strata in a tiny colony like Belize were anything but cohesive and monolithic, and they had their own internal cultural politics. For example, most of the European expatriate elite of Belize actually came from relatively modest middle-class backgrounds in the home countries; they might drink French champagne and eat turtle soup regularly while working abroad, but could never afford them regularly at home. With their true status insecure, especially when they were faced with real metropolitan nobility, consumption of all kinds became an important performance: they made elaborate shows of expensive and fashionable clothes, foods, and public entertainments. Their efforts were frustrated by slow communications and irregular shipping, which left them far behind metropolitan fashion despite their best efforts.

The multiethnic working class were equally divided and diverse, but their dire economic circumstances left them unable to take a regular part in the cultural hierarchy of colonial consumption. They simply could not afford to eat imported food as a regular diet, and because of restrictions on land tenure, even rural people were often hard-pressed to grow enough food for their own consumption. Instead imported luxuries became part of annual festivities concentrated at the end of the mahogany-cutting season, when male workers streamed out of the forest into town for the Christmas holidays. Even under slavery the annual Christmas 'bacchanal' saw woodcutters parading through the streets arrayed in fine European clothes, dining on roast beef and swilling imported liquors, much to the discomfort of their masters. These events were carnivalesque transgressions, where the speakers of the lower-ranking dialect presumed to use (through public consumption) the dialect of the elite class.

The idea of culinary diglossia reflects some important similarities between the symbolic content of language and food; the notion of taste, and the sense of what makes a proper meal are naturalized at both conscious and unconscious levels, just like language. We can liken the habitus of taste to the unconscious grammatical structures and knowledge that make it possible to generate and understand language.[18] At the same time that much of language is unconsciously generated, we are also capable of using it intentionally and expressively at a number of levels – of course including explicit content and meaning, but also with subtleties of accent, emphasis, volume, rhythm and the like. Similarly, within a community that shares a culinary 'language' food has expressive meaning communicated in many registers beyond the simple ingredients.

While it is useful to think about the similarities between language and cuisine as reflections of social order that are also constitutive of that order, there are also important differences between language and cuisine that reflect the persistent material nature of foodstuffs.[19] Unlike language, cuisines are connected directly to the cultural and physical ecology of food production, to structures of trade and politics that are far beyond the control of cooks and diners. One could also argue that the constraints of nutrition and regularity make food an inherently different medium of cultural expression and communication from speech. None of these differences necessarily weakens the utility of the concept of dietary diglossia as a way of discussing social distinction; but they should prompt us to think further about the different potential roles that speech, dress, cuisine and other forms of consumption can play in social systems of categorization.

From Diglossia to Creolization

During the frequent economic depressions in the timber economy at the end of the nineteenth century the rigid social and economic boundaries of colonial Belizean society began to change. Instead of diglossia, a situation with just two distinct and separate dialects, a better metaphor for this period is the Creole language, which has a range of dialects.[20] In postcolonial situations creole languages typically include several *mesolects* that occupy the space between a high-ranked foreign-standard *acrolect* and the locally specific low-ranking *basolects*. In culinary terms, while the cultural superiority of European food was not challenged, a variety of cuisines developed that were intermediate in status between European and local rural (often 'ethnic') cuisines.

The social group who spanned the middle ground came to be called Creoles, a group whose origins in Belize have been discussed by many recent historians. Even the lightest skinned and best educated of Creoles began to have serious political and cultural differences with the sojourning colonial government officials, technicians and functionaries who planned to retire to the home country. Their long local history gave them many kinship, commercial and sexual relationships with the urban and rural middle and working classes. Rather than developing a single blended or hybridized culture and language, they performed a kind of cultural 'code switching', mastering different 'registers' in a range from formal to informal, competently English to fully local. At one end was European formal dining, with the full range of elaborate silver tableware, china plate, overcooked meats smothered in sauces and all the other delights of stiff colonial dining. At the other end were dishes like armadillo stewed in a spicy Yucatan-style black sauce, with conch fritters and plantain dumpling. The local Creoles did not just to learn to appreciate ('speak') and understand the full range, but knew their appropriate settings and uses, and could use them in sophisticated and expressive ways.

There was never, in this scheme, any question of which end of the scale was highest ranking, for the only permissible food in all formal public events like receptions, weddings, government functions and balls was European. Local food was a private pleasure that appeared in public only at popular entertainments like sporting events, village fiestas, and horse races. Creolization, like other aspects of the colonial class system, created many anxious pleasures and ambiguous events. The cultural richness of neighbouring countries and immigrant ethnic groups also provided some opportunities to escape from the limits of the colonial hierarchy, from the polarity of local and foreign. Refugees from the Caste Wars of Yucatan in the mid-nineteenth century brought a variety of dishes that were relatively free of class associations, so 'Spanish' food entered easily into all levels of the food/class system. Some East Indian, Mayan and Garifuna dishes also entered the Creole mix, though they tended to carry more rural and working-class connotations. In the early twentieth century Chinese restaurants also began to play a similar role as sources of food with fewer class connotations.

Linguists have observed that upwardly striving middle-class speakers often adopt 'hyper-correct' pronunciation, showing much less tolerance for dialect variation than elites.[21] The standard explanation is that elites are more secure in their status, while the working class has no status to lose by speaking in stigmatized ways. We can see a similar kind of dynamic in the colonial range of food 'dialects' in early twentieth-century Belize, leading to a phenomenon I have called a *style sandwich*.[22] Wild game and fish provide a good example. Animals like deer, ducks and snappers that had close cognates or relatives in England were acceptable to most people. On the other hand, local game meats like armadillo and iguana and seafood like crabs and shark, widely eaten in the countryside, were shunned at middle-class tables, where imported tinned sardines were preferred to any local fresh fish. The elite, on the other hand, were free to indulge in game meat as part of sporting entertainment, which included mass pigeon and parrot hunts. Unlike the striving middle class, high-status people could indulge in many local foods (as well as other forms of marginal social behaviour) without endangering their respectable social position.

Progress

The superior ranking of European food always had an anchor in the global geography of empire, since it radiated outward from the cultural centre. Technological 'progress' was one of the key concepts that organized the colonial world spatially and temporally into centre and periphery, leading and backward, civilized and primitive. The competition between colonies for position in this temporal/spatial position led government and business leaders in places like Belize to organize expensive entries for exhibits at international shows, fairs and exhibitions. The arrival of the first steamship in the harbour was a huge event, which simultaneously brought Belize 'forward' into the present, and emphasized just what a distant backwater it really was. There were similar celebrations on the opening of the first local brewery, bottling works for local 'aerated waters', the installation of the first refrigerator, and the arrival of the first frozen meat.

Ice was a particularly important indication of civilization in the later nineteenth century. In the early 1860s, Belize City developed as a trading centre for both the Union and Confederate sides in the American Civil War. Frequent and rapid sailings to American ports brought the first bulk shipments of ice, packed in sawdust in wooden barrels.[23] Newspaper editorials claimed that ice had health-giving properties for white people in the tropics, and commended it as an essential article of civilization. By 1866 ice chests were on sale, and a regular shipping schedule established. As a local taste developed for iced drinks and ice cream, the expense and inefficiency of importing ice led to a major public debate. The Governor and the legislative council argued in 1883 over building a local ice factory. The council said that with such a small local market, a privately owned factory would never be a viable business. As a matter of public health and as a sign of civilization the government should provide a subsidy to build it. The governor dismissed the proposal on the grounds that ice was no more than a luxury, and the government did not have the money anyway.

Undaunted, ice cream and iced drink shops opened, using imported ice and canned milk. Throughout the 1880s and 1890s churches and civic charities held ice-cream socials and parties as fund-raisers, though they had to contend with an unreliable ice supply. Finally in 1897 an American entrepreneur opened the Belize Ice and Distilled Water Works. The irony was that while this ostensibly made Belize more modern and self-sufficient, capable of supplying its own needs, in reality it created a continuing demand for ever-more complex imports, not only of equipment, fuel, bottles and processed ingredients, but also for new tastes and the expertise to satisfy them. In the colonial status system, peripheral areas could never 'catch up' with fashions and tastes that came from the centres of empire, no matter how hard they tried, leading to a permanent state of cultural 'embarrassment' about a backwardness that could never be remedied by the products that were ostensibly the agents of modernity.

Conclusion

I have only discussed a few of the close connections between the economy of food supply and the culture of cuisine in this corner of the colonial system. The food connection exposes fundamental conflicts between the goals of making colonies *economically* self-sufficient and capable of funding their own government and services, and at the same time maintaining cultural and political connections to the home country. This contradiction fuelled a cycle in which every increase in the value of exports (which broadened to include sugar and bananas in the 1920s) led to increases in the demand for imported food. While the prices of raw commodities exported stagnated (in competition with those produced by other colonies), new packaged and processed foods grew increasingly expensive. New tastes became the key indicators of progress and civilization, which could never stand still despite dire financial consequences, which ended up starving the colony of the capital that could have been used to expand or diversify the economy.

In the concluding chapters of my book on Belizean food I argue that a variation of the same destructive cycle continues today, despite (or perhaps even because of) a fundamental economic shift away from export agriculture and towards tourism. Today the global tastes of empire come in glossy tubes of Pringles chips, which sit on shelves close to some hardy survivors of the British Empire, like Johnny Walker whisky and Crosse & Blackwell's salad cream. Today the range of imported food has broadened considerably, and modern Belizean supermarkets sell cans of imported tropical fruit and American-made frozen 'Chinese' rice dinners (made with Mexican vegetables). Though local food production has increased, and local cuisines are thriving, Belizean food products can never keep up with the incredible variety of new food products pouring out of the Northern industrial food system, at low prices thanks to subsidies. Millions of development dollars are still wasted on 'agricultural diversification', while imports are now more than double exports by value.[24]

The taste of and for foreign food continues to play an essential role in this system. Historians could make a major contribution by tracing the histories of particular products that have enduring significance in colonial trade, brands that have maintained loyalty and visibility over centuries. We might then learn why and how certain tastes become so deeply embedded in culture that they endure through dramatic political and economic transformations, while many other tastes change quickly and follow the whims of fashion. In a world where McDonalds and Coca Cola are following in the cultural footsteps of earlier global foods, we have a great deal to learn from the past. And as Sidney Mintz has convincingly argued, the puzzle of food conservatism vs labile food fashion has special importance as the world's population presses harder and harder on the limits of sustainable food production.[25]

Notes

1. Intellectual and visual culture have been particularly well studied; see for example F. Driver, *Geography Militant: Cultures of Exploration and Empire* (Oxford, 2001); D. Cannadine, *Ornamentalism: How the British Saw Their Empire* (Oxford, 2002); and J. Ryan, *Picturing Empire: Photography and the Visualization of the British Empire* (London, 1997).

2. W. Anderson, 'Excremental Colonialism: Public Health and the Poetics of Pollution', *Critical Inquiry*, 21 (1995): 640–69; W. Anderson, *Colonial Pathologies: American Tropical Medicine, Race, and Hygiene in the Philippines* (Durham, NC, 2006), W. Anderson, *The Cultivation of Whiteness: Science, Health, and Racial Destiny in Australia* (New York, 2003).

3. L. Collingham, *Curry: A Tale of Cooks and Conquerors* (Oxford, 2006) focuses on the relationship between pre-colonial and colonial cuisine, while I. Cusack's 'African Cuisines: Recipes for Nation-Building?', *Journal of African Cultural*

Studies, 13(2) (2000): 207–25 takes up the connection between colonial and post-colonial national foodways.

4. J. Watson (ed.), *Golden Arches East* (Cambridge, MA, 1997) includes a series of essays by anthropologists about the way different countries in East Asia have adapted McDonald's chain restaurants to local culture; the lesson is that the persistence of national cultures requires even multinational corporations to change. Yet in the end the authors never address the cultural impact of fast food, as a genre, on local cuisines, nor the economic impact of franchise chains on diverse independent merchants and restaurants.

5. I develop these themes at greater length in R. Wilk, 'Learning to Be Local in Belize: Global Systems of Common Difference', in D. Miller (ed.), *Worlds Apart: Modernity through the Prism of the Local* (New York, 1995), pp. 110–33.

6. The best histories of Belize are O. Bolland, *The Formation of a Colonial Society* (Baltimore, MD, 1977) and O. Bolland, *Belize: A New Nation in Central America* (Boulder, CO, 1986), and more recently A. Sutherland, *The Making of Belize* (Westport, CT, 1998).

7. During this period food comprised between 40 and 80 per cent of total imports by value.

8. The popular explanation is typified by the statement on the Schweppes website that 'As the British Empire grew, Englishmen, longing for a taste of home, brought Schweppes to distant countries in every corner of the world' (http://www.dpsu.com/brands/schweppes.html). This is not to say that food doesn't play an important role in maintaining contact and identity among diasporic groups, as ably documented, for example, by D. Sutton in *Remembrance of Repasts* (Oxford, 2001).

9. I discuss some of the contradictory advice about healthful diets given to Europeans in Belize in *Home Cooking in the Global Village* (Oxford, 2006), pp. 110–12. Medical opinion also changed over time, and local folklore developed in each colony and region. About the only consistent advice was that Europeans should eat 'light' meals and avoid overeating, though it is hard to judge what would have been considered overindulgence on the part of Victorians, for whom normal breakfast might have three kinds of meat; highly spiced foods were generally shunned as well. On Victorian dining in general see S. Freeman, *Mutton and Oysters: The Victorians and Their Food* (London, 1989).

10. A. McCants, 'Exotic Goods Popular Consumption and the Standard of Living: Thinking About Globalization in the Early Modern World'. Published online, 2006, available at http://web.mit.edu/kayla/Public/ToPrint/globaltrade.pdf (2006, pp. 3–4).

11. W. Lindsay, *History of Merchant Shipping and Ancient Commerce* (v. II., London, 1874).

12. O. Jones, 'Commercial Foods, 1740–1820', *Historical Archaeology*, 27(2) (1993): 25–41.

13. Among food imports it is important to distinguish between raw materials, which can be anonymous, and recognizable processed foods, which have a great deal more cultural meaning. In Belize, for example, wheat could not be grown locally, and wheat flour was an important imported food, but it came interchangeably from many different countries, while *Huntley & Palmer* or *Uneeda* tinned biscuits were respectively British and American.

14. The defining cases of linguistic diglossia include early twentieth-century Greece and Egypt, countries where educated and literate elites spoke 'classical' languages, while the largely illiterate masses used a demotic popular dialect. My discussion here builds on J. Goody, *Cooking Cuisine and Class* (Cambridge, 1982), which forcefully argues that only cultures with true class distinctions can develop a class-based cuisine that differentiates an elite from an agricultural working class.

15. See M. Douglas, 'Deciphering a Meal', in C. Geertz (ed.), *Myth, Symbol and Culture* (New York, 1971), pp. 61–82.

16. For example wheat flour and biscuit imports rose from 45.2 kg/capita in 1886 to 52.3 kg/capita in 1935.

17. A 1900 advertisement for the International Hotel claims 'The meat, vegetables, and fruit are imported from the U.S.A. ... The hotel has an unlimited supply of ice and American lager and English beer, several kinds of Aerated and Mineral waters and at least two brands of Champagne are always to be had cold': *Colonial Guardian*, 19(30) (1900).

18. Whether or not we accept Chomsky's notion of a biologically-based 'language acquisition device' underlying our ability to generate language, we know that the generative capacities of grammar, syntax and lexicon that make language possible are not consciously accessible to its users; we do not know how we generate speech. In a similar way, we know that certain things taste right and others are unpleasant or disgusting, but as eaters we are not conscious of the cognitive and biological structures that generate that knowledge and the physical experiences of pleasure, distaste or disgust we experience when eating.

19. Like language and other aspects of culture, cuisine is a system that simult-aneously projects order on to the world and reflects the internalized ordered classification of cultural actors, what Pierre Bourdieu calls 'a structuring struc-ture' or a ' a system of classified and classifying practices' in *Outline of a Theory of Practice* (Cambridge, 1977), p. 170. But as yet we do not understand the patterns of changes in cuisines that would be analogous to the well-recognized laws of syntactic and sound shifts (like Grimm's law) used by historical linguists to describe language change.

20. The concept of creolization (or the Hispanic equivalent of *mestizaje*) has a long and complex intellectual history in the social science of the New World that is

summarized well by M. Sheller in *Consuming the Caribbean* (London, 2003) and by R. Burton, *Afro-Creole: Power, Opposition, and Play in the Caribbean* (Ithaca, NY, 1997). The term has a much narrower use in linguistics, where a creole is specifically a new language that develops from a mixed pidgin used for intercultural communication.

21. The classic observation of this tendency is described by W. Labov in *Socio-linguistic Patterns* (Philadelphia, PA, 1973).

22. I discuss the style sandwich in more detail in *Home Cooking in the Global Village*; similar observations were made by S. George in *Ill Fares the Land: Essays on Food, Hunger and Power* (Washington DC, 1984).

23. On the development of the ice trade from the United States, and the ingenious marketing techniques used to create demand, see G. Weightman, *The Frozen Water Trade* (New York, 2003).

24. The 2005 official import figures show that about US$40 worth of food is imported into the country each month for each of the 250,000 Belizean residents, which may not sound like much except that average per capita monthly income is only about US$150.

25. S. Mintz, *Tasting Food, Tasting Freedom* (Boston, 1996), and 'Food at Moderate Speeds', in R. Wilk (ed.), *Fast Food/Slow Food* (Walnut Creek, CA, 2006), pp. 3–14.

–7–

Americanizing Coffee

The Refashioning of a Consumer Culture[1]

Michelle Craig McDonald and *Steven Topik*

Introduction

The spread of luxury goods has driven the expansion of the world economy for thousands of years. Fashion-conscious elites and their imitators in search of distinction or utility joined profit-seeking merchants, shippers and manufacturers to fuel the global dispersal of silks and porcelain, as well as sugar, tea and coffee, producing new trade patterns and markets.[2] Culture, in this sense, was as important as economics to the growth of long-distance transactions and the shaping and defining of luxury goods through socially constructed desires. But the complicated and ambiguous processes of consumption 'can only be properly recovered', as one editor of this volume notes, by analysing 'the links that connect the different places in which goods are produced, distributed, purchased or consumed and given meaning'.[3]

Foods, in particular, have played central roles in the creation of national identities, for though consumption became diffuse, ingestion remained tempered by local rituals and adaptations. Coffee, the subject of this chapter, symbolized independence from British authority and culture in North America since 1776, an example of what Sidney Mintz has called 'tasting freedom'.[4] Coffee appears in US nationalist and internationalist iconography – as a patriotic proxy for tea during the economic embargoes of the 1760s; as diplomatic leverage during the early republic; as a symbol of US expansionism; and as a vehicle to spread the 'American way of life'.[5] Thus coffee is linked to US state-formation, nation-building, continentalism and globalism. By the nineteenth century, it was as quintessentially American as tea was British or Chinese, beer German and wine French.

But coffee starred in a global drama as well, entering America's diet and character at the same time that it saturated the world economy. It was part of the explosion in caffeinated hot drink consumption that William Clarence-Smith details in this volume for England and the Americas, it supplemented the sugar-driven energy Sidney Mintz emphasizes and helped drive the 'green international' Alexander Nützenadel describes. What distinguishes coffee in North America's history is its tenacious and contradictory relationship to ideas of freedom. How did an African plant, transplanted to the Caribbean and Central and South America, become a symbol of American freedom? Coffee's assimilation and nationalization were neither predestined nor organic, but resulted from a confluence of historically specific cultural, social, political and economic influences.

The transformation from luxury beverage in the seventeenth century to mass consumer drink by the mid-nineteenth century reinforced coffee's egalitarian and democratic symbolic significance to eighteenth- and nineteenth-century pamphleteers and chroniclers such as Thomas Paine, Hector St. John de Crévecoeur, Domingo Faustino Sarmiento, Alexis de Tocqueville and other purveyors of the American story of equality.[6] And political tracts and travellers' accounts are only one way to gauge coffee's increasing importance in American life. Merchant account books document coffee's sale to mariners, brewers, labourers and widows by the 1760s; elite Boston and Philadelphia women like Abigail Adams and Elizabeth Drinker describe its popularity among the well-to-do in the 1780s and 1790s; and even enslaved labourers received coffee as payment for overwork in Virginia iron works by the 1820s.[7] So common were coffee pots and cups on US tables that European visitors considered the commodity an indelible part of the new nation's identity within years of independence. 'Our supper was rather scanty', wrote François Jean Chastellux, a French traveller to Virginia in 1787, 'but our breakfast the next morning was better … we are perfectly reconciled to this American custom of drinking coffee.'[8]

By the mid-nineteenth century, the United States led global coffee importation, though the commodity's overseas pedigree was usually erased. Domestic coffee roasters chose American landscapes or the familiar face of Uncle Sam over exotic or foreign imagery for their trade cards.[9] On the rare occasions advertisements divulged provenance, they mentioned Java or Mocha, which held historical appeal. Indeed, on the western frontier coffee was known as 'jamoca', a combination of 'java' (Indonesia) and 'mocha' (Yemen), though nearly all of it came from Latin America.[10] Overall, however, coffee became divorced from its origins in the nineteenth century – geographically sanitized – in the campaign to supplant tea as the all-American drink.

Military campaigns also assisted in coffee's assimilation into American daily life. During the American Civil War, Union troops considered coffee necessary for martial victory. General Sherman called it 'the essential element of the ration', concluding that 'the coffee and sugar ration be carried along, even at the expense of bread, for which there are many substitutes'.[11] Those shirking their duty became known as 'coffee coolers', an epithet for 'shiftless, superannuated loungers'.[12] By the early twentieth century, coffee was renamed 'cup of Joe' in honour of its close identification with 'GI Joe' in the First and Second World Wars and in recognition of its contributions to America's overseas efforts. When the wars ended, coffee drinking spilled over into civilian life. A 1937 *Fortune* magazine article reported that 'a blending of old socialites and new celebrities called Café Society' was on the rise and other sources noted the increasing appearance of 'coffee breaks' among both white- and blue-collar workers.[13] Coffee became a US custom – civilian and military, elite and proletarian, male and female alike. But America's destiny as a vehicle for the globalization of coffee would have surprised early English colonists. This is an overview of that unexpected, centuries-long path.

Coffee and the Boston Tea Party

America's interest in coffee began almost as early as colonization itself. John Smith, one of England's first settlers in Virginia, described 'coffa' or 'coava' in his travel accounts from Turkey almost twenty years before England's first coffeehouse opened. Pilgrims migrating from Holland, Europe's main coffee entrepôt, might well have brought beans with them and Dutch settlers in New Amsterdam and French settlers in New Orleans imported coffee by the mid-seventeenth century and early eighteenth century respectively.[14] Despite this early introduction, coffee-drinking in North America grew slowly. Coffeehouses clustered in port cities, limiting the opportunities for rural Americans to participate in public consumption and cost curbed its incursion into private homes. William Penn complained in 1683 that British taxing and transport policies raised the price of coffee to a stunning 18*s*. 9*d*. per pound, well beyond the means of most colonial families. Though the price of coffee dropped over the next century coffee consumption remained low, only one-eighteenth of a pound per head by 1783, or enough to brew a few cups of coffee per person annually.[15]

Both popular and scholarly histories point to the Boston Tea Party as the watershed event that forever changed America's relationship to coffee. 'It is sufficient here to refer to the climax of agitation against the fateful tea tax,' observed William Ukers, long-time editor of *The Tea and Coffee Journal*, 'because it is undoubtedly responsible for our becoming a nation of coffee drinkers instead of tea drinkers, like the English.' The Boston Tea Party of 1773, he argued, left Americans 'with a prenatal disinclination for tea' and 'caused coffee to be crowned 'king of the American breakfast table' and 'the sovereign drink of the American people'.[16] Recent popular coffee studies by Mark Pendergrast, John Beilenson, and Gregory Dicum and Nina Luttinger agreed with Ukers.[17] Dicum and Luttinger even proposed that 'European colonialism seemed to dictate where coffee was cultivated and drunk', but, 'in the case of the United States, it was the end of colonialism, dramatically reflected in the Boston Tea Party, that marked its rise to prominence.'[18]

At first glance, manuscript sources seem to support these interpretations. Certainly revolutionary leaders such as Paul Revere and Samuel and John Adams, and patriotic groups like the 'Sons of Liberty', used Boston's Green Dragon Coffee House and New York's Merchants' Coffee House to protest against the Stamp and Townsend Acts.[19] Nor was coffee's patriotic potential limited to cities. During the summer of 1774,

John Adams wrote that when he asked an innkeeper, 'Is it lawful … for a weary Traveller to refresh himself with a Dish of Tea, providing it has been honestly smuggled, or paid no Duties?', the proprietess replied, 'No sir … we have renounced all Tea in this Place. I can't make tea … but [can] make you Coffee.'[20] Adams' recollection is one of the few to compare coffee and tea in writing during the colonial period and implies that the two caffeine beverages were, if not equally desirable, at least gastronomically interchangeable. More importantly, it demonstrates that some Americans – in this case a rural innkeeper and Continental Congressional representative – identified coffee with American ideas of freedom.

But the association was short-lived. America's 1765 and 1769 embargoes of British goods focused on Britain and Ireland; but a third inter-colonial boycott in 1774, beginning just months after Adams' Massachusetts excursion, included the British Caribbean, America's chief coffee supplier. Coffee, in other words, became as politically charged as tea. Some colonial representatives pleaded that banning West Indian trade 'must produce a national Bankruptcy'; but their arguments received short shrift from those who considered Caribbean commodities like coffee 'intoxicating poisons and needless luxuries' that should be sunk at sea 'rather than [brought] ashore'.[21] By 1777, even Adams changed his mind about coffee, writing to his wife, Abigail: 'I hope the females will leave off their attachment to coffee. I assure you, the best families in this place have left off in a great measure the use of West India goods. We much bring ourselves to live upon the produce of our own country.'[22]

Coffee as the Drink of Diplomats

Before the boycott, most North Americans' coffee came from Britain's colonies in Jamaica, Grenada, Saint Vincent and Dominica. But in 1783 Parliament banned shipments of British colonial produce in US vessels and did so precisely when American interest in the commodity was booming.[23] Pre-Revolutionary coffee imports peaked at just over US$1 million in 1774, but British West Indian coffee imports alone into the United States were worth US$1,480,000 per annum from 1802 to 1804, while coffee imports from the rest of the world topped US$8 million.[24]

Over half America's coffee imports left shortly after they arrived. Coffee had moved between Britain's mainland colonies during the colonial period, but America's re-export trade by 1800 was international. Table 7.1 compares domestic and re-exported coffees as a percentage of total trade. Initially, many of these re-exports went to Amsterdam, Paris and London; but after 1790 US traders made new inroads into Germany, Italy and Russia. Because tropical goods generally and coffee especially, were important to American interests, US access to the West Indies was a serious concern. Some merchants turned to smuggling to meet demand; many more relied on international competition, legal loopholes and especially government intervention to expand their businesses.

Table 7.1 US Coffee Imports and Re-exports, 1800–1805

Year	Domestic Imports (lb)	Per cent of Total	Re-exports (lb)	Per cent of Total	TOTAL
1800	36,709,317	43.6	47,389,946	56.4	84,099,263
1801	44,890,182	43.9	57,383,904	56.1	102,274,086
1802	36,162,859	46.9	40,886,861	53.1	77,049,720
1803	10,105,240	37.5	16,828,493	62.5	26,933,733
1804	48,105,304	49.7	48,638,382	50.3	96,743,686
1805	45,823,329	44.9	56,141,320	55.1	101,964,649

Source: Percentages derived by comparing total coffee re-export revenue of $7,302,000 to total re-export revenue of $28,533,000 as they appear in ASPCN, V: 612–72.

Merchants and farmers bitterly debated the pros and cons of tariffs for goods that competed with American manufactures, but more often agreed on trade concessions for commodities America did not produce. Tea and coffee figured prominently in these discussions, since Congressional delegates recognized that both 'enter largely into the consumption of the country and have become articles of necessity to all classes'.[25] In 1774 they created a three-man European Commission – John Jay, John Adams and Benjamin Franklin – to oversee negotiations and authorize treaties with several European nations and the Barbary Coast.[26] The 'plan of treaties' was an ambitious endeavour for any nation. With only a small army and no formal navy, the United States could not achieve its objectives militarily. Instead, Congress equipped its European commissioners with the strongest weapon at its disposal – American purchasing power – and declared that nations refusing trade treaties with the United States would face discriminatory tariffs and market restrictions. During the Commission's first two years, however, only Prussia agreed to a treaty based on the model of free trade.[27]

Thomas Jefferson replaced Jay on the committee in 1784 and recommended that nations with Atlantic colonies become the Commission's first priorities.[28] American diplomats hoped Amsterdam might be receptive to American interests. Colonial officials in the Dutch colony of Saint Eustatius had been the first government body to recognize North American claims to independence, followed by France and then Holland.[29] But though Holland's liberal commercial policies allowed American vessels into its West Indian colonies, it limited what Americans could bring to the colonies and what they could take from them – especially coffee and sugar.[30]

Other options were scarce. Denmark imposed fewer considerations, but the Danish West Indies were ultimately insufficient for America's burgeoning coffee industry.[31] The Commission also approached the Portuguese Ambassador about establishing trade with Brazilian coffee plantations, but was told that Portugal 'admitted no nation to the Brazils'.[32] North American thirst would only be slaked by Brazilian coffee after the colony freed itself from Portugal.

Frustrated, as 1785 drew to a close, America's European Commissioners found themselves haggling with places like Austria that offered no prospects of profits from tropical goods, prompting Jefferson and his colleagues to promote a preferential treaty with France early in 1786.[33] This move aligned the United States with the only military force able to challenge Britain. 'It will be a strong link of connection', Jefferson wrote, 'the more [so]with the only nation on earth on whom we can solidly rely for assistance till we stand on our own legs.'[34] Moreover, it gave US importers access to the French Caribbean colonies, especially Saint Domingue, the leading producer of sugars and coffee in the Caribbean since the early eighteenth century.

American merchants rallied behind Jefferson's plan and in October 1786 France agreed to a series of trade concessions, including use of American ships and lowered tariffs in both France and the French Antilles.[35] The shift to French coffee suppliers is obvious in Table 7.2.

Table 7.2 US Coffee Imports from the West Indies, 1790–1791

Region	Coffee (lb)	Per Cent of Total US Coffee Imports
French West Indies	3,432,385	77.0
Dutch West Indies	559,613	13.0
British West Indies	346,875	7.0
Spanish West Indies	51,689	1.0
Danish West Indies	28,715	0.7
East Indies	25,138	0.6
Swedish West Indies	8,895	0.1
Portuguese West Indies	1,108	<0.01
West Indies (General)	8,472	0.1
Other	15,783	0.4
TOTAL	4,478,676	100.00

Source: ASPFR, 1:195.

Britain continued to exclude America from its Caribbean colonies; but war in Europe undermined the Royal Navy's ability to patrol the region.[36] American neutrality was more than a diplomatic objective; it had been essential to the nation's future prosperity ever since the first overtures of the European Commission.[37] Without trade agreements Americans could not conduct their budding business with the lucrative Caribbean colonies and without neutral shipping they were unable to bring tropical produce to their consumers – at a time when war between Britain and France provided prime opportunities to enter European markets.[38] So while the nascent nation expanded its continental territory westwards, it also extended its commercial influence southward. The re-export trade – with coffee as its flagship product – became essential to the national economy and political advocates portrayed re-export merchants as 'patriots' whose trade was 'a necessary link in the chain of our society and of our place in the world'.[39] Re-exportation of foreign-grown coffee, like coffee drinking for those few years in 1770s, became a patriotic act that inspired national and international attention.

Coffee and Slavery

Patriotic Americans tended to conflate 'independence' and 'freedom', just as they confused commercial and civil liberties. Slavery, however, posed the biggest challenge to coffee's association with American freedom. Throughout the eighteenth and nineteenth centuries Caribbean and Latin American slaves produced most of the coffee Americans drank and even East Indian coffee labourers, while not technically enslaved, could hardly be called free. At times, the relationship was even more direct – some coffee importers traded in slaves as well. Both British and American emancipationists recognized the powerful cultural connections between commodities and the labour that produced them in their boycotts of slave-produced sugar; but coffee, like tobacco and cotton, never faced a similar embargo.[40] By 1800, the cost of a coffee embargo would have been too high for America. The new nation made more from the re-export of coffee overseas than from re-exports of tea, sugar and molasses combined; coffee represented 10 per cent of all US trade income and 25 per cent of its re-export income – high figures for a commodity that North America did not produce itself.[41]

Coffee cultivation had not always been synonymous with slave labour. It was first commercially produced in Yemen, which monopolized world coffee production until Dutch cultivation began in Java at the end of the seventeenth century.[42] Slave labour entered the still small world coffee market only in 1718, with the first Atlantic experiments in Dutch Surinam. Thereafter coffee planters, slaves and cultivation techniques rapidly crossed imperial boundaries until almost all European empires in the west – British, French, Spanish, Portuguese and Dutch – boasted important coffee export economies. Some 2.6 million Africans eventually populated the small islands that dotted the Caribbean Sea, constituting the majority of the population in most colonies.[43] The numbers of slaves working in coffee varied by colony, but most early farms were small. One contemporary source estimated as few as 250 acres (100 hectares approx.) and 'a few slaves' could produce coffee profitably and though coffee planters undoubtedly had higher aspirations, most owned fewer than fifty slaves.[44]

Smaller start-up costs in land and labour made coffee planting accessible to a socially and economically diverse group of people. Unlike the great sugar planters, many of whom left the management of their Caribbean estates to attorneys and bookkeepers and lived in London or Paris, coffee growers often lived in residence in the Caribbean and their letters offer one perspective on coffee slaves' experiences in the remote, highland areas where coffee grew best.[45] 'The negroes in my district never went abroad', wrote Pierre Joseph Laborie, a refugee Saint Domingue coffee planter, who likened his coffee farm in the Blue Mountains of Jamaica to an island. Rather than allow his slaves to purchase provisions at local markets he 'brought from the Cape all the articles which my negroes desired'.[46] Only the handful of mule drivers responsible for bringing coffee to market regularly left Laborie's plantation. Small-scale coffee farmers used similar tactics, though in the case of Matthew Smith, who lived near the Jamaican port of Savannah la Mar, slaves replaced mules as beasts of burden. When British port officials complained that Smith's coffee bags were underweight – colonial law mandated that coffee be shipped in bags of 112 pounds, while Smith's weighed between 72 and 79 pounds – he replied that he had no mules or horses and 79 pounds was 'as much as a Negro can carry upon his head'.[47]

Travel narratives, a popular eighteenth- and early nineteenth-century literary genre, included several accounts of coffee plantation slavery, suggesting that Americans were well aware of how their coffee was produced; but no public backlash occurred.[48] A few writers noted with irony the duplicity of abolitionists' boycotts of slave-produced sugar while consumption of other slave products continued apace. 'Oh, they say, do not use the polluted thing; beware of sweetening your coffee with slave-grown sugar', wrote the Reverend Robert Burns, a member of Glasgow Young Man's Free Trade Association. But how could 'slave-grown tobacco, cotton and coffee' be acceptable, he reasoned, 'while slave-grown sugar must be productive of moral disease?'[49] Most writers, however, remained silent. In fact, public reaction to the incongruity of coffee's connotations of freedom and its origins in slavery remained largely unexplored in public debate before 1848, when protests came – not from socially conscious American consumers – but from disgruntled British planters. These planters, forced to use non-slave labour after Britain's abolition of slavery in 1838, protested against the prospect of competing for the American market with slave-produced coffee from Brazil.[50] American reactions, however, remained tepid; an 1859 *New York Times* article noted only that coffee together with some other tropical goods formed 'necessaries of life' for the 'northern latitudes which embrace the largest civilized portions of the human race'; its unfree origins were ignored.[51] Ironically for the protesting British planters, one of the fastest-growing British colonial coffee-consumer markets was the labour force that had formerly produced it. Edward Bean Underhill noted in his 1862 account of the West Indies that 'the vast increase in the use of these articles [sugar and coffee] is the result of freedom... With such an internal demand, it is no wonder that coffee cultivation is growing into favour among the negroes.'[52]

In reality, French, rather than British, Caribbean colonies had supplied most of America's coffee needs for decades by the time Underhill wrote his report. In French Saint Domingue, the principal exporter of coffee to the United States until 1803, *gens de couleur* (free people of colour) dominated the colony's coffee industry, owning one-third of the plantation property and one-quarter of the slaves in Saint Domingue in 1789.[53] Saint Domingue's dominant place in American commerce dramatically declined, however, after Toussaint l'Ouverture led revolutionary forces against French colonial troops. Saint Domingue, renamed Haiti, became the second European colony in the Americas to gain independence and the first to abolish slavery. Rather than applaud this double freedom, the United States government refused to recognize Haiti's independence or to send an ambassador to the new nation until 1862.[54] America's domestic north–south sectional conflict shaped its international commercial and diplomatic policy towards the former colony, leading the federal government to encourage coffee importation from slave-rich Brazil rather than from emancipated and free Haiti.

Coffee Becomes Americanized

Eighteenth-century tea boycotts whetted the North American appetite for coffee, but did not guarantee that the United States would become known as a nation of coffee drinkers. Although colonists briefly abandoned tea drinking, they soon returned. In 1859, the United States imported more than 29 million pounds of tea, which rose to 47 million pounds in 1870 and 81 million in 1881. That was more than a pound per head. True, Americans imported 455 million pounds of coffee in 1881; but tea imports had been growing rather than shrinking. Some traders estimated that four times as much coffee grounds as tea leaves were needed to produce the same amount of beverage.[55] Since coffee imports were 5.5 times tea imports, the amount of coffee and tea brewed and presumably consumed was quite similar. Independent Americans drank far more tea than had colonial Americans. Indeed, most coffee roasters, such as Chase & Sanborn, Folgers, or White House, advertised tea as much as coffee. Only in 1890 did nationalists regularly proclaim coffee 'the national beverage' of the United States, arguing that the United States had set aside tea definitively and become a 'coffee loving country'.[56] So if the true divide in the hot beverage war was well after independence, what explains coffee's triumph once the Boston Tea Party is dismissed as the cause?

For international merchants, the issue had been how much coffee and tea Americans imported, not how much they drank; here coffee towered over tea. The United States imported one-third of the world's coffee in the 1880s as annual per capita consumption ballooned from well under one pound at independence to nine pounds by 1882. Factoring in population increases from under 4 million to 50 million during that century, total coffee consumption increased over a hundredfold. The import price of coffee in the United States during the nineteenth century averaged about one-half of what it had been at Brazil's independence in 1821. By 1906, when Brazil exported almost 90 per cent of the world's coffee in terms of volume, the price had fallen to one-third of the 1821 price.[57] Brazilians used their near-monopoly position to expand foreign consumption vertiginously rather than to extort monopoly rents. Supply-driven demand meant that per capita consumption in the United States continued to grow until 1902, when it reached 13.3 pounds. After 1870, coffee grew at the expense of tea, since per capita tea consumption declined almost 40 per cent between 1870 and 1900, while coffee consumption grew by over 50 per cent.[58] The primary reason for coffee's vigorous growth was Brazil's ability to increase production without increasing price; the 'forest rent' of vast, fertile little-cultivated lands yielded historic coffee crops once put to the plough.

By 1900 America was the world's greatest coffee market and coffee the third most important internationally traded commodity. Caribbean trading had created the necessary preconditions to spread and deepen the coffee-drinking habit, but the monumental and unprecedented expansion of American coffee drinking in the nineteenth century depended on two additional developments: the drink had to be Americanized and it had to become a mass beverage.

Interestingly, for a product so closely tied to Americanism, both needs were met by forces outside America. First, Brazil gained its independence and opened up the largest coffee plantations the world had seen; then Northern European immigration brought millions of northern Europeans to the United States, particularly Germans and then Scandinavians predisposed to drinking coffee. The two might have simply been coincidental, but the availability of inexpensive coffee – and sugar – probably sweetened the prospects of emigrating to the United States rather than to Canada or South America or of remaining in Europe (see Table 7.3).

Table 7.3 Share of World Coffee Exports and Imports, 1850–1900 (5-year averages)

Years	Exports	Imports		
	Brazil Share (per cent)	US Share (per cent)	Europe Share (per cent)	US per capita Consumption (lb)
1800	0	1.0	93	
1851–55		28.2	65	
1856–60	53.0	32.2	61	
1861–65	49.4	17.5	75	
1866–70	47.8	24.9	69	5.01
1871–75	50.1	31.2	62	6.86
1876–80	47.6	34.7	58	6.93
1881–85	51.8	37.6	55	8.63
1886–90	56.8	38.1	48	8.62
1891–95	57.1	46.8	45	8.31
1896–1900	62.4	31.9	60	9.93

Sources: Edmar Bacha and Robert Greenhill, 150 Anos de Café (Rio de Janeiro: 1992) passim. For Columns 1,2 and 3, Ukers, All About Coffee; p. 529 for Column 4.

The refashioning of foreign-produced goods into American products appealed to an increasingly vocal constituency who lamented what they considered the dangerous trend of US investment in re-exported commodities. 'Independence has been the theme', wrote the newspaper editorialist James Tilton as early as1819, 'from the days of 1776 to this time.' During the Revolution, political independence, 'as it was emphatically styled, was the rage, from Georgia to Maine', he noted, 'and yet strange to tell, few or more of us think of *eating and drinking independently*. Is it not a thousand times more ridiculous to send to the West Indies for breakfast or supper' because of our 'inhabitants of cities and towns … obstinate adherence to tea, coffee &c.?'[60] If people like Tilton bought coffee it would have been best to de-emphasize its foreign origins, an easier strategy after the Louisiana Purchase, when some entrepreneurial marketers promoted 'New Orleans' coffee as a 'national' American alternative, hoping buyers would not realize that New Orleans was the port of coffee importation rather than a coffee producer.[61] Coffee's Americanization grew even more blatant in the late nineteenth and early twentieth centuries. Arbuckles Coffee included pictorial histories of Britain's thirteen North American colonies on the back of their coffee brewing instructions. Schnull-Krag & Co. tacitly promoted American coffee by denigrating non-American coffees, damning with faint praise, for example, 'fine' but 'expensive' Java coffee. But coffee purveyors Thomas Wood & Co.'s Americanization went further still, graphically demonstrating the seller's support of American expansionism and the simultaneous de-exoticization of Puerto

Figure 7.1 Advertising Tin – Uncle Sam's High Grade Roasted Coffee. *Source*: Thomas Wood and Company Importers and Roasters, Boston, *c*.1880. Photo courtesy of James D. Julia, Inc., Auctioneers, Fairfield, ME

Rico, Hawaii and Manila, which now, according to their advertisements, fell under the umbrella of Uncle Sam as 'his own possessions'.[62]

They Have a Lot of Coffee in Brazil

Neither New Orleans nor small West Indian islands could realistically hope to meet America's swelling demand. Brazil, however, had both ample land and slave labour.[63] Coffee arrived in Rio de Janeiro in the 1760s via French Guyana and Pará. The *arabica* came, not from export merchants, but through Portuguese officials and religious orders, especially the Capuchins, the Bishop of Rio de Janeiro and French and Dutch immigrants and was originally planted beside other experimental crops like ginger and pepper in small orchards.[64]

Coffee, as an export product, was not an inevitable development in Brazil.[65] Some economists estimate that 80 per cent of all coffee exported in Brazil's 322-year-long colonial period shipped between 1810 and independence in 1822, reflecting its minor role in the colonial period. This changed only after Napoleon Bonaparte invaded Portugal in 1808, forcing the prince-regent, Dom João VI, to conduct the largest trans-oceanic migration of an imperial capital in history.[66] In Rio de Janeiro, some newly arrived aristocrats and merchants, as well as Caribbean transplants, stripped of their traditional sources of income, turned to tropical agriculture and managed to send their first cargo of coffee to Boston that same year.[67] Though Dom João had tea, not coffee, planted in the royal Botanical Garden that he ordered built, coffee was quickly more successful. Independence, first of the United States and then of Haiti, opened up new markets to Brazil. Political liberty, ironically, also led to a flood of African slaves.

Relations between the United States and Brazil grew stronger still after American merchants and shippers supplanted the British in the Atlantic slave trade, integrating Brazil and Africa into a United States-based triangular trade after Brazilian independence in 1822. A spurt in commercial relations between newly free Brazil and the recently freed United States was based mostly on the flourishing slave trade. Brazil had long been the world's leading importer of African slaves, first via the Portuguese and then via Dutch, Angolan, Brazilian and British slavers. American slavers, forbidden from importing into the United States after 1808, benefited from anti-slavery campaigns that hindered British competition in the chattel trade, even though Brazil awarded British shippers of other goods preferential treatment to the extent that Brazil has been considered a central part of the United Kingdom's 'informal empire'.[68] North American merchantmen carried some of the greatest annual slave importations Brazil had known – until the Atlantic slave trade was terminated by the British navy in 1850.[69] The role of the US merchant marine in the Brazil trade and in the Atlantic in general, declined with the prohibition of the Atlantic slave trade. American investors turned to the home market and developed its west as railroads reached ever further towards the Pacific. But Americans' reorientation from the Atlantic to the western frontier did not thwart their budding romance with coffee. Brazil's coffee exports jumped 75-fold by volume between independence in 1822 and 1899 as Brazilians responded to – and stimulated – new opportunities and British bottoms took the place of Yankee traders. British moralists who subdued the lucrative trans-oceanic commerce in humans in the first part of the 1800s were not able to convince their countrymen to forgo profiting from a slave-grown crop, an industry much larger after 1850 than before. Coffee exports, three-quarters of which went to the United States, constituted over 40 per cent of Brazil's exports after 1830, eclipsing sugar.[70] The growing capitalist economy of the United States gave rise to scores of 'coffee barons' and slave baronies in Brazil.

Brazil's ability to escalate coffee production without increasing retail prices explains part of the American fascination with the bean; but the immigration to the United States of millions of northern Europeans predisposed to buy coffee was important as well. Settlers from what is today Germany started arriving in the British North American colonies in 1683, around the time that immigrants from other northern European areas also began trickling in. Although not a majority, they constituted a large share in states such as Pennsylvania and New York, the two leading coffee ports in the eighteenth century and later in Illinois and Minnesota. The 1830s and 1840s were key years for German immigration. Data for coffee consumption by ethnicity does not exist; however, anecdotal evidence suggests that they played a role disproportionate to their 15–20 per cent share of the total US population.

Eighteenth- and nineteenth-century taxation policies in Germany put coffee beyond the reach of most of the population; but desire for the commodity is evident in the number of coffee substitutes that developed.[71] Germans and other northern Europeans were influenced in part by their cold climate and in part by a desire to emulate the coffee-drinking aristocracy and bourgeoisie (some of whom, in turn, imitated French café society). But what Jan de Vries has called the 'industrious revolution', with longer days, urbanization and more work outside the house also contributed to the urge for caffeine.[72] By the beginning of the nineteenth century, Germany was the second largest importer of coffee behind the United States. In absolute figures, it led European imports, though it still fell behind the Scandinavian countries, Belgium and the Netherlands in per capita terms.[73] At the middle of the nineteenth century the German desire for coffee probably encouraged many poor immigrants to think that an important part of 'making America' was the simple luxury of occasionally drinking coffee. Certainly there is scattered evidence of ethnic coffeehouses in major American cities. There were even advertising campaigns directed to a German-American audience, such as one by Lion's Coffee, one of the largest brands at the end of the nineteenth century, announcing 'All Germans like it!'[74]

But though Latin American suppliers and western European consumers were key components of coffee's diffusion in American culture, they remained almost invisible in how America's coffee industry marketed itself to its ever-growing consumer base. United States corporations continue to spread coffee-drinking world-wide, though now through roasting houses, advertising and coffee houses rather than via merchant shippers. US troops spread the coffee-drinking habit to Japan, the Philippines and Korea. Starbucks is making incursions into China. Elsewhere countries whose coffee-drinking history had been all but forgotten, such as Turkey and India, are returning to the *arabica*.

Conclusion

National identity through consumption and international networks through trade have long been closely related. Coffee is clearly an important commodity to America's economy, but its historical and social development reveals larger cultural connotations that need to be reconsidered. Coffee was a democratic drink in so far as consumption was widely disseminated in the United States, but its ties to liberty and equality are tenuous if not hypocritical when provenance is taken into account. The patriotic American drink came via Caribbean and Latin American slavocratic colonies. Though it contributed to the independence of Brazil's government, it also perpetuated that society's dependence on slavery until 1888. American purveyors erased coffee's Janus face by recasting the commodity as an all-American consumable and American consumers likewise paid little attention to the form of labour or the US imperialist policies that brought them their morning wake-up call. By the late nineteenth century, the 'literary men about town and strangers of distinction', wrote one society columnist, 'discuss the latest topics of the world and day' over 'the fumes of coffee and a slice of French rolls'. The news and food still had international cachet; but coffee had become thoroughly domesticated.[75]

Notes

1. The authors thank Frank Trentmann, Alexander Nützenadel and the members of the Food and Globalization seminars held at Wassenaar, NL and Cambridge, England in 2005 and 2006 for their helpful insights. In particular, we thank Sidney Mintz for his comments and suggestions.
2. J. Willis, 'European Consumption and Asian Production in the Seventeenth and Eighteenth Centuries, pp. 133–47, S. Mintz, 'Changing Roles of Food', p. 266 and C. Shammas 'Consumption from 1550 to 1800', p. 199, in J. Brewer and R. Porter (eds), *Consumption and the World of Goods* (London, 1993).

3. J. Brewer and F. Trentmann, 'Introduction', in *Consuming Cultures, Global Perspectives: Historical Trajectories, Transnational Exchanges* (Oxford, 2006), p. 13.

4. S. Mintz, *Tasting Food, Tasting Freedom* (Boston, 1996), pp. 13–14.

5. See F. Fulgate, *Arbuckles: The Coffee that Won the West* (El Paso, 1994) and M. Pendergrast, *Uncommon Grounds* (New York, 1999).

6. J. H. St John de Crévecoeur, *Letters from an American* Farmer (Philadelphia, 1793); D. F. Sarmiento, *Estados Unidos* (Buenos Aires, 1849–51 rpt. 1945); A. de Tocqueville, *Democracy in America* (New York, 1840); T. Paine, *The American Crisis* (Norwich, CT, 1776).

7. Mifflin and Massey, Ledger, 1761–63, Historical Society of Pennsylvania; A. Adams to J. Adams, July 5, 1775, *Adams Family Papers*, Massachusetts Historical Society; E. Forman Crane, *et al.* (eds), *The Diary of Elizabeth Drinker*, 3 vols (Boston, 1991), Vol. 3, pp. 1081, 1081n and 2016; C. B. Dew, *Bonds of Iron; Master and Slave at Buffalo Forge* (New York, 1994), p. 114.

8. François Jean de Beauvoir, Marquis de Chastellux, *Travels in North America*, 2 vols (Dublin, 1787), Vol. 2, p. 52.

9. See the Warshaw Collection and Hills Brothers archives in the Museum of American History at the Smithsonian in Washington, DC, for examples of nineteenth-century trade cards. Also see Fulgate, *Arbuckles*, pp. 117–37.

10. Fulgate, *Arbuckles*, p. 68; J. Rischbieter, 'Globalizing Consumption: Coffee Trade and Consumption in Imperial Germany', delivered at the Food and Globalization: Markets, Migration and Politics in Transnational Perspective Seminar, Leipzig, Germany (September 2005). For US ads see: *The Tea and Coffee Journal* and *The Spice Mill*. For the appearance of foreign coffee workers in commercials see M. Seigal, 'Trading Races: Transnational Conversations and Construction of Race in the US and Brazil after WWI', unpublished manuscript; P. Munoz, 'Juan Valdez: The Story of 100% Colombian Coffee', unpublished paper, (University of California, Irvine, Winter 2006); and M. C. McDonald, 'The Real Juan Valdez: Opportunities and Impoverishment in Global Coffee', Harvard Business School Working Paper Series, No. 9-806-041 (November 2005), pp. 1–23.

11. W. T. Sherman, *Memoirs of General W. T. Sherman* (Rpt, New York, 1990), p. 882. We thank Madeleine Foote for this quote.

12. J. D. Billings, *Hardtack and Coffee: The Unwritten Story of Army Life* (Chicago, 1923), p. 123 and *Oxford English Dictionary Online*, entry for 'coffee'.

13. *Fortune* (December 1937), p. 123; the *OED* claims that coffee breaks were written into labour contracts after 1951. The Pan American Coffee Bureau popularized the concept after 1952, according to Mark Pendergrast, *Uncommon Grounds* (New York, 1999), p. 242.

14. 1603–30 CAPT. SMITH *Trav. & Adv.* 25 'Their [Turkes'] best drinke is Coffaa of a graine they call Coava' (cited in the *Oxford English Dictionary Online*); W. Ukers, *All About Coffee* (New York, 1922).

15. F. B. Thurber, *Coffee: From Plantation to Cup* (London, 1881), p. 212. By contrast, tea imports at the time were only one-twelfth of a pound per head.
16. W. Ukers, *All About Coffee*, p. 102–3; W. Ukers, *All About Tea*, Vol.1 (New York, 1935), p. 65.
17. M. Pendergrast, *Uncommon Grounds: The History of Coffee and How it Transformed the World* (New York, 1999), p. 15; J. Beilenson, *The Book of Coffee* (White Plains, NY, 1995), p. 24; G. Dicum and N. Luttinger, *The Coffee Book: Anatomy of an Industry from Crop to the Last Drop* (New York, 1999), p. 34.
18. G. Dium and N. Luttinger, *The Coffee Book*, p. 35.
19. Ukers, *All About Coffee*, pp. 106, 116.
20. J. Adams to A. Adams, July 6, 1774, *Adams Family Papers*.
21. J. Adams, *Autobiography*, 'Travels and Negotiations,' p. 20 (entry dated May 6, 1778).
22. J. Adams to A. Adams, July 6, 1775 and August 11, 1777, *Adams Family Papers* and *Adams Family Correspondence*, Vol. 2, pp. 295–6.
23. *American State Papers: Documents, Legislative and Executive, of the Congress of the United States*, 38 vols (Washington, DC, 1832–61). Hereafter to be cited as *ASPCN* (Commerce and Navigation) or *ASPFR* (Foreign Relations), with volume and page numbers. The above reference is from *ASPCN*, V: 640.
24. *ASPCN*, V: 640–2.
25. US *Congress, Journal of the House of Representatives* (Washington, DC, 1829). 21st Cong., 1st sess., 8 December, p. 18.
26. These included France, the United Netherlands and Sweden, with whom the United States already had treaties of commerce, as well as England, Hamburg and Saxony, Prussia, Denmark, Russia, Austria, Venice, Rome, Naples, Tuscany, Sardinia, Genoa, Spain, Portugal and the Barbary States of the Porte, Algiers, Tripoli, Tunis and Morocco (nations listed in T. Jefferson, *Diaries*, entry for 4 January 1784, part of the online collection of Congressional papers at the Library of Congress); M. D. Peterson, 'Thomas Jefferson and Commercial Policy, 1783–1793', *William and Mary Quarterly* 3rd ser., 22(4) (1965): 590–1.
27. J. Adams to R. Livingston, 13 August 1783, *Revolutionary Diplomatic Correspondence of the United States*, 6 vols (Washington, DC, 1889), Vol. 6, pp. 649–50 (hereafter *RDC*).
28. T. Jefferson to J. Adams, 7 August 1785 in L. Cappon (ed.), *The Adams–Jefferson Letters: The Complete Correspondence Between Thomas Jefferson and Abigail and John Adams*, 2 vols (Chapel Hill, NC, 1959), Vol. 1, p. 51.
29. A. O'Shaughnessy, *An Empire Divided: The American Revolution and the British Caribbean* (Philadelphia, 2000), p. 214.
30. J. Adams to Livingston, 23 July 1783 and 31 July 1783, *Adams–Jefferson Letters*, Vol. 2, p. 623.

31. See St Croix between 1781 and 1783, recorded in the Records of the Philadelphia Custom House, Records Group 36, Inward and Outward Entry Volumes, 1781–1787.
32. Peterson, 'Jefferson and Commercial Policy,' p. 593. See also, Thomas Jefferson Papers, Series 1, General Correspondence, 1651–1827, 'United States Treaties, 1786, Amity and Commerce Treaty between Portugal and the United States', in the collections of the Library of Congress (hereafter TJP)
33. T. Jefferson to J. Jay, 27 January 1786, in Julian P. Boyd (ed.), *The Papers of Thomas Jefferson*, Princeton, NJ, Vol. 9, 1954, p. 235.
34. T. Jefferson to R. Izard, 18 November 1796, in Boyd, *Papers of Jefferson*, Vol. 10, 1954, pp. 541–2.
35. C. Alexandre de Calonne to T. Jefferson, 22 October 1796, TJP, Series 1, General Correspondence, 1651–1827; T. Jefferson, Observations on Charles Alexandre de Calonne's Letter of 22 October 1786, on Trade between the United States and France (22 October 1796), TJP, Series 1, General Correspondence, 1651–1827. See also M. Peterson, 'Jefferson and Commercial Policy', p. 599; and J. F. Stover, 'French–American Trade during the Confederation, 1781–1789', *North Carolina Historical Review*, 35 (1958): 399–414.
36. Bernard Mayo (ed.), *Instructions to the British Ministers to the United States, 1791–1812*, Washington, DC, Government Printing Office, 1941, p. 35.
37. Deane to the Committee of Secret Correspondence, undated, *RDC*, 2: 118.
38. A. Clauder, *American Commerce as Affected by the Wars of the French Revolution and Napoleon, 1793–1812* (Philadelphia, 1932) and John H. Coatsworth, 'American Trade with European Colonies in the Caribbean and South America, 1790–1812', *The William and Mary Quarterly*, 3rd Ser., 24(2) (1967): 243–66.
39. B. Schoen, 'Calculating the Price of Union: Republican Economic Nationalism and the Origins of Southern Sectionalism, 1790–1828,' *Journal of the Early Republic* 23(2) (Summer 2003): 184.
40. A. Hochschild, *Bury the Chains. Prophets and Rebels in the Fight to Free an Empire's Slaves* (Boston, 2005), pp. 192–6.
41. 'U.S. Revenue from Commodity Re-Exports, 1802–1804,' *ASPCN*, V: 642.
42. B. Cowan, *The Social Life of Coffee: The Emergence of the British Coffeehouse* (New Haven, CT, 2005), pp. 55–77.
43. Thurber, *Coffee,* p. 19.
44. Wimpffen, *A Voyage to Santo Domingo*, pp. 319–320. Edgar Corrie offers similar figures in his *Letters on the Subject of the Duties of Coffee* (London, 1808), p. 8.
45. R. Dunn, *Sugar and Slaves: The Rise of the Planter Class in the English West Indies, 1624–1713* (Chapel Hill, NC, 1972), pp. 10–103, 142–143, 161–163, 200–201, 213–222.

46. P. J. Laborie, *The Coffee Planter of Saint Domingo: With an Appendix Containing a View of the Constitution, Government, Laws and Statutes of that Colony prior to the Year 1789* (London, 1797), pp. 178–9.

47. NA/T 1/484/323a–b and 324. Memorial of Stephen Fuller, Esq., Agent of Jamaica, 1770; NA/T1/484/325a–b Letter from Jno. Morse to Stephen Fuller Esq., Agent for Jamaica, 1770.

48. R. Bisset's two-volume history of the slave trade confirms Laborie's account of coffee slaves' isolation. R. Bisset, *The History of the Negro Slave Trade, in its connection with the Commerce and Prosperity of the West Indies and the Wealth and Power of the British Empire*, 2 vols (London, 1805), Vol. 1, p. 392.

49. R. Burns, *Restrictive Laws on Food and Trade Tried by the Test of Christianity: A Lecture Delivered ... December 6, 1843* (Glasgow, 1848), pp. 8–9.

50. See, for example, R. Paterson, *Remarks on the Depressed State of Cultivation in the West India Colonies* (Edinburgh, 1848), p. 15.

51. *New York Times* (10 November 1858), p. 4.

52. E. Bean Underhill, *The West Indies: Their Social and Religious Condition*, London, 1862, p. 333.

53. M.-R. Trouillot, 'Motion in the System: Coffee, Color and Slavery in Eighteenth-Century Saint Domingue', *Review* 3 (Winter 1982): 349–54; C. Fick, *The Making of Haiti: The Saint Domingue Revolution from Below* (Knoxville, TN, 1990), p.19.

54. See, for example, L. Dubois, *Avengers of the New World* (Cambridge, MA, 2004) and *A Colony of Citizens* (Chapel Hill, NC, 2004), M.-R. Trouillot, *Silencing the Past, Power and the Production of History* (Boston, 1995).

55. F. Thurber, *Coffee, from Plantation to Cup* (New York, 1886), pp. 205–6. The *Spice Mill* Convention Supplement (November 1911), p. 989.

56. The *American Grocer* cited in the leading coffee trade journal, *The Spice Mill* (July 1891), p. 172 and (February 1890), p. 37. We thank Sarah Gingles, who pointed out tea's continuing popularity in her excellent unpublished essay, 'Social Beverages: Ale's Condemnation Creates Coffee's Public Glory' (University of California, Irvine, May 2006).

57. Marcellino Martins and E. Johnston, *150 Anos de Café* (Rio, 1992), p. 335.

58. Calculated from Ukers, *All About Coffee*, p. 521.

59. In pounds per head, five-year average from Ukers, *All About Coffee*, p. 529.

60. J. Tilton, 'Variety and Observations,' *The American Journal* (Oct. 16, 1819).

61. J. T. Magill, 'New Orleans' Coffee Connection,' *Louisiana Cultural Vistas* (Fall 2005): 45–55.

62. Arbuckles Coffee Co., 'Illustrated Atlas,' Donaldson Bros. Lithographers (1889); Schnull-Krag Coffee Co., 'It is the Best Coffee Ever Sold,' Indianapolis, IN (undated); 'Washington's Coffee.' *New York Tribune*, 22 June 1919. Library of Congress, Serial and Government Publications Division; Thomas Wood & Co., 'Uncle Sam's High Grade Roast Coffee' (1880).

63. V. Stolcke, *Cafeicultura. Homens, Mulheres e Capital (1850–1980),* trans. D. Bottmann and João Martins Filho (SP: Editóra Brasiliense, 1986), p. 189. M. Nolasco in *Café y sociedad en México* (Mexico D.F., Centro de Ecodesarrollo, 1985), p. 42 has a similar finding for Mexico. S. Stein, *Vassouras, a Brazilian Coffee Municipio* (Princeton, NJ, 1985), p. 12.

64. A. de E. Taunay, *História do Café no Brasil* Vol. 2, tomo 2 (Rio: Departamento Nacional de Café: 1939; B. de Magalhães, *O Café nah História, no Folclore, e nas Belas-Artes* (São Paulo: Cia. Editora Nacional, 1939).

65. Whereas Haiti after 75 years of cultivation reached a yearly export total of 80 million pounds, Brazil in 1830, some ninety years after coffee's first introduction, only exported 14 million pounds. In that same year of 1820 Cuba, benefiting from the flight of Haitian planters with their slaves, was exporting some 25 million pounds: Thurber, *Coffee from Plantation to Cup* (New York, 1881), p. 125.

66. N. P. Macdonald, *The Making of Brazil, Portuguese Roots, 1500–1822* (Sussex, 1996), p. 358.

67. D. Gomes, *Antigos Cafés do Rio de Janeiro* (Rio, 1989), pp. 18–20.

68. R. Miller, *Britain and Latin America in the Nineteenth and Twentieth Centuries* (London, 1993), pp. 53–4; P. R. de Almeida, *Formação da diplomacia econômica no Brasil* (Brasilia, 1998), pp. 69–70, 368, 369.

69. J. F. Rippy, *Rivalry of the United States and Great Britain over Latin America* (Baltimore, MD, 1928); A. K. Manchester, *British Preeminence in Brazil: Its Rise and Decline* (Chapel Hill, NC, 1933), p. 266; L. Bethel, *A Abolição do trafico de escravos no Brasil* (São Paulo, 1976), pp. 272, 273.

70. E. Bacha and R. Greenhill, *150 Anos de Café no Brasil,* Rio de Janeiro, 1992, p. 355.

71. U. Heise, *Kaffee und Kaffeehaus, Eine Kulturgeschichte* (Leipzig, 1987); H.E. Jacob, *Sage und Siegeszug des Kaffees: Die Biographie eines Weltwirtschaftlichen Stoffes* (Hamburg, 1952); R. Sandgruber, *Die Anfänge der Konsumgesellschaft* (Vienna, 1982); W. Schivelbusch, *Tastes of Paradise: A Social History of Spices, Stimulants and Intoxicants* (New York, 1992).

72. Jan de Vries, 'Purchasing Power and the World of Goods', in J. Brewer and R. Porter (eds), *Consumption and the World of Goods* (London, 1993), pp. 95, 107, 115.

73. Thurber in *Coffee* p. 241 shows Hamburg's imports to be second to the United States in 1877. M. Samper and R. Fernando in *The Global Coffee Economy in Africa, Asia and Latin America 1500–1989* (New York, 2003), pp. 443, 446–7 have the same finding. Ukers, *All About Coffee,* p. 527 shows how German imports towered over other European totals between 1853 and 1933.

74. In Warshaw Collection of Business Americana, Smithsonian Museum of American History, 'Coffee' box 2.

75. *Philadelphia Gazette,* 18 October 1844.

–8–

Transnational Food Migration and the Internalization of Food Consumption

Ethnic Cuisine in West Germany

Maren Möhring

In the field of food, globalization has often been discussed as an internationalization of foods and food consumption habits. Besides quantitative and qualitative adaptations in food consumption it is, above all, the growing importance of 'foreign', imported foods and the decreasing relevance of regional foods for local markets that is considered a characteristic of internationalization.[1] Regionalization, nationalization, internationalization and globalization, however, are not separate phenomena, succeeding one another but, I would argue, in a sense *parallel* and interacting processes. From a historical perspective, the emergence of distinct national as well as regional cuisines is an effect of what we today call globalization. In most European countries, national cuisines were invented in the nineteenth century, during the first phase of globalization and the decisive stages of nation-building.[2] National cuisines tied together the manifold regional and local cuisines, which, nevertheless, did not disappear. In Germany, a national cuisine, claiming simplicity and naturalness, was constructed mainly to distinguish it from the internationally dominant and refined French cuisine.[3] Whereas the emergence of national cuisines in the nineteenth century was an answer to intensified international contacts and political and economic as well as cultural competition, the immense diversification of cuisines today can be interpreted as an answer to global processes of generic standardization, epitomized in the idea of a McDonaldization of food culture.[4] Since the 1990s, the idea of a global homogenization of foods and food consumption patterns has been criticized for underestimating 'the local' and its complex connections with 'the global'. Roland Robertson's concept of 'glocalization'[5] tries to grasp this mutual constitution of 'the local' and 'the global', enabling descriptions of local adaptations of globally traded goods and their social and cultural re-coding.[6]

My study of ethnic restaurants in West Germany addresses similar processes, focusing on transnational food migration, and thus combining research on consumerism and migration to postwar Germany. When I speak of food migration, I am not primarily considering the function of food as an 'agent of memory' or changes in food habits occurring within the new homes of migrants.[7] Analysing the ethnic restaurant entails a focus on the *public* production and consumption of ethnic food, that is, on the emergence of migrant cuisines in the marketplace and their effects on the food consumption patterns of the non-migrant population.

The growing popularity of eating out as a social and cultural practice, and eating out in ethnic restaurants, in particular, will be outlined in the first part of this chapter, followed by a section on the spread of ethnic restaurants and snack-bars in West Germany. Ethnic cuisine, however, did not only become more and more important in the restaurant sector, it also changed home cooking, an aspect that will be discussed in the third part of this chapter. The last section deals with the cultural meanings surrounding ethnic food, focusing on the political dimension of ethnicized commodities.

Eating Out

The restaurant is an establishment where ready-made eatables and drinks are not only bought, but also consumed and where – in contrast to traditional inns – the patrons choose their meals from a menu and eat them at separate tables.[8] This is a genuinely modern phenomenon. Restaurants originated in Paris at the end of the eighteenth century,[9] and developed relatively late in Germany, their real spread beginning only in the 1870s, becoming fully established in the years just before the First World War.[10] The war led to a decline in the number of restaurants, partly compensated for in the inter-war years.[11] Because of the growing distance between home and workplace in urban areas, the reduction of time for lunch breaks and the increasing percentage of women joining the workforce, more and more people became dependent on public eateries offering lunch.[12] Besides this, in the course of the twentieth century, eating out has become an essential part of leisure time.

Since the 1950s, and especially since the 1960s, an increasing proportion of household food expenditure has been devoted to eating out, not only in Germany, but in all Western countries, as well as Japan. In 1978, *c.*50 per cent of the German population had lunch or dinner outside their homes: 91.2 per cent of these went to restaurants and snack-bars, and 20.7 per cent also to canteens. Men ate more often in canteens than women, who went to restaurants more frequently.[13] In 1983, on average, every household had seven meals per month, in 1988 eight in a restaurant, whereas in 1993 the number had dropped to 5.7. (In the new *Bundesländer* only 4.8 meals were eaten outside the home in 1993.) From 1993 to 1998, however, expenditure for individually consumed food outside the home nearly doubled.[14] Whereas in 1983 the main meals were mostly eaten in restaurants (*c.*80 per cent), the smaller meals were mostly bought in snack-bars (*c.*70 per cent).[15] In the year 2000, every German spent on average nearly 42 German Marks on meals outside the home three times per week, with small snack-bars being a little more popular than restaurants.[16] Take-away meals have become increasingly popular in recent years, a trend that reached Britain a little earlier. From 1975 to 1984, the number of take-away meals in the UK rose from 14 per cent to 27 per cent of all meals.[17]

Though eating out is popular all over Europe, the differences between the European countries are significant. Consumers in Scandinavia generally eat out less often than their counterparts in the rest of Western Europe, though the practice is significantly more popular in Sweden than in Norway. Today, *c*.10 per cent of the Norwegian population never go to a restaurant, while about 60 per cent eat out in a restaurant three to eleven times a year, 35 per cent once a month, and only 12 per cent once a week.[18] While place of residence and income may be considered material factors influencing the decision to eat out, age and education are the main cultural factors.[19] As in other European countries, the typical restaurant guest in Norway is young and/or highly educated, and 'definitely urban'.[20] This holds true even more where visiting *ethnic* restaurants is concerned.[21] In Germany, more than 40 per cent of the patrons of ethnic restaurants are under the age of 35, compared with less than 30 per cent in German restaurants.[22]

Since the 1980s, eating in *ethnic* restaurants and snack-bars has become 'one of the hottest segments of the food service industry'.[23] The ethnic food market in France, Germany, Italy, Spain and Britain grew to 924 million pounds in 1997, the UK having the largest ethnic food market in Europe, accounting for two-thirds of the sales figures.[24] British surveys demonstrate that consumption of ethnic foods, above all Indian and Chinese, have risen steadily since 1995, though major regional differences have to be taken into account, expenditure being highest in London and much lower in Northern England and Scotland.[25]

Eating in an ethnic restaurant is a social and cultural practice that has often been described as a 'substitute for travel'.[26] Whereas for the migrant restaurateur and the migrant patron the ethnic restaurant might represent some form of (diasporic) 'home', for the other guests it is associated with vacation and/or the exotic. Meeting the expectations of the non-migrant patrons, many ethnic restaurants choose their style of furniture and decoration according to a specific 'architecture of desire', underlining the importance of aestheticization and the imagination in the act of dining out as a modern form of entertainment.[27]

It is not only the touristic experience of an increasing part of the population,[28] but also the mostly moderate prices and informality of many ethnic restaurants that have been the decisive factors in the success of these enterprises.[29] But what is an ethnic restaurant? Wilbur Zelinsky defines it as follows: A 'self-consciously ethnic restaurant will show its colours in one of three places: in its name, in its inclusion under an ethnic heading in a special section of the telephone directory, or by listing the specialties of the house in a display ad'.[30]

Since the distinction between German and foreign food – between here and there – is anything but self-evident, the processes of constructing these positionings need to be explored, thus questioning and historicizing the whole concept of the ethnic restaurant and ethnic cuisine. In Germany, the term 'ausländische Gastronomie' is used for 'ethnic cuisine', and, at least from 1950 to 1980, the ethnic restaurant was called *ausländisches Spezialitätenrestaurant* (restaurant offering foreign specialities), thus stressing the food's origin in a foreign country. At the same time, German cuisine was not considered as one ethnic cuisine among others, but was left ethnically unmarked. In today's telephone directories we sometimes find headings announcing German cuisine. This is a new development, arising from an understanding that German cuisine forms (just) one part of a multicultural gastronomic landscape. Before the 1990s, German cuisine was categorized according to the kind of dishes the restaurant specialized in, for example, fish restaurants, or – and this holds true for most of the German restaurants – classified as *(gut)bürgerlich*, that is, both home-style and middle-class, thus indicating the outlet's claimed social status – a form of social differentiation that is lost when a restaurant is simply labelled 'foreign'. The adjective *bürgerlich* was and sometimes still is used as a synonym for 'German (cuisine)'. This becomes apparent in an article on 'foreign' cuisine, published in the *Leverkusener Anzeiger*, the local newspaper of the city of Leverkusen near Cologne, in July 1980. Under the headline 'Türken und Thais rühren im Küchentopf' (Turks and Thais stir the cooking pot) the author emphasizes that foreign restaurateurs 'speak German and cook foreign (but also *bürgerliche*) dishes', meaning that they offer German food, too.[31] Especially in the early stage of ethnic cuisine in postwar Germany, menus often combined foreign and German dishes, presenting them next to each other, as the 1965 menu of a Greek restaurant in Munich demonstrates, offering Greek 'specialities' as well as 'Wurstsalat'. In practice, the dishes were often adapted to each other or fused, bringing forth a new, transnational cuisine.[32]

Taking into account the 'heterotopic effect' of migrant cuisines, the ethnic restaurant has to be conceptualized as a local place of food consumption, the locality of which is transnational from the outset.[33] Whereas the generic term *Lokal* in German refers to any kind of eatery or bar (not only to the neighbourhood pub), the ethnic *Lokal* could be called a *Trans-Lokalität*. Here, transnational networks and intercultural transfers of foodstuffs, technologies and information can be analysed within the sphere of everyday life. The social actors – migrant and non-migrant owners of the restaurant, cooks, waiters, and (illegal) kitchen workers as well as migrant and non-migrant patrons – all participate in the transnational space of the ethnic restaurant, though with differing investments.[34] It is precisely this transnational setting that makes the ethnic restaurant a pre-eminent place – like cookbooks – for (re-)inventing national, ethnic and regional cuisines.[35] Here, certain dishes, formerly typical of only one region or another, are stylized in such a way that they become the embodiment of national cuisines. Which dishes are selected depends on the specific local conditions and the availability of the necessary ingredients, as well as the likes and dislikes of the non-migrant population frequenting the restaurant. The construction of national dishes, therefore, not only takes place within a national, but also within a transnational framework, with feedback effects on the 'homeland'. Pizza is one of the most prominent examples for these processes. In Italy, pizza was 'the' typical food in Naples, eaten by the poor on the streets, and the Neapolitan form of pizza was the one introduced by migrants from southern Italy to the United States, where its international career started when migrants from southern Italy transformed the pizza in several ways to meet American tastes – with extremely successful results.[36] In Germany, pizza became relatively widely known during the years of occupation, when American soldiers introduced it to German prisoners of war, as well as to civilians. [37] In the 1960s and 1970s, pizzerias spread all over Germany. They were tremendously successful, as they offered modestly priced dishes and a less formal, child-friendly atmosphere. German tourists also wanted their pizza when visiting Italy.[38] Touristic considerations led to the establishment of pizzerias in the whole of Italy.

The Spread of Ethnic Restaurants in West Germany

It was at the end of the nineteenth century that the demand for new types of reasonably priced eateries emerged; early forms of convenience restaurants opened up, such as *Aschinger* in Berlin, where you could get a quick and inexpensive lunch. During periods of food rationing, during the two world wars, scarce food could be eaten there, making public eateries an indispensable part of city life.[39] Whereas Aschinger offered German or, more precisely, Bavarian cuisine, restaurants with 'foreign' cuisine were rare in the German *Kaiserreich*. There existed a few Italian restaurants in big cities, such as Berlin, and in seaports, such as Hamburg, we find a number of Chinese restaurants; but these places were exceptions rather than the rule.[40] All in all, it was the Italian cuisine that functioned as a kind of door-opener for other ethnic cuisines, itself predated by the success of Italian ice-cream parlours, which spread across middle and Western Europe in the late nineteenth and early twentieth centuries.[41] At this time, Germany was already the prime importer of Italian products,[42] especially of food, with cheese and rice the goods most in demand. The German–Italian food trade played a pivotal role during the 'Third Reich', and although national socialist policy was opposed to 'foreign' influences, including cuisines, and instead, sought to propagate German cookery, Germany relied heavily upon food imports from the allied axis power in Europe.[43]

Even though there is some continuity in terms of restaurants offering 'foreign' cuisine throughout the twentieth century, the significant spread of ethnic cuisine took place only in postwar West Germany. Whereas ethnic restaurants had been an almost exclusively metropolitan phenomenon before the Second World War, the picture started to change in the 1960s and 1970s. Many restaurants, most of them offering Mediterranean cuisine, were established by immigrants, some of them former 'guest-workers' (*Gastarbeiter*), that is, immigrants who had been recruited on a contract-labour basis between 1955 and 1974.[44] Many of the migrants starting a restaurant or snack-bar already had working experience as waiters or waitresses, cooks or kitchen helpers: 17,000 'guest-workers' had been hired specifically for work in German catering.[45] The spread of ethnic restaurants, which started in the 1960s, accelerated in the 1970s and 1980s. Between 1975 and 1985, the number of ethnic restaurants doubled from *c*.20,000 to *c*.40,000; in 1985, every fourth restaurant was run by a non-German owner.[46] In 1992, of the 55,000 foreign restaurateurs in Germany, approximately 18,000 were Italian; the second biggest group were Turkish restaurateurs.[47] Today, there are about 7,000 Italian restaurants and *c*.9,000 pizzerias in Germany.[48]

The data I collected for the cities of Cologne and Leverkusen shows that a considerable spread of ethnic restaurants took place no earlier than the late 1960s. While in 1950 only three existed in Cologne (one Italian and two Chinese), in 1955 there were five ethnic restaurants, in 1960 eleven, and in 1968 fourteen. By 1973, the number had increased to sixty-two.[49] In Leverkusen in 1977, seventy-six of the 445 restaurants were ethnic restaurants, run by foreign residents, mainly from Italy, Yugoslavia, Greece and China.[50] Except for the food offered in so-called *China-Restaurants* – a term only known in Germany and suggesting an experience of a miniature China as well as Chinese food – other non-European cuisines were not available in Germany at this time. This is in marked contrast to the UK.[51] Whereas in London, Indian restaurants were already fashionable in the 1950s, in Germany Indian cuisine was considered absolutely exotic.[52] In 1951, a German businessman, living in India, suggested to the Chamber of Commerce in Cologne that one or more of the city's hotels should offer Indian food, prepared by an Indian cook, so that businessmen from India were no longer forced to stay in London when travelling around Europe. Employing an Indian cook, however, was beyond the imagination of Cologne restaurant managers in the early 1950s: *Ein solcher Vorschlag ist natürlich für uns unannehmbar* ('Such a proposal is, of course, unacceptable for us').[53]

The increasing number of migrants opening up restaurants soon alarmed German restaurateurs. In 1977, the director of the Northern Rhenish trade association for the restaurant and hotel business proclaimed that though the restaurant scene in Leverkusen was not in foreign hands (*in fremder Hand*), nevertheless a huge number of non-German businesses existed, giving rise to 'legitimate fears'. According to the director, it was no longer certain that the city's authorities would be able to guarantee observance of German laws and regulations. The authorities reacted to this intervention in a very restrained way, however, emphasizing that there was no problem with the supervision of restaurants in Leverkusen, whether they were run by German or non-German owners.[54]

The migrant businesses were often situated, within urban areas, in decaying inner cities or red-light districts, unalluring to German entrepreneurs. These areas were not suitable for a *gutbürgerliches* (German) restaurant, but provided the ethnic restaurants with a new clientele: besides other migrants, people (especially the young) indulging in night-life activities were attracted to these eating-places with full meals served at moderate prices, and late at night when 'traditional' restaurants had already shut their doors. Opening a restaurant in a non-migrant residential area was not at all easy, especially, I would argue, for immigrant entrepreneurs. Archival records demonstrate that the (German) neighbours of proposed, as well as existing, ethnic restaurants often objected to such places, mostly on the grounds of noise.[55]

Despite the sometimes openly hostile atmosphere, many migrants chose to open up their own businesses. What were the reasons for this decision? In the 1970s, economic restructuring in the aftermath of the oil crisis affected immigrants in particular; the unemployment rates of foreign residents were disproportionately high. Non-EEC nationals, that is, until the 1980s, all 'guest-workers' (except for Italians), were at risk of losing their residence permits on becoming dependent on social welfare (after the expiry of their eligibility for unemployment benefits). Opening up your own business was often the only way to make a living in Germany, for oneself as well as for family members who came to Germany in the course of family reunification policies. Whereas the German government developed various measures to persuade 'guest-workers' to return to their home countries, migrants created jobs for themselves and their families, made their stay in Germany permanent, and successfully resisted the government's repatriation (*Rückführung*) campaigns. In becoming self-employed, many migrants also fulfilled their desire for independence, attaining control over their lives and escaping from at least some forms of institutional and everyday racism encountered at many workplaces in Germany. The question of migrants' self-employment (with its risks of unemployment) is central to debates over the ethnic economy. Whereas research on ethnic business in the United States tends to stress the socioeconomic chances and the success of self-employed immigrants, the European debate tends to see ethnic business as a reaction to discrimination in the labour market. In Germany, the job market is highly regulated, and institutional barriers make access to the formal labour market difficult for migrants. Whereas in the United States immigrant business has been supported by the ideology of free enterprise and the myth of the 'self-made man,' in Germany (an immigration country in denial, with a migration regime based on rotation) ethnic business has a very different history – a history still to be written.[56]

Until 2005, migrants residing in Germany for less than five or eight years needed straw men, or figureheads, to establish themselves in business.[57] Both the precarious legal status of migrants and stringent business regulations (such as formal testing within crafts – *Deutsche Handwerksordnung*) have hindered self-employment. Despite these restrictions, many migrants have managed to start their own businesses, mainly in the 'small business' sector. The largest part of the immigrant economy in Germany belongs to the food and especially the restaurant sector: 27 per cent of the foreign self-employed work in the catering field, and another 15 per cent in retail businesses.[58] The main reason for the greater inclination to enter these sectors is the comparatively small financial capital that is required.[59]

Grocery stores and restaurants belong to an unstable and labour-intensive sector, strongly affected by trade recessions and with a high turnover of labour.[60] These characteristics are considered typical for what is classified as ethnic business. There are, according to Felicitas Hillmann, four main features that define an ethnic business: horizontal and vertical co-ethnic networks; the employment of mainly co-ethnic workers, often (unpaid) family members; a predominantly co-ethnic clientele; and co-ethnic suppliers (sub-contractors).[61] A business is labelled 'ethnic' when belonging to an ethnic community influences socioeconomic decisions, and when 'ethnic solidarity' functions as a substantial resource.[62]

In contrast to other (ethnic) businesses, in restaurants the percentage of employees who do not belong to the family is high; but these (mostly co-national) workers have often been recommended by friends or kin.[63] Whereas the characteristics of an ethnic business hold true in the case of ethnic restaurants in Germany, these presumably specific qualities are also found in other small businesses not viewed as ethnic, in businesses where kinship networks and the unpaid work of family members are common features.[64]

Another problematic aspect of the concept of ethnic business is the (sometimes) underlying essentialist notion of 'ethnic communities.' In many case studies dealing with ethnic economy, ethnic communities appear to be more or less homogeneous and static, with clear-cut borders; differences within these imagined communities are often overlooked, as is their transformation over time, an aspect that is especially relevant in the context of migration processes. Nevertheless, ethnicity may, in historically specific situations and for a certain period, function as a resource that can be used economically.[65] But instead of explaining socioeconomic or cultural processes by recourse to ethnicity, strategies of ethnicization and self-ethnicization have themselves to be examined, taking into consideration the fluidity and variability of ethnicities. The whole debate on the so-called ethnic economy itself forms part of the discourses that have to be analysed in a study on ethnic restaurants.

The Internationalization of Home Cooking

In a survey on eating-out preferences in Germany in 2003, 56 per cent of the respondents said they liked foreign cuisine most. Almost 50 per cent preferred Italian restaurants, followed by Chinese and Greek restaurants (21 per cent and 18 per cent, respectively). French cuisine was named by only 2 per cent, and Spanish cuisine by 1 per cent.[66]

Foreign dishes also score high when food preferences at home are at stake. In Germany, spaghetti has become the most popular home-cooked dish, with Italian pasta and olive oil also selling very well.[67] This is a new trend: in the 1950s and 1960s, German consumers preferred Italianized convenience food, such as *Maggi*'s canned ravioli or *Kraft*'s spaghetti 'Miracoli'.[68] In his study on food consumption in Germany in the 1950s, Michael Wildt has analysed the market research undertaken by *Maggi*, and highlighted the following trends: a move towards more digestible food, and the increasing popularity of international specialities, in general, and Italian specialities, in particular.[69] *Maggi*'s canned ravioli were tested with great success in two German cities in summer 1957 and, because of their great success, introduced all over Germany only a year later. By autumn 1961, more than 75 per cent of German housewives interviewed by the Nuremberg *Gesellschaft für Konsumforschung*, researching consumer choices, knew of the new product.[70] Internationality and the fast food aspect were, according to Wildt, the two main elements for the success of canned ravioli.[71]

It was, however, not just instant food, promising internationality and modernity, that was promoted in the 1950s. The cooking columns of women's magazines and *Hausfrauenblätter* (housewives' magazines) show an increasing interest in 'foreign' cuisine. In the journal *Die kluge Hausfrau* (The Wise Housewife), edited by *Edeka* – a retail association with an average circulation of 1 million in the mid-1950s[72] – the first Italian recipe appeared in December 1950: an Italian salad.[73] The Italian salad is a standard recipe, included in almost all cookbooks of the 1950s to 1980s, and not merely found in cookery books dedicated to 'international specialities'.[74] The Italian salad in *Die kluge Hausfrau* was meant for the New Year's Eve buffet,[75] demonstrating that, in contrast to highly tradition-bound festive meals such as Christmas, parties were opportunities for a more experimental style of cooking.[76]

Certain vegetables, typical of Mediterranean cuisines, such as eggplants and zucchini, were not easily available on the German market. Bedriye Furtina, who had come from Turkey to Germany in 1959, recollects:

> There were no vegetables in the beginning. Only later spinach as I knew it was introduced here. And even later eggplants, red peppers, all kinds of vegetables came to Germany. On the market, merchants handed out recipes: eggplants are cooked this way, zucchini are prepared like this – so that the Germans knew how to prepare all this.[77]

Since some of the ingredients needed for cooking an 'exotic' dish were not available in Germany, or too expensive, recipes often suggested substitutes. In 1953 we find the first allegedly 'Chinese' dish, 'Nasi-Goreng', recommended in *Die kluge Hausfrau*, followed by 'Schweinefleisch süßsauer (chinesisch)' ('pork sweet and sour (Chinese)'), which consisted of diced ham, ketchup and canned pineapple.[78] By using familiar ingredients and tastes, these 'exotic' dishes became assimilated to the German palate, producing a hybrid dish that is neither purely Chinese nor purely German. Instead, transnational food migration transgresses these clear-cut boundaries.

An analysis of cookbooks of the twentieth century demonstrates that on the one hand there had been a tradition of 'international cooking', predating the appearance of ethnic restaurants in Germany. Many cookbooks had, for example, a recipe for 'Hammelpilaw' (pilaf, a mutton and rice dish) long before Turkish restaurants and snack-bars were established in German cities.[79] On the other hand, the spread of eateries offering 'foreign' cuisine fostered the popularity of recipes for 'exotic' dishes:

> By now, *China-Restaurants* are to be found in many cities in Germany. In some cities there are even a number of them. This way, over the years, a wide circle of people have learnt about the diversity and tastiness of the Chinese cuisine. Therefore, it is understandable that now one wants to eat Chinese at home, too.[80]

From the 1960s, in addition to 'international speciality' cookbooks, a new genre of cookery books started to proliferate, dedicated to a single specific 'foreign' cuisine.[81] The public and private consumptions of ethnic food reinforced each other's success. In both spheres, an internationalization, or to be more precise, a transnationalization and hybridization of food consumption has taken place. Redefinitions of taste in postwar Germany were initiated, therefore, not only by migrant restaurateurs, but also by (German) housewives who were key players in these transformation processes, situated as they were at the interface of public and private consumption.[82]

As in the United States, the 1960s in Germany brought forth a new interest in cooking. Cooking, and cooking 'adventurously', in particular,[83] became a status symbol in the 1970s, attracting many middle- and upper middle-class people, some of whom were or had been part of the counterculture or New Left.[84] These 'most-travelled', 'best-read' and 'most discerning' consumers[85] searched for new means of social distinction and self-expression; cooking and food consumption in general were considered appropriate means to find and demonstrate one's place in society – for men, as well as for women. Convenience food was increasingly viewed as unhealthy by this group of consumers,[86] and as an embodiment of capitalist alienation. A revival of 'traditional' forms of production was propagated. Besides cooking at home, the small ethnic restaurant around the corner became a place where such consumers hoped to escape mass production and processed food. Today's Slow-Food movement, reacting to processes of global standardization, is part of this tradition of criticism of mass production and consumerism, epitomized by the fast-food industries.

Food and Identities

Whereas consumerism in general plays a fundamental role in processes of social distinction and self-expression, this is particularly true of food. Eating is an incorporation of what is considered as 'the (kn)own' and 'the other', and thus functions as a primary means of producing ethnic identities. With the greatly increased availability of ethnic foods in the 1960s, images of 'exotic' foodstuffs and narratives about their origins started to proliferate widely. For a cultural biography[87] of specific ethnic foods, not only the commodity-specific characteristics have to be considered, but also the changes of cultural meanings over time and between different social contexts.[88]

In their descriptions of the cuisine offered in ethnic restaurants, restaurant guide books – proliferating massively over the last few decades – often refer to imaginary places, untouched by modern Western civilization.[89] The ethnic restaurant is represented as part of a foreign country. The tavern *Fidias* in Leverkusen, for example, is described as a *Stück Klein-Griechenland* ('a little bit of Greece'), as an *Erinnerung vielleicht an schöne Urlaubstage in der Ägäis* ('a recollection of a lovely vacation on the Aegean Sea').[90] Authenticity and genuineness are the two central attributes with which restaurateurs choose to characterize their restaurants and dishes. Advertisements for the opening or re-opening of restaurants frequently use phrases like 'authentic specialities from the Balkans' (*echte Balkanspezialitäten*)[91] or 'genuine Greek cuisine' (*Original griechische Küche*).[92]

An ethnic restaurant is viewed as authentic, offering 'genuine' dishes, when it is frequented not only by Germans, but also by co-nationals of the restaurateur. Together with the staff, the decoration and the furnishings, these guests are considered guarantors for the authenticity of the food. Both the material dimensions of the place and the social interactions between patrons and staff point to the performative aspect of ascribed ethnicity. The ethnic restaurant can be conceptualized as a theatrical space, with the kitchen as backstage and the dining-hall as centre stage, where a certain ethnic performance is expected and practised by both sides, whether intended or not. An exceptionally complex ethnic performance takes place when, for example, a pizzeria is managed by Turks.[93] Ethnic drag and ethnic passing are going hand in hand here, making visible the mechanisms of 'normal' ethnic performances.

These ethnic performances are highly political acts, but are rarely viewed as such. In what follows, I will discuss an example of an overt, explicit political use of an ethnicized food item in contemporary Germany: the *Döner Kebab*. The doner kebab (in short: 'the Döner') is the most successful fast food in Germany today, selling better than hamburgers.[94] As eaten in Germany, the doner kebab is a Berlin invention.[95] It consists of lamb or beef, salad and *pide*, a bread associated with Ramadan in Turkey, but that lost this meaning for German Turks when it became an essential part of the doner kebab. Consisting of imported and non-imported ingredients, combined in a new way formerly unknown in Turkey, it is an entirely transnational food item,[96] produced not only for co-nationals, but very soon also for the so-called open market.

It is important to stress that in the process of commodification of the doner kebab, no pre-existing ethnicity is simply reproduced. Instead, a specific German Turkishness is invented, transcending the conceptions of 'Turks in Germany' and engraving new significations on the social landscape. In this sense, I would argue, the production and consumption of ethnic food is always involved in actual representational politics. Whereas the doner kebab functions as a 'positive symbol in multiculturalist discourses', it is also used for debasing (German) Turkish culture.[97]

Specific ethnic food items – and most often a national cuisine is reduced to one or two well-known dishes[98] – can be used for symbolic battles over social positions. A slogan such as *Bockwurst statt Döner* ('bockwurst instead of doner kebab'), printed on sweatshirts worn by Neo-Nazis, expresses rejection of 'the Turkish' and/or the hybridization of 'the German', and thus exemplifies the paranoid discussions of the incommensurability of the two cultures.[99] According to this logic, the supposedly original *Bockwurst* should replace the 'foreign' doner kebab. It is either/or, both foods standing in for strongly defined 'us and them' images.[100] Without historical narratives, without biographies of the food items, the slogan is incomprehensible. Furthermore, the word *statt* (instead), that is 'in place of', invokes images of placing and re-placing, referring to spatial politics and suggesting the inseparability of real and imaginary geographies.

The attacks on Turkish snack-bars in Germany – or, similarly, on Asian food stores in the UK – are the more violent outcome of these racist attempts at replacement, indicating the strong identification of a migrant group with 'its' food. As the example of the doner kebab demonstrates, ethnic food is intrinsically involved in contemporary discourses on ethnic identities and undoubtedly serves as a 'powerful metonym for national cultures'[101] and a 'source of racial stereotyping'.[102] Although, of course, 'ethnic business' in general is under attack, here, the restaurant or snack-bar is the most, or sometimes the only, visible 'institutional embodiment of cultural difference'.[103]

Conclusion

An analysis of the various discourses and practices dealing with ethnic food in Germany, including eating out at ethnic restaurants and ethnic cooking at home, addresses the question of what the consumption of 'foreign' food means in the context of the reconfiguration of German society and its relation to 'the other' after 1945.

When eating ethnic food is understood as a 'way of making some kind of declaration' the question is: what kind of declaration is it?[104] Interpretations of the consumption of the foods of different migrant groups vary widely. It has been seen to symbolize 'the acceptance of each group and its culture',[105] or as a way of learning 'some minimal lessons in cultural relativity'.[106] Others have criticized such optimistic accounts, stressing the fact that 'consuming the other' (the fantasized constructions of 'the other') has historically often been linked to exploitation. Commodifying and consuming 'the other' is an ambiguous process, open to resignifications of various kinds. In relation to the ethnic restaurant, I would argue, we see both a consumerist, more or less peaceful multiculturalism and the persistence of racist traditions, a nexus symptomatic of the handling of cultural differences in Germany after 1945.

In the postwar German context, eating out in ethnic restaurants might have been instilled by the desire to become cosmopolitan, to internationalize German identity after 1945. After years of exclusion from global (consumer) culture during the Nazi period, at least during the Second World War, many Germans wished once again to participate in a Western life-style, to which eating out had become more and more important.[107] Furthermore, it seems no coincidence that, as Dieter Richter has pointed out, ethnic cuisine had its breakthrough in West Germany in the late 1960s and 1970s. Not only was there a growing number of immigrants opening restaurants and snack-bars, for the first time enabling consumers in many parts of Germany to try ethnic food; in addition, this newly available supply was met by a generation of (young) consumers looking for political, but also culinary alternatives. In his song 'German Sunday' (*Deutscher Sonntag*), the left-wing songwriter Franz-Josef Degenhardt characterized German cuisine as the *Blubbern dicker Soßen* ('the bubbling of thick sauces'), and thus as immobile, bourgeois, narrow-minded and, in a sense, fascist. Italian cuisine, by contrast, seemed to offer a modern, light and healthy food option.[108] For alternative milieus, the outlets of the left-wing 'Italian around the corner', the 'left-wing Greek' (escaped from the Greek military regime), and, later on, the persecuted 'Turk' or 'Kurd' were popular meeting-places, not least because they demonstrated international solidarity through consumer choice.[109]

As well as political opinion, class, ethnic and gender differences are articulated in the act of eating out. This takes place in sometimes conflicting ways, suggesting that food consumption practices are precariously flexible markers of identity.[110] Tracing the transnational consumption in ethnic restaurants and at home is, of course, but one arena for discussing ethnic identities in West Germany. The omnipresence of ethnic food, however, makes it an ideal object for studying the re-negotiations of cultural differences in everyday life. It brings to the fore the complex processes of glocalization entailed in transnational food migration. In this sense, food – and ethnic food, in particular – functions as a lens for understanding global processes. What is especially interesting about food in this context is its connection with the body. Eating is about boundaries being transgressed, about something from the outside taken inside, and maybe it is this corporeal dimension that makes food such a powerful symbol in struggles over places and territories, over social and personal identities. Food is materially incorporated and, therefore, possesses a complexity not shared by (all) other consumer goods.

Notes

1. S. Köhler, *Internationalisierung der Verzehrsgewohnheiten in ausgewählten europäischen Ländern* (Frankfurt/M., 1993), p. 12.

2. E. Barlösius, *Soziologie des Essens: Eine sozial- und kulturwissenschaftliche Einführung in die Ernährungsforschung* (Weinheim, 1999), p. 147.
3. U. Spiekermann, 'Europas Küchen: Eine Annäherung', *Mitteilungen des Internationalen Arbeitskreises für Kulturforschung des Essens*, 5 (2000): 31. See also U. Spiekermann, 'Deutsche Küche – Eine Fiktion: Regionale Verzehrsgewohnheiten im 20. Jahrhundert', in K. Gedrich and U. Oltersdorf (eds), *Ernährung und Raum: Regionale und ethnische Ernährungsweisen in Deutschland* (Karlsruhe, 2002), pp. 47–73.
4. G. Ritzer, *The McDonaldization of Society: An Investigation into the Changing Character of Contemporary Social Life* (Thousand Oaks, CA, 1993).
5. R. Robertson, 'Glocalization: Time–Space and Homogeneity–Heterogeneity', in M. Featherstone, S. Lash and R. Robertson (eds), *Global Modernities* (London, 1995), pp. 25–44.
6. For a case study on the entanglement of local food and cuisine with the global food trade, see R. Wilk in this volume.
7. H. Diner, *Hungering for America: Italian, Irish, and Jewish Foodways in the Age of Migration* (Cambridge, MA, 2001), p. 8.
8. H.-J. Teuteberg, 'The Rising Popularity of Dining Out in German Restaurants in the Aftermath of Modern Urbanization', in M. Jacobs and P. Scholliers (eds), *Eating Out in Europe: Picnics, Gourmet Dining and Snacks since the Late Eighteenth Century* (Oxford, 2003), p. 284. In pre-modern times, eating out did not form part of the experience of a considerable number of people, and the inns providing food for travellers did not offer choice from a range of dishes.
9. R. L. Spang, *The Invention of the Restaurant: Paris and Modern Gastronomic Culture* (Cambridge, MA, 2000).
10. C. Drummer, 'Das sich ausbreitende Restaurant in deutschen Großstädten als Ausdruck bürgerlichen Repräsentationsstrebens 1870–1930', in H.-J. Teuteberg and G. Neumann (eds), *Essen und kulturelle Identität: Europäische Perspektiven* (Berlin, 1997), p. 304. The German term *Restaurant*, borrowed from the French in the second half of the nineteenth century, at first referred only to the highest level of cuisine, but today comprises more or less all eateries where you can have your meal at a table; it is used synonymously with *Gaststätte* (Teuteberg, 'Rising Popularity', p. 281). On the history of gastronomy in Germany, see A. Jenn, *Die deutsche Gastronomie: Eine historische und betriebswissenschaftliche Betrachtung* (Frankfurt/M., 1993).
11. Teuteberg, 'Rising Popularity', p. 283.
12. K. R. Allen, *Hungrige Metropole: Essen, Wohlfahrt und Kommerz in Berlin* (Hamburg, 2002), p. 13.
13. K. Gedrich and M. Albrecht, *Datenrecherche der Entwicklung der Haushaltsausgaben für Ernährung in der zweiten Hälfte des 20. Jahrhunderts* (Freising-Weihenstephan, 2003) (Materialienband Nr. 3), p. 48.
14. Gedrich and Albrecht, *Datenrecherche der Entwicklung der Haushaltsausgaben*, p. 49.

15. Gedrich and Albrecht, *Datenrecherche der Entwicklung der Haushaltsaus-gaben*, p. 80, Table 11.
16. Teuteberg, 'Rising Popularity', p. 281.
17. D. J. Oddy, 'Eating without Effort: The Rise of the Fast-Food Industry in Twentieth-Century Britain', in Jacobs and Scholliers, *Eating Out*, p. 309.
18. V. Amilien, 'The Rise of Restaurants in Norway in the Twentieth Century', in Jacobs and Scholliers, *Eating Out*, p. 185. In the UK, the percentages of people eating out weekly or monthly are double the Norwegian figures.
19. Yet the general increase in eating out cannot be attributed to rising incomes alone. It is also the spread of non-luxurious eateries that has enabled a growing proportion of Europeans to go out for lunch or dinner. For the Netherlands, Adri Albert de la Bruhèze and Anneke H. van Otterloo have emphasized this aspect (A. Albert de la Bruhèze and A. H. van Otterloo, 'Snacks and Snack Culture in the Netherlands', in Jacobs and Scholliers, *Eating Out*, p. 330).
20. Amilien, 'Rise of Restaurants', p. 186.
21. Research undertaken in the UK suggests that students and other highly educated social groups form the largest part of the patrons of ethnic restaurants. Cf. A. Warde and L. Martens, *Eating Out: Social Differentiation, Consumption and Pleasure* (Cambridge, 2000). For a discussion of the restaurant as a pre-dominantly urban phenomenon, see D. Bell and G. Valentine, *Consuming Geographies: We are Where We Eat* (London, 1997).
22. Zentrale Markt- und Preisberichtstelle für Erzeugnisse der Land-, Forst- und Ernährungswirtschaft (ZMP) (ed), *Essen außer Haus 2000* (Bonn 2001), p. 22. Women go to foreign restaurants more frequently than men.
23. W. Zelinsky, 'You Are Where You Eat', in B. G. Shortridge and J. R. Shortridge (eds), *The Taste of American Place: A Reader on Regional and Ethnic Food* (Lanham, MD, 1998), p. 243.
24. A. Basu, 'Immigrant Entrepreneurs in the Food Sector: Breaking the Mould', in A. J. Kershen, *Food in the Migrant Experience* (Aldershot, 2002), pp. 149f.
25. Whereas in London in 1999, 90 grams of ethnic foods were eaten per week, only 17 grams were consumed in Yorkshire (Oddy, 'Eating without Effort', p. 310). In the Netherlands, it is Chinese-Indonesian food that is eaten much more frequently than other types of foreign cuisine (De la Bruhèze and van Otterloo, 'Snacks', p. 328, Table 19.3).
26. S. Peckham, 'Consuming Nations', in S. Griffith and J. Wallace (eds), *Consuming Passions: Food in the Age of Anxiety* (Manchester, 1998), p. 172.
27. J. Finkelstein, *Dining Out: A Sociology of Modern Manners* (New York, 1989), p. 3.
28. For the German case, statistical data on travelling abroad, especially to Italy, and the growing market for Italian restaurants in the 1960s seem to confirm the correlation of travelling and eating out in an ethnic restaurant, thereby indicating that the movement and transfer were not, and are not, unidirectional. For a

history of postwar German tourism, see C. Pagenstecher, *Der bundesdeutsche Tourismus, Ansätze zu einer Visual History: Urlaubsprospekte, Reiseführer, Fotoalben 1950–1990* (Hamburg, 2003).

29. In almost all accounts of ethnic restaurants in Germany their competitive prices are mentioned. Cf. 'Neues italienisches Restaurant eröffnet', *Lokale Informationen (Lev)*, 7/2/90. Also in Britain, ethnic restaurants 'mostly catered for the less expensive end of the market' (S. Mennell, *All Manners of Food: Eating and Taste in England and France from the Middle Ages to the Present* (Urbana, IL, 2nd edn, 1996), p. 326).

30. Zelinsky, 'You Are Where You Eat', p. 246. I follow this definition to the extent that telephone directories represent an essential part of my source material for reconstructing when and where ethnic restaurants were established in Germany.

31. 'Sie sprechen deutsch und kochen ausländisch (aber auch bürgerlich)' (W. Dipp, 'Türken und Thais rühren im Kochtopf: Ein Jugoslawe fühlt sich als Rheinländer', *Leverkusener Anzeiger*, 8/7/1980).

32. Furthermore, already fused dishes were imported into Germany. 'Mulligatawny-Suppe', for example, was classified as coming from India and England, and has been described as a 'sort of soup-odyssee' (R. Gööck, *Die 100 berühmtesten Rezepte der Welt: Das Farbbild-Kochbuch der internationalen Spezialitäten* (Bonn, 1971), p. 55).

33. K. Ray, *The Migrant's Table: Meals and Memories in Bengali-American Households* (Philadelphia, PA, 2004), p. 6.

34. 'They may occupy its spaces momentarily (during the consumption of a meal, for example) or for a lifetime (as members of ethnically defined transnational communities)' (P. Jackson, P. Crang and C. Dwyer, 'Introduction: The Spaces of Transnationality', in P. Jackson, P. Crang and C. Dwyer (eds), *Transnational Spaces* (London, 2004), p. 3).

35. In this sense, national cuisines are the result of intercultural encounters (D. Richter, 'Reisen und Schmecken: Wie die Deutschen gelernt haben, italienisch zu essen', *Voyage. Jahrbuch für Reise- und Tourismusforschung*, 2002, p. 25).

36. In 1984, the *Associazione Verace Pizza Napoletana* was founded. In their charter, rules for baking an 'authentic' pizza are formulated ('Die Pizza als Weltkulturerbe? Interview with Antonio Pace, president of the Associazione Verace Pizza Napoletana', *Voyage*, 2002, pp. 89–95).

37. Personal conversation with Mr. S., 2/8/2006, in Leverkusen.

38. On the Italian restaurant business in Germany see E. Pichler, *Migration, Community-Formierung und ethnische Ökonomie: Die italienischen Gewerbetreibenden in Berlin* (Berlin, 1997).

39. Allen, *Hungrige Metropole*, p. 108

40. L. Amenda, *Fremde – Hafen – Stadt: Chinesische Migration und ihre Wahrnehmung in Hamburg 1897–1972* (Munich, 2006), p. 323.

41. Even today (in 2000), Italian cuisine is the most popular in Germany. When eating out in foreign restaurants, 40 per cent choose Italian restaurants or pizzerias and another 16.4 per cent go to Greek restaurants (ZMP, *Essen außer Haus 2000*, p. 25).

42. P. Bernhard, 'L'Italia nel piatto. Per una storia della cucina e della gastronomia italiane in Germania nel XX secolo', in G. Corni and C. Dipper (eds), *Italiani in Germania tra Ottocento e Novecento: Spostamenti, rapporti, immagini, influenze* (Bologna, 2006), p. 264.

43. Bernhard, 'L'Italia nel piatto, p. 271.

44. A comprehensive account of the history of the *Anwerbestopp* (recruitment stop) is given by U. Herbert, *Geschichte der Ausländerpolitik in Deutschland: Saisonarbeiter, Zwangsarbeiter, Gastarbeiter, Flüchtlinge* (Munich, 2001), pp. 223ff.

45. Jenn, *Die deutsche Gastronomie*, p. 70.

46. H. H. Grimm, *Das Gastgewerbe in der Bundesrepublik* (dpa Hintergrund; Nr. 3245, 21/7/1987), p. 11. In marked contrast to Germany and Britain, ethnic cuisines 'made fewer inroads among restaurants in France' (Mennell, *All Manners of Food*, p. 330).

47. H. D. von Löffelholz, A. Gieseck and H. Buch, *Ausländische Selbständige in der Bundesrepublik Deutschland: Unter besonderer Berücksichtigung von Entwicklungsperspektiven in den neuen Bundesländern* (Berlin, 1994), p. 78 and pp. 45f. Whereas, until the 1970s, Italians constituted the largest segment of migrants in West Germany, the Turkish population has formed the largest group since 1971.

48. World-wide, approximately 60,000 Italian restaurants exist (R. Wachter, 'Bella Italia', *Hessische Gastronomie. Fachmagazin für die Hotellerie und Gastronomie*, 12 (2003): 19).

49. Greven's Kölner Adreßbücher (Cologne address books), 1955, 1960, 1968 and 1973.

50. In 1980, 70 of the 570 restaurants were run by migrants, i.e. a little more than 12 per cent ('Ausländer zieht's hinter die Theke: Jeder achte Wirt spricht eine fremde Sprache', *Leverkusener Anzeiger*, 4/7/1980). Only 18.7 per cent go to Asian restaurants when eating in ausländische Spezialitätenrestaurants (ZMP, *Essen außer Haus 2000*, p. 25).

51. Amenda, *Fremde*, p. 340. See also Note 91 for the similar term *Balkan-Grill*.

52. Though outside London in the early 1950s a restaurant devoted to a non-European cuisine was 'almost wholly unfamiliar' (C. Driver, *The British at the Table, 1940–1980* (London, 1983), p. 74). In Germany the already-mentioned Chinese restaurants in seaports, such as Hamburg, formed an exception.

53. Rheinisch-Westfälisches Wirtschaftsarchiv, Cologne, Gaststättengewerbe – Allgemeines, Bd.1: 1945–1952 (Abt. 1, Nr. 176, Fasz. 3) [53], *Kölner Hof* to Dr. Rüther, Chamber of Commerce in Cologne, 4/7/1951.

54. H. Mai, 'Furcht vor zu vielen fremden Gastwirten: Leverkusener Gastronomen an getrennten Tischen', *Kölnische Rundschau (Lev)*, 3/24/1977.

55. 'Grieche baut Restaurant: Anwohner protestieren', *Leverkusener Anzeiger*, 5/4/1992.

56. D. Schmidt, 'Unternehmertum und Ethnizität – ein seltsames Paar', *Prokla: Zeitschrift für kritische Sozialwissenschaft*, 30(3) (2000): 339.

57. Only after eight or, if they were married to a German national, after five years, did migrants have the chance to get an unlimited residence permit. Since the 1980s, this regulation has not been a major problem, because in most cases at least one member of a migrant family has resided in Germany for more than five years (J. Blaschke and A. Ersöz, 'The Turkish Economy in West Berlin', *International Small Business Journal*, 4(3) (1985): 40).

58. Löffelholz, Gieseck and Buch, *Ausländische Selbständige*, p. 51.

59. Basu, 'Immigrant Entrepreneurs', p. 152.

60. Because of its labour-intensity in catering work, David Parker calls into question the idea of time-space compression in the age of globalization, stressing differing perspectives through the example of fast food – time-saving for the consumers, but implying the surrender of much time on the part of those selling fast food all day and even at night (D. Parker, 'The Chinese Takeaway and the Diasporic Habitus: Space, Time and Power Geometries', in B. Hesse (ed.), *Un/Settled Multiculturalisms: Disaporas, Entanglements, 'Transruptions'* (London, 2000), pp. 89f.).

61. F. Hillmann, 'Ethnische Ökonomien als Schnittpunkte von Migrationssystem und Arbeitsmarkt in Berlin', *Prokla*, 30(3) (2000): 417.

62. Hillmann, 'Ethnische Ökonomien als Schnittpunkte'. These features apply to businesses run by first-generation male entrepreneurs, in particular; generational and gender differences are of utmost importance in this context (F. Hillmann, *Türkische Unternehmerinnen und Beschäftigte im Berliner ethnischen Gewerbe* (FS I 98-107, discussion paper, December 1998)).

63. Blaschke and Ersöz, 'Turkish Economy', p. 41.

64. Schmidt, 'Unternehmertum', p. 352.

65. I prefer the term nationality to ethnicity, which, in the German context, connotes bloodline descent and is to some extent a substitute for 'race', a term that has been more or less extinguished from public discourse since 1945.

66. Wachter, 'Bella Italia', p. 20. According to a survey undertaken by the *Allensbach-Institut*, of young people under 30 years of age, 65 per cent prefer Italian restaurants (R. Lücke, 'Für die italienischen Momente im Leben, Pizza, Pasta, Parma-Schinken: Vor 50 Jahren kam La Dolce vita nach Deutschland – und mit ihm eine neue Esskultur', *Welt am Sonntag*, 1/16/2005). Similarly, in the Netherlands, Italian restaurants by far outsell other Mediterranean restaurants, such as Yugoslavian and Spanish (A. van Otterloo, 'Foreign Immigrants and the Dutch at the Table, 1945–1985: Bridging or Widening the Gap?', *The Netherlands Journal of Sociology*, 23(2) (1987): 132).

67. Sales figures of Italian pasta in Germany have almost doubled in the past five years, the Netherlands, France and Germany being the three biggest importers of Italian food (Lücke, 'Für die italienischen Momente'). For the history of Italian food imports to Germany, see Bernhard, 'L'Italia nel piatto'.

68. Patrick Bernhard speaks of 'l'autoitalianizzazione' in this context (Bernhard, 'L'Italia nel piatto', p. 279).

69. M. Wildt, *Vom kleinen Wohlstand: Eine Konsumgeschichte der fünfziger Jahre* (Frankfurt/M., 1996), p. 144.

70. Wildt, *Vom kleinen Wohlstand.*

71. Wildt, *Vom kleinen Wohlstand*, p. 145.

72. Wildt, *Vom kleinen Wohlstand*, p. 177.

73. M. Blasche, *Das kleine Kochbuch für Schülerinnen, Lehrlinge und junge Hausfrauen* (Hiltrup, 4th edn, 1950), p. 52.

74. E. Schuler, *Mein Kochbuch: Über tausend Rezepte für die einfache und feine Küche* (Stuttgart, 6th edn, 1949), p. 209. For an early example of a German compilation of Italian recipes, see 'Italienische Spezialgerichte', *Frauen-Genossenschafts-Blatt*, 3 (1904).

75. Wildt, *Vom kleinen Wohlstand*, pp. 184f.

76. Within the daily meal cycle, marginal meals, such as breakfast in Western societies, are more prone to change.

77. 'In Deutschland nannten sie mich Ayse: Die Tellerwäscherin Bedriye Furtina', in M. Richter, *Gekommen und Geblieben: Deutsch-türkische Lebensgeschichten* (Hamburg, 2003), p. 126: 'Gemüse gab es am Anfang nicht. Erst später kam Spinat hierher, so wie ich ihn kannte. Und noch später kamen Auberginen, Paprika, alle Arten von Gemüse nach Deutschland. Auf dem Markt verteilten die Händler damals Rezepte: Auberginen werden so gekocht, Zucchini so zubereitet – damit die Deutschen wussten, wie man alles zubereitete.'

78. Wildt, *Wohlstand*, pp. 188f. Nasi goreng soon became one of the most popular canned dishes, in a way similar to ravioli. In the Netherlands, popular woman's magazines started to publish the first Chinese-Indonesian recipes in 1950 (Otterloo, 'Foreign Immigrants', p. 131), i.e. just after Indonesia's independence.

79. Blasche, *Das kleine Kochbuch*, p. 33.

80. 'China-Restaurants sind heute bereits in vielen Städten Deutschlands anzutreffen. In manchen Städten gibt es sogar eine ganze Reihe. Weite Kreise haben so hier im Laufe der Zeit die Vielfalt und Schmackhaftigkeit der chinesischen Küche schätzen gelernt [...]. Es ist daher verständlich, dass man nun zu Hause ebenfalls chinesisch essen möchte' (The Amoy Canning Corporation (ed.), *Rezepte für AMOYCAN Chinesische Leckerbissen* (Hong Kong, 1974), p. 2).

81. Similarly, in the United States in the 1950s, more and more Americans became interested in 'foreign' cuisines, and speciality cookbooks made 'significant inroads into the cookbook market' (J. Neuhaus, *Manly Meals and Mom's Home Cooking: Cookbooks and Gender in Modern America* (Baltimore, MD, 2003), p. 165).

82. Implicitly or explicitly, the cookbooks of the 1950s to 1970s mainly addressed middle-class housewives and did not refer to working-class or migrant women's different experiences.

83. 'Essen als Abenteuer – warum eigentlich nicht?' (Eating as adventure – why not?) asks Horst Schaffenberg in his cookbook *Zu Gast an fremden Feuern: Das KARL-MAY-Kochbuch* (Bamberg, 1975), p. 5.

84. H. Levenstein, *Paradox of Plenty: A Social History of Eating in Modern America* (New York, 1993), pp. 217, 219.

85. Levenstein, *Paradox of Plenty*, p. 219.

86. Changes in food consumption patterns are partly the result of the dissemination of nutritional information – an aspect that is beyond the scope of this chapter. For the growing mistrust of the food industries and their products from the 1960s onwards, see Mennell, *All Manners of Food*, p. 340; for a very similar development in the US see W. Belasco, *Appetite for Change: How the Counterculture Took on the Food Industry* (Ithaca, NY, 1993).

87. A. Appadurai, *The Social Life of Things: Commodities in Cultural Perspective* (Cambridge, 1986).

88. Foods in general share the following traits, above all: variability and transitoriness (A. Zingerle, 'Identitätsbildung bei Tische: Theoretische Vorüberlegungen aus kultursoziologischer Sicht', in Teuteberg and Neumann, *Essen und kulturelle Identität*, p. 69).

89. The general proliferation of guidebooks is a response to the enormous variety of consumer goods and to the problems of choosing from this wide range of available goods. Cf. A. Warde, 'Continuity and Change in British Restaurants, 1951–2001', in Jacobs and Scholliers, *Eating Out*, p. 241.

90. H. Schonauer, 'Hermes und Poseidon laden in die antike Taverne: Neues griechisches Lokal mit Ansprüchen', *Rheinische Post (Lev)*, 6/25/1983. In an advertisement for the tavern *Sorbas* in Leverkusen, the Mediterranean Sea and Greek folklore (men in Greek costumes dancing *sirtaki*) represent the longing for Hellas and the authenticity of the restaurant ('Sorbas', *Leverkusener Anzeiger*, 8/30/1980).

91. Advertisement of the *Zagreb-Grill* in Leverkusen (*Leverkusener Anzeiger*, 6/22/1968). The *Balkan-Grill* was a very popular institution in the 1970s and early 1980s, but has been increasingly under attack as 'outdated' in recent years. Germany's 'guest-workers' cuisine' (*Gastarbeiterküche*) in general has had its day, according to P. Peter, 'Bye-bye, Balkan-Grill', *Frankfurter Allgemeine Sonntagszeitung*, 1/18/2004.

92. Advertisement for the restaurant *Sorbas* in Leverkusen (*Lokal-Anzeiger*, 9/23/1980).

93. This is a typical situation, especially in Eastern Germany, but also elsewhere. Cf. D. Soyez, 'Der "Kölsche Chinese" und andere Hybride: Kölner Restaurants als Bühnen von Glokalisierungsprozessen', *Kölner Geographische Arbeiten*, 82 (2004): 32.

94. F. Hillmann and H. Rudolph (1997), 'Redistributing the Cake? Ethnicisation Processes in the Berlin Food Sector', *Discussion Paper FS I 97-101* of the Wissenschaftszentrums Berlin für Sozialforschung, Berlin, p. 19.
95. A. Caglar, 'McDoner: Doner Kebap and the Social Positioning Struggle of German Turks', in J. Costa and G. Bamossy (eds), *Marketing in a Multicultural World: Ethnicity, Nationalism, and Cultural Identity* (Thousand Oaks, CA, 1995), pp. 209– 30.
96. I prefer this characterization to the conceptualization of the Döner-kebap as a creolized product. The concept of creolization is in danger of reifying the assumption of two pure, distinctive cultures mixing. Cf. I. Cook and P. Crang, 'The World on a Plate: Culinary Culture, Displacement and Geographical Knowledges', *Journal of Material Culture*, 1(2) (1996): 131–53. 'Translocal' might be an even more appropriate term here, since it is not necessarily national contexts, but specific localities (such as Berlin) that merge with other localities to produce something new (cf. Maren Möhring, 'TransLokal. Ausländische Gaststätten in der Bundesrepublik Deutschland', *traverse* 41(2) (2007)).
97. Caglar, 'McDoner', p. 209.
98. In the case of migrant cuisines, these dishes are often placed at the bottom of the culinary hierarchy. Cf. Barlösius, *Soziologie des Essens*, p. 163.
99. A kind of response to the Nazi slogan is a T-shirt now available in several shops in Germany and via e-bay, promising that 'Döner makes you more beautiful' ('Döner macht schöner').
100. M. Featherstone, 'Global and Local Cultures', in J. Bird *et al.* (eds), *Mapping the Futures: Local Cultures, Global Change* (London, 1993), p. 184.
101. Peckham, 'Consuming Nations', p. 172. This 'intimate connection between alimentary imagery and national identity' is also stressed by Parker, 'Chinese Takeaway', p. 78.
102. A. J. Kershen, 'Introduction: Food in the Migrant Experience', in A. J. Kershen, *Food in the Migrant Experience*, p. 8. In Germany, Italians were and are sometimes still called 'Spaghettifresser'.
103. Parker, 'Chinese Takeaway', p. 79. Christina Hardyment speaks of restaurants as 'the most public face of the new communities' (C. Hardyment, *Slice of Life: The British Way of Eating since 1945* (London, 1995), p. 139).
104. S. W. Mintz, *Tasting Food, Tasting Freedom: Excursions into Eating, Culture, and the Past* (Boston, 1996), p. 13.
105. S. Kalcik, 'Ethnic Foodways in America: Symbol and Performance of Identity', in L. Keller Brown and K. Mussell (eds), *Ethnic and Regional Foodways in the United States: The Performance of Group Identity* (Knoxville, TN, 1984), p. 61.
106. R. Abrahams, 'Equal Opportunity Eating: A Structural Excursus on Things of the Mouth', in Keller Brown and Mussell, *Ethnic and Regional Foodways*, p. 23.

107. 'To be at the leading edge of modern capitalism is to eat fifteen different cuisines in any one week' (S. Hall, 'The Local and the Global: Globalization and Ethnicity', in A. McClintock, A. Mufti and E. Shohat (eds), *Dangerous Liaisons. Gender, Nation, and Postcolonial Perspectives* (Minneapolis, MN, 1997), p. 181).

108. Richter, 'Reisen und Schmecken', p. 27. For the 'stereotype of the healthy other on the shores of the Mediterranean' see A. James, 'How British Is British Food?', in P. Caplan (ed.), *Food, Health, and Identity* (London, 1997), p. 73.

109. On the 'longing for Italy' in the German New Left, see S. Sackstetter, 'Vogliamo tutto – Wir wollen alles: Italiensehnsucht der deutschen Linken', in H. Siebenmorgen (ed.), *Wenn bei Capri die rote Sonne ... Die Italiensehnsucht der Deutschen im 20. Jahrhundert* (Karlsruhe, 1997), pp. 124–9.

110. According to Elspeth Probyn, eating is less a confirmation than a questioning of identity; eating, as a process of connecting one's body to others, animate and inanimate, entails becoming different, 'reworking the categories that once defined us' (E. Probyn, *Carnal Appetites: Foodsexidentities* (London, 2000), p. 32).

Part III
Transnational Knowledge and Actors

–9–

A Green International?

Food Markets and Transnational Politics, *c*.1850–1914
Alexander Nützenadel

The period between the middle of the nineteenth century and the First World War is often characterized as the 'first globalization' in modern history.[1] International investments and trade soared, and world-wide migrations peaked. Cultural exchanges intensified, as new technologies of transport and communication – railways and the telegraph – were diffused. The shift from sailboats to steamers along with the construction of the Panama and Suez canals shortened oceanic shipping routes. Transport costs of international trade and migration fell precipitously and the volume of trade rose. The world's shipping tonnage increased from roughly 4 million tons in 1800 to 47 million tons in 1913. Global trade expanded considerably faster than output: between 1820 and 1913, the production per capita grew at an average rate of 7.3 per cent, while the volume of foreign trade increased by 33 per cent.[2] The creation of transoceanic telegraphy linked the financial markets in London, Paris and New York. Political and economic elites with access to these networks were informed more swiftly about remote events than ever before. By the turn of the century, there was barely a place on the globe where prices were not influenced by foreign trade, where railways were not financed by foreign investments, where technology and manufacturing skills were not imported from abroad, and where labour markets were not influenced by long-distance migration flows.[3]

Food markets played a prominent role in nineteenth-century globalization. Even though coffee, sugar, tea and other commodities had been part of international trade networks for much longer, it was only by the middle of the nineteenth century that staple foods for mass consumption, such as wheat, rice or wine, were shipped from one continent to another in large quantities and at competitive prices. After the invention of mechanical refrigeration (around 1880) the same was true for perishable goods like meat, fish, and fresh produce.[4]

At the same time the global trade system was hotly contested in agriculture. Especially in continental Europe, nationalist movements began to organize farmers. By the late nineteenth century, the United States and most European countries had moved back to protectionism. This is generally viewed as a first sign of a 'globalization backlash', leading to the collapse of the international political order and the economic disintegration in the era of the world wars.[5]

This thesis is based on the idea of an antagonistic or dialectical relation between global economic trends on the one hand, and national political orders on the other. Both historians and political scientists have suggested that the nation-building of the nineteenth century was in many ways a reaction to global changes.[6] In this view, the emergence of the welfare state, the redefinition of national borders and citizenship and the corporatist organization of economic interests were closely linked to the legacies and challenges of a globalizing world. New territorially bounded systems of social and economic relations emerged in a period when markets stretched well beyond national boundaries.[7]

This chapter offers an alternative narrative. It shows how new forms of 'global governance' emerged in the food sector in the late nineteenth century beyond national arrangements and institutions. These embryonic forms of transnational governance were not promoted by states but by producers trying to cope with the effects of a global market. Producers became aware that they shared common interests and that they could best solve their problems through cooperation rather than through unilateral efforts by individual countries. The internationalist spirit that emerged everywhere during the late nineteenth century was not limited to civil society and humanitarian movements, but also affected interest groups.

The first part of this chapter analyses the development of global food chains and their repercussions on European agriculture between 1850 and 1914. The second part deals with the role of cross-border networks and institutions such as the *International Institute of Agriculture* in Rome, founded in 1905. While these institutions were initially created to defend European producers against imports from overseas, a more global vision of food markets and governance gained ground in the years before the First World War. Internationalism was not, as Akira Iriye has argued, limited to social movements and non-profit bodies 'engaged in activities that were sometimes at odds with the interests of global capitalism'.[8] Capitalism itself became a powerful force of transnational cooperation, using often the same political strategy and moral rhetoric as civic initiatives and movements in this field.

European Food Markets and the 'First Globalization', *c*.1850–1914

In the *The Economic Consequences of the Peace,* John Maynard Keynes in 1919 described the deep impact of the First World War on the global economic system:

> What an extraordinary episode in the economic progress of man that age was which came to an end in August 1914! ... The inhabitant of London could order by telephone, sipping his morning tea in bed, the various products of the whole earth ... he could at the

same moment and by the same means adventure his wealth in the natural resources and new enterprises of any quarter in the world ... or he could decide to couple the security of his fortunes with the good faith of the townspeople of any substantial municipality in any continent that fancy or information might recommend. ... But, most important of all, he regarded this state of affairs as normal, certain, and permanent, except in the direction of further improvement, and any deviation from it as aberrant, scandalous, and avoidable.[9]

This picture of a peaceful and prosperous system of economic exchange drawn by Keynes is obviously biased by his British perspective. Global market integration had different outcomes and effects in different parts of the world, depending on market access, factor endowment or geography. The notion of a united 'world economy' that Marx and Engels had envisioned already in the *Communist Manifesto* of 1848 was deeply influenced by the experiences of the Western world.[10] Access to technology, infrastructures and communication networks was often limited to merchants in North America and Europe. The massive expansion of international trade that is apparent from the overall statistical data was only partly due to overseas exchange. It was mainly the industrialized countries that traded with each other. The regional distribution of commercial exchange reveals a clear European dominance during the nineteenth and early twentieth centuries. World trade consisted primarily of intra-European exchange of goods and of European trade with overseas countries of European settlement. Around 1900, the combined shares of Africa, Asia and South America did not exceed 16 per cent of world exports.[11]

However, a closer look at the composition of trade shows that this picture has in part to be revised. While markets for industrial commodities, services and capital were almost exclusively concentrated on the Western world, this was not the case for food and raw materials. Between 1870 and 1913, output of agriculture grew at a high rate all over the world, but this growth was particularly strong in South America and the Western colonial settlements of Europe (see Table 9.3). Agricultural products, such as coffee, tea, cotton and sugar especially, as well as staple foods such as rice, wheat and meat, became integrated into a truly global trade system that also involved the southern hemisphere (see Table 9.1). New developing nations such as Argentina, Australia, and Brazil experienced an export boom, and fully participated in the nineteenth-century expansion of world trade. Between 1840 and 1900, per capita exports in South America increased from US$2 (at constant prices) to $15, while the respective increase for Oceania was from $2.50 to $46.35.[12] As a consequence, the share of exports in the national product of South America surged to 18 per cent in 1900, surpassing the percentages in Britain (13.0 per cent), the United States (6.7 per cent) and Germany at that time.[13]

An increasing proportion of food exports from Asia, Africa and South America went to Europe and North America.[14] Table 9.2 shows the geographical distribution of the destinations of exports from these areas between 1840 and 1900. Although

Table 9.1 Value of Less Developed Countries' Exports of Selected Products (US$ millions)

Commodity	1860	1880	1900	1913
Cocoa	2.1	2.9	17.0	84
Coffee	53.7	114.5	153.6	336
Cotton	35.8	96.9	107.7	300
Jute	1.5	22.0	26.2	105
Oilseeds	7.7	29.5	42.6	220
Rice	20.1	55.3	88.5	242
Rubber	2.0	8.5	73.1	210
Sugar	75.1	99.8	85.0	132
Tea	26.4	65.2	67.4	133

Source: Hansen, Trade, p. 36.

Table 9.2 Approximate Geographic Distribution of Exports of Asia, Africa, and South America, 1840–1900 (percentage)

Region	1840	1860	1880	1900
United Kingdom	44	49	40	24
Other Western Europe	22	18	22	31
North America	7	8	12	15
Asia	24	20	18	21
Other	4	5	8	9

Source: Hansen, Trade, p. 55

Table 9.3 Rates of Change in Gross Output of Agriculture, 1870–1938

	1870–1913	1913–1938
Europe	1.34	0.76
Northwestern Europe	1.02	1.50
Southern Europe	0.81	1.19
Eastern Europe	2.13	0.36
Asia	1.11	0.58
South America	4.43	3.05
Western Settlements	2.20	0.74
World	1.56	0.67

Notes: Northwestern Europe: UK, France, Sweden, Denmark, Belgium, the Netherlands, Germany, Finland, Switzerland. Southern Europe: Italy, Greece, Spain, Portugal. Eastern Europe: Austria-Hungary and Russia. Asia: Japan, India, Indonesia. Western Settlements: Canada, Australia, USA. South America: Argentina, Uruguay, Chile.
Source: G. Federico, Feeding the World. An Economic History of Agriculture, 1800–2000 (Princeton, NJ, and Oxford, 2005), p. 18.

the underlying data are fairly rough, they illustrate a rise in exports to the United Kingdom until 1860, and a subsequent decline of the British share that accelerated at the end of the century. The data further point to a decline in the export share of most other regions, with the prominent exception of North America, followed by an increase that is most pronounced in the case of Western Europe. Even though these aggregated statistics have to be treated with caution, they reveal a remarkable trend. Not the industrialized and free-trading nation of Britain, but continental Europe and North America, with expanding food sectors and long traditions of agricultural protectionism, were increasingly absorbing food imports from overseas.

According to modern trade theory, globalization implies more than cross-border trade. It means, first of all, the emergence of globally integrated markets of commodities, capital and labour. Early modern trade stretched across continents, but was for the most part limited to luxury and non-competing goods. 'Colonial goods' such as tea, coffee, sugar, spices and tobacco were traded because they required different climates for their production. Furthermore, intercontinental trade remained largely monopolized or at least controlled by mercantilist regulations, and huge price gaps characterized distant markets even in the face of improving transport technologies. Even within Europe, the grain trade remained highly segmented until the end of the eighteenth century.[15] Market integration, measured in terms of factor and commodity price convergence, was by and large a phenomenon that developed after 1820, mainly driven by the transport and communication revolution that minimized the 'natural protection of space' and created stable networks of global trade. Between 1850 and 1913, world trade in agricultural products grew at a faster pace then ever before, a yearly average rate of 3.44 per cent.[16]

Econometric studies of various commodity markets show that price convergence is particularly discernible for primary commodities where transportation costs and technology played a decisive role. According to Harley, the freight rates between Britain and North America dropped by roughly 70 per cent between 1840 and 1910 in real terms.[17] From 1870 to 1912, the price gap between Chicago and Liverpool fell from 60 per cent to 14 per cent for wheat, from 93 to 18 per cent for meat and animal fats, and from 14 to 1 per cent for cotton textiles. At the same time, the price difference for vegetables declined from 55 to 17 per cent between Sweden and Britain.[18] Convergence was not limited to the Atlantic World. Price cleavages between Europe and Asia were narrowed by the opening of the Suez Canal in 1869, by the shift from sail to steam, and by other improvements on long-distance routes. The cotton price gap between Liverpool and Bombay declined from 57 per cent in 1873 to 20 per cent in 1913, while the gap for rice between London and Rangoon fell from 93 to 26 per cent during the same period. This had a deep impact on the creation of an Asian market for rice and wheat, and furthermore, for the formation of a global market for cereals.[19]

A similar development can be observed for other basic foodstuffs, including perishable goods such as meat, butter, cheese and other fresh produce, where long-distance trade was accompanied by a fundamental adjustment of traditional methods of distribution.[20] To ship freshly slaughtered beef thousands of miles from Argentina or Australasia to Europe, artificially cooled cargo space was fundamental. The transportation of frozen lamb and mutton from Australia, New Zealand and Argentina was reorganized along the same distributional paths. At the same time, transport innovations revolutionized national distribution systems and stock keeping in general. At the end of the nineteenth century, refrigerated railway wagons moved the meat from and to ports, where it was stored in specialized warehouses.[21]

Moreover, fundamental changes took place in industrial organization. With new forms of distribution came larger firms and vertical integration in the food sector. The emergence of a modern agro-industrial complex was thus closely related to globalization, and this would have far-reaching consequences for market organization, economic interests and political action in this sector.[22] The division between agriculture, trade and industry that had characterized earlier periods declined in importance, while new forms of integrated firms appeared, especially in the highly commercialized sector of the international food trade.

All this leads to a more differentiated picture of trade policy and economic interest organization. Traditionally, the role of agriculture has been described in terms of economic backwardness and political conservativism. According to this view, for example, the traditional Prussian Junkers continued to dominate politics and society in Germany until the First World War.[23] In France, Italy, and the Habsburg monarchy landed elites and rural middle classes began to organize themselves in nationalist movements in order to gain protection against the consequences of industrialization and economic change.[24]

It is true that, after a free-trade interlude of three decades, most European states raised their trade barriers as agricultural prices declined and producers felt the blast of overseas competition. Germany's reconversion to protection began with the tariff of 1879, which restored duties on wheat and other food products. In the following years, similar duties were adopted by France, Austria-Hungary, Sweden, Spain and Portugal, and, finally, by the United States, which extended protectionism to agriculture with the McKinley Tariff of 1890.[25] Trade was also hampered by new forms of non-tariff barriers such as veterinary meat-import restrictions in Germany or the introduction of the *Appellation d'origine* in France to protect the quality of wine.[26] Only a few European nations abstained from the temptation to protect their food sector. This was the case for small countries with a shortage of natural resources and a highly commercialized agriculture, such as Denmark, Belgium and the Netherlands, as well as Great Britain, where Free Trade was deeply rooted in the political culture.[27]

Some recent studies have linked different outcomes of trade policy to the distributional effects of globalization. As trade produces losers as well as winners, political scientists like Ronald Rogowski have argued that choices for or against trade protectionism depended largely on the respective factor endowments of different countries.[28]

From a historical perspective, however, the standard models of public choice and collective action seem far too reductive. Even though battles over trade policy often evolved along class lines, and coalitions were frequently fuelled by distributional conflicts, theories of political economy rarely match with historical reality. In the case of agriculture, political coalitions and social formations were much more complex and fragmented, and they hardly mirrored clear-cut economic interests.[29] For example, recent accounts of the role of the Prussian Junkers have shown that traditional extensive wheat production went often hand-in-hand with modern commercialized forms of agriculture.[30] German agriculture, and continental agriculture as a whole, experienced enormous productivity gains during the decades before the First World War. This was assisted by global developments: prices for inputs such as fodder, machines and chemical fertilizers declined,[31] while the lengthening of food chains and the increasing demand in Europe and overseas created new markets for German products. As a consequence, many farmers favoured a moderate tariff for some items, while at the same time trying to gain access to global markets.

Even though state intervention in favour of agriculture became more pronounced after 1880, its impact should not be overstated. Tariffs continued to rise, but their real effect faded, as international prices declined faster and the structure of imports shifted to non-protected commodities.[32] Moreover, falling transport costs over-compensated for the effects of new tariffs. European duties affected mainly wheat, which accounted for roughly one-sixth of gross output before 1914. As a result, the total subsidy from protection amounted to some 5–9 per cent of production. It must be stressed that protection was not even particularly manifest in continental Europe.[33] For example, in 1909–13 the general tariff quota amounted to 8.6 per cent in Germany and 8.7 per cent in France, while the United States and Russia peaked with quotas of respectively 21.4 and 29.5 per cent.[34]

Moreover, there is no empirical evidence for a significant correlation between the level of protection in a country and the development of foreign trade. For instance, countries with relatively high duties, like Germany or the United States, experienced a disproportionate growth of foreign trade, while some low-tariff countries, such as the Netherlands or Belgium, faced severe problems at the same time. More generally, exports grew faster in continental Europe after the abandonment of free trade than in Great Britain, which abstained from tariffs.[35]

Protectionist movements thrived, as Atack and others have argued, for mainly political reasons, pushed through by 'a few vocal losers [who] can win the support of a majority if the majority perceives itself just one step away from joining the losers'.[36] In other words: since globalization had far-reaching distributional effects, societies had to compensate those social groups and economic sectors that suffered most from external competition. As Knut Borchardt has argued, moderate tariffs were thus not an anti-globalizing force, but, on the contrary, an essential precondition for integrating modern economies into world markets.[37]

Transnational Cooperation

These findings are important, as they change some standard interpretations regarding the development of the North American and European food sectors. The following section will pay attention to the transnational perceptions, strategies and policies of agrarian producers. Historical research in this area has mainly focused on the role of national associations and interest groups. In Germany, the *Bund der Landwirte*, founded in 1892, was able to integrate different agricultural groups and became the most important mass organization of the *Kaiserreich*. Beyond giving technical assistance, the *Bund* was able to mobilize rural voters on a large scale and to control a considerable part of the conservative electorate.[38] Similar institutions and movements emerged in France, Italy and Austria-Hungary.[39] According to conventional wisdom, these movements were not only committed to economic protection but also formed a social breeding ground for an aggressive 'integral' nationalism in the run-up to the First World War. In the case of Germany, social historians have characterized agrarian nationalism as a precondition for the emergence of fascism in the Weimar Republic.[40]

However, this historiography has overlooked that agrarian organizations were also involved in international cooperation and exchange, especially in Europe, but also beyond. The second half of the 'long nineteenth century' was a period where new forms of internationalism and intensified cross-border transfers of political ideas, institutions and cultural practices appeared. Civic groups and social movements emerged in various fields, striving to create international identities and to reform society and politics through transnational cooperation. International congresses, world exhibitions and informal networks made knowledge about other countries more easily available and contributed to the formation of common languages and the spread of tastes and fashions. In addition, international agencies were created to regulate common problems and concerns, including postal and navigation systems, weights and measures, money, and passports, as well as telegraphic communication.[41]

In the field of agriculture, such forms of transnational cooperation and exchange were less apparent at first sight, but nevertheless played an important role. On one side, the emergence of well-organized interest groups and associations in different European countries was a closely related phenomenon. For example, the foundation of the German *Bund der Landwirte* was influenced by the model of the French *Société des agriculteurs*, while Italian landowners were impressed by German rural associations and their highly developed system of cooperative banks and rural consortia.[42] Knowledge about efficient economic institutions and modern forms of interest organization circulated among European farmers and their representatives, triggering a process of knowledge transfer.

On the other side, a series of international meetings took place. More stable types of cooperation developed. In 1878, the first International Congress of Agriculture took place in Paris. The following years saw international congresses and exhibitions that served as forums for the exchange of ideas, networking and the popularization of knowledge.[43] Initially, most participants came from continental Europe, bringing together representatives of national associations, politicians, and businessmen from the food industry as well as experts from universities, statistical offices and commercial organizations. While at the first congresses in Paris (1878) and Budapest (1885) activities barely reached beyond the exchange of information, debates had shifted to more general political and economic concerns by 1889. There was growing awareness that European farmers shared certain interests and goals beyond national boundaries and that these could best be served by pooling their resources and promoting transnational cooperation, instead of preoccupying themselves with their respective national interests.

This transnational awareness was not driven by internal European problems and conflicts alone, but also responded to global challenges. As Jules Méline, the French Minister of Agriculture, emphasized at the opening speech of the International Congress in Paris 1889, the consequences of market integration were 'disastrous for the old nations, crushed by the burdens of the past, who, from time immemorial, have bruised the bowels of the earth and can render it fertile only by dint of work and sacrifice.'[44] Méline, one of the most fervent supporters of protectionist tariffs, saw European cooperation as the only way to resolve the crisis of the food sector. Similarly, the President of the Republican *Société nationale d'encouragement à l'agriculture* argued that the difficulties of agriculture had to be treated 'on a European scale ... instead of dealing with these questions at purely local or national level'.[45]

Although the word 'globalization' was unknown at the time, the phenomenon itself was at the heart of discussion among European farmers. It was more than a coincidence that the first international congress was organized in conjunction with the World Fair in Paris 1878, where commercial representatives from all over the world convened. The main question was the impact of international flows of food and other commodities on European societies. Would trade liberalization lead to falling wages and profits, and what countermeasures should be taken against the threat of foreign competition? Closing borders by tariffs and other import restrictions was only one response discussed by the representatives of European agriculture. The debate about global trade revolved around a set of assorted topics and problems such as better credit, new forms of market organization and the role of diverging monetary systems (bimetallism in France, the gold standard in Germany) and their influence on the food trade. Often, these debates were permeated by a language of anti-capitalism and conservative morality. For example, German farmers promoted the idea of bimetallism as a bulwark against the 'great powers of international capital', while French and Italian representatives endorsed 'sane' and locally based cooperative banks with the same argument.[46]

A major issue was the regulation of the stock market for agricultural commodities. In 1896, the German Reichstag had passed a bill that entailed far-reaching controls for the stock market, including the public registration of brokers and a prohibition on futures trading in grains and flour. German landowners, who had been engaged in the battle against 'evil speculators' for many years, used the international congresses to obtain similar legislation in other countries. Farmers in Europe, suggested the German representative Gustav Ruhland in Budapest in 1896, should 'walk shoulder to shoulder in the battle against the international of gold and the predatory practice of stock markets'.[47] Ernst Lauer, secretary of the Swiss Farmers' Association, used the congress in Lausanne as a platform for his agitation against futures trading.

> Only if the supremacy of the stock market and its harmful influence is broken, will producers and consumers be able to decide on prices, and the solid and honourable merchant replace the speculator... For this purpose, we shall proclaim from farm to farm, from village to village, from country to country and from continent to continent: Farmers of all nations, unite.[48]

However, not all congress members shared the aggressive anti-capitalist stance expressed by Lauer and Ruhland. The French representatives, for instance, were pleading for a more differentiated treatment of stock markets, arguing that only excessive forms of market distortion should be suppressed. Combining national regulations with international coordination, speculation could be efficiently controlled without abandoning a free market system.[49] Claims for more regulation against the risk and volatility of international markets went hand-in-hand with a rhetoric of internationalism that, surprisingly, was not dissimilar from that of other civic groups like workers or of the women's international.

Until the turn of the century, the 'green international' was mainly a European enterprise. All congresses took place on the European continent, and representatives from other continents – including Great Britain – were rarely invited. This European perspective also shaped the campaign for a common trade and tariff area, inspired by the model of the German *Zollverein* of 1834. Tariff policy should aim at reducing trade barriers within Europe, with an external wall of protection against the rest of the world. This meant that trade agreements, including the most-favoured-nation clause, were to be limited to European states.[50] Discrimination against extra-European producers also inspired plans to establish a European grain board. In 1903, the agrarian associations of Germany, France, Portugal, Austria-Hungary, Spain, Switzerland and Serbia set up an International Commission to coordinate the wheat and flour trade through self-governed marketing boards, conceived mainly as a response to the problem of containing the 'invasion' of cheap grain from overseas. Even though the Commission had only limited success, as most farmers refused to sign agreements with the newly created boards, the concept of international cooperative marketing influenced debates on the reorganization of European markets during the years to come.

In other sectors, however, European initiatives appeared less defensive. In 1902, the International Sugar Convention was established in Brussels, aiming to abolish both export subsidies and import restrictions. Especially in Germany, France and Austria-Hungary a modern agro-industry had emerged in this sector, integrating sugar beet cultivation, refinery and commercial distribution within a few firms.[51] In the last decades of the nineteenth century, European sugar production had expanded considerably, and producers preferred to maintain their hold on international markets rather than insisting on subsidies from their national governments.

Farmers' economic interests became more differentiated, as did attitudes towards international trade. Even groups who aimed at protectionism were increasingly intrigued by global developments. Tariffs did raise domestic prices beyond the general world level, but – as earlier sections have shown – did not isolate markets completely from international developments. Price fluctuations abroad continued to influence domestic markets, and thus the profit margins of producers.

A major problem consisted in the lack of information on global markets. From the late nineteenth century on, a vast literature emerged. National statistical offices began to produce data on world-wide crop production, price flows and acreages. Moreover, the International Commission of Agriculture, founded in 1889 in Paris, fostered the development of an international knowledge exchange.[52] However, in most cases, the data of these reports and statistics were retrospective and did not supply reliable information on current trends.

It was against this background that plans for more sophisticated reporting emerged among North American and European farmers at the turn of the nineteenth and twentieth centuries. In 1904, the American farmer and entrepreneur David Lubin proposed the creation of an International Chamber of Agriculture in order to improve the collection and circulation of economic data. Lubin, who had made a fortune with several department stores and a mail order firm in California,[53] regarded market information as the most important prerequisite to stabilize agrarian incomes in a globalizing economy. Without any knowledge on price movements and production data, farmers were subject to the uncertainty and risks of international markets.

So long as there is no general knowledge of the world-factors, and so long as there is no shaping of these factors by the farmer, then so long must his production and his distribution be a pure matter of chance and guess-work, and so long as this is the case the industry of farming must give place to the speculator, and with power to employ the group of facts which the speculator is able to master but which the farmer is not. Once the International Chamber of Agriculture master these facts and the speculative phase will be largely replaced by certainty, and certainty is much more likely to bring about equity in exchange than uncertainty.[54]

Complaints about the inferior position of agrarian producers relative to powerful industrial trusts and financial speculators were not a novel phenomenon, but they were now framed within a wider context of transnational action and coordination. As 'the principal factors which govern the economic production and distribution of agriculture are international', Lubin argued, the political interests of farmers could not be effectively secured within national organizations.[55] At the same time, Lubin – who was deeply rooted in the American antitrust movement – envisioned a new coalition between 'farmers of the world and the consumers of the world'. Both sides would gain from more stable prices and more transparency in global markets.[56]

This is not the place to analyse in detail the history and structure of the International Institute of Agriculture (IIA), founded in Rome in 1905 with initially forty-one member nations.[57] Yet it is worth mentioning that the IIA was an official intergovernmental institution with formal statutes, offices, committees and a general assembly, which could pass resolutions and present them to the adhering states. After a period of internal conflicts and disagreements among the member states, the Institute started work in 1908. While American leaders had shown little interest in endowing an international agency with headquarters in Europe, the Italian King, and subsequently most European governments, supported the IIA.[58]

Unlike earlier institutions in this field, the IIA encompassed numerous nations from the non-Western world, including Japan, Turkey, Russia, Egypt, Australia, Persia and almost all the South American states.[59] Even though Europeans were still in a majority, a more global perspective progressively replaced the once-dominant European self-understanding of the 'Green International'. This was also one reason why IIA bodies were barely involved in the tariff debates, which would necessarily have threatened the internationalist spirit of the IIA. Rather, Lubin and other members stressed the 'common interests of farmers' all over the world against powerful industrial, bank and trade organizations. Even though the IIA abstained from official statements in this matter, there was a broad consensus about the fundamental importance of freer trade in the ranks of the IIA.

During the early years, the IIA was mainly an international clearing-house for agricultural information. Member states had to report to the IIA current statistical data on acreages, expected (and realized) harvest yields and prices. These were then compiled, published and distributed through the IIA's Statistical Bulletin. The IIA offices integrated all data within a 'single numerical statement' for each commodity in order to provide producers with an overall picture of world market developments.[60] If all producers and consumers had full knowledge of the 'natural' price of a specific merchandise, speculations would become impossible. This would not only lead to a fair 'bargaining of producers and producers' but also to more stable prices.[61] Even though the reliability of this 'single numerical statement' was controversial, it became an important source of information in the years before the war, and, in addition, served as the basis for more sophisticated statistical surveys during the inter-war period.[62]

However, the activities of the IIA were not limited to information and technical advice alone. According to Lubin, the IIA should serve as an 'International Parliament of Agriculture' in order to give the agrarian sector a voice in a globalizing world.[63] Apart from agronomic and technical questions, the IIA promoted the idea of an International Commission to regulate freight rates, and the establishment of new forms of distribution through mail order (the 'Parcel Post Plan'), as well as the creation of new credit institutions in agriculture.[64] Much work was dedicated to the establishment of international marketing boards for specific commodities such as tobacco or sugar.[65] All these initiatives were framed by the vision of a new global system that would combine free trade with more ethical principles of commerce and social justice. For Lubin, the political agenda of the IIA was not merely dedicated to the interests of a specific group, but inspired by the principles of 'economic ethics' (he coined the term 'etheconomics'). In this view, market transparency, free access to resources and international regulation of trade was 'not merely an advantage to any one nation, but an advantage to all the nations. The seeming advantage has thus become equity. The former unjust, unethical system has now become just, hence ethical.'[66]

Conclusion

It could easily be argued that Lubin's vision of a world order, where free commerce was embedded in a system of international regulation and economic justice, had little to do with reality. The IIA remained a relatively weak institution, and had only limited influence on international agreements and trade regulations. The statistical information service worked fairly well until 1914, when governments interrupted the circulation of economic data for reasons of warfare. In the final analysis, economic internationalism had only limited success before the First World War. Like many other transnational movements and civic organizations, the IIA was not able to realize its ambitious reform agenda in this period.[67]

From a broader historical perspective, however, international cooperation and governance has become a powerful source of economic organization and political action. To this very day, no other sector is more regulated by international institutions and agreements than agriculture. The history of the European 'Common Agricultural Policy' is an exercise in transnational cooperation and institution-building, even though the relation between state and non-state actors is less clear-cut in agriculture than elsewhere. Farmers and other economic actors often refer to the same tools of transnational politics as social movements and humanitarian organizations.

This chapter has shown how the institutional framework for coping with transnational issues has evolved over time. The IIA cooperated closely with the League of Nations during the inter-war period and formed the nucleus for more serious forms of global food governance after the First World War.[68] More historical research is needed to understand how these traditions and legacies have affected policies and conflicts over food supply and consumer demand, international trade orders and famine relief in the present era of globalization.

Notes

1. See, for example, S. Berger, *Notre Première Mondialisation: Leçons d'un échec oublié* (Paris, 2003); Ch. Davies, 'The Rise and Fall of the First Globalisation', *Economic Affairs* 25(3) (2005): 55–7; C. K. Harley (ed.), *The Integration of the World Economy, 1850–1914* (Aldershot, 1996).
2. R. Fremdling, 'European Foreign Trade Policies, Freight Rates and the World Markets of Grain and Coal during the 19th Century', *Jahrbuch für Wirtschaftsgeschichte*, 2 (2003): 83.
3. K. H. O'Rourke and J. G. Williamson, *Globalization and History: The Evolution of a Nineteenth-Century Atlantic Economy* (Cambridge, MA, 1999); K. Borchardt, *Globalisierung in historischer Perspektive* (Munich, 2001).
4. R. Perren, *Taste, Trade and Technology: The Development of the International Meat Industry since 1840* (Aldershot, 2006).
5. A. Estevadeordal, B. Frantz and A. M. Taylor, 'The Rise and Fall of World Trade, 1870–1939', *Quarterly Journal of Economics*, 118 (2003): 359–407.
6. S. Berger, 'Globalization and Politics', *Annual Review of Political Science*, 3 (2000): 43–62; S. Conrad, *Globalisierung und Nation im Deutschen Kaiserreich* (Munich, 2006); J. Osterhammel and N. Peterson, *Globalization: A Short History* (Princeton, NJ, 2005).
7. Ch. S. Maier, 'Consigning the Twentieth Century to History. Alternative Narratives for the Modern Era', in *American Historical Review*, 105 (2000): 807–31.
8. A. Iriye, *Global Community. The Role of International Organizations in the Making of the Contemporary World* (Berkeley, CA, 2002), p. 18. See also the chapters by Wilk and Trentmann in this volume.
9. J. M. Keynes, 'The Economic Consequences of the Peace (1919)', in Keynes, *Collected Writings*, vol. 2 (Cambridge, 1971), pp. 6–7.
10. K. Marx and F. Engels, *The Communist Manifesto*, introduction by M. Malia (New York, 1998).

11. J. R. Hansen, *Trade in Transition. Exports from the Third World, 1840–1900* (New York, 1980), p. 20.

12. L. J. Zimerman, 'The Distribution of World Income 1860–1960', in E. de Vries (ed.), *Essays on Unbalanced Growth* (The Hague, 1962), pp. 52–3.

13. Hansen, *Trade*, p. 23.

14. See also P. Bairoch and B. Etemad, *Structure par produits des exportations 1830–1937* (Geneva, 1985).

15. See W. Abel, *Crises agraires en Europe, XIIIe–XXe siécle* (Paris, 1973), p. 315; D. Jacks, 'Market Integration in the North and Baltic Seas, 1500–1800', London School of Economics, Working Papers in Economic History no. 55/00 (London, 2000); see also K. O'Rourke and J. Williamson, 'When Did Globalization Begin?', *European Review of Economic History*, 6 (2002): 23–50.

16. W. A. Lewis, 'The Rate of Growth of World Trade 1870–1913', in S. Grassman and E. Lundberg (eds), *The World Economic Order: Past and Prospects* (London, 1981); see also S. Pollard, 'Free Trade and the World Economy', in M.H. Geyer and J. Paulmann (eds), *The Mechanics of Internationalism: Culture, Society, and Politics from the 1840s to the First World War* (Oxford, 2001), pp. 29–30.

17. K. Harley, 'Ocean Freight Rates and Productivity, 1740–1913: The Primacy of Mechanical Invention Reaffirmed', *Journal of Economic History*, 48 (1988): 851–76; K. Harley, 'North Atlantic Shipping in the Late Nineteenth Century: Freight Rates and the Interrelationship of Cargoes' in L. Fisher and H. Nordvik (eds), *Shipping and Trade, 1750–1950: Essays in International Maritime Economic History* (Pontefract, 1990), pp. 147–72; see with similar results D. North, 'Ocean Freight Rates and Economic Development 1750–1913, *Journal of Economic History,* 18 (1958): 538–55.

18. Pollard, *Free Trade*, p. 38.

19. See A. J. Latham and L. Neal, 'The International Market in Rice and Wheat, 1868–1914', *Economic History Review*, 36 (1983): 260–80; L. Brandt, 'Chinese Agriculture and the International Economy 1870–1913: A Reassessment', *Explorations in Economic History*, 22 (1985): 168–80; K. Sugihara, 'Patterns of Asia's Integration into the World Economy, 1880–1913' in W. Fischer, R. M. McInnis and J. Schneider (eds), *The Emergence of a World Economy 1500–1914, Part II: 1850–1914* (Stuttgart, 1986), pp. 709–28; O'Rourke and Williamson, 'When Did Globalization Begin?', p. 38.

20. Ch. Nonn, 'Fleischvermarktung in Deutschland im 19. und frühen 20. Jahrhundert', *Jahrbuch für Wirtschaftsgeschichte,* 1 (1996): 53–76.

21. Perren, *Taste*, pp. 30–87; B. Loheide, 'Beef Around the World: The Emergence of a Global Food Market 1870–1914', *Comparativ* (forthcoming).

22. K. Harley, 'The World Food Economy and Pre World War I Argentina', in S. Broadberry and N. Crafts (eds), *Britain in the World Economy: Essays in Honour of Alec Ford* (Cambridge, 1992), pp. 244–68.

23. H.-J. Puhle, *Agrarische Interessenpolitik und preußischer Konservatismus im wilhelminischen Reich (1893–1914). Ein Beitrag zur Analyse des Nationalismus in Deutschland am Beispiel des Bundes der Landwirte und der Deutsch-Konservativen Partei* (Hanover, 1967); S. B. Webb, 'Agricultural Protection in Wilhelmine Germany: Forging an Empire with Pork and Rye', *Journal of Economic History*, XLII (1982): 309–26. A. Gerschenkron, *Bread and Democracy in Germany* (Berkeley, CA, 1943).

24. H.-J. Puhle, *Politische Agrarbewegungen in kapitalistischen Industriegesellschaften. Deutschland, USA und Frankreich im 20. Jahrhundert* (Göttingen, 1975); R. Aldenhoff-Hübinger, 'La politisation des campagnes à travers agrarisme et protectionnisme. À la fin du 19e siècle en Europe (Allemagne, France, Italie)', in J.-L. Mayaud and L. Raphael (eds), *Histoire de l'Europe rurale contemporaine. Du village à l'État* (Paris, 2006), pp. 163–76.

25. For an overview see M. Tracy, *Government and Agriculture in Western Europe 1880–1988* (New York, 1989), pp. 20–5.

26. Webb, 'Agricultural Protection', pp. 317–19; L. Loubère, *The Red and the White: The History of Wine in France and Italy in the 19th Century* (Albany, NY, 1978), pp. 104–9; for a general discussion of French protectionism see H. Lebovics, *The Alliance of Iron and Wheat in the Third French Republic, 1860–1914: Origins of the New Conservatism* (Baton Rouge, LA, 1988).

27. Tracy, *Government*, p. 23; Denmark, Belgium and the Netherlands, however, had some industrial tariffs. For the unique place of Britain, see F. Trentmann, *Free Trade Nation: Commerce, Consumption, and Civil Society in Modern Britain* (Oxford, 2008).

28. R. Rogowski, *Commerce and Coalitions. How Trade Affects Domestic Political Alignments* (Princeton, NJ, 1989); see also D. A. Irwin, *Against the Tide: An Intellectual History of Free Trade* (Princeton, NJ, 1996); O'Rourke and Williamson, *Globalization and History*, pp. 77–117.

29. See the excellent study by R. Aldenhoff-Hübinger, *Agrarpolitik und Protektionismus. Deutschland und Frankreich im Vergleich 1879–1914* (Göttingen, 2002). For the analytical problems of economic approaches , see F. Trentmann, 'Political Culture and Political Economy', *Review of International Political Economy*, 5(2) (1998): 217–51.

30. See H. Winkel, 'Zur Anwendung des technischen Fortschritts in der Landwirtschaft im ausgehenden 19. Jahrhundert, *Zeitschrift für Agrargeschichte und Agrarsoziologie*, 27 (1979): 19–31; P. Wagner, *Bauern, Junker und Beamte. Der Wandel lokaler Herrschaft und Partizipation im Ostelbien des 19. Jahrhunderts* (Göttingen, 2005).

31. Germany, for example, became the main importer of animal food world-wide; C. Torp, *Die Herausforderung der Globalisierung. Wirtschaft und Politik in Deutschland 1860–1914* (Göttingen, 2005), p. 100.

32. See also P. Bairoch, 'Free Trade and European Economic Development', *European Economic Review*, 3 (1972): 273–45; Bairoch, *Economics and World History: Myths and Paradoxes* (Chicago, 1993).

33. G. Federico, *Feeding the World: An Economic History of Agriculture, 1800–2000* (Princeton, NJ, 2005), p. 190.

34. Bairoch, *Economics and World History*, p. 26; see also Torp, *Herausforderung der Globalisierung*, p. 368.

35. Bairoch, *Economics and World History*, p. 51.

36. J. Atack, F. Bateman and W. N. Parker, 'The Farm, the Farmer and the Market', in S. Engerman and R. Gallman (eds), *The Cambridge Economic History of the United States*, vol. 2, (Cambridge, 2000), p. 282.

37. Borchardt, *Globalisierung*, p. 23.

38. S. R. Tirell, *German Agrarian Politics after Bismarck's Fall: The Formation of the Farmers' League* (New York, 1951); Puhle, *Agrarische Interessenpolitik*.

39. M. Malatesta, *I signori della terra. L'organizzazione degli interessi agrari padani (1860–1914)* (Milan, 1989); P. Barral, *Les Agrariens français, de Méline à Pisani* (Paris, 1968).

40. See H.-J. Puhle, *Von der Agrarkrise zum Präfaschismus. Thesen zum Stellenwert der agrarischen Interessenverbände in der deutschen Politik am Ende des 19. Jahrhunderts* (Wiesbaden, 1972). This interpretation was at the core of the *Sonderweg* debate; see, for a critical discussion, H. Grebing, *Der 'deutsche Sonderweg' in Europa 1806–1945: Eine Kritik* (Stuttgart, 1986); D. Blackbourn and G. Eley, *The Peculiarities of German History* (New York, 1984).

41. See M. Geyer and J. Paulmann (eds), *The Mechanics of Internationalism: Culture, Society and Politics from the 1840s to World War I* (Oxford, 2001); W. Kaiser, 'Transnational Mobilization and Cultural Representation: Political Transfer in an Age of Proto-Globalization, Democratization and Nationalism 1848–1914', *European Review of History*, 12 (2005): 403–24; Iriye, *Global Community*, pp. 9–36; C. N. Murphy, *International Organization and Industrial Change: Global Governance since 1850* (New York, 1994).

42. Aldenhoff-Hübinger, *Agrarpolitik und Protektionismus*, pp. 87–8.

43. Between 1878 and 1913, 12 congresses were organized in different European cities: Paris (1878, 1889 and 1900), Budapest (1885 and 1896), The Hague (1891), Brussels (1895), Lausanne (1898), Rome (1903), Vienna (1907), Madrid (1911) and Ghent (1913); see M. Rieul Paisant, 'La Commission Internationale d'Agriculture et son rôle dans l'économie européenne', *Annales de la Commission Internationale d'Agriculture*, 5 (Paris, 1936): 69–192.

44. My translation, *Congrès international d'agriculture tenu à Paris du 4 au 11 juillet 1889* (Paris, 1889), p. 64 ; quoted from Aldenhoff-Hübinger, *Agrarpolitik und Protektionismus*, p. 42.

45. My translation, *Congrès international d'agriculture*, p. 155; quoted from Aldenhoff-Hübinger, *Agrarpolitik und Protektionismus*, p. 43.

46. President of the German *Bund der Landwirte* Berthold v. Ploetz in *Congrès international d'agriculture tenu à Budapest du 17 au 20 septembre 1896. Comptes-rendus* (Budapest, 1897), pp. 396–7.

47. *Congrès international d'agriculture tenu à Budapest*, p. 208.

48. *Cinquième Congrès international d'agriculture. Réuni à Lausanne du 12 au 17 septembre 1898* (Lausanne 1898), p. 20; quoted from Aldenhoff-Hübinger, *Agrarpolitik und Protektionismus*, p. 53.

49. See the comments on Laur's speech by the President of the 'Société des agriculteurs', Marquis de Vogüé, *Cinquième Congrès international d'agriculture*, p. 155.

50. Aldenhoff-Hübinger, *Agrarpolitik und Protektionismus*, pp. 54–69; H.-U. Wehler, *Deutsche Gesellschaftsgeschichte*, Vol. 3 (Munich, 1995), p. 656.

51. See for Germany K.-P. Ellerbrock, *Geschichte der deutschen Nahrungs- und Genussmittelindustrie 1750–1914* (Stuttgart, 1993), pp. 388–94.

52. F. Houillier, *L'Organisation internationale de l'agriculture. Les institutions agricoles internationales et l'action internationale en agriculture* (Paris, 1935), pp. 9–14; Rieul Paisant, 'La Commission'.

53. See O. Rossetti Agresti, *David Lubin: A Study in Practical Idealism* (Boston, 1922).

54. D. Lubin, The International Chamber of Agriculture, 13th March 1905, FAO, David Lubin Archives, vol. 1-I-1.

55. D. Lubin, The Welfare of the State and the International Chamber of Agriculture, Sacramento 6th October 1904, FAO, David Lubin Archives, vol. 1-I-1.

56. D. Lubin, Speech at the International Statistical Congress in London 1905: 'for under the present system the farmers have no voice at all in determining prices so long as they are determined for them by the manipulator and by the exploitator. Under the proposed parliament – the International Institute for Agriculture – it will be the farmers of the world and the consumers of the world who will determine the price between them,' in FAO, David Lubin Archives, vol. 1-I-1.

57. See, on the foundation and structure of the IIA, A. Hobson, *The International Institute of Agriculture: A Historical and Critical Analysis of its Organization, Activities, and Policies of Administration* (Berkeley, CA, 1931).

58. See FAO, David Lubin Archives, vol. 4-I-1, 2 and 4: Letters to the President of the USA, Correspondence with Members of Congress and US Dept of Commerce; 1-VII-13: Correspondence with Italian leaders.

59. See International Institute of Agriculture in Rome, Convention, 7th June 1905, in FAO, David Lubin Archives, vol. 1-I-1. The number of member states rose to 56 in 1914 and 68 in 1939.

60. See documents in FAO, David Lubin Archives, vol. 1-VIII-17: Crop reporting.

61. See, e.g. the report by Prof. Arthur J. Sargent (London School of Economics), 'The International Institute of Agriculture and the world's price of the staples

of agriculture, and the influence governing the same, 10th March 1908'; John Hubbard, 'Some observations on the gathering, summarizing and disseminating of information on the staples of agriculture, 11th February 1905', in David Lubin Archives, vol. 1-I-1.

62. During the First World War many nations (including the USA after it entered the war) refused to deliver statistical information on food markets; see Herbert Hoover to Ass. Secretary of State, Alvey A. Adee, 10th December 1917, in FAO, David Lubin Archives, vol. 1-VIII-17. For the inter-war period see, for example, International Institute for Agriculture, *The First World Agricultural Census (1930). A Methodological Study on the Questions Contained in the Forms Adopted for the Purposes of Census in the Various Countries* (Rome, 1937).

63. FAO, David Lubin Archives, vol. 1-I-1I: Lubin, Speech at the International Statistical Congress London 1905.

64. FAO, David Lubin Archives, vol. 3-II-2: Ocean Freight rates; vol. 3-II-3: Marketing by Parcel Post Plan.

65. FAO, David Lubin Archives, vol. 3-II-4.

66. Lubin to Felix Adler (Columbia University), 22nd December 1912; see also Lubin to L. S. Rowe, President of the American Academy of Political and Social Sciences, 26th November 1913, as well as other letters in FAO, David Lubin Archives, vol. 3-I-1.

67. See, for example, L. J. Rupp, *Worlds of Women: The Making of an International Women's Movement* (Princeton, NJ, 1997).

68. L. Tosi, Alle origini della FAO: Le relazioni tra l'Istituto Internazionale di Agricoltura e la Società delle Nazioni (Milan, 1989); F. Trentmann and F. Just (eds), Food and Conflict in Europe in the Age of the Two World Wars (Basingstoke, 2006); A. L. S. Staples, The Birth of Development. How the World Bank, Food and Agriculture Organization, and World Health Organization Changed the World, 1945–1965 (Kent, OH, 2006).

–10–

Starvation Science

From Colonies to Metropole

Dana Simmons

'With the advent of the Second World War', the English nutrition expert Frederick Prescott recalled in 1947, 'clinicians in Europe were able to study deficiency disease first hand without having to go to tropical countries'.[1] Across Europe, particularly in the East, in Greece, and in Holland, the Second World War forced entire populations to confront hunger and even starvation. Doctors in occupied cities, camps, and asylums observed the symptoms of malnutrition. Dietary deficiency, once the purview of colonial health research, became an urgent medical issue on the European continent. War and genocide created the conditions – and the research subjects – for a vastly expanded science of starvation.

In a pair of important articles, Michael Worboys and David Arnold have debated whether nutrition science should be viewed as an 'importation' from the metropole to the colonies. Worboys suggests that nutrition surveys travelled in the inter-war period from Europe to the colonial context.[2] Arnold traces a longer history of nutrition study that he identifies as uniquely within the field of colonial medicine.[3] It seems clear that, at least from the nineteenth century, nutrition science experienced parallel developments in the metropolitan laboratory and the colonial field.

I argue in this chapter that the world wars brought a properly colonial style of medicine into the metropole. Doctors in wartime Europe employed techniques of coercive selection and human experimentation in large-scale human experiments, following an established colonial model. Colonial methods entered Europe at precisely the moment when mass starvation and bare life – the limit between life and death – touched wide populations. In the process, starvation became a 'disease', and medical researchers entered into the politics of bare life.[4]

In the colonies, beginning in the late nineteenth century, chemical studies of nutrition gave way to medical pathologies. Instead of measuring individual input and output, nutrition scientists turned to describing aetiologies. Medical doctors, not chemists, shaped this new field. They sought to diagnose the physiological and behavioural symptoms of malnutrition, which had only recently been identified as a 'disease'. Whereas chemists were concerned only with fluctuations of their subjects' energy, weight and excrement, the medicine of malnutrition covered a wide range of facts and symptoms. Above all, in the colonies, this disease was connected to frequent mortality among workers, prison inmates, and soldiers. Where metropolitan studies were concerned with managing health and productivity, colonial medicine sought to explain the causes of widespread death. Metropolitan nutrition science sought to optimize the body; colonial studies sought to identify its pathologies.

The World Wars greatly expanded the field of human dietary observation, which until that time had been restricted to penal experiments, hunger artists and colonial subjects. In modern war, food supply became a strategic flashpoint and starvation a weapon. Military and civilian authorities created a typology of diets and applied them on a mass scale. Doctors compared the physiological and moral effects of rations on civilians, soldiers and prisoners. The war transformed nutrition into a medical population science, with human experiment at its core.

The Calorimeter and the Temple Ration: Two Models of Nutrition

In the nineteenth century, a new and growing field of nutrition science attracted the attention of physiologists, chemists and doctors. European scientists centred their activities in the laboratory. Colonial medical officers, on the other hand, developed a very different scientific programme based on large-scale population study. The next section will outline the contrast between these two zones of medical research.

European and American dietary standards, in this period, referred to chemical input–output measures. The first studies designed to quantify minimal nutritional requirements were performed on farm animals. Chemists weighed and analysed animals' feed and excrement in order to optimize their diet. Scientists of nutrition measured minimum needs by universal chemical units, derived from laboratory analyses. These same measures were soon applied to people in prisons, schools, and factories. Such studies concentrated on maintaining body weight and maximizing productivity. Their goal was to render bodies more economical and efficient. Nutrition appeared here as a chemical-economic question.[5]

This model of nutrition is best exemplified by its favourite instrument: the respiratory calorimeter. A kind of oversized bell jar, the chamber was used to capture and weigh every sweat droplet, breath of air, excretion and foodstuff that passed in and out of a single individual. Calorimeters, in theory, accounted for everything that a person ingested and used up in a given period. The laboratory subject stuck in this apparatus became the model for the recommended calorie measurements still used today.[6]

When the American physiologist Francis Benedict undertook a seminal 'study of prolonged fasting' in the early twentieth century, he engaged a flashy Italian 'professional faster' and hooked the man to a calorimeter for thirty days. The subject was weighed, his members were measured, blood pressure and temperature were monitored, and exhalations and excrements analysed. All this served to determine, as Benedict put it, the 'balance of income and outgo'.[7] This one faster's ordeal formed the basis for standard measures of 'basal metabolism' and minimum calories. Subsequent works on starvation rarely fail to cite Benedict's experiment. The calorimeter, with its precise accounting and hermetic laboratory conditions, typified Western nutrition science in the nineteenth century.

Nutrition, in this context, was characterized by physiological measurement and economic calculation. Laboratory research focused on a single, ideal experimental subject. Bodily weight, excrement and respiration served as the primary indexes for nutrition quality. Input–output analyses quantified every element that entered and exited that body, seeking a universal minimum measure. Such standards served to calculate the least expensive means to feed both people and animals. State administrators in institutions from prisons to schools weighed their subjects, recorded their diets and adjusted the daily rations accordingly.

Colonial doctors, by contrast, lacked the ideal laboratory conditions and elaborate instruments to undertake comparable studies. Administrators there, as elsewhere, hunted for corners to cut and costs to save. Their attention focused on state-administered institutions, particularly prisons. In Europe, most such officials were content to compare their charges' diets with those developed in laboratory experiments. They adjusted official rations in order to optimize input and output. In the colonies, however, a more forceful tack developed. A specifically colonial approach to diet began to take shape in the late nineteenth century. Subjects in prisons, work groups and camps were selected and exposed to large-scale human experimentation.

The prison was a crossover institution, at the centre of nutritional concern in Europe and its colonies.[8] Governments everywhere were involved in the daily upkeep of prisoners to an extent unprecedented in any other institution. Penal administrators in the early nineteenth century adopted a punitive approach to diet. Prison meals were set without medical consultation. Deterrence, not dietary science, was the focus. By the 1850s, chemical input–output studies offered a new perspective. Prison doctors in England and France gained significant influence over their charges' living conditions. In colonial zones such as India, however, dietary research struggled to gain legitimacy.

Colonial officials debated the merit of two opposing models of nutrition: diet as chemical balance, and diet as discipline. Sanitary officers such as Madras's Dr. William Cornish argued strenuously that chemical measures of diet applied equally to Europeans and Indians.[9] His superiors in the Indian government stuck with a racialized, disciplinary model. Medical workers in India, colonial doctors and sanitary officials, were held in lower regard than their counterparts in England. An oversupply of medical school graduates in the metropole allowed the Colonial Office to hire at will and under stringent conditions.[10] In addition judges and trained administrators held much broader power over state institutions. Even when England

and France began to adopt medical recommendations for prison diet, Indian colonial judges rejected them.[11]

During the famine of 1877–8 the Madras government extended the disciplinary model beyond the prison. Administrators undertook a starvation study within their own relief camps.[12] This policy came to be known as the Temple Ration after its initiator, Delegate Sir Richard Temple. Temple was not a doctor by training, and took a strong stand against the prevailing dietary science. A consummate colonial administrator, he was educated at the East India Company's Haileybury College and rose up the ranks of the Indian government, from foreign secretary to finance minister to Governor of Bengal.[13] Temple was put in charge of managing the relief of starving Madras residents, under the quite explicit directives 'that no waste was to be permitted; that extravagance was to be sternly checked; that lavish expenditure was not to be sanctioned for a moment'.[14] In response he raised the possibility of lowering rations in the camps for starving Madras civilians.

Where other Madras health officials sought to approximate relief to already established chemical standards, Temple proposed a new tack. Why not decrease the food distributed, he asked, and observe the results? 'There might indeed be question whether life cannot be sustained with one pound of grain *per diem*', he wrote, 'and whether the Government is bound to do more than sustain life. This is a matter of opinion; and I myself think that one pound *per diem* might be sufficient to sustain life, and that the experiment ought to be tried.'[15] The outcome of the 'experiment' would become apparent when labourers in the camps did or did not 'fall off' in the weeks following their change of diet. The Madras Presidency solicited the participation of local surgeons in and around relief camps to gather data. They were to observe any changes in camp inmates' bodily condition, and to note any 'loss of power or flesh in the coolies'.[16]

Temple's experiment showcases two key aspects, which described colonial nutrition medicine in the following decades. First, he adopted a racial attitude toward dietary science.[17] European standards and their chemical-economic logic simply could not apply to natives. The universal laboratory subject may offer insights into Western diet, he allowed, but not Indian. Where his opponents raised objections based on European scientific standards for health and productivity, he refused to admit their validity. 'However valuable' such studies may be 'in the abstract', they 'are not strictly and exactly applicable to the poorer classes of the Madras Presidency'.[18]

Second, and most important, the endpoint of Temple's initiative was not to optimize body weight or productivity. Rather, he quite explicitly aimed to bring internees to the absolute limit between life and death. The 'trial' he proposed was not to maintain his subjects' health, but barely to avoid mortality. 'The one purpose [of such a trial]to which is admitted', he explained, was no more than 'the staving off of danger by starvation'.[19] Temple's nutrition experiment defined its subjects literally in terms of their bare life.

Colonial Malnutrition: The Beriberi Experiments

Beriberi was a classic colonial malady. Widespread outbreaks struck regions across Southeast Asia, troubling doctors from Java to Siam. Though relatively rare in the nineteenth century, its frequency increased alongside the spread of industrial rice mills. Although doctors trained in Pasteurian tropical medicine first inclined to view it as an infectious disease, many observed a correlation between the sickness and processed white rice. Medical officers tested subjects for beriberi in numerous institutions. In their reports – first published in specialized Southeast Asian journals, then in prestigious metropolitan publications like *The Lancet* – we find a specifically colonial dietary science. The beriberi experiments were characterized by involuntary selection among incarcerated 'natives'. In most cases – unlike vaccine trials undertaken in the same context – the goal was not therapeutic, but purely to observe rates of illness and mortality.[20] The beriberi studies showcase the development of a colonial nutrition science.

Some of the first human beriberi trials were undertaken by the Dutch inspector of prisons in Java in the 1890s. Adolphe Vorderman was struck by the nervous disorders that his friend and colleague Christian Eijkman obtained by feeding milled rice to hens. Vorderman surveyed the prisons under his purview, in order to compare the type of rice used for inmates' rations and the frequency of beriberi illness.[21] He found that prisoners served processed white rice were far more likely to fall ill than those fed with brown or parboiled rice. The Japanese naval surgeon Kanehiro Takaki undertook similar dietary surveys on military ships, and ordered a change in their diet.[22]

Beginning in the 1900s, incidental observations gave way to systematic human experiments. These took place mainly in Southeast Asian prisons, asylums and indentured labour camps, where large groups of men lacked control over their own food supply. Often these were sites of earlier mortal outbreaks of beriberi. Each study repeated essentially the same protocol: doctors randomly separated inmates into two or three groups, each to receive a different type of rice diet. Those who fell ill were closely examined, occasionally treated, and tallied.

The British medical officer William Fletcher undertook one such trial at the Kuala Lumpur Lunatic Asylum in 1906, following a beriberi episode that claimed two dozen lives. 'The chief constituent of the rations supplied to the inmates of the asylum was uncured (Siamese) rice', reported Fletcher in *The Lancet*. 'In view of the fact pointed out by Dr. Braddon that beri-beri occurs chiefly amongst communities with whom such rice is the staple of diet it was decided, with the sanction of the government, to place half the lunatics on cured (Indian) rice...'.[23] The hundred-odd patients who drew a place in the parboiled rice group were secured from further illness. Of the group receiving milled white rice, however, thirty fell ill and eighteen perished.[24] Fletcher's work repeated a trial conducted five years earlier by Hamilton Wright in the Kuala Lumpur municipal jail.[25]

Henry Fraser and A. T. Stanton reported on the same experiment applied to groups of indentured construction workers in a remote corner of Malaya. The workers' employer, aware of current medical findings, had imposed a diet of parboiled rice following several occurrences of the disease. The authors persuaded him to allow them to divide the group and try out diets of various types of rice. The published report claimed that the subjects were warned of the danger of illness attaching to it, but chose the white rice diet through a predilection for its taste. Half the participants received the white rice diet, while the other half received parboiled rice against their will. Of the first group, twenty were struck by the disease and were sent to local hospitals.[26]

In at least one case, this experiment was carried through to death without any attempt to treat the suffering subjects. Richard Pearson Strong, director of the Manila Bureau of Laboratories and future Harvard Professor of Tropical Medicine, applied the typical beriberi test to inmates at the Bilibid Prison. Strong had a history of coercive human experimentation; an earlier deadly vaccination trial had raised a minor controversy in the United States.[27] The Bilibid Prison had been completely free of beriberi before 1912, when the experiment was launched. Strong and his coauthor selected death-row prisoners and offered twenty-nine of them unlimited cigarettes in exchange for their signed consent to participate in the study. 'They were told that the experiments were for the purpose of testing the comparative value of different kinds of rice as a food; the articles of food comprising the diet that would be given to them were enumerated, and they were also told that perhaps they might contract beriberi.'[28] The authors set out to resolve whether beriberi, as had been shown elsewhere, had a dietary cause also in the Philippines. As in previous trials, half of those prisoners fed with milled white rice became ill. One perished without treatment.[29]

The beriberi experiments contributed to define insufficient diet in medical terms. Malnutrition appeared here not as a function of economic relations, poverty or coercive institutions, but as a disease. The field of research was dominated by medical officers. Many considered deficiencies as endemic to the environment or the race; particular races (the Chinese versus the Tamil, or the Bengali versus the Sikh) were thought more susceptible than others, by inheritance or because of habits like the consumption of milled rice.[30] When in 1912 Casimir Funk related beriberi and other deficiency diseases to factors he called vitamins, the possibility arose that individual vitamin preparations might provide a cure. With the promise of simple chemical treatments, malnutrition appeared more than ever as a medical question.

Other such diseases, pellagra in particular, were objects of research during the early twentieth century. Doctors in Africa, South America and the southern United States recorded observations of dietary habits and physiological symptoms.[31] Public health officers investigated beriberi in Louisiana, and medical researchers recorded cases of hunger oedema and 'night blindness' in rural Tennessee.[32] The nutritionist W. R. Aykroyd toured rural Romania in 1935 and diagnosed widespread cases of pellagra.[33] In the South of the United States, as in the colonies, insane asylums were primary sites for controlled dietary trials. Doctors entered mental institutions in the early 1900s to determine the cause of pellagra. Indeed, a 1909 experiment at the Peoria State Hospital for the Insane appears very similar to colonial studies: inmates were divided into separate groups, given controlled diets and had their physical condition monitored.[34] Likewise twelve Mississippi convicts in 1915 were recruited with the promise of early release to expose themselves to a pellagra-inducing diet.[35]

Beriberi and other deficiency disease studies left a legacy for medical research. Medical officers involved in beriberi research imposed diets on selected human subjects. Though the trials generally did not intentionally damage their subjects, they took place in structurally coercive environments. Colonial inmates of prisons, asylums and indentured labour camps were exposed to insufficient diets. These studies took place on the margins of colonial society, and at the edges of death.

The Second World War: Colonial Medicine Enters the Metropole

Colonial beriberi experiments underwent a role reversal during the Second World War. Military and civilian doctors interned in Japanese prisoner of war camps between 1942 and 1945 repeated the same observations on themselves and their fellow inmates. In one such case 52,000 British soldiers were marched into the Changi, Singapore prison camp in February 1942. Medical officers among the men 'were from the first alive to the opportunities of study likely to be presented'.[36] They anticipated an outbreak of deficiency disease, given the similarity of their camp's white rice diet with that in previous studies. 'The occurrence of beriberi was foreseen for some time before it actually appeared', reported one, 'and attempts were made immediately to minimize the danger.'[37] Doctors monitored rice cooking to preserve the vitamins in the rice husks, and mixed together *ad hoc* dietary supplements of yeast and leafy vegetables.

As one finds in so many reports of wartime starvation research, the doctors marvelled at the spectacle of so many deprived bodies. 'An opportunity for placing a large number of healthy adults simultaneously on a standardized deficient diet and observing the results over a period of years is one which the many workers on the vitamin-B complex must have coveted', wrote the author of a study on 'cerebral beriberi'. 'To some extent the capitulation of Singapore supplied these conditions...'.[38] The author found laboratory facilities in the camp hospital lacking, and regretted that the same disease rendered the researchers themselves somewhat less capable than they could have been. Nevertheless, he successfully carried out autopsies of patients who had suffered from neurological decline due to diet.

The doctors who published these studies were conscious of their relation to earlier colonial work. One suggested that the internment camps, in contrast to earlier cases, offered a 'unique opportunity for studying the effects on a white population of a semi-starvation diet'.[39] Racial views of diet clearly showed through in the text. The author was aware of colonial studies on 'native' races, as testified by the list of publications on deficiency disease in Southeast Asia and the Southern United States in his bibliography.

In a comprehensive study of the POWs at Changi and the civilian internment camp in Hong Kong, medical officers Smith and Woodruff recorded episodes of beriberi, nutritional oedema, neurological problems, pellagra and riboflavin deficiency. They compared their observations with earlier literature and found their case studies to 'correspond fairly well with textbook descriptions'.[40] They wondered about the 'bewildering' variety of symptoms associated with these maladies, and entered into great detail concerning curative measures. On an optimistic note, they suggested that the British officers' preventive distribution of groundnuts, yeast, rice polishings and beans should provide a model for 'application to oriental dietaries'.[41] The emphasis on therapy here contrasts strikingly with 'native' studies, which concentrated nearly exclusively on symptoms and mortality.

The Japanese POW studies portray most obviously how the war turned colonial experiments back upon European subjects. Yet they by no means presented the only 'opportunity' to observe masses of starving Western populations.[42] World war brought starvation to the centre of the metropole. Spanish doctors treated hundreds of pellagrans and oedema sufferers in civil war Madrid.[43] Famine conditions in the winter of 1941–42 pushed the excess mortality in the Greek cities of Athens and Piraeus into the tens of thousands. Starvation claimed more lives there than violence.[44] Urban residents of the Western Netherlands, cut off from rail supplies near the end of the war, suffered massively from hunger oedema. Doctors in Amsterdam alone counted over 5,000 excess deaths in early 1945.[45] Everywhere in Western Europe the poor, elderly and imprisoned risked death by hunger. Hospitals in Brussels and Paris reported oedemas, hypoglycaemic comas and mortality among 'deprived populations'.[46] The situation in Eastern Europe was worse. One to two million Russian prisoners of war perished from lack of food in German camps. The POW camps, Jewish ghettos and concentration camps were the most extreme sites of total starvation.

These European studies had few local precedents. A British medical officer in the Boer concentration camp on St Helena Island reported in 1902 on cases of oedema among the interned civilians there. Later studies cited this as a reference on deficiency in white populations.[47] Doctors imprisoned in the Warsaw ghetto compared the Boer case to the mass starvation they observed among their own fellows.[48] German physiologists during the First World War found among Central European civilians and prisoners of war a pathology, which they named 'hunger sickness' (*Hungerkrankheit*).[49] Medical aid workers in the Russian famine of 1921–2 also recorded their observations of starvation and disease.[50] Uncertainty remained, however, as to whether hunger illness should be attributed to diet alone, or also to infection.

Far more than medical studies, dietary science in inter-war Europe was dominated by the nutrition survey.[51] Sociologists and economists surveyed various populations on their household expenditures and their daily menus. These surveys generally conformed to a chemical-economic view of nutrition. They compared the daily intake of urbanites, factory workers, families or rural peasants with physiological standards. The studies brought laboratory standards into the realm of social science. The celebrated nutritionist John Boyd Orr, for example, concluded during the Depression that Europeans suffered from a lack of vitamin A and calcium.[52]

The surveyors' goal, generally, was to aid these consumers to improve their diets and to select nutritious items. This aim intensified during the wars, as consumer choice became a matter of optimizing scare resources. Pamphlets and cookbooks suggested means by which housewives might keep up their family's health by judicious purchasing and preparation. Like earlier calometric studies, this branch of nutrition was most concerned with minimizing expense and maintaining productivity.

With the exception of areas on the margins of the metropole such as the American South and Eastern Europe, Western nutrition science did not describe pathologies or mortality. This would change with the Second World War.

During the war, pathological malnutrition entered mainstream medicine. A flood of medical publications described deficiency and starvation illnesses. Case studies were rife. Just as in the colonial context, state institutions stood at the centre of this development. Places like prisons and asylums, which before had attracted the attention of economizing administrators, became sites of large-scale death. Civilians living in scarcity experienced terrible hunger and, in a few regions, high mortality. Institutionalized populations, by contrast, bore a disproportionate burden of illness and death.

In 1943 a French medical student defended a thesis entitled 'the study of dietary supplements in times of war'. The young man noted that new experimental data had become available over the past two years: 'it has happened that in certain institutions (psychiatric hospitals, prisons, etc.), the boarders do not receive any foodstuffs beyond products counted on their ration card. In this way, we see some of the most perfect examples of illnesses related to nutritional deficiency (starvation oedema, pellagra); these cases are as clear as those created in experiments.'[53] Perhaps only a student thesis would state the matter so baldly. Doctors in France treated their institutional patients like colonial experimental subjects. Medical treatments served mainly to provide data on causes and effects, and perhaps to slow the inevitable decline of starving internees.

Like colonial doctors, those in French wartime institutions took the stance of observers, not nurses. They monitored their subjects' decline and described their symptoms but did little to alter the situation. Some entered the asylum specifically with the object of gathering data. Members of the Institut de Recherches d'Hygiène, for example, received permission from the attending doctor at the Charenton psychiatric hospital in 1941 to undertake research on starving subjects there. Researchers followed the diet and condition of asylum patients there for nearly two years, during which more than one-third of them (120 of 320 patients) died of starvation.[54]

The status of bare life was even more pronounced in French Jewish and gypsy internment camps. By 1944 three major camps for 'undesirable foreigners' contained Jewish internees, seven sites imprisoned gypsies, and nineteen others held a mixed, primarily Jewish, population for labour or deportation. Formally, the internment camps functioned like other state institutions. In the Puy de Dôme, the Departmental Directorship of Provisioning informed its subordinates in December 1943 how to account for 'the supervised groups of "controlled labourers" ... regrouping foreigners, Israelites or expatriates from the forbidden zone, assembled in camps. ... The mechanism is the same as in prisons, but the rations are different.'[55] The difference in quantity was pronounced: in September 1940 the Ministry of Provisioning reduced camp meals by one-third.[56] Intendants and administrators congratulated themselves on economizing food costs far below the official rates.[57]

As in French psychiatric asylums, starving internees were selected for temporary treatment and then sent back to suffer once again the same symptoms. Doctors from the Jewish charity *Oeuvre de Secours aux Enfants* [OSE] were allowed to enter the camps and diagnose the internees' state of health systematically. In the winter of 1941–2 volunteer doctors recorded an average rate of two deaths per day in all the camps. In June 1942 Dr Joseph Weill estimated an average daily ration in the camps to equal 958 calories. As time passed, however, the caloric level in some places fell to 500.[58]

Weill persuaded the Inspector General of Camps to allow his team to treat the most serious starvation cases. Beginning in February 1942, OSE medical volunteers 'methodically examined 85 to 95% of the camps' total population'.[59] The OSE team classified internees according to a pathology of cachexia, or severe weakness and wasting of the body. Weill gave a checklist of symptoms for each of his clinical labels. People in the most severe category 'strike one from afar because of their miserable appearance, extreme thinness and characteristic mask. Their skeletal thinness is impressive and they have generalized muscular atrophy... Many of these adults of average size weigh no more than 40 kilograms.'[60] Camp doctors, by contrast, refused to admit that the internees' condition resulted from dietary deficiencies. One attributed the internees' oedemas to their 'sedentary' lifestyle.[61]

Camp administrators permitted the OSE to treat selected patients in the most serious class of his clinical diagnosis. Weill rejoiced at the recovery of several apparently wasted patients. However, he vigorously warned administrators, the organization could not change the camps' underlying condition. 'The alarming dietary deficiencies resulting from the internees' rations call all our work into question. The cachexia cases and pre-cachexia cases who we release back into the camp [after treatment] fall ill again because they are exposed to the same pathogenic agent: hunger.'[62] Despite Weill's protestations, camp administrators limited medical efforts to diagnosis and stopgap treatment.

The camps lead one to conclude that starvation experiments, and the conditions of extreme scarcity in which they were performed, focused on populations deemed without social value. Like those of colonial subjects, the existences of internees seem to have held no great interest for administrators. They sought neither to exterminate them nor, necessarily, to ameliorate the condition of their charges. Rather, internees were treated as medical pathologies in formation. Treatment was not withheld, nor was it directed in a manner designed to maintain health efficiently.

German concentration camps and Jewish ghettos present the most emblematic, and most complex, picture of starvation science during the Second World War. It is well known that concentration camp organization functioned largely through food denial, as a means of discipline and of mass extermination.[63] Food bore power both to protect and to murder. In both labour camps and death camps, internees not selected for immediate execution generally perished of hunger-related diseases within six months.[64] Withdrawal of food from the Jewish ghettos was also a form of extermination. Wrote one Warsaw resident, 'hunger was the principal motor of daily life within the ghetto walls', and the result was a 'generalized mass murder by famine'.[65] Doctors in the ghetto in early 1943 numbered deaths by starvation at 43,000.[66] There is perhaps no clearer story of coercive, programmatic, institutionalized food deprivation.[67]

The camp and ghetto were spaces between life and death, in which existence meant no more than the absence of death. As Giorgio Agamben notes, this limit zone at the edge of the mortal is occupied by two figures: the sovereign and the doctor.[68] Starvation in the camps and ghettos had an economic logic, not of productivity but of extermination. Any research occurring in these places, by their very structure, could not produce any lasting therapeutic effects. Its only product could be a detailed observation of the types and stages of hunger disease. In all these aspects starvation studies in camps and ghettos echoed earlier colonial medical research. Doctors performed triage, selection, detailed observation, and limited or experimental treatment, and by desire or necessity returned their subjects to an organization geared for their death.

Using the same experimental techniques, physiological analyses, and aetiological questions, doctors both inside and outside the camp performed research on hunger disease. As had not happened in any other case, hunger studies in the camps and ghettos were undertaken from three opposing perspectives. Nazi doctors at Auschwitz initiated a programme of starvation research on internees. Physicians from outside the camps following their liberation treated, studied and reported on the emaciated survivors. Finally, doctors interned within the camps and ghetto themselves undertook studies on themselves and their fellow prisoners. Three types of starvation science emerged from the camps: self-reflexive testimonials of conditions suffered; a coercive, exterminatory programme of human experimentation; and a therapeutic attitude adopted by doctors outside the camps seeking to diagnose and cure survivors.

The Dutch and Jewish physician Lucie Adelsberger published an article in *The Lancet* in 1946, detailing her participation in starvation research by camp doctors at Auschwitz-Birkenau. Adelsberger survived for two years there, and then in Ravensbruck and Neustadt. At Birkenau she was assigned to work in a women's sick station under the authority of an unnamed 'camp doctor', whom scholars later identified as Joseph Mengele.[69] Adelsberger puzzled at the camp doctor's hypocrisy in selecting gas chamber victims while next haranguing her and the other interned physicians with 'earnest lectures … on the treatment of diarrhea and famine-oedema'.[70] Under his command, she made detailed observations of several deficiency diseases and aided in analysis of blood samples from starving patients. Some developed famine oedema, while others became dehydrated. 'When able to speak, they complained of exhaustion; precordial pain and pains in the muscle and bones; constant thirst; disturbances of taste; and a longing for potatoes. Tachycardia, circulatory weakness, apathy and stupor were among the signs recorded.'[71] Adelsberger reported on skin lesions, some which ate parts of the face away completely, and which a Dr B. Epstein identified as vitamin B deficiency. She also noted cases of pellagra. She was able to treat some of her patients with vitamin supplements and extra rations, before they were sent back to the camp.

Finally, Adelsberger recorded the results of blood work performed on selected groups of internees. The *Lancet* article provides no context for this data. However, a memoir written in the 1950s offers a clue as to its origin. She describes how two of her favourite young girls, patients in her sick ward, were 'wangled [*sic*] into a series of experiments on the scientific study of the composition of blood under starvation. Prisoners involved in experiments were protected from selection and received an additional ration of milk, not enough to make them fat, but enough to keep them alive.'[72] Presumably Adelsberger herself managed their admission in order to save their lives, at least temporarily.

Prisoners selected for the blood project were divided into seven groups. These included a few in relatively good health: 'New arrivals, recently arrested', '"Aryan" Polish women in receipt of food parcels, well nourished', and 'Prisoners employed at least 6 months in the kitchen'. In addition the study selected subjects on the edge of death: 'Dehydrated starvation cases', 'Cases of famine-oedema' and 'Pellagra cases'. A final selection consisted of 'Jewish prisoners from the sewing and weaving shops, who had been living on the official rations only. Most prisoners in this group did not survive long beyond six months.'[73] Under the camp doctor's direction, Adelsberger found that starvation patients had low levels of protein in their blood and a high blood sedimentation rate. The protein deficiency became increasingly marked in dehydrated, oedema and pellagra patients. The study's selection and differential treatment of experimental groups, the lack of any therapeutic intervention, and detailed observation of subjects' decline all recall the colonial model of human dietary experimentation.

A few of the hunger studies performed under extermination conditions were self-reflexive. Some of the starving undertook upon themselves the same kind of medical research as that forced upon their group by doctors associated with their oppressors. The medical reports shared the same references and methods and often the same data and conclusions. Yet these were composed by the hungry themselves.

Between February 1942 and January 1943, a group of doctors associated with the Jewish hospital in the Warsaw ghetto composed a remarkable scientific and literary artefact. In it they described the aetiology of their community's decline. The report itself appears much like a standard starvation study: a review of the literature, discussion of symptoms, possible diagnoses, photographs and autopsy results. Its liminal texts and testimonies reveal its extraordinary nature. All of its authors were dead by the end of 1946.

The research took place at the 'Czyste' hospital during the Warsaw ghetto's first phase; all activity ended abruptly when the German police moved all Jews into a small section of the ghetto and cut off access to the hospital. Researchers decided to restrict their study to children between six and twelve years of age and adults between the ages of twenty and forty, in order to eliminate any physiological distortions resulting from early childhood growth or puberty. They selected their subjects from residents of a refugee asylum. They chose only those suffering from 'pure starvation', without any other discrete maladies.[74] These subjects then underwent the standard range of physiological tests, of bodily measurement, blood sampling, and chemical analysis. A number of the reports contain postmortem results. In two and a half years, doctors in the hospital's Institute for Pathological Anatomy performed 3,658 autopsies.[75]

These self-reflexive famine reports share a striking similarity: the authors give precedence to quantity over quality. They viewed starvation as a single disease, not as a set of distinctive pathologies. Conventional medical wisdom on hunger illnesses, drawn from colonial research, dealt almost exclusively with specific deficiencies. As we have seen, beriberi research provides an exemplary case. A group of symptoms were matched to a circumscribed aetiology. Doctors searched for the individual 'causes' of beriberi, pellagra, scurvy and other individual hunger diseases: a lack of protein, sugar, fat, vitamin B/thiamin, riboflavin, or vitamin C.

Studies from the camps and ghettos, the work of those within them, emphatically overturned this view. 'Pioneers of nutritional research have outlined entities of specific deficiency diseases, such as beriberi in the Far East, pellagra in parts of America and Southern Europe, and scurvy in the Polar regions', acknowledged the Danish doctors. Yet these studies did not provide any guidance for their experience in the camps. 'Personally', they wrote, recalling their medical training, 'the authors came to the KZ-camps much better fitted to understand what they did not see: avitaminoses, than to grasp the scope of that which they did see, viz. famine disease'.[76] The Warsaw study specifically eliminated all subjects suffering from individual deficiencies from their observations. From the population in the refugee centre, researchers chose only 'pure cases, without complications (tuberculosis, avitaminoses, diarrhea...)'.[77]

Warsaw doctor Joseph Stein argued for the existence of a 'specific pathological unity', which he named 'famine disease'. Distinct from 'qualitative' dietary diseases, which corresponded to vitamin deficiencies, starvation had its own proper aetiology. 'What interests us here are the troubles caused by quantitative hunger, that is the changes caused by the general absence, or at least a lack, of all the fundamental components of food.'[78] He defined the symptoms of famine disease by emaciation, the disappearance of fats, the decomposition of proteins in the body and the atrophy of internal organs. 'Given that the clinical symptoms offer an absolutely characteristic picture, we can treat the symptoms caused by a prolonged lack of calories as a pathological unity – from the biological, clinical and anatomical point of view – which it is completely justifiable to call by the name "famine disease".'[79]

Starvation was a single disease. Clinicians who treated concentration camp survivors in Switzerland and Denmark concurred with the interned doctors' assessment. Though qualitative deficiencies played a role, and could be identified as distinct pathologies, hunger itself was also a malady. 'The question today, is whether hunger disease should be explained purely quantitatively or qualitatively. Do other factors act in tandem with the absolute decrease in the number of calories...?'[80] The author, studying survivors of Mauthausen, Gusen, Linz and Auschwitz, inclined to define hunger as a unitary disease. 'According to its metabolic-chemical definition, the hunger condition [*Hungerzustand*] begins when the organism begins to deconstruct its own bodily substance.'[81] The Swiss physician identified a series of symptoms ranging from extreme emaciation to slow movement and respiration, apathy and low pulse and temperature. His Danish counterparts concurred: 'Famine disease ... is undoubtedly the most common disease in the world and it presents social and medical problems of far-reaching compass. In spite of this, it is only through the conquests of recent years that knowledge of the pathology of chronic undernutrition has been brought into line with the other advances in medicine...'[82]

Dr Charles Richet, a French nutrition scientist and survivor of the Buchenwald concentration camp, recalled after the war that 'as long as dietary deficiency loomed far away from Europe, we barely worried about it. One knew, without fully believing, that for the disinherited ... the ration barely reached a vital minimum... One lamented that a famine struck Mongolia or Turkestan, but only for good form; for many doctors, dietary deficiency was a formula used to explain ... tuberculosis or typhus.'[83] The Second World War altered this attitude indelibly. Famine, he moralized, killed more people than bombs.

World war brought colonial starvation science into the metropole. This was a turning-point in nutrition science, when hunger became a disease and medical researchers entered the politics of bare life. Beginning in the 1890s, doctors in the colonies developed an experimental medicine specifically concerned with starvation and death. They undertook human experiments characterized by a lack of therapeutic value and selection of subjects in a coercive context. Regimes of bare life crossed from colonial to metropolitan science at a moment when Europe itself became subject to imperial war and occupation. Along this trajectory, nutrition shifted from a chemical-economic equation to a medical pathology, from the management of life to the management of death.

Notes

1. F. Prescott, 'Preface', in E. F. Simonart (ed.), *La Dénutrition de guerre: étude clinique, anatomo-pathologique et thérapeutique* (Brussels, 1947), p. 6.
2. M. Worboys, 'The Discovery of Colonial Malnutrition between the Wars', in D. Arnold (ed.), *Imperial Medicine and Indigenous Societies: Studies in Imperialism* (Manchester, 1988).
3. D. Arnold, 'The "Discovery" of Malnutrition and Diet in Colonial India', *The Indian Economic and Social History Review*, 31(1) (1994): 1–26.
4. On 'bare life', see G. Agamben, 'Homo Sacer: Sovereign Power and Bare Life', in W. Hamacher and D. E. Wellbery (eds), *Meridian: Crossing Aesthetics* [trans. D. Heller-Roazen] (Stanford, CA, 1998).
5. D. Simmons, 'Minimal Frenchmen: Science and Standards of Living, 1840–1960' (University of Chicago Ph.D. thesis, 2004).
6. For an overview of energetic science, see A. Rabinbach, *The Human Motor: Energy, Fatigue and the Origins of Modernity* (Berkeley, CA, 1990). See also K. Carpenter, *Protein and Energy: A Study of Changing Ideas in Nutrition* (Cambridge, 1994), pp. 70–105.
7. F. G. Benedict, *A Study of Prolonged Fasting*, Carnegie Institution of Washington no. 203 (Washington, 1915).
8. David Arnold suggests that prisons were essentially the only site of nutrition research in India through the early twentieth century, and provided state officials with previously unknown data on regional eating habits. See D. Arnold, *Colonizing the Body: State Medicine and Epidemic Disease in Nineteenth-century India* (Berkeley, CA, 1993), p. 111.
9. W. Digby, *The Famine Campaign in Southern India (Madras and Bombay Provinces and Province of Mysore) 1876–1878*, 2 vols, Vol. 2 (London, 1878), p. 175.
10. D. Haynes, 'The Social Production of Metropolitan Expertise in Tropical Diseases: The Imperial State, Colonial Service and the Tropical Diseases Research Fund', *Science Technology and Society* 4(2): 205–38, especially pp. 206–8.
11. Arnold, *Colonizing the Body*, p. 99.
12. Arnold points to this precedent to establish a specifically colonial Indian dietary science. Arnold, 'The "Discovery" of Malnutrition', p. 6. See also M. Davis,

Late Victorian Holocausts: El Niño Famines and the Making of the Third World (London, 2002), pp. 23–116.

13. 'Temple, Sir Richard, Bart.' in *Encyclopaedia Britannica* (Cambridge, 1911), p. 601.

14. Digby, *The Famine Campaign in Southern India*, p. 172.

15. Digby, *The Famine Campaign in Southern India*.

16. Digby, *The Famine Campaign in Southern India*, p.179.

17. Temple, of course, was not the only author to express racial opinions about diet. A longstanding literature, dating from the eighteenth century, classified races and nations according to food consumption. English meat-eaters, for example, appeared favourably in contrast to feeble Indian vegetarians and Irishmen with sluggish 'potato blood'. (On 'potato blood' see F. Gregory, 'Scientific Materialism in Nineteenth-Century Germany', in R.. Cohen, E. Hiebert and E. Mendelsohn (eds), *Studies in the History of Modern Science* (Dordecht, 1977), p. 90.)

18. Digby, *The Famine Campaign in Southern India*, p. 180.

19. Digby, *The Famine Campaign in Southern India*, p. 173.

20. Comparable human experiments with contagious disease can easily be found in contemporary tropical medicine, most famously in Walter Reid's yellow fever trials in Cuba.

21. K. Carpenter, *Beriberi, White Rice and Vitamin B: A Disease, A Cause and A Cure* (Berkeley, CA, 2000), p. 61.

22. Carpenter, *Beriberi, White Rice and Vitamin B*, pp. 10–12.

23. W. Fletcher, 'Rice and Beri-beri: Preliminary Report on an Experiment Conducted at the Kuala Lumpur Lunatic Asylum', *The Lancet* 69(4374) (1907): 1776.

24. Fletcher, 'Rice and Beri-beri'.

25. Carpenter, *Beriberi, White Rice and Vitamin B*, pp. 66–70.

26. H. Fraser and A. T. Stanton, 'An Inquiry Concerning the Etiology of Beri-beri: A Preliminary Communication', *The Lancet* 173(4459) (1909).

27. K. A. Campbell, 'Knots in the Fabric: Richard Pearson Strong and the Bilibid Prison Vaccine Trials, 1905–1906', *Bulletin of the History of Medicine* 68(4) (1994).

28. B. C. Crowell and R. P. Strong, 'The Etiology of Beriberi', *Philippine Journal of Science* 7B (1912): 291. Strikingly, this report was used in the Nuremberg medical trials, apparently as evidence for a pre-existing protocol that required doctors to obtain consent from human experimental subjects. B. C. Crowell and R. P. Strong, 'Extract from an article concerning medical experiments conducted on prisoners in the Philippines', in Karl Brandt *et al.* (eds), *Trial Name: NMT 01. Medical Case – USA v.* (Cambridge, 1947).

29. Carpenter, *Beriberi, White Rice and Vitamin B*, p. 91.

30. Medical Officer Hamilton Wright compared the dietary habits of Tamil, Chinese and Malay people in Malaya in 1902; in 1912 the Calcutta physiology professor D. McCay unfavourably contrasted Bengali diet and physique to that of Sikhs and Rajputs. See respectively: Arnold, 'The "Discovery" of Malnutrition ', p. 12; and Carpenter, *Beriberi, White Rice and Vitamin B*, p. 66.
31. Carpenter, *Beriberi, White Rice and Vitamin B*.
32. R. H. Kampmeier, 'John B. Youmans (1893–1979) Biographical Sketch', in W. J. Darby and T. H. Jukes (eds), *Founders of Nutrition Science: Biographical Articles from The Journal of Nutrition* (Bethesda, MD, 1992), p. 1139.
33. W. R. Aykroyd, I. Alexa and J. Nitzulescu, 'Study of the Alimentation of Peasants in the Pellagra Area of Moldavia (Romania)', in K. Carpenter (ed.), *Pellagra* (Stroudsburg, PA, 1981), pp. 31–46.
34. Pellagra Commission of the State of Illinois, 'General Summary, Report of the Pellagra Commission of the State of Illinois', ibid., pp. 129–30.
35. J. Goldberger and G. A. Wheeler, 'Experimental Pellagra Brought about by a Restricted Diet', ibid., pp. 131–4.
36. H. E. Wardener and B. Lennox, 'Cerebral Beriberi (Wernicke's Encephalopathy): Review of 52 Cases in a Singapore Prisoner-of-war Hospital', *The Lancet* 249(6436) (1947): 11.
37. R. C. Burgess, 'Deficiency Diseases in Prisoners-of-war at Changi, Singapore, February 1942 to August 1945', *The Lancet* 248(6421) (1946): 416. Burgess gives the figure of 52,000 troops; Wardener counts 32,000 British soldiers.
38. Wardener and Lennox, 'Cerebral Beriberi', p. 11.
39. D. A. Smith and M. A. Woodruff, *Deficiency Diseases in Japanese Prison Camps, Medical Research Council Special Report Series no. 274* (London, 1951), p. 169.
40. Smith and Woodruff, *Deficiency Diseases in Japanese Prison Camps*.
41. Smith and Woodruff, *Deficiency Diseases in Japanese Prison Camps*, p. 173.
42. Another striking example of the transfer of colonial treatments for starvation to European subjects may be found in British troops' application of the "Bengal Famine Diet" to liberated prisoners at the Bergen-Belsen concentration camp. This mixture of rice and sugar was originally given as relief for starving Bengalis during the Famine of 1943–1944. See Captain A. Pares, Adjutant of the 113th Light Anti-Aircraft Regiment, *The Story of Belsen* (London, c.1945), p. 8. Frank Trentmann argues in this volume that wartime food shortages in Europe also instilled a sense of global solidarity with far-off famine victims suffering. See Chapter 14, p. 262.
43. E. A. Vallejo, 'Sur le traitement des oedèmes par déséquilibre alimentaire par la suralimentation lactée', *Bulletins et mémoires de la Société médicale des hôpitaux de Paris* 58(17-18-19) (1942). See also E. Garcia-Albea Ristol, 'Las neuropatías carenciales en Madrid durante la Guerra Civil', *Neurología (Ars medica, Barcelona)* 14(3) (1999).

44. V. G. Valaoras, 'Some Effects of Famine on the Population of Greece', *Milbank Memorial Fund Quarterly* 24(3) (1946): 215–16.

45. *Malnutrition and Starvation in Western Netherlands: September 1944–July 1945*, 2 vols, Vol. 1 (The Hague, 1948), p. 24.

46. P. Govaerts, 'Pathogénie de l'oedème de famine', in E. J. Bigwood (ed.), *Enseignements de la guerre 1939–1945 dans le domaine de la nutrition, médécine et biologie* (Paris, 1947); P.-A. Bastenie, 'Pathologie de guerre et dénutrition à Bruxelles', in *Enseignements de la guerre 1939–1945 dans le domaine de la nutrition*, pp. 231–46; P. Durand, 'Comment, pourquoi et chez qui sont apparus les oedèmes par carence alimentaire?', *La Presse Médicale* 18–19 (1942): 233–4; L. Justin-Besançon, 'L'Ostéopathie de famine', *Paris médical* 32(33) (1942): 259–63; G. Laroche, E. Bompard, and J. Trémolières, 'A propos de huit cas d'oedèmes par carence alimentaire', *Bulletins et mémoires de la Société médicale des hôpitaux de Paris* 57(23) (1941): 631–5; Roudinesco and Imbona, 'A propos d'un cas d'œdème par carence alimentaire', *Bulletins et mémoires de la Société médicale des hôpitaux de Paris* 58(12-13-14-15-16) (1942): 155–7.

47. F. Simonart (ed.), *La Dénutrition de guerre, étude clinique, anatomo-pathologique et thérapeutique*, p. 14.

48. J. Stein and H. Fenigsten, 'Anatomie pathologique de la Maladie de Famine', in E. Apfelbaum (ed.), *Maladie de Famine: Recherches cliniques sur la famine exécutées dans le ghetto de Varsovie en 1942* (Warsaw, 1946), p. 24.

49. A. Schittenhelm and H. Schlecht, 'Ueber Oedemkrankheit mit hypotonischer Brachykardie', *Klinische Wochenschrift (Berlin)* 55 (1918): 1138.

50. C. Salzmann, 'Historisches zur Hungerkrankheit', in A. Hottinger *et al.* (eds), *Hungerkrankheit, Hungerödem, Hunger tuberculose* (Basle, 1948), p. 10.

51. The nutrition survey itself has a history going back to the statistical work of Frédéric Le Play and his disciple Ernst Engel in the mid-nineteenth century.

52. Carpenter, *Protein and Energy*, p. 137.

53. M.-L. Démeusy, *Thèse pour le Doctorat en Médecine (Diplôme d'Etat). Etude des aliments de complément à la ration du temps de guerre*, ed. Faculté de médecine de Paris (Paris, 1943), p. 16.

54. M. Bachet, *Thèse pour le Doctorat en Médecine (Diplôme d'Etat). Etude des troubles causés par la dénutrition dans un asile d'aliénés* (Travail du service du Docteur Baruk, à la Maison de Charenton, et de l'Institut de Recherches d'Hygiène dirigé par le Professeur agrégé H. Gounelle) (Paris, 1943), p. 23.

55. Direction départementale du Ravitaillement Général du Puy de Dôme, 'Réunion plénière des Chefs de District' 18 December 1943. Archives Nationales F23 410.

56. A. Grynberg, *Les camps de la honte: les internés juifs des camps français, 1939–1944, Sciences humaines et sociales* (Paris, 1999), p. 151.

57. J. Weill, *Contribution à l'histoire des camps d'internement dans l'Anti-France, Etudes et Monographies* (Paris, 1946), p. 37.

58. Weill, *Contribution à l'histoire des camps d'internement dans l'Anti-France*, pp. 55, 65, 38.
59. Weill, *Contribution à l'histoire des camps d'internement dans l'Anti-France*, pp. 55, 57.
60. Weill, *Contribution à l'histoire des camps d'internement dans l'Anti-France*, p. 58.
61. Weill, *Contribution à l'histoire des camps d'internement dans l'Anti-France*, p. 123.
62. Weill, *Contribution à l'histoire des camps d'internement dans l'Anti-France*, p. 60.
63. P. Levi, *Survival in Auschwitz* (New York, 1996).
64. L. Adelsberger, 'Medical Observations in Auschwitz Concentration Camp', *The Lancet* 247(6392) (1946): 318. P. Helwig-Larsen *et al.*, 'Famine Disease in German Concentration Camps, Complications and Sequels', *Acta Medica Scandinavica* 144(274) (1952): 13.
65. I. Milejkowski, 'Introduction', in Apfelbaum (ed.), *Maladie de Famine*, pp. 9–10.
66. Milejkowski, 'Introduction', p. 11.
67. H. C. Gerlach, *Krieg, Ernährung, Völkermord : Forschungen zur deutschen Vernichtungspolitik im Zweiten Weltkrieg* (Hamburg, 1998).
68. Agamben, *Homo Sacer*, p. 159.
69. L. Adelsberger, *Auschwitz: A Doctor's Story*, ed M. Yalom, trans. S. Ray, *Women's Life Writings from Around the World* (Boston, 1995), p. 141. Historical footnote by A. J. Slavin.
70. Adelsberger, 'Medical Observations in Auschwitz', p. 317.
71. Adelsberger, 'Medical Observations in Auschwitz', p. 318.
72. Adelsberger, *Auschwitz: A Doctor's Story*, p. 96.
73. Adelsberger, 'Medical Observations in Auschwitz', p. 318.
74. E. Apfelbaum (ed.), *Maladie de Famine*, p. 16.
75. Stein and Fenigsten, 'Anatomie pathologique de la Maladie de Famine', p. 33.
76. Helwig-Larsen *et al.*, 'Famine Disease in German Concentration Camps', p. 73.
77. Apfelbaum (ed.), *Maladie de Famine*, p. 16.
78. Stein and Fenigsten, 'Anatomie pathologique de la Maladie de Famine', p. 23.
79. Stein and Fenigsten, 'Anatomie pathologique de la Maladie de Famine', p. 25.
80. Salzmann, 'Historisches zur Hungerkrankheit', p. 10.
81. Salzmann, 'Historisches zur Hungerkrankheit', p. 11.
82. Helwig-Larsen *et al.*, 'Famine Disease in German Concentration Camps', p. 72.
83. C. Richet, *Leçon inaugurale, Chaire des Problèmes Alimentaires* (Corbeil, 1947), p. 8.

–11–

Illusions of Global Governance
Transnational Agribusiness inside the UN System
Christian Gerlach

A series of famines swept the world from West Africa to Bangladesh after 1972, linked to a shortage of grain in world markets and to tripling grain prices that seemed to herald a new age of scarcity. In retrospect, this World Food Crisis – as it was called then – can be connected not only with the sudden appearance of the USSR as a large-scale buyer in world markets, or to an El Niño event, or to the enlargement of a protectionist European Economic Community. It has also to be seen against the background of the crisis of the international monetary system in the early 1970s, the global economic crisis of 1973–5 and intensified international economic competition. Moreover, the crisis resulted from the abrupt commercialization of the world grain trade by exporters and a change in trade patterns, with the socialist and the non-industrialized countries newly emerging as massive importers of grain, suddenly generating novel conceptions of 'food security' and initiating a feverish quest to implement them. Given the huge anticipated import requirements of Asian, African and Latin American countries for basic foodstuffs for which they would hardly be able to pay, filling economic niches such as the supply of fruit and vegetables for export would not eliminate the urgent need to step up the production of staple foods.[1]

The crisis also served as a catalyst for the breakthrough of new concepts in international development policies. Instead of industry and infrastructure, as in older approaches, the new policies put more emphasis on agriculture in general and called not merely for production-oriented 'green revolution' concepts (which favoured large-scale production) but identified the rural poor – and above all small peasants, more than landless workers, tenants and share-croppers – as the key to both the hunger problem and staple food production. International organizations, agencies in industrial nations, authorities in non-industrialized countries and non-governmental organizations (NGOs) set out to 'help' the rural poor in the 'Third World' by modernizing their production. Subsistence farmers were to produce for the market and to use modern inputs such as fertilizer, high-yielding seeds, pesticides, irrigation and machinery. Up to 100 million self-sufficient families, or one-fifth of the planet's population, were thus expected to be integrated into national markets and national systems of commercial exportation, thereby conveniently enlarging the monetized world economy: a piece of true 'globalization'.

If the rural poor in non-industrialized countries were to be integrated into market relations, this, of course, did not only concern governments and international organizations. Massive business interests were involved as well. Who was to expand capitalist structures if not private companies? In the evolving economic crisis of the matured economies since 1973, for many of them it proved all the more important to tap new markets. No organization is better suited to demonstrate what came out of such efforts than the Industry-Cooperative Programme (ICP) of the Food and Agriculture Organization of the UN (FAO). Founded in 1966 and dissolved in 1978, the ICP was described by FAO Director-General Boerma as a 'joint venture' between transnational agribusiness corporations and the UN. Members explicitly had to be *Multis* operating internationally.[2] ICP has so far remained unique – the only institutional business representation within the UN system. For the transnationals, this was an ideal strategic base to launch expansive projects from, in close contact with the development community. The chapter that follows analyses the structures and activities of ICP, the purposes of its member companies, and their cooperation with the UN, and tries to evaluate ICP's influence, and to find indications of how far massive international business expansion in the field of staple food (mainly grain) production in non-industrialized countries materialized. Moreover, the case of ICP raises questions about the chances for 'global governance', which are discussed at the end.

Structures and Objectives

ICP was founded in the context of FAO's changing orientation from data collection and technical advice into a development organization under Director-General Binay Ranjan Sen (1956–67). Several new investment-focused programmes were introduced in the mid-1960s, also including the FAO/IBRD Cooperative Programme; under Sen's successor Boerma (1967–75), who was even more favourable to investment-oriented field programmes, the FAO/Bankers Programme and the FAO Investment Centre followed swiftly. All this served to give FAO's policies more thrust and make them more operational through direct links to sources of economic power and financial resources when most of its projects were financed through the UN Development Programme. Sen had explored possibilities for cooperation with industries in meetings with several executives on trips to Chicago, New York, Paris, and Rome between April and June 1965. In 1966, 18 companies, mostly from the USA and Britain, formed the nucleus of ICP.[3]

In the mid-1970s, ICP membership comprised about 100 corporations from nearly 20 countries. Among them were prominent names such as Hoechst, Bayer, BASF, Ciba-Geigy, Sandoz, International Minerals and Chemicals (IMC), Dow Chemical,

Pfizer, Imperial Chemicals Inc. (ICI), BP, Royal Dutch/Shell (for pesticides and/or fertilizer, and increasingly for seeds), Massey-Ferguson, Caterpillar, John Deere, Ford, Fiat, Voest-Alpine (tractors and machinery), Cargill (as the only major grain trader, also interested in seeds), Mitsubishi, Mitsui, Ralston Purina, Del Monte, Castle & Cook, Pillsbury, Heinz, Nestlé, and Unilever.[4] ICP had a small secretariat at the FAO in Rome, managed by an Executive Secretary. While administratively placed in the Development Department of FAO, the programme was financed by membership fees. Its elected Chairman was a corporate leader who served for two years.[5] General Committee meetings in which senior executives represented their companies were held twice a year. Working groups that met irregularly but more frequently were established for pesticides (the biggest section, uniting companies with 90 per cent of world production), seeds industry development, farm mechanization training, agricultural by-products, protein foods, dairy production, meat, forestry and fisheries, and on the use of plastics in agriculture.[6]

What FAO hoped to get from ICP was to increase the flow of capital into 'Third World' agriculture, and the spread of technology, expertise, training and advice at all levels from local practice to national government.[7] Transnational companies, above all, through ICP wanted to gain access to data and knowledge about planned projects from FAO and non-industrialized countries, about agricultural production data, statistics, trade, policies and legislation in various countries. In part, they also used information from FAO's Country Representatives in the field as a channel. From March 1970 to March 1971, member companies sent 950 requests for a total of 2,400 documents, and brought 250 emissaries to FAO headquarters.[8] Likewise firms used FAO as a gateway to the entire UN system to obtain similarly strategic information. (In 1972, ICP's official name was changed to 'Programme of Agro-Allied Industries with FAO and other UN organizations'). Plans to go beyond 'the confines of agriculture, forestry and fisheries', however, failed. FAO also served corporations for public relations, for acquiring a reputation as respected partners in development, and for improving the international investment climate. Moreover, they aimed at 'solid contacts' with government authorities in non-industrialized countries. The preferred result, of course, was to generate specific business opportunities, ideally with governments or international organizations taking over financial risks and preventing undesirable nationalizations.[9]

When going south, it was generally not unusual that firms cooperated with national or international development agencies, seeking subsidies for the company's business, as a historian of Mitsui, the Japanese general trading and production firm, pointed out in 1973: 'In carrying out overseas projects it is often necessary to work through international organizations such as World Bank, The International Development Association, Asian Development Bank or Private Investment Company for Asia, as well as through national development banks and regional associations.' Negotiations required local knowledge, 'sophistication and infinite tact'.[10]

The Power of the Multis

Critical scholars have described ICP as an ideal avenue by which multinationals could enter and manipulate the UN system and thereby penetrate non-industrialized countries. This suggested that transnational companies had gained massive power and substantial freedom of manoeuvre through the organization.[11] 'It is, of course, the type of organization which gets a bad press from untidy young ladies with their heads full of sociology', as a former ICP Chairman suggested.[12] Indeed, several facts suggest that ICP had substantial influence on development policies in the UN system in the 1970s. A number of business-friendly resolutions at the crucial UN World Food Conference in November 1974 came into being as a result of direct input by some of the 69 corporate leaders who – operating from a couple of suites in a hotel opposite the conference venue – were allowed to participate via ICP. This included the resolutions on pesticides, fertilizer, nutrition, the combating of trypanosomiasis in Africa, and the World Soil Charter.[13] Susan George has even sarcastically argued that ICP could be regarded as the biggest delegation to the World Food Conference, ahead of the USA, although the names of ICP members at the event miraculously vanished from the official list of individual participants between the provisional and the final version.[14] In addition, ICP companies at least planned to exercise a discreet influence beforehand on the positions of their home governments at that conference.[15] At a meeting in Toronto in preparation for the conference, about 180 corporate leaders (not all involved in ICP) discussed ways to increase business in non-industrialized countries that could be related to the World Food Crisis. Nonetheless, papers remained at a quite unspecific level, and no substantial steps toward action concerning 'subsistence level farmers' were demonstrated.[16] ICP also had an official representation at a conference of the UN Industrial Development Organization (UNIDO) in Lima in March 1975.[17]

Moreover, in 1970 Paul Cornelsen, Vice President of Ralston Purina and then Chairman of ICP, launched the election of the US fisheries expert Roy Jackson to the post of Deputy Director-General of FAO (1972–7), which took place in late 1971. Private business thus managed to get the second highest official in the biggest UN sub-organization appointed. In office, however, Jackson seems to have been 'largely left aside' by FAO leaders.[18] From FAO, ICP managed to establish cooperative agreements with other UN sub-organizations and regularly to obtain confidential information on planned projects.[19] It was because of protests against multinationals – particularly pesticide producers successfully penetrating the UN – issued by scientists, NGOs and the International Confederation of Free Trade Unions, that the FAO Director-General Edouard Saouma dismantled ICP in 1978. FAO's official administrative history, published in 1981, concealed the fact that ICP, a political embarrassment, had ever existed.[20]

Unexpected Limits to Growth: Inner Criticism and Conflicts

Arguably FAO's US$2 billion 40-year project to 'control' trypanosomiasis with the help of DDT and other chemicals over an area of 7 million square kilometres in Africa (in order to develop an export-oriented cattle industry for the European market) and the contribution to the 'development' of Brazil's Amazonian region can be regarded as ICP's biggest commercial successes.[21] However, many other big projects, such as making Sudan (among other regions, the province of Darfur) the granary and meat supplier for Arabia, or in the field of protein-enriched foods for the poor of the South (especially the 'protein from mineral oil' projects, the darling of international capital) largely did not materialize.[22] Even those that did were usually not related to staple food production, although ICP often spoke of and declared their profound interest in supporting the rural poor. Very few companies actually educated their employees about the world food problem and the specific repercussions it could have for the corporation's work, as Caterpillar did.[23] Projects such as 'tractors for Africa' remained unrealistic. '[M]arket economics are often a source of frustration', noted ICP's Deputy Executive Secretary with regard to the development of adjusted technologies for small farmers.[24] Generally, the problem of small-scale credit and the indebtedness of small agricultural producers who invested in modern input packages could rarely be overcome. Rather, companies focused on food processing and the marketing of higher-priced processed foods, including dairy products for urban consumers, and on capital-intensive government development projects concerning plantations (while disposing of many estates a company itself owned), forestry and fisheries. And they preferred minority equities, consultancy contracts or doing feasibility studies as against massive investments, which were seen as risky in a time of expropriations, nationalizations and anti-multinational attitudes.[25] Industry was 'increasingly convinced that its major role is in the transfer of planning and management skills, technology, and of marketing and distribution systems', as ICP's Executive Secretary put it. Managerial expertise was flamboyantly presented as the 'scarcest input' that industry had to offer.[26]

Different industries could arguably assess the successes or failures of ICP in very different ways. Aside from the food-processing industry, which is of less interest here, pesticide-producing corporations were clearly the most active, using ICP as a powerful public relations instrument. They also urged UN organizations not to approve documents unfavourable for the chemical industry, and Swiss firms championed conspiratorial efforts to secure the position of ICP against critics within the UN and to silence critical journalists.[27] By contrast, the activities of the fertilizer companies through ICP were very limited (owing to the older forms of cooperation with FAO of a dozen major companies that were already in existence), those of the producers of agricultural machinery remained mostly restricted to advertising and promotional films, and the seeds producers started to organize effectively within the programme only in 1976. With one exception, the secretive major grain-trading firms did not even join ICP. In addition to showing films such as Caterpillar's 'Lands of Promise, Fields of Hope', Hoechst's 'Food for Six Billion', and Ciba Geigy's 'Beacon in the Night' (on fighting the rice stem borer in Indonesia), the main activity of members in direct cooperation with ICP seems to have consisted of the organization of workshops and conferences, such as the seminars 'on the safe and effective use' of pesticides with FAO in Sao Paulo, Colombo and Nairobi.[28]

For a couple of years, companies were ready to treat ICP like a subsidiary that first needed to get established before it began to pay off. Then they started to complain. Records show, aside from bickering about payment of the modest membership fees (US$3,000 annually at first; later US$5,000), a substantial fluctuation in membership. For example, from 1970 to March 1972, twenty-nine companies terminated their membership and twenty-six joined. From February 1976 to October 1977, nineteen firms left the organization (nine from the United States), among them Cadbury, Del Monte, General Mills, Heinz, Mitsui, Pfizer, Renault and Sumitomo Trading, while nine were added to the membership list (only two from the United States).[29] The relative lack of interest in collaboration of US companies was a constant concern. Except in the initial years, they represented only 20–30 per cent of the participants while Western European firms dominated.[30] Opening an office in New York in 1973 under Walter Simons did not help much. All the Chairmen of ICP after 1972 were Europeans.

Anyone who had expected a vast array of business projects emerging directly from ICP's activities was bitterly disappointed. 'ICP is not an important factor in social and economic development in developing countries, nor does business view ICP as an effective link with developing countries', a paper by ICP's secretariat gloomily stated.[31] ICP's consulting firm concluded: 'Majority of ICP members discouraged and disillusioned. Most members have a faint idea of what ICP is doing. ICP has failed to influence FAO, UN agencies or individual governments.' When taking over ICP's chairmanship in 1972, Anthony Hugill said that members were always asked, 'what on earth you are doing in the Programme, what is it doing for your shareholders, what use is it'; this 'shouldn't go on for ever'.[32] His predecessor Umbricht judged that ICP had not 'made the grade' especially because FAO officials lacked the interest or were too business-sceptical to approach ICP for advice, and ICP had failed to serve as a consultant for UNIDO, WHO, and the 'World Bank'. Criticism that meetings and reports were filled with idle talk was widespread. Only part of the members participated in a committed way; dynamics rested on the personal dedication of two dozen business leaders.[33] On the other hand, complaints tended to target group (plenum) activities, which needed to be more 'specific', more than criticizing ICP as a channel available to individual companies.

Such objections also applied to ICP's country missions, planned since 1967 but finally introduced only five years later in order to shift the programme's focus toward direct business investment. Between 1972 and 1977, ICP teams including two to four high-level corporate representatives, and some staff were sent to ten countries: Dahomey (Benin), Venezuela, Liberia, Sri Lanka, Brazil (twice), Cameroon, Colombia, Pakistan, Tanzania, and Senegal. (A dozen more trips were organized by the Working Groups.) However, expeditions spent usually only two or three weeks in the country, reviewing government projects and broader long-term planning as well as making their own proposals for projects. Preparations were often flimsy, the groups lacked local and sometimes agricultural expertise, and their reports, though listing potential projects, remained thin. Above all, hardly any projects involving transnational companies ever resulted from them, a fact criticized not only by ICP members but also by governments of the countries visited.[34] The country missions were a short-lived phenomenon: there was only one after 1974.[35] Unlike similar studies by the US-based Agribusiness Council sketched below, ICP's missions reflected Western European capital interests, focusing on Africa and Latin America, and visited, with two exceptions, small or medium-sized countries without large potential markets. This was to explore and open up smaller, otherwise less interesting economies – ironically, in particular by gaining influence over government planning. Mostly the countries who expressed interest in such visits belonged to that group. FAO also tried to exercise some influence over the missions.[36] But given a strictly national project framework in host countries, this did not apparently lead to glorious business prospects. Outside the country missions, the fact that existing projects proposed by governments or the FAO were tailored for public funding cooled down corporate enthusiasm and led to a reversal – ICP member companies were asked to bring forward their own project ideas. From March 1970 to March 1971, however, they initiated no more than 18 of them.[37]

Even three affirmative studies between 1970 and 1976 came to similar results: the enthusiasm of member corporations for ICP was strictly limited. Many even stated that ICP had failed in the very fields that were found most important after directly generating business opportunities: information sought was often not available or considered of low value when it arrived, it came upon request only, and contacts and information channels into the UN system beyond the FAO left much to be desired, too.[38]

Separate Ways: The Agribusiness Council

World organizations do not operate in a nation-free vacuum. Among the reasons for the failure of international cooperation in ICP was an excessive nationalism in the hegemonic capitalist country that also played major roles in the international grain trade and international development policies. Corporations from the United States preferred to organize in a separate, private national organization to increase private investment in the agribusiness sector in non-industrialized countries: the Agribusiness Council, still existing today. When it was founded on the initiative of the US Department of Commerce one year after ICP, in 1967, this took place under already changed conditions in the international agricultural economy. On the one hand, the Indian food crisis of 1965–7, which seemed to offer new opportunities for grain exports as well as input industries, given that the 'green revolution' was quite suddenly to be expanded to Asia, had not become fully manifest before ICP had been founded, and certainly not when it was initiated, in the spring of 1965. Second, the recession of 1966–7 in several industrial nations also suggested benefits in finding new markets and possibly also new investment opportunities beyond the capitalist North.[39] In this situation, the organization was formed 'by a group of business, academic, foundation, and government leaders' under the auspices of US President Johnson,[40] demonstrating the cooperation between corporations and state and research institutions.

Aside from US agribusiness firms, membership also comprised non-profit groups, international organizations and individuals. In 1970, the Agribusiness Council had about seventy member companies (fifty-nine in 1975). There was only a small overlap of nine firms that were also members of ICP.[41] The Agribusiness Council, cooperating with the US Agency for International Development, explored the investment climate in non-industrialized countries, identified general sectors favourable for agribusiness investment, and, not unlike ICP, organized country explorations, resulting in recommendations for companies and governments, based on project ideas from both sides. By contrast with ICP, the Agribusiness Council expeditions focused, and still seem to focus, on Asia, in accord with US capital interests.[42] In the case of foreign requests for technical and managerial assistance, the Agribusiness Council was approached by US government officials asking for statements on the 'suitability' of pursuing certain projects.[43]

In the early 1970s, the Nixon administration encouraged corporations to expand their exports in order to improve the US balance of trade. At the same time, there were hot debates about the costs and benefits, from a national point of view, of private capital investments by US companies abroad. Government officials acknowledged that they had neglected ICP as a way to stimulate US-based business; yet ICP's wooing remained of little avail. On the other hand, facing stronger international competition, corporations complained about Washington because of a lack of federal support for their operations, citing Western European governments allegedly doing more for their business clientele.[44] In February 1974, addressing links between the world food problem and international investment, the Agribusiness Council organized a conference of corporate leaders, researchers, development experts and foundation officials, 'Science and Agribusiness in the Seventies'. However, of the more than 150 participants meeting in London, only forty-five came from the United States, among them no more than thirteen corporate executives.[45] This indicates that the 'problem' lay not only with the government. Compared with their Western European counterparts, US companies themselves also felt less inclined to use international fora or channels for their business expansion.

The FAO/Bankers Programme

FAO's separate unit for cooperation with private financial institutions shows parallels to ICP.[46] The oil boom that started in 1973 resulted in huge sums of money not invested by OPEC countries domestically, but deposited with Western European and US commercial banks. Given a lack of promising investment opportunities in the sluggish industrial economies, many of these petrodollars flowed as credits to non-industrialized countries. Increasingly these were commercial short-term credits that would start to cause national debt crises in the late 1970s. Much of the recovery of industrial economies between 1975 and 1979 can actually be ascribed to exports financed by such loans.[47]

Some scholars have argued that this also led to a 'discovery' of smallholders as recipients of credits by commercial banks. For example, Continental Bank organized a conference in Chicago in 1974 'Feeding the World's Hungry: A Challenge to Business'.[48] Yet there is little evidence for the direct involvement of multinational private credit institutions in any corresponding financial operations. In fact, the FAO/Private Banks Programme had been established in 1970 to facilitate investment in non-industrialized countries for commercial banks. However, the number of private banks within that programme (nine in 1973, seventeen as of 1978 – though some were prominent)[49] and the scope of the corresponding activities remained so limited that, from 1972 on, national development banks and international financial institutions were admitted, too, and the programme's orientation (now it was called the FAO/Bankers Programme) switched toward the operations of the public institutions. Reputed as it was to be more project-oriented than the ICP, between 1975 and 1977 eight projects worth US$163 million were implemented through the Programme. Nevertheless, most of them failed to reach small 'Third World' staple food producers.[50] 'If ICP can identify a project, the Bankers Programme can finance it', a representative of Barclays Bank was quoted as saying.[51] In reality, again, little of this materialized directly.

Still, the wider picture is a different story. To analyse the financial streams in the economic upheaval of the 1970s would go beyond this short study. Yet, for example, private banks played a decisive role in financing the private grain-trading companies that needed enormous short-term credits, lacking – family businesses as they were – the financial assets to cover their enormous transactions.[52] In any case, private credits to non-industrialized countries were massive. About half the US$35 billion balance of payments deficits of non-oil-exporting countries in 1975 were financed by private banks.[53] Much of it concentrated on a small number of Latin American and Asian countries, but the share of others, including African countries, invested mostly in public institutions, was still substantial, and financing rural development programmes was among the purposes of such loans. The FAO/Bankers Programme facilitated some of the cooperation between financial institutions in industrial and those in non-industrialized countries.

Conclusion

Among the core advantages corporations saw in their ICP participation were access to information and data from the UN, contacts with other UN agencies, and gaining credibility thanks to the ability to operate under the UN umbrella. The discontinuation of ICP announced in the autumn of 1977 hit collaborating corporate leaders hard as they saw their hopes betrayed. For long they had realized threats to their interests in the shape of UN enquiries into multinationals concerning other activities; but apparently ICP was thought to be a less vulnerable bastion. In fact, in these examinations ICP had been confidently presented as a forward-looking model for serious and mutually fruitful cooperation with the UN on a larger scale.[54] In 1978, ICP was terminated but replaced by the Industry Council for Development (ICD) with some of the old ICP staff; yet the attempt to make ICD part of the UN Development Programme (UNDP) failed. Though housed in their New York headquarters, ICD was only unofficially associated with UNDP and hence less attractive (and less focused on agriculture). Only thirty-two of ICP's former 100 member companies joined. Swiss corporate leaders judged that after the 'ICP debacle', 'not much positive will come out of [ICD]'.[55] ICD's star waned in the early 1980s.

Despite the benefits already discussed, the ICP, supposed to work like a catalyst, yielded few tangible results, which also prompted criticism by the FAO.[56] More importantly, an even smaller proportion of those projects addressed the production or consumption of staple foods in non-industrialized countries. Firms avoided risks and still preferred large markets, Western European capital interests prevailed, and conflicts between UN impartiality, very partial business interests, and national policies hampered the programme. Organizational deficiencies added to the difficulties. Ironically, companies chose, and got caught in, the usual bureaucratic development framework ('the style of business and bureaucracy are basically incompatible', as an ICP evaluation complained), stressing the necessity to collaborate with governments in order to influence their development planning: following the project approach, efforts remained confined to national boundaries, which rendered undertakings in smaller states economically unprofitable.[57] That small farmers in the affected countries lacked credit was a hurdle never quite overcome. And companies in the 1970s, while disinvesting from some of their large estates, preferred to be active in the form of management contracts and feasibility and pre-investment studies, or to engage in the more lucrative business of food processing.[58] Thereby precisely reinforcing existing mechanisms that lacked practicability, agribusiness mostly did not infuse the practical capitalist spirit FAO had hoped for into staple food production, at least not through ICP. Direct capital investment in input industries in countries of the South remained low, while ICP as a marketing channel helped exports of agrochemicals (more than machinery and even seeds) grow. Not surprisingly, often corporate cost–profit and market size considerations were incompatible with development projects, let alone social concerns.

The organizational approach chosen here may create the impression that plans for getting inputs, goods and capital into the staple food sector of non-industrialized countries in substantial amounts failed miserably. A closer look at the development in different industries would uncover a more differentiated, but not an entirely different picture. Transnational agribusiness did not conquer the countryside of the 'Third World' in the 1970s, but did play a role in the market integration of 'Third World' subsistence farmers and staple food production, yet in other ways than development experts planned, far from everywhere, yet still preferably utilizing public funding.

It comes as no surprise that the international capitalist system cannot solve the problems of inequality and world hunger. Nor is it stunning that FAO supported capitalist business. In fact, the preamble of FAO's 1945 constitution – visible to every employee of the organization as it hangs in the entrance hall of the headquarters in Rome – requires it to engage in 'contributing to an expanding world economy', implying capitalist expansion in what has been one of the most government-regulated sectors of the economy of most nations; and the organization has ever since been geared towards that goal.[59] What is amazing, though, are the difficulties, even the partial inability, of FAO and transnational companies in the 1970s to spread capitalism. A market integration of small farms in Asia and Africa as massive as had been envisioned was beyond their reach. The spread of technology remained limited.

The 'world food crisis' of the early 1970s was a prime example of an emergency of a perceived global scope that required an international response, as identified by proponents of 'global governance' theories. The crisis actually did lead to the emergence of a number of new global bodies in the field (such as the International Fund for Agricultural Development, the World Food Council, and the Consultative Group on Food Production and Investment; the two latter were dissolved in 1996 and 1979, respectively), and it transformed FAO, and not only because of the competition that that organization felt threatened by. Yet these institutional responses and the adopted policies can be viewed as ineffective acts in the face of mighty economic transformations in the world food system.[60] They belong in the context of a more general growth of intergovernmental organizations in the 1970s that has been linked to the rise of multinational companies and closer international economic ties,[61] and, of course, economic crises.

Blame for the failure of ICP – if that term is admitted[62] – would in case of doubt probably be put on the FAO. Indeed, criticism of the Director of the programme, Marcel Latour, an FAO career functionary, by member companies was widespread until he was sacked in 1972 and not replaced. The fact that ICP remained so poorly managed and amateurishly organized afterwards finds less of an explanation in FAO's shortcomings and had more to do with the lack of engagement of companies as opposed to certain corporate leaders. Some 'global governance' concepts put much emphasis on non-state actors.[63] ICP did provide a sphere where government sovereignty counted little and non-governmental actors directly interacted with a world organization. In the end, ICP was also brought down by criticism from individual intellectuals and international NGOs. But as long as the programme existed, transnational companies used it – among other purposes – to get into contacts with 'Third World' governments and influence their planning policies. Many participant corporate officials evaluated such efforts through ICP as moderately successful at best. As the example of the Agribusiness Council suggests, not all *Multis* seem to have found the absence of state authority very beneficial to their interests; and often they preferred to rely on state support.

There may be the objection that the term 'global governance' – often used in reference to the era after the breakdown of European socialism around 1989[64] – should not be applied ahistorically to a time when it was not yet invented, anyway. However, in the past fifteen years, decisive progress has not been made toward eradicating world hunger, nor in modernizing the staple food production in many African or Asian countries, especially as far as rainfed agriculture is concerned (whatever the connection between these two facts may be). All deadlines for achieving certain goals for global poverty reduction, be it the ones adopted at the World Food Conference in 1974 or at the World Food Summit in 1996, have been missed, demonstrating continuity in this field.[65] This ongoing failure in a question of overwhelming importance may suggest that 'global governance', with its many overtones of 'control' and 'governing', may just be too grandiose a term.

Notes

1. See C. Gerlach, 'Die Welternährungskrise 1972 bis 1975', in *Geschichte und Gesellschaft* 31(4) (2005): 546–85. This chapter draws on material from my forthcoming book *Making the Village Global: The Change of International Development Policies and the World Food Crisis, 1972–75*, see which for further discussion. This project received financial support from the Hamburger Stiftung zur Förderung von Wissenschaft und Kultur, the Deutsche Forschungsgemeinschaft, the German Historical Institutes in Rome, Washington and London, the University of Freiburg and the Center for Historical Studies, University of Maryland, College Park.
2. Extract of statement by Mr. A. H. Boerma at 6th Session of General Committee, ICP, 23–24 March 1970, in paper dated 15 July 1971, FAO Archives, 9 Subject Files I/ICP IV. – Multinationals: J. A. C. Hugill, 'Agribusiness and the Industry Cooperative Program', in *Agricultural Initiative in the Third World: A Report on the Conference: Science and Agribusiness in the Seventies* (Lexington, MA, 1975), p. 108, and ICP, 44th and 45th Sessions of the Executive Committee, 24 and 26 May 1977 of 24 June 1977, FAO 9, DDI, IP 22/5.1.

3. FAO, Circular letter no. 90, August 1965, Political Archive of the German Foreign Office, IIIA2, Nr. 140; Secretary Note to Item 9, Cooperation with Industry (1965), German Federal Archive B116/20218; Hugill, 'Agribusiness', p. 108; J. Carroz, 'Le Programme de Cooperation F.A.O.–Industrie', in *Annuaire Francais de droit international* XIII, 1967, pp. 469–71; speech of Boerma on Private Banks Program meeting, 8–9 May 1969, FAO 9, SF I, IBRD III.

4. Membership lists: Carroz, 'Programme', p. 472, Note 21 (1 January 1968); W. Simons, 'Government–Industry Partnership in the Third World: A United Nations Experiment Begins to Pay Off', in *Columbia Journal of World Business* 3 (1975): 43–4; A. G. Friedrich and V. G. Gale, *Public–Private Partnership Within the United Nations System: Now and Then* (Bielefeld, 2004), pp. 109–11.

5. Chairmen were E. F. Schroeder of CPC International, 1966–8; Victor Umbricht of Ciba Geigy, 1968–70; Paul Cornelsen of Ralston Purina, 1970–2; J. A. C. Hugill of Tate & Lyle, 1972–4; Luigi Deserti of Oltremare, 1974–6; and George Bishop of Booker McConnell, 1976–8. The Executive Secretary in the 1970s was the West German forestry expert Alexander Gunther Friedrich; Walter Simons headed the ICP office in New York: Friedrich and Gale, *Partnership*, p. 54.

6. 'How big business has started to feed Africa', in *Africa*, 71 (1977): 95; Friedrich and Gale, *Partnership*, p. 62 and 71–2.

7. FAO, Circular letter, August 1965 (see Note 3); paper of 15 July 1971 (see Note 2).

8. 'Programme Achiev[e]ments', 12 March 1971, FAO 9, SF I, ICP IV; see 20-page list of inquiries by ICP members, enclosure to a memo by V. E. Gale of ICP, 25 November 1975, FAO 9, DDI, IP 22/8. Sample requests for 18 and 9 project papers, respectively, of UNDP and other agencies in: Ciba Geigy to Latour (ICP), 10 August 1971 and 23 March 1972, FAO 9, DDI, IP 22/8, Box 11, Ciba Geigy I; correspondence between BP and FAO 1972/73, ibid., Box 10, BP I.

9. Paper of 15 July 1971, see Note 2; 'Business International Report on ICP', December 1970, FAO 9, SF I/ICP IV; 'Political Exploitation of Economic Efficiency', n.d., FAO 9, Misc., DDI; K. Albright *et al.* 'Cooperation between agroindustry and the UN', in *Food Policy* 2 (1977): 44–59; L. D. Solomon, *Multinational Corporations and the Emerging World Order* (Port Washington, NY, 1978), pp. 161–226; G. Maaß, 'Internationale Entwicklungsagenturen in der Weltgesellschaft: Die Rolle der FAO bei der Herausbildung des Weltagrarsystems', in T. Siebold and R. Tetzlaff (eds), *Strukturelemente der Weltgesellschaft* (Frankfurt a.M., 1981), pp. 228–36; 'Friedrich Heads FAO's Industry Cooperative Program', *Delegates World Bulletin* 3(3) (1973); Friedrich and Gale, *Partnership*, p. 85. Sometimes companies even asked for FAO's 'co-operation and backing' for sales of specific products: Douglas-Pennant (BP) to Simons, ICP, 'Nu-Way Benson Mini Drier', 22 September 1971, FAO 9, DDI, IP 22/8, Box 10, BP I. Or they tried to use ICP to prevent the establishment of Third World industries as unwelcome competition:

'Aktennotiz' Umbricht of 23 March 1968, Archiv für Zeitgeschichte, Zurich, NL Umbricht, UNO, FAO Meetings, Nov. 1967–1972.

10. J. Roberts, *Mitsui: Three Centuries of Japanese Business* (New York, 1973), pp. 486–7.

11. See S. George, *How the Other Half Dies: The Real Reasons for World Hunger* (Montclair, NJ, 1977), pp. 184–204, and Maaß, 'Entwicklungsagenturen'.

12. A. Hugill, *Sugar and all that… A History of Tate & Lyle* (London, 1978), p. 280.

13. W. Simons, 'Implementing World Food Conference Decisions – A Role for Agro-Industry' (March or April 1975), FAO 9, ICP/ UN 43/1 II; 'The Follow-Up – ICP Proposals', FAO 9, DDI, PR 4/75; Solomon, *Multinational Corporations*, pp. 170–2; Simons, 'Government–Industry Partnership', p. 40. For mixed conclusions of an ICP member from the World Food Conference, see Kettle (Massey Ferguson) to Friedrich, n.d., FAO 9, DDI, IP 22/8, Box 13, Massey Ferguson II.

14. George, *How the Other Half Dies*, p. 189; see UN World Food Conference, Provisional list of delegates, 11 November 1974, Addendum: International Organizations, FAO 22, WFC Docs, Docs. of the Preparatory Committee, fourth file.

15. Kettle (Massey Ferguson) to Friedrich, 4 October 1974, FAO 9, DDI, IP 22/8, Box 13, Massey Ferguson II; Neil Schenet (IMC) to Butz (October 1974), NARA, RG 16, USDA Gen. Corr., Box 5847, Food 2, 1 October–26 November 1974; Henry J. Heinz to Vidal Naquet, 10 June 1974, FAO 22, UN-43/3A Regional meetings.

16. UN/World Food Conference, DDI:G/74/89, Consultation with Agro-Industrial Leaders, 10–11 September 1974, Toronto, of 26 September 1974, FAO 12, UN 43/2B ICP-General; material in FAO 12, UN 43/2B Consultation with Agro-Industrial Leaders; Simons to Horst Genting, UNDP Senior Agricultural Advisor, FAO 9, DDI, UN 43/1 II; AfZ, NL Umbricht, UNO, World Food Conference.

17. Friedrich and Gale, *Partnership*, p. 78.

18. See R. H. Dean, Chairman of the Board and CEO, Ralston Purina, to US Secretary of Agriculture Hardin, 15 December 1970, and Hardin's answer, 15 February 1971, US National Archives (NARA), RG 16, 170/10/7/2, USDA Gen. Corr. 1971, Box 5402, Foreign Relations 1 (FAO), Jan.–Nov. 19, 1971. For US Government efforts to get Jackson elected, see exchange in NARA, RG 59, SNF, 1970–73 Economic, Box 459, 2/1/71. Quotation: J. Abbott, *Politics and Poverty: A Critique of the Food and Agriculture Organization of the United Nations* (London, 1992), p. 44.

19. Cooperative agreements were signed with 11 UN sub-organizations from 1969 to early 1971: 'Programme achiev[e]ments', 1971 (see note 8); Albright *et al.*, 'Cooperation'. Information: Latour (ICP) and Ergas, note for file 'FAO

Investment Centre and FAO Industry Cooperative Programme', 22 December 1969, FAO 9, SF I, Investment Centre 1969–70.

20. See R. Philipps, *FAO: Its Origins, Formation and Evolution 1945–1981* (Rome, 1981); for the discontinuation of ICP, see the files FAO 9, DDI, IP 22/5.1, *Tagesanzeiger*, 18 April 1978, and *Neue Zürcher Zeitung*, 21 June 1978, FAO 13, GII, IN 2/1, brown file Criticisms, Vol. III. For the role of the ICFTU cf. correspondence of 1977 in FAO 9, DDD, BK 51/1; less than impartial: Friedrich and Gale, *Partnership*, pp. 81 and 83.

21. B. Dinham and C. Hines, *Agribusiness in Africa* (London, 1983), pp. 41–2; George, *How the Other Half Dies*, pp. 186–7; FAO 9, DDI, PR 4/44; M. Linear, 'Gift of Poison – The Unacceptable Face of Development Aid', in *Ambio* 11(1) (1982): 1–8; O. Matzke, 'Die Welternährungskonferenz heute und morgen', *Neue Zürcher Zeitung* (7 July 1974).

22. C73/LIM/15, Agricultural Adjustment: Sudan, August 1974, FAO 6, Reel 537; Agenda for the meeting of the London Group, 27 May 1974, FAO 9, ICP, IL 3/235; cf. FAO 12, PAG, PAG Matters-Policy 1971–6.

23. See FAO 9, DDI, IP 22/8, Box 11, Caterpillar I and II.

24. Quotation: Simons, 'Government–Industry Partnership', p. 42. UN/WFC, DDI: G/74/89, 'Consultation with Agro-Industrial Leaders, 10–11 September 1974, Toronto, Canada', FAO 12, UN 43/2B ICP-General; Walter Simons (ICP), 'The World Food Problem – A Role for the Private Sector', speech, Dallas, 3 April 1975, NARA RG 16, USDA Gen.Corr. 1975, Box 5974, Food 2. Tractors: Simons to Friedrich, 2 April 1976, and snappish comments by Weitz to Yriart, 21 April 1976, FAO 9, DDI/ICP/PR 15/49.

25. Simons, 'Government–Industry Partnership', p. 42.

26. Friedrich to Huyser, 6 June 1975, FAO 9, DDC, PR 4/69, vol. II; second quotation: telegram, Friedrich to Marei, 12 September 1974, FAO 12, UN 43/2B Consultation with Agro-Industrial Leaders.

27. Büttiker to Latour, 'International Convention for Plant Protection', 8 August 1972, Rohmer to Friedrich, 18 July 1973 and 2 February 1974 (on UNIDO's 'Workshop on Pesticides' in May 1973), FAO 9, DDI, IP 22/8, Box 11, Ciba Geigy I and II; telling data are to be found in *Die Unterwanderung des UNO-Systems durch multinationale Konzerne: Auszüge aus internen Protokollen und Briefwechseln* (Zurich, 1978).

28. FAO's Fertilizer Industry Advisory Committee (FIAC) had been created in the 1960s. For members, see Gardner-McTaggart to Minnick, 24 October 1975, FAO 9, DDI, PR 7/2. Machinery: L. D. Solomon, 'Industry Cooperative Programme of the Food and Agriculture Organization of the United Nations: A Catalytic Organization Bridging Multinational Agribusiness Corporations and Developing Nations', in *Texas International Law Journal* 13(69) (1977): 81. Seeds: Hendrie (Shell) to Nagashima (Mitsubishi Europe), 1 July 1976, FAO 9, DDI, IP 22/8, Box 13, Mitsubishi. Films: FAO 9, DDI, IP 22/8, Box

11, Caterpillar I; description of films in ibid., Ciba Geigy II; Redlhammer to Friedrich, 10 September 1975, and Friedrich's letter, 3 February 1976, ibid., Box 12, Hoechst; 'New Partners', *Wall Street Journal* (18 March 1975).

29. 'Programme achiev[e]ments' (see Note 8); Wrigley (BP) to Friedrich, 17 October 1972, FAO, 9 DDI, IP 22/8, Box 10, BP I; materials in FAO 9, DDI, IP 22/4 and 22/5.1.

30. Friedrich (ICP) to Weitz, 6 April 1973 and draft of 27 May 1976, FAO 9, DDI, PR 15/49; Paul J. Byrnes, U.S. Permanent Representative to FAO, to Simons, 30 January 1973, FAO 9, DDI, IP 22/4; Walton to Cottam, 2 March 1973, FAO 12, ES FA 8/6 II ('an increasingly critical matter'). Of 108 members in 1975, thirty were from the United States, severnteen from Britain, thirteen from France, eight each from Italy and the Netherlands, seven from Switzerland, six from Japan, five from West Germany, and fourteen from other countries: Simons, 'Government–Industry Partnership', pp. 43–4; list in NARA, RG 59, SNF, Economic 1970–3, Box 458, 12/1/70; Friedrich and Gale, *Partnership*, p. 57.

31. 'ICP – A strategy for accomplishment' (so-called Bignami report), FAO 9, DDI, IP 22/5.3, Business International I.

32. 'Business International Report on ICP, December 1970: Summary, conclusions and recommendations', FAO 9, SF I, ICP IV; 'Statement J. A. C. Hugill on March 10, 1972, upon his election as chairman [...]', FAO 9, DDI, IP 22/4; Osvaldo Ballarin (Nestlé of Brazil), 'What do we get out of it?', April 1976, AfZ, NL Umbricht, UNO, FAO, ICP, 1972–.

33. 'Business International Report on ICP' (see Note 32); 'ICP – A strategy for accomplishment' (see Note 31); Umbricht to Hugill, 23 May 1973, AfZ, NL Umbricht, UNO, FAO, ICP, 1972–.

34. Plans: Carroz, 'Programme', pp. 480–1. Introduction: exchange in FAO 9/SF I/ICP IV and V. Problems: Wrigley to Friedrich, 17 October 1972 (see Note 29); ICP, General Committee, 10th session – Conference, Summary Record, 22 March 1974, FAO 22, UN-43/2B; Solomon, *Multinational Corporations*, pp. 178–84. However, a paper of 1977 claimed 101 commercial projects of ICP members existed in target countries of country missions '[a]lthough it would be difficult in every case to prove close correlation between missions and project implementation': Review of ICP Country Missions and Working Parties 1972–1977, FAO 9, DDI, IP 22/5.1. See also FAO 9, ICP, Collection of Mission Reports I and II; 'ICP – Guidelines for Missions', n.d., FAO, 9, DDI, IP 22/9 General I.

35. Cf. Friedrich and Gale, *Partnership*, p. 60.

36. For the interest in influencing planning see US Embassy Rome to State Department, 'FAO: The Industry-Cooperative Program', 28 January 1972, NARA, RG 59, SNF Economic, 1970–73, Box 460, 1/1/72. Selection: 'Discussion on proposed high level industry missions', 4 August 1971, FAO

9, SF I, ICP IV; 'Consultation with Agro-Industrial Leaders' (see Note 24). Countries' requests: 'Industry Cooperative Programme', 10 November 1972, FAO 9, IP 22/9 general, vol. I; Hugill's circular, 11 May 1972, FAO 9, SF I, ICP V. FAO: Solomon, 'Industry Cooperative Programme', p. 83.

37. Simon, 'Government–Industry Partnership', p. 37; 'Programme Achiev[e]ments', 1971 (see Note 8).

38. See Albright *et al.*, 'Cooperation', esp. pp. 53–4; 'Business International Report on ICP', December 1970, FAO 9, Subject Files I/ICP IV; Solomon, *Multinational Corporations*; Olsen, Vice President, FMC, to Simons, 6 March 1974, FAO 12, UN 43/2B ICP-General.

39. For the preparatory phase, see R. Goldberg, 'Agribusiness for Developing Countries', in *Harvard Business Review* (September–October 1966): 81–4 and 89.

40. See www.agribusinesscouncil.org, 'History', accessed 29 April 2005. The quotation is from *Agricultural Initiative* (a publication by the Agribusiness Council), opposite title page.

41. Membership: Second World Food Congress, Commission VI, Private Sector Support, February 1970, FAO, 9 V Misc./2nd World Food Congress; Agribusiness Council, Membership list, January 1975, FAO 9, DDI, IL 3/235. Overlap: Yohalem, Senior Vice President, CPC International, to Hugill, 11 April 1973, FAO 9, ICP, IL 3/235.

42. Up to 1971, nine countries were visited (six in Asia, three in Latin America), among them six larger markets (Iran, Pakistan, Indonesia, South Korea, Mexico, Turkey). 'The Agribusiness Council, Inc.' with cover letter of 19 May 1971, NARA, Nixon, FO, Box 50, GEN FO 4-3, Int. Investments 1971–72, file 1. Sample report: The Agribusiness Council, 'Agribusiness Prospects in Sudan: Summary Report', 22 September 1972, FAO 9, DDI, IL 3/235. For general operations, see Agribusiness Council, Report of Activities 1976, ibid. For recent times, see www.agribusinesscouncil.org, 'Scope of Activities', accessed 29 April 2005.

43. Telegram US Embassy Manila, 'Agri-Business Council', 6 April 1971, NARA, RG 59, SF, Economic, 1970–3, Box 471, AGR Phil 1/1/1970.

44. Mair (USDA) to Palmby (Vice President, Continental Grain) and to Hardin (Vice President, Ralston Purina), 21 February 1973, NARA, RG 16, 170/10/13/4, USDA Gen.Corr. 1973, Box 5714; 'FAO Activities of Interest to the U.S. Government – Industry Cooperative Programme', 20 June 1972, FAO 9, Subject Files I/ICP V.

45. See the contributions in *Agricultural Initiative in the Third World* (for participants, pp. 197–207); and report of Donald Paarlberg (USDA), 22 February 1974, FAO 9, DDI, IL 3/235. At a similar meeting, the conference 'World Food Supplies' organized by British Airways and the *Financial Times*, 1–2 May 1974, only one representative of a US company spoke (FAO 12, UN-43/5 GB).

46. See 'Rules Governing Objectives, Organization and Operating Procedures, FAO/Bankers Programme', April 1973, FAO 9, Misc., DDC.

47. E. Mandel, *Die Krise: Weltwirtschaft 1974–1986* (Hamburg: Konkret Literatur Verlag (1987)), pp. 85–8, 297–301 and 322.

48. S. George, *Warum die Hungernden die Satten ernähren: Nahrung unter der Kontrolle der Konzerne* (n.p., n.d.), pp. 47–50; M. Perelman, *Farming for Profits in a Hungry World: Capital and the Crisis in Agriculture* (Montclair, NJ, 1977), p. 122, Note 52.

49. In 1974, the only 23 participant institutions included Bank of America, Bankers Trust, Barclays Bank International, Banco Commerciale Italiana, and Wells Fargo Bank: FAO/Bankers Programme, List of Members (as at 14 March 1974), FAO 9, Misc., DDC.

50. See FAO 9, DDD, BK 51/1, esp. 'Note for the discussion on policy for the FAO/Bankers Programme' [May 1978]and address R. Jackson, 26 May 1977; cf. FAO 9, V (Misc.), Private Banks 1972–3; ICP, 13th Session of the General Committee, 25 and 26 May 1977, Summary Report, FAO 9, ICP, Summary Reports of the General Committee; FAO/Bankers Programme, List of Members (14 March 1974), FAO 9, Misc., DDC; *The Times*, 8 April 1976, Special report, p. II.

51. 'How big business has started to feed Africa', in *Africa*, no. 71, 1977, p. 96.

52. North American Congress on Latin America (NACLA), *Weizen als Waffe: Die neue Getreidestrategie der amerikanischen Außenpolitik* (Reinbek, 1976), pp. 66–7; R. Burbach and P. Flynn, *Agribusiness in the Americas* (New York, 1980), pp. 239–41.

53. Address by Henry Kissinger before the Fourth Ministerial Meeting of UNCTAD, Nairobi, 6 May 1976, p. 16, Gerald D. Ford Presidential Library, Ann Arbor, MI, L. William Seidman files, Box 189, Kissinger, Henry A, 5/6/76 UNCTAD speech.

54. ICP, General Committee, 10th session – Conference, Agenda, 11 March 1974, and Summary Record, 22 March 1974, FAO 22, UN-43/2B; ICP, Annual Report April 1973/March 1974, FAO 9, Misc., DDI; FAO, DDI G/74/S, 18 December 1973, FAO 12, UN 43/2B Divisional Contributions Gen.; *Neue Zürcher Zeitung*, 21 June 1978; see also *Die Unterwanderung des UNO-Systems*, esp. pp. 52–5; the ICP paper on which their Geneva presentation was based is published in Friedrich and Gale, *Partnership*, pp. 113–29.

55. D. Weir and M. Schapiro, *Circle of Poison: Pesticides and People in a Hungry World* (San Francisco, 1981), pp. 54f.; S. Dillon, 'Increased investment in LDCs', in *Food Policy* 9, 4, 1984, p. 281; Maaß, 'Entwicklungsagenturen', pp. 235–6. Cf. AfZ, NL Umbricht, UNO, FAO, Sub-groups + ICP/ICD, esp. Bodmer (Ciba-Geigy) to Umbricht and response, 25 and 27 January 1979, and ICP Ex.Committee, 49th session, 24 July 1978; ibid., FAO, ICP, 1972–, esp. ICD, First Annual General Meeting, 12–13 July 1979.

56. Yriart (Director of FAO's Development Dept.) to Yohalem, Vice President, CPC International, 17 April 1974, FAO 9, Misc., DDI; Pierre Terver, Statement for ICP's General Committee's 8th session, 18 September 1972, FAO 9, DDI, IP 22/5.1.

57. Different criticisms of taking the project approach in Freeman (Business International) to Friedrich, 4 August 1975, FAO, 9 DDI, IP 22/5.3 Business International I, and Olsen (FMC) to Simons, 6 March 1974, FAO 9, DDI, IP 22/8, Box 12, FMC. Quotation: 'ICP – A strategy for accomplishment' (see Note 31). Cf. also Summary report of ICP General Committee meeting of 11 to 12 February 1975, 28 February 1975, FAO 9, ICP, Summary Reports of the General Committee.

58. Dinham and Hines, *Agribusiness in Africa*; George, *Warum*, pp. 56–7.

59. Constitution of the FAO of 16 October 1945, in *Basic Texts of the Food and Agriculture Organization of the United Nations* (Rome: FAO, 2000), p. 3; the full quotation is 'contributing to an expanding world economy and ensuring humanity's freedom from hunger'. For an excellent analysis of FAO's work for capitalist interests cf. Maaß, 'Entwicklungsagenturen'.

60. For FAO, see S. Marchisio and A. di Blasé, *L'Organisation pour l'Alimentation et l'Agriculture (FAO)* (Geneva: Georg, 1986), pp. 83–106; otherwise C. Gerlach, 'Der Versuch zur globalen entwicklungspolitischen Steuerung auf der *World Food Conference* 1974', in *WerkstattGeschichte* 31 (2002): 67–77.

61. A. Iriye, *Global Community: The Role of International Organizations in the Making of the Contemporary World* (Berkeley, CA., 2002), pp. 129–30.

62. In Friedrich and Gale, *Partnership* two former functionaries of the programme present ICP as a success model suitable for future cooperation between UN and big business.

63. For example, J. N. Rosenau, 'Governance in a New Global Order', in David Held and Anthony McGrew (eds), *Governing Globalization: Power, Authority and Global Governance* (Cambridge, 2002), pp. 72–3, 77.

64. M. Hewson and T. J. Sinclair, 'The Emergence of Global Governance Theory', in T. J. Sinclair (ed.), *Global Governance: Critical Concepts in Political Science* (London, 2004), Vol. 1, pp. 227–39.

65. The objectives declared were, in 1974, to eradicate world hunger within ten years, and in 1996, to reduce world hunger by half within twenty years. The latter target figure has already been 'adjusted' to realities again.

Part IV
Trade and Moralities

–12–

Postcolonial Paradoxes

The Cultural Economy of African Export Horticulture
Susanne Freidberg

Imagine a plane taking off in the middle of the night from a town seemingly in the middle of nowhere. The time was January 1994, the place Bobo-Dioulasso, Burkina Faso, and the plane was full of premier-quality French beans, headed north to Paris. Within several hours, they would be put up for sale at Rungis, the wholesale market outside the French capital. The flight was a singular event in that it was the first to export the region's produce in more than ten years. But many other cargo jets followed parallel routes, from poor countries in the global South to rich ones in the global North. This flight represented, moreover, hopes for a more lasting take-off, the kind that might lift Burkina Faso's predominantly rural population out of poverty and perennial food insecurity. The country's foreign donors shared these hopes, drawing on evidence from countries such as Kenya, where high-value fresh vegetable exports had brought about one of Africa's all-too-rare rural development 'success stories.'[1]

Now imagine another small yet significant event, around the same time but very far away. In a farmyard in, say, Wales, a crazy-eyed cow fell to her knees. Her brain was full of holes, and she would die soon. Like the airplane's flight, the cow's collapse recurred elsewhere, and represented, unfortunately, something much bigger. Mad cow disease itself, as well as the mass culling intended to staunch its spread, would ultimately fell millions of cattle. And with them collapsed Europeans' confidence in both their own governments' food regulatory capacity and in the broader agro-food industry.

A plane taking off and a cow falling down: these two very different events belonged to histories that became increasingly interwoven over the next decade, as the aspirations of Africa's agro-exporters collided with the anxieties of European consumers and retailers, and globalized commerce came under the scrutiny of the globalized media and the activist community. This decade saw dramatic changes not only in Europe's supermarkets, but also in the African regions that sold them food, and in those regions' prospects for economic development and poverty reduction through high-value export food production.

These changes, however, were not uniform, nor easily predictable. They showed that analyses of contemporary South–North fresh-produce trades – and of the 'post mad cow' global food economy more generally – must look beneath the macro-level, and beyond the purely economic. To illustrate this point, this chapter examines the fresh vegetable trades linking two sub-Saharan African countries to their former colonial powers. The francophone trade sells Burkina Faso's green beans to France, while the anglophone trade brings an assortment of pre-packaged fresh vegetables from Zambia to Great Britain. Broadly similar in some ways, they differ radically in others – including the ways that they experienced Europe's late-twentieth- century food scares.

This chapter makes two broad arguments. First, it shows how cultural economy analysis can provide unique insights into the trade and investment relationships that make up the globalized food economy. Here, the analysis helps us understand why one trade fuelled an unsustainable boom, while the other proved an enduring bust. Second, this chapter argues that the standards that corporate supermarkets impose on their suppliers in Africa (and elsewhere in the global South) constitute a little-recognized form of postcolonial power. It is postcolonial in that it not only operates through relationships that date from the colonial era (see Trentmann, Chapter 14, this volume) but also, like the colonial 'civilizing mission', focuses on the intimate details of daily life. In particular, it focuses on the way that horticultural farms attend to the health, housing and hygiene of their workers.[2] In theory, the supermarkets' standards simply respond to demand for good safe food as well as 'ethical' and 'accountable' food trading, at a time when globalization has made both appear in short supply. In practice, these standards mask disciplinary processes that are globalizing in scope and aim, and that are hardly 'accountable', but are also, as we shall see, not always very successful.

The chapter begins with a brief discussion of how cultural economy analysis can help us understand the workings of transnational food commerce. The next section provides background on the events framing the research, which was conducted in Burkina Faso, Zambia, France and Britain between 1999 and 2005.[3]

Culture and Nature in Transnational Food Trades

At the most general level, cultural economy analysis assumes not that economic practices are simply 'embedded' in social and cultural contexts, but rather that the economic and cultural are mutually constitutive.[4] From this basic premise follow a number of methodological and analytical assumptions central to any cultural economy study of transnational food trading.

First, 'culture' within any transnational food trade network refers not to one society's taken-for-granted customs, nor to a single organization's learned discourses and behaviours, but rather to the norms, practices and social institutions recognized and shaped by the network's members. It is culture that revolves around commerce, but encompasses many activities besides basic commercial negotiations and transactions. While particular institutions may dictate its norms of product quality and professional conduct, individual members do not necessarily believe in or adhere to them. Equally important, the geographic breadth of many trade networks – their passage through different places and institutions – subjects them to diverse, potentially contradictory normative influences, as well as practical contingencies that demand improvisation and compromise. Thus whatever makes them culturally distinctive may also be internally inconsistent, contested and unstable.

Second, the cultural economy of any transnational food trade must be understood in the light of multiple and connected histories – of the trade itself, but also of the regions it connects (see Trentmann, Chapter 14, and Jackson and Ward, Chapter 13, this volume). The comparative research described here, for example, paid particular attention to histories of agrarian change and food provisioning, during and since Europe's colonial conquest of Africa. Zambia's history of settler colonialism and 'company town' development produced a postcolonial landscape of export food production vastly different, both physically and politically, to the one that emerged from France's nominally 'pro-peasant' policies in Sahelian West Africa.

Third, cultural economy analyses of food assume that food differs fundamentally from other commodities, owing at least partly to the very nature of its production and consumption – in other words, the natural (or 'organic') processes involved in agriculture and eating, and the uncertainties and risks associated with both.[5] Food's unique nature has made it uniquely central to human social life (in gardens and markets as well as homes and restaurants) and therefore a carrier of historically-constructed meanings both intimate and geopolitical.[6] These meanings in turn enter into food markets, broadly understood, at a variety of levels. Different societal definitions of food purity and danger, of the 'proper meal' and the proper treatment of farmland and livestock, of government's responsibility to protect producers and consumers' from food risks – all these norms influence not simply market supply and demand but also food trade politics and policies. They have also repeatedly confounded international efforts to harmonize food quality and safety standards.[7]

Cultural economy analysis also considers how the natural qualities of specific foodstuffs (such as perishability or bacterial content) and the specific ecologies of their production pose risks and uncertainties that trade networks, in turn, handle in culturally specific ways. Farmers and food traders in agrarian societies have historically dealt with nature's vagaries partly through the relations and norms of reciprocity, trust and justice commonly described as the moral economy.[8] In Burkina Faso, for example, both local and foreign fresh produce merchants are expected to appreciate (and if possible, provide aid for) the calamities, natural and otherwise, that can delay or ruin growers' harvests: the storms, the sicknesses, the mechanical breakdowns. Those who neglect such expectations risk losing their suppliers' loyalty, without which they rarely do well. The moral economy's ongoing relevance to fresh produce exporting is hardly unique to Burkina Faso; elsewhere in Africa farmers and merchants cope with harsh environments and poor infrastructures in similar ways.[9] In the overseas markets, however, the popular media tends to portray 'Africa in chaos', not coping – a stereotype about the continent that has arguably influenced European consumers' and retailers' concerns about the safety of its fresh produce.[10]

In industrialized societies, technological and institutional forms of risk protection (i.e. cold storage, crop insurance) have perhaps made personal trust less central to the marketing of relatively stable, standardized food commodities (soya beans, pork bellies), especially when all parties enjoy such protections. In trades that span hemispheres and deal in highly perishable food commodities, however, nature poses multiple risks, and protections tend to be uneven. So even when the trading partners are all multinational corporations, personal trust still matters; it is just assessed and accorded differently. More to the point, even the most technical and impersonal forms of risk protection are produced and used according to culturally specific norms about who and what can be trusted.

Supermarkets and Standards

Supermarket standards rank among those seemingly objective risk protection tools that in fact have clear cultural and historical roots. Although such standards are increasingly harmonized on a global scale, British retailers have developed and wielded them much more enthusiastically than their counterparts in most other countries. Through these standards and other technologies of 'audit culture', British supermarkets have sought protection against not just the natural hazards of transnational fresh food sourcing, but also the social and political risks.[11] While traditionally such risks have been associated with the production regions (where, for example, a coup d'état or labour strike might disrupt supply) these days British supermarkets must also prepare for unpredictable events in the home country, such as food scares and scandals.

Such concerns are due in part to legislation such as Britain's 1990 Food Safety Law, which requires that food businesses of all kinds demonstrate due diligence.[12] In brief, this means that a business found selling unsafe food must be able to trace that food back to its source and show that everything possible was done to keep it safe. Yet, liability considerations aside, British supermarkets have sought to prevent their supply chains from generating any product or event that might damage their brand image. Substantial research suggests that this concern has become a greater day-to-day preoccupation at the management level than the task of complying with the letter of the law.[13] And it is a concern that managers themselves tend to trace quite directly to Britain's history of food scares, mad cow among others.[14] This was at least partly because the scares raised doubts about the country's globalized, industrialized food supply that went well beyond mere safety – doubts that the media and certain non-governmental organizations (NGOs), they said, helped to feed.

A widely-viewed 1997 television documentary called Mangetout, for example, portrayed Tesco as a neo-imperial power, extracting profits from a Zimbabwean export farm where a worker could be fired if she let a lone caterpillar into a package of peas. That same year, the NGO Christian Aid published a report on the British supermarkets' Third World supply farms that exposed, among other things, the use of child labour.[15] It then collected some £17 million worth of shopper receipts and presented them to the supermarkets as evidence of consumer demand for more ethical sourcing practices. The campaign got more media coverage than any in Christian Aid's fifty-year history, according to its organizers, helping convince the country's top food retailers to join NGOs and the government in what became known as the Ethical Trading Initiative.[16] Christian Aid was just one of many British charities that called for reforms in supermarket food supply practices in order to advance other causes, from social justice and child nutrition to animal welfare and countryside protection. People involved in these campaigns acknowledged that the mad cow crisis had, in fact, helped them. It not only helped build public support for reform, but also pushed retailers to show that they, unlike the government ministries that had so utterly failed to protect the public against the dangers of BSE, were accountable.[17]

Among the ways the supermarkets sought to demonstrate accountability was to develop standards of supplier 'best practice' that, at least at the level of food safety, typically exceeded government baseline regulations. While they originally developed most of these standards in-house, by the late 1990s they were joining and initiating industry-wide efforts to codify best practice. These ranged from the aforementioned Ethical Trading Initiative to the British Retail Consortium (which produced a 'global standard') to EurepGAP (which produced a 'protocol' specifically for European retailers' horticultural suppliers, aimed at responding to 'consumer concerns on food safety, animal welfare, environmental protection and worker health, safety and welfare) to the Global Food Safety Initiative (which formed in 2000 in order to create 'a global set of voluntary but universally recognized standards of food safety, quality and security').[18]

As this list suggests, the retailers were not simply concerned to keep their products free of microbes and detectable pesticide residues. Rather, they wanted codes that would enable them to assess, rank and if necessary discipline their suppliers according to multiple standards of 'best practice'. They also wanted to be able to monitor compliance with these standards in a thorough but efficient fashion. Thus emerged a particular sort of 'audit culture,' populated by a variety of in-house and third-party auditors (including firms such as Price Waterhouse), transmitted through supplier checklists, site visits, and faxed requests for traceability records, and documented in annual corporate 'social responsibility' reports, among other places.[19]

In sub-Saharan Africa, the on-the-ground consequences of the supplier standards first appeared in Kenya, the continent's biggest exporter of green beans. In the early 1990s, the World Bank touted Kenya's horticultural sector as a model of non-traditional export-led development, primarily because 75 per cent of the produce came from smallholders, most of them women, cultivating under contract for firms that appreciated their cheap and careful labour.[20] Green beans didn't interfere with staple grain production, and even a one-tenth hectare plot generated enough income to make a real difference in growers' households and local economies. It helped them feed their children, and generated jobs for rural people who might otherwise end up in Nairobi's slums. In short, Kenya's horticultural 'success story' seemed to show that luxury export food crops, contrary to common assumptions in the critical development literature,[21] could in fact improve rural food and land tenure security.

A few years later, however, the World Bank's optimism – at least regarding the prospects of smallholders – looked equally premature. Kenya's horticultural exports continued to increase and diversify, but the bulk of production (70 per cent) now lay in the hands of large, typically white-owned farms. Dolan and Humphrey's research makes clear that the British supermarkets were the driving force behind this rapid back-to-the-plantation shift. The retailers' produce managers said as much: given their anxious and intensely competitive home market, they only wanted to deal with suppliers who could reliably meet their standards of food safety, quality, and ethics, and continue to meet them as the standards inevitably got tougher. And in their view, the only suppliers who could do this were the large farm operations. One Institute for Development Studies report thus concluded that smallholders would probably survive in the horticultural export sector only as outgrowers for 'benign dictators', meaning 'major, well-established' firms capable of 'assuming responsibility for the rigid enforcement of standards'.[22]

But did events in Kenya reflect broader trends in food trading between Africa and Europe, and between global South and North? The research described in the rest of this chapter sought to answer this basic question. It started with certain doubts about the likelihood that similar changes could have taken place in Burkina Faso, which had long been sub-Saharan Africa's number two green bean exporter. This was partly because the country has no big white-owned farms – the arid climate didn't appeal to many settlers – nor many big farms, period. Rural development policy during and since the colonial period had always sought, at least in principle, to modernize rather than expropriate the peasantry.[23] But it was also doubtful because Burkina Faso, like its francophone neighbours, exported to France, a market that had undergone its share of food scares and supermarket mergers, but was structurally and culturally very different from the British one.

Exporting Against All Odds

In the early 1970s, the 'pro-peasant' priorities of Burkinabé and French rural development policy, combined with the perennial French appetite for haricots verts, made the export green bean seem like a logical weapon in the Sahelian country's battle against rural poverty, hunger, and apparent desertification. This high-value crop had been cultivated in Burkina Faso since the early colonial era, sometimes on forced-labour farms intended to provision the local French population.[24] Small-holders could cultivate it during the long (October–April) dry season, using land on donor-funded irrigation schemes.[25] Organized in cooperatives and provided with the proper inputs, smallholders could (in theory) use cheap family labour to assure the best care for the fragile bean. If timed right, their harvests could hit the French market during the lucrative winter holiday season, and then again in early spring, right before the green bean harvests in North Africa and southern France. With their earnings, growers could buy staple grains to supplement their own production, which was inadequate during the frequent drought years.

This rural development logic gave rise to an export sector that appeared, in almost any other light, geographically illogical, in that the production sites were remote, widely scattered, and in some cases six hours or more (on bad roads) from the airport in Ouagadougou, the capital city. Such distances were especially problematic given the fragility and perishability of fine-grade green beans, and the poor state of the (non-refrigerated) trucks that carried them.

For several years the state, with help from foreign donors, handled all green bean exports; but by the early 1990s it had withdrawn from the business and encouraged private enterprise to takes its place. And indeed, a handful of self-proclaimed 'agro-entrepreneurs' got those green beans aboard the 1994 flight mentioned at the chapter's beginning. During the 1990s, they shared packhouse and air cargo space with anywhere from one to two dozen other small (i.e. family or even individual) export operations.

This remained the basic arrangement in 2000. The exporters still contracted with peasant cooperatives for a certain tonnage of green beans per month, at a pre-agreed price, and they still depended on financing from French importers in order to supply the co-ops with seeds and other inputs for peasant cooperatives. And across the entire francophone network, 'traceability' was still a foreign concept, pronounced with a purposefully anglo accent. Altogether, Burkina Faso's green bean business seemed little affected either by European food scares or by a recent injection of US$2.75 million worth of French aid, aimed at 'professionalizing' export activities. The significance of this aid programme will be discussed again below.

Ye certain things had changed a lot since 1994, and not for the better. Thanks to increasing international competition, green bean prices had declined, but thanks to World Bank-mandated economic liberalization, growers' production and basic living costs had risen. Aesthetic standards had too, meaning that more green beans never made it past the packhouse. The region's air transport, on the other hand, had grown increasingly scarce and unreliable, so shipments that reached the runway often never took off, and ended up either sold in local markets or fed to goats.

The resulting disappointment and uncertainty both encouraged and was compounded by an assortment of 'risk management' strategies undertaken by growers, exporters and importers alike. Growers, perennially underfinanced and unsure whether they'd get paid what they considered their due, would often either sell the fertilizer intended for their green beans, or put it on their millet. In place of the intended pesticides, some would use the much cheaper but also more toxic chemicals used on cotton (which, if detected by inspectors in France, could be grounds for an indefinite ban on Burkina's produce).

Perhaps most commonly, growers would sell beans to anyone who would pay cash, even though their crops had almost always been contracted to and financed by someone else. Exporters, for their part, would buy up those 'leaked' beans whenever they lacked the tonnage they owed clients in France. Since this was a roundabout form of theft, it often took place in the middle of the night. And since green bean earnings were seasonal at best, exporters' alternative revenue sources tended to be diversified to the point of distraction: in between real estate ventures, mango farms, sesame exports, and consulting gigs, they had little time to check up on their green bean growers, who, consequently, saw little point in sticking to their contractual obligations.

Meanwhile, most French importers managed the risk of dealing with Burkina's beans by only accepting them on commission and, in some cases, by convincing themselves that it was fair to *voler les africains* ('steal from the Africans'), who otherwise, they said, would have stolen from them. Few were still willing to provide the kind of financing on which the entire Burkina Faso green bean business depended. In fact, by 2000 a third of the country's production was financed by one French import company, Selection. The company's owner and founder, Yves Gallot, was the first to buy Burkina Faso's green beans some thirty years before, and he claimed he still did business there only because his clients were his friends.

In short, the entire network was a mess, fraught with irregularities in quantity and quality that corporate supermarkets (which dominated fresh produce retailing in France as they did in Britain) no longer tolerated. They no longer had to, because Burkina Faso's exports now competed with those from several African countries. Yet year after year, the green bean planes took off. Why did the trade survive? What kept people participating when they faced such uncertain returns on their investments?

Clean and Corporate

Burkina Faso's tenuous but stubborn toehold in the global green bean market seemed all the more remarkable given the recent emergence of horticultural industries in countries such as Zambia. There, white landowners have dominated commercial farming since the early twentieth century, when settlers from Britain and South Africa were permitted to buy huge tracts of fertile line-of-rail land, and the land's African inhabitants were relocated to Native Reserves. Although the settler population remained small compared to Zimbabwe's or Kenya's (and got much smaller after independence), white farmers made sure that the colonial government favoured their interests over African smallholders'.[26] And although many of them left at independence, ongoing neglect of smallholder agriculture left Zambia dependent on white farming for the bulk of its export and food crops.[27]

Zambia's government got away with this neglect because mining, not farming, generated much of the country's employment and most of its wealth. Indeed, the most tangible signs of development in Zambia owed to the investments of Ernest Oppenheimer's Anglo-American Corporation and the American-owned Roan Selection Trust. Beginning in the 1920s, they built not just mines in the country's Copperbelt region, but entire company towns, complete with schools, hospitals and sports fields. Strong world copper prices helped the companies accommodate workers' demands for raises and benefits in the 1940s. At independence in 1964, Zambia was one of Africa's wealthiest countries. By 1971, the mines were nationalized and their workers earned an average of £1,000 annually – on a par with wages in Europe, and at least five times more than Zambian farm labourers.[28]

The prosperity didn't last. When world copper prices crashed in the mid-1970s, so did the Zambian economy. Heavily indebted as well as dependent on imported foodstuffs, the country underwent a World Bank structural adjustment programme, which liberalized the economy but failed to revive growth. Zambia had descended into the ranks of world's poorest countries by the time foreign investment began trickling back in during the early 1990s. Among the new arrivals were two companies intent on producing high-value, pre-packaged vegetables for the British market.

One, York Farms, was owned by CDC Capital Partners, a 'public–private' equity investor partly funded by the British government (and formerly known as the Commonwealth Development Corporation). The other, Agriflora, was the creation of TransZambezi Industries, an investment firm active in southern Africa but incorporated in the British Virgin Islands. Both companies were expatriate-managed, and both bought up prime irrigated land on the outskirts of Lusaka. Agriflora, by far the larger of the two, also bought produce from outgrowers, all white Zambians farming around either Lusaka or other nearby line-of-rail towns.

Both companies built their facilities expressly to meet the standards of the British supermarkets. Retailers in continental Europe either didn't want pre-packaged baby vegetables or didn't offer high enough prices. So for the Zambian export firms, the British market amounted to the only market. And they worked hard to please it. In addition to state-of-the-art irrigation and cold storage, they invested in an impressive social welfare infrastructure: on-farm clinics and kindergartens, housing for permanent employees, soccer fields for employee matches, and free lunches (or, in the case of one company, a daily high-protein drink). Some of these amenities of course, served the companies' own interest in maximizing labour productivity and attentiveness. As one manager admitted, 'let's be fairly hard about it. If our people are not healthy and happy, we're not going to get the work from them.'

It's worth noting that most of the field and packhouse workers were not considered permanent employees, and earned about a dollar a day. But this was considered a decent wage relative to the alternative of no wage at all. And indeed, managers at Agriflora were proud to offer such employment, and especially proud that their company ranked among the African horticultural enterprises farthest along in compliance with both the Ethical Trading Initiative 'base code' (which focused on labour standards) and the much more technical EurepGAP protocol. Recognizing that their overseas customers took compliance with codes seriously, both Agriflora and York Farms were eager to demonstrate a similar commitment. So they drew up a voluminous national code of horticultural conduct. Its standards covered most of the same issues as the external codes, but helped emphasize, as one company's technical manager put it, that 'Zambia's clean'.

Certainly it looked that way. The fields were orderly, the packhouses immaculate. Agriflora even kept a guard posted in the washroom, to make sure workers scrubbed their hands after using the toilets. Managers and outgrowers, for their part, kept meticulous records of their field and packhouse operations, so that in the event of an unannounced audit by one of their supermarket clients (typically sent by fax) they could demonstrate total traceability within a matter of hours. Technical managers prided themselves on their bookkeeping prowess. As one of them said,

> Anybody can come on to this farm any time without notice and they can see our records and I'll guarantee you they'll be as damn near 100 percent as they'll ever be, and they won't be fixed, they won't be pretty, you know, they'll be accurate. We have to be.

The companies' top management described this kind of work as stressful but fruitful. They knew that, if they slipped up, a supermarket might abruptly take its business elsewhere. On the other hand, said the managers, look what the supermarkets' standards had helped to create: a technically sophisticated and socially responsible export industry in one of the poorest countries on earth. Agriflora's director went so far as to say that companies like his would 'revolutionize Africa.'

Agriflora's outgrowers, however, were less impressed by what they saw as bureaucratic meddling. In fact their complaints sounded very similar to those voiced decades earlier by white settler farmers, who resented the taxes and policies (particularly regarding labour) of Britain's Colonial Office.[29] Longtime farmers, they hated the paperwork. While agreeing with the basic goals of the supermarkets' codes – reduced pesticide use, environmental sustainability, worker welfare, and of course high quality produce – they found nitpicky directives concerning, say, field toilets and chemical storage annoying. They said they knew how to look after their land and 'their people'. Most considered the supermarkets' categorical ban on under-16 labour hypocritical and senseless, given that many 14-year-olds in Zambia were AIDS orphans and heads of households.

Not least, the outgrowers did not like how the supermarkets' prices had remained the same for several years even as the costs of complying with their standards had risen. As the profits that had originally drawn them into high-value horticulture diminished, so had the outgrowers' numbers: by 2000, all but five or six (versus more than two dozen a few years before) had given up on the baby veg business. They'd refocused their efforts on dairy, beef and maize farming, or taken up export crops that were not subject to such intense foreign oversight.

Agriflora's top management claimed to be unfazed by the loss of so many outgrowers. It bought and planted additional acreage, and rounded up donor aid for a programme that would contract out some production to smallholder (meaning black Zambian) cooperatives. In keeping with the 'benign dictator' model of contract farming described above, the management emphasized that company employees would handle all pesticide spraying on the smallholders' fields.[30] Meanwhile, Agriflora won the 'exporter of the year' award in 2003, and boasted annual sales increases of more than 600 per cent. In an otherwise stagnant national economy, the company's success appeared too good to be true. In fact, it was.

The Enduring Bust...

Let's return to the question of why Burkina Faso's green bean trade puttered on, against increasingly unlikely odds. One part of the answer lies in the priorities of the French supermarkets, which differ considerably from those of their British counterparts. Traditionally patronized for their convenience and cut-rate prices, French *hypermarchés* such as Carrefour were trying, by the end of the twentieth century, to pretty up their fresh produce aisles. So they cared more about grading and packaging than before. But their food safety worries, like those of the French public, remained much more food-specific those in Britain. Mad cow disease, dioxin-tainted chickens and trafficked animal feeds had shaken French confidence in the livestock industry.[31] But as the French retailers saw it, beef and green beans were very different things, and surveys showed that consumers still considered fruits and vegetables relatively safe and 'natural', especially if they came from small farms.[32] So their chief concern about imported fresh produce was getting reliable, uniform shipments, as cheaply as possible.[33] They didn't really want to know what was happening down on the farms and in the packhouses of Africa, and certainly didn't intend to send high-level managers to find out (a standard practice of the top British supermarkets).

The French supermarkets' single-minded emphasis on price drove many French importers out of business, and favoured large firms such as Dole. But it also left the mid-sized importers, like the company Selection and its founder Yves Gallot, free to continue doing business with long-time suppliers in Burkina Faso. It did not matter to Carrefour that the country's infrastructure was abysmal, and that its green bean growers were mostly illiterate peasants. What mattered was that Gallot and his suppliers – the Burkinabé exporters – delivered the goods. Put somewhat differently, the key to the unlikely survival of the Burkina Faso green bean trade, in an age of intense competition and stringent standards, lies in the motives and relationships between these groups of intermediaries. As always, these must be understood in context.

The Burkinabé exporters, for example, persisted in this trade at least partly because of the moral status and economic entitlements it brought. The moral status derived from their purported roles as the patrons of the peasantry. Several exporters described great satisfaction in 'helping' their growers earn a decent living. Although their 'help' was perhaps unreliable at best, the exporters' role still carried a certain moral weight among urban educated Burkinabé, many of whom supported needy rural kin. This moral status also had practical value back in the rural areas themselves. In general, the exporters with the most loyal and reliable growers (and thus the best beans) were those most willing and able to act as benefactors rather than just buyers.

The economic entitlements came in the form of the 'help' the exporters themselves received from the Agence Française du Developpement (AFD). The AFD's aforementioned US$2.75 million aid programme aimed to revitalize smallholder green bean export production by 'professionalizing' the exporters. The hope was that if these businessmen acted somehow more businesslike, then this would boost smallholders' confidence and productivity. While the French AFD official in charge of the programme in 2000 readily admitted that progress was slow, the exporters had not been idle. Rather, they had taken advantage of everything the aid programme offered – an office and secretary, loans, 'learning tours' to Paris and East Africa – to broaden their personal social networks and sources of income. In their view, this was a legitimate use of aid moneys. A good agro-exporter (meaning good at both making money and redistributing it to the peasantry) was a diversified and well-connected one.

Even though the aid programme was relatively new, the exporters' strategies for tapping its resources had much in common with those employed by the region's mercantile elite for the past half-century. In other words, they used rural patron–client relations to build personal business careers that were both subsidized and justified by the cause of peasant-based development. Many members of this elite worked for government ministries and foreign aid agencies before starting their own businesses; they rented trucks to those agencies and houses to their expatriate employees.[34] The exporters, in this sense, were professional middlemen, and proud of it! Ultimately the historical role of such middlemen in rural development helps explain why green exporting remained appealing even when it was no longer profitable in any reliable, conventional sense. Beans were means to other ends.

But what about Yves Gallot, who insisted that he only kept doing business in Burkina Faso because his friends were there? This would ordinarily seem like a suspiciously sentimental claim from a businessman of his stature; since his first trips to Burkina thirty years earlier, Gallot had built one of the world's biggest green bean import–export trades. But given the complicated meanings and obligations of 'friendship' in the West African societies where he had long worked, it made sense. In other words, in exchange situations bound by neither kin nor contract, your friends are those who won't cheat you, or at least not too much.[35] They expect favours and sympathy, but they also expect to grant them. Gallot's businesses practices reflected this notion of friendship. If he had not 'become African', as he sometimes joked, he had at least learned how to work profitably in an African country where most other importers had given up.

It helped that Gallot had a diversified supply base; he bought green beans from all over Africa, and sold to retail clients with a range of quality expectations. The size of his enterprise, in other words, gave him a buffer. But his loyalty to Burkina Faso, where people called him le roi d'haricot vert (the green bean king) also gave him power. He could set prices, and reward competence with big contracts. In turn, he could count on his 'friends' (who were known to be country's most respected and reliable exporters) to work very hard procuring beans that would meet the market's rising standards. He took losses sometimes, but overall he managed to find quality on the cheap in Burkina Faso. And like the Burkinabé exporters, he found satisfaction in playing the role of the patron.

So that's the story of the enduring bust – which, it is worth noting, still endured three years after Gallot's death in 2003. His son took over the business, and maintained relations with his father's suppliers. According to Gallot Jr., however, the story may end definitely with aeroplanes, just as it began. Senegal and Morocco are now able to send green beans to France in rapid refrigerated container vessels, one of the more recent innovations in 'cool chain' technology. Ocean shipping has always been much cheaper than airfreight, and in a post-9/11 era of diminishing air service and escalating costs, this differential has become decisive. Despite cheaper labour costs, land-locked green bean exporters such as Burkina Faso may soon stand no chance. This will be too bad, said Gallot's son, 'because our friends are there.'

…and the Unsustainable Boom

Meanwhile, back in Zambia, scandal rocked the baby veg industry in mid-2004. TransZambezi Investments, Agriflora's owner, discovered that its director (the one who boasted that his industry would 'revolutionize Africa') had committed 'massive financial irregularities' – so massive that he'd fled the country. It turned out that for the past three years he and his number-two man had padded the account books by several million dollars. They wanted the figures to look good so that banks would continue to lend them money, which Barclays and others in fact did. By the time the irregularities were exposed, Agriflora owed the banks US$23 million, and went immediately into receivership. At the end of 2004, TZI sold it off to another

British-financed fresh-produce company. The investment firm's shareholders lost several million dollars, and eventually many of Agriflora's 5,000-plus workers lost their jobs.[36]

Clearly one must be careful not to read too much into the actions of a few unscrupulous individuals. But it can be argued (and has been, by industry insiders) that the episode confirmed what the Zambian outgrowers figured out a few years earlier: the whole enterprise was not really financially viable, given the dazzling imported equipment, the expatriate management's salaries, the airfreight from southern Africa, and not least, the cost meeting the supermarkets' ever more rigorous standards of safety, quality and 'ethics'.

Yet expectations – on the part of investors, clients, and not least Zambians – were high, and meeting them (or at least appearing to) was straightforward. It just required going through all the routines of accountability (the record keeping, the audits) with just a little more creativity than would otherwise be necessary. Who would know? Not the accounting firm KPMG, which audited Agriflora's finances. In fact in the wake of the scandal this firm (which ranks alongside Price Waterhouse as one of the world's biggest auditors) defended its own accountability. Said KPMG's Zambia representative: 'We applied internationally recognized standards in our audit process and we stand by that.'[37]

So what does corporate transparency conceal, besides how easily top managers can cook the books? It conceals the power relations that make it possible. The British supermarkets, in other words, can demonstrate 'transparency' in their transnational supply chains because they can demand that their suppliers comply with and pay for standards defining (according to the supermarkets) 'best practice'. This power is both economic and politico-cultural. More precisely, it is rooted in both the supermarkets' near-monopoly control of the national food retail market and in British norms of corporate social responsibility.

These norms can be traced at least as far back as the antislavery movement (see also Jackson and Ward, Chapter 13, and Trentmann, Chapter 14, this volume).[38] They have gained renewed currency, however, in an era when a combination of corporate consolidation and state liberalization (especially in the global South) has given the biggest retailers more *de facto* regulatory power over food production and distribution than the governments of the countries where they operate.[39] So the same processes of economic globalization that have helped to create the South–North high-value food trades discussed in this chapter have also fuelled popular expectations that retailers can and should act 'ethically' on a global scale. The great irony, of course, is that the retailers now invoke these expectations to justify standards aimed, above all, at higher profits. In Africa, these standards have excluded small farmers, and squeezed larger suppliers to the point where real improvements in worker welfare – higher pay, greater job security – appear less likely.

This comparison of the anglophone and francophone trades has not intended to portray the latter, with its emphasis on trust and friendship, as somehow better.

In fact, smallholders in this trade endured years of unreliable and inadequate remuneration. By January 2005, many long-time green bean growers had given up on export production altogether, and instead grew vegetables for the poor but less risky domestic market. Rather, the comparison highlighted the culturally specific, historically rooted norms and relationships through which power is exerted and exploitation justified. More broadly, it showed that globalization has not erased cultural difference in the world of food and trade, but instead has stretched it to a transnational scale.

That said, large retailers are likely to increase their domination over transnational food trading. They will probably also attempt to globalize their 'best practice' standards further, supposedly in the consumers' interest.[40] Cultural economy analysis can help to show that such efforts to dictate goodness are rarely all that benign.

Notes

1. S. Jaffee, 'The Many Faces of Success: The Development of Kenyan Horticultural Exports', in S. Jaffee and J. Morton, *Marketing Africa's High-Value Foods: Comparative Experiences of an Emergent Private Sector* (Dubuque, IA, 1995), pp. 319–74.
2. R. Abrahamsen, 'African Studies and the Postcolonial Challenge', *African Affairs* 102 (2003): 189–210; M. Foucault, G. Burchell, C. Gordon and P. Miller, *The Foucault Effect: Studies in Governmentality* (London, 1991).
3. The National Science Foundation, the Radcliffe Institute for Advanced Studies, the Nelson Rockefeller Center at Dartmouth College, and the Rahr Foundation all provided support for this research. For a more in-depth explanation of the research methodology see S. Freidberg, 'On the Trail of the Global Green Bean: Methodological Considerations in Multi-Site Ethnography', *Global Networks* 1 (2001): 353–68. For a more in-depth discussion of the research findings, see S. Freidberg, *French Beans and Food Scares: Culture and Commerce in an Anxious Age* (New York, 2004).
4. J. Dixon, A Cultural Economy Model for Studying Food Systems, *Agriculture and Human Values* 16 (1999): 151–60; P. Du Gay and M. Pryke, *Cultural Economy: Cultural Analysis and Commercial Life* (London and Thousand Oaks, CA, 2002).
5. D. Goodman and M. Redclift, *Refashioning Nature: Food, Ecology and Culture* (New York, 1991); B. Fine, 'Towards a Political Economy of Food', *Review of International Political Economy* 1 (1994): 519–45.

6. S. Mintz, *Sweetness and Power: The Place of Sugar in Modern History* (New York, 1986); M. Weismantel, 'Enfants Et Soupes, Hommes Et Taureaux: Les Répas Et Le Temps Pour Les Femmes De Zumbagua', in M. Aymard, C. Grignon and F. Sabban, *Le Temps De Manger: Alimentation, Emploi Du Temps, Et Rythmes Sociaux* (Paris, 1993), pp. 151–82.

7. M. French and J. Phillips, *Cheated Not Poisoned? Food Regulation in the United Kingdom, 1875–1938* (Manchester, 2000); M. A. Echols, *Food Safety and the WTO: The Interplay of Culture, Science, and Technology* (London, 2001).

8. J. Scott, *The Moral Economy of the Peasant: Rebellion and Subsistence in Southeast Asia* (New Haven, CT, 1976); M. Watts, *Silent Violence: Food, Famine, and Peasantry in Northern Nigeria* (Berkeley, CA, 1983).

9. See for example G. Clark, *Onions Are My Husband: Survival and Accumulation by West African Market Women* (Chicago, 1994); N. Horn, *Cultivating Customers: Marketwomen in Harare, Zimbabwe* (Boulder, CO, 1994); B. House-Midamba and F. K. Ekechi (eds), *African Market Women and Economic Power* (Westport, CT, 1995); J. MacGaffey and R. Bazenguissa-Ganga, International African Institute, *Congo–Paris : Transnational Traders on the Margins of the Law* (London and Bloomington, IN, 2000).

10. S. Freidberg, 'Of Cows and Men', *Transition* (1999), pp. 100–10; S. Freidberg, Tradeswomen and Businessmen: The Social Relations of Contract Gardening in Southwestern Burkina Faso, *Journal of African Rural and Urban Studies* 3 (1996); S. Freidberg, 'Contacts, Contracts and Green Bean Schemes: Liberalisation and Agro-Entrepreneurship in Burkina Faso', *Journal of Modern African Studies* 35 (1997): 101–28.

11. M. Power, *The Audit Society: Rituals of Verification* (Oxford, 1997); M. Strathern (ed.), *Audit Cultures: Anthropological Studies in Accountability, Ethics, and the Academy* (New York, 2000).

12. S. Henson and J. Caswell, 'Food Safety Regulation: An Overview of Contemporary Issues', *Food Policy* 24 (1999): 589–603.

13. S. Freidberg, *French Beans and Food Scares: Culture and Commerce in an Anxious Age* (New York, 2004); T. Marsden, A. Flynn and M. Harrison, *Consuming Interests: The Social Provision of Foods* (London, 2000); A. Hughes, 'Responsible Retailers? Ethical Trade and the Strategic Re-Regulation of Cross-Continental Food Supply Chains', in N. Fold and B. Pritchard, *Cross-Continental Agri-Food Chains: Structures, Actors and Dynamics in the Global Food System* (New York, 2005), pp. 141–54.

14. P. Shears, F. Zollers and S. Hurd, 'Food for Thought: What Mad Cows Have Wrought with Respect to Food Safety Regulation in the EU and U.K.', *British Food Journal* 103 (2001): 63–87.

15. L. Orton and P. Madden, *The Global Supermarket: Britain's Biggest Shops and Food from the Third World* (London, 1996).

16. A. Hughes, 'Multi-Stakeholder Approaches to Ethical Trade: Towards a Reorganization of U.K. Retailers' Global Supply Chains', *Journal of Economic Geography* 1 (2001): 421–37; ETI, Purpose, Principles, Programme, http://www.ethicaltrade.org/Z/lib/ppp/ppp_en.shtml, May 30, 2006.

17. S. Ratzan (ed.), *The Mad Cow Crisis: Health and the Public Good* (New York, 1998); D. A. Powell and W. Leiss, *Mad Cows and Mother's Milk: The Perils of Poor Risk Communication* (Montreal, 1997); S. Freidberg, 'The Ethical Complex of Corporate Food Power', *Environment and Planning D-Society and Space* 21 (2004).

18. H. Campbell, 'The Rise and Rise of EurepGAP: European (Re)Invention of Colonial Food Relations?', *International Journal of Sociology of Food and Agriculture* 13 (2005): 1–19; K. Jason, M. Michael and H. Maki, 'Governance in the Global Agro-Food System: Backlighting the Role of Transnational Supermarket Chains', *Agriculture and Human Values* 22 (2005): 291–302.

19. For a detailed discussion of audit culture as well as case studies, see M. Power, *The Audit Society: Rituals of Verification* (Oxford, 1997); M. Strathern (ed.), *Audit Cultures: Anthropological Studies in Accountability, Ethics, and the Academy* (New York, 2000); M. Power, *The Audit Explosion* (London, 1994); A. Hughes, 'Global Commodity Networks, Ethical Trade and Governmentality: Organizing Business Responsibility in the Kenyan Cut Flower Industry', *Transactions of the Institute of British Geographers* 26 (2001): 390–406.

20. S. Jaffee, 'The Many Faces of Success: The Development of Kenyan Horticultural Exports', in S. Jaffee and J. Morton, *Marketing Africa's High-Value Foods: Comparative Experiences of an Emergent Private Sector* (Dubuque, IA, 1995), pp. 319–74; S. Jaffee, 'Contract Farming in the Shadow of Competitive Markets: The Experience of Kenyan Horticulture', in P. D. Little and M. J. Watts, *Living under Contract: Contract Farming and Agrarian Transformation in Sub-Saharan Africa* (Madison, WI, 1994), pp. 97–139.

21. For example, see M. Mackintosh, *Gender, Class, and Rural Transition: Agribusiness and the Food Crisis in Senegal* (London, 1989).

22. C. Dolan and J. Humphrey, 'Governance and Trade in Fresh Vegetables: The Impact of UK Supermarkets on the African Horticulture Industry', *Journal of Development Studies* 37 (2000): 147–76; IDS/NRI, Enhancing the Development Impact of Export Horticulture in Sub-Saharan Africa, 1999.

23. This policy had parallels in France's own modern history of rural development. See E. J. Weber, *Peasants into Frenchmen: The Modernization of Rural France, 1870–1914* (Stanford, CA, 1976); R. Delavignette, *Les Paysans Noirs* (Paris, 1931); P. Muller, *Le Technocrate et le Paysan: Essai sur la politique francaise de la modernization de l'agriculture* (Paris, 1984).

24. S. Freidberg, 'Making a Living: A Social History of Market-Garden Work in the Regional Economy of Bobo-Dioulasso, Burkina Faso', Ph.D. thesis, University of California-Berkeley, 1996; S. Freidberg, 'To Garden, to Market: Gendered

Meanings of Work on an African Urban Periphery', *Gender, Place and Culture* 8 (2001): 5–24.

25. V. Compaore *et al.*, *Burkina Faso: Développement des Cultures Irriguées* (Ouagadougou 1987).

26. On colonial era land policies, see K. P. Vickery, *Black and White in Southern Zambia: The Tonga Plateau Economy and British Imperialism, 1890–1939* (Westport, CT, 1986); R. Palmer, 'Land Alienation and Agricultural Conflict in Colonial Zambia', in R. I. Rotberg, *Imperialism, Colonialism and Hunger: East and Central Africa* (Lexington, MA, 1983).

27. D. J. Dodge, *Agricultural Policy and Performance in Zambia: History, Prospects, and Proposals for Change* (Berkeley, CA, 1977).

28. M. Burawoy, *The Colour of Class on the Copper Mines, from African Advancement to Zambianization* (Manchester, 1972); J. Ferguson, *Expectations of Modernity: Myths and Meanings of Urban Life on the Zambian Copperbelt* (Berkeley, CA, 1999).

29. D. Kallman, 'Projected Moralities, Engaged Anxieties: Northern Rhodesia's Reading Publics, 1953–1964', *The International Journal of African Historical Studies* 32 (1999): 71–117.

30. Most of the 'smallholders' turned out to be relatively affluent black Zambian civil servants and retirees, who owned land on the outskirts of Lusaka. Most had no experience in horticulture, much less farming. Those interviewed in 2000 complained that Agriflora was providing too little technical help, not too much.

31. N. Mamère and J.-F. Narbonne, *Toxiques Affaires: de la Dioxine à la Vache Folle* (Paris, 2001).

32. M.-A. Moreau-Rio, 'Crises Alimentaires et Environmentales: les Fruits et Légumes Aussi!', *Infos-Ctifl* (1999), pp. 20–4.

33. C. Ducrocq, *Distribution Alimentaire: Enjeux Stratégiques et Perspectives 1994–1998* (Paris, 1996).

34. E. Gregoire and P. Labazée (eds), *Les Grands Commercants d'Afrique de l'Ouest* (Paris, 1993); P. Labazée, *Entreprises et Entrepreneurs du Burkina Faso* (Paris, 1988).

35. K. Hart, 'Kinship, Contract and Trust: The Economic Organization of Migrants in an African City Slum', in D. Gambetta, *Trust: Making and Breaking Cooperative Relations* (New York, 1988), pp. 176–93.

36. H. Saburi, 'Axe Falls on Two Senior Agriflora Directors', *Financial Gazette* (Harare, 3 June 2004); K. Kaswende, 'TZI Planning to Take Agriflora's Top Management to Court', *The Post* (Lusaka, 31 January 2005).

37. K. Chambwa, 'International Standards were used in Auditing Agriflora—KPMG', *The Post* (Lusaka, 28 July 2004).

38. S. Drescher, *Capitalism and Antislavery: British Mobilization in Comparative Perspective* (Oxford, 1987).

39. S. Freidberg, 'The Ethical Complex of Corporate Food Power', *Environment and Planning D-Society and Space* 21 (2004); S. Drescher, *Capitalism and Antislavery: British Mobilization in Comparative Perspective* (Oxford, 1987); T. Marsden, 'Creating Space for Food: The Distinctiveness of Recent Agrarian Development', in D. Goodman and M. Watts, *Globalizing Food: Agrarian Questions and Global Restructuring* (New York, 1997), pp. 169–91.
40. On the spread of corporate supermarkets into new regions, see T. Reardon, P. Timmer, C. Barret and J. Berdegué, 'The Rise of Supermarkets in Africa, Asia and Latin America', *American Journal of Agricultural Economics* 85 (2002): 1140–6; L. Dries, T. Reardon and J. Swinnen, 'The Rapid Rise of Supermarkets in Central and Eastern Europe: Implications for the Agrifood Sector and Rural Development', *Development Policy Review* 22 (2004): 525–56.

–13–

Connections and Responsibilities
The Moral Geographies of Sugar
Peter Jackson and *Neil Ward*

Introduction

In his classic study of the place of sugar in modern history, Sidney Mintz drew attention to the mysterious connection that exists between a field of sugar cane in Puerto Rico and the refined white sugar that sweetens a cup of tea or coffee in Europe or the United States. The connection, he argued, was not simply one of technical transformation but also involved 'the mystery of people unknown to one another being linked through space and time – and not just by politics and economics, but along a particular chain of connection'.[1] These links connect the Caribbean to the rest of the world, as the region and its people have for more than 500 years been 'caught up in skeins of imperial control, spun in Amsterdam, London, Paris, Madrid, and other European and North American centers of world power'.[2] The genius of Mintz's study was to link the supply of sugar from the Caribbean with the growth of demand in Europe. Similar connections were drawn by Stuart Hall regarding the colonial origins of the British taste for sugar and tea, which constitute 'the outside history that is inside the history of the English'.[3]

This chapter is about the different kinds of connection that exist within the history and geography of the British sugar industry and the sense of moral responsibility that stems from an appreciation of those connections. The chapter adopts the metaphor of the commodity chain to analyse these multiple and contested connections.[4] Unlike most commodity chain analyses, however, which seek to identify the points along the chain where value is added and profit extracted, this chapter – like the wider project from which it is drawn – seeks to analyse the points at which *meaning* is manufactured along the chain as the commodity travels from source to sales-point.[5] As we shall see, the meanings of sugar include its nutritional and culinary properties, its effects on dental health and childhood obesity and its historical associations with slavery and empire. Understanding these meanings involves a cultural analysis as much as an economic one, though one might argue that an effective analysis of commercial culture requires us to move beyond such conventional distinctions.[6] Tracing the links between those involved in different ways in the global trade in sugar, this chapter seeks to map the moral geographies of connection and disconnection, to understand our sense of responsibility for 'distant strangers' and the strategies that are employed to accept or deny such responsibilities.[7]

According to the food writer Jenny Linford, interviewed as part of this project, sugar is 'an invisible food': 'it's taken for granted – we don't really think about it, we don't think about how it's produced … its presence in our households'.[8] Likewise, a former sales and marketing executive at Tate & Lyle argued that the public perception is that 'sugar just happens, you know, nobody makes it, it's just there'.[9] Such consumer indifference is remarkable when one considers the extent to which the history of sugar is mired in the politics of slavery and empire. Its production, trade and regulation continue to provoke questions of economic dependency and inequality.[10] Despite recent reforms, European sugar producers continue to attract significant subsidies, protected from foreign competition by a complex system of production quotas, price guarantees and external tariffs that critics see as contributing to the distortion of world trade in sugar.[11] Sugar is also associated with public health issues such as dental decay and childhood obesity, leading one author to describe the product as 'pure, white and deadly'.[12] Besides the granular form of sugar that is familiar to most consumers, sugar is used as an additive in soft drinks, baked goods and many other processed foods. Its everyday use rarely provokes serious thought about issues of provenance, quality, price or value, unlike many other food products where these issues have become increasingly prominent in recent years. Campaigning groups like Oxfam have made numerous interventions about sugar; but it has never attained the public profile of other commodities, such as the sweatshop conditions associated with textile production or the ethical campaigns that have been organized around other 'fair trade' products such as coffee, tea and chocolate.[13]

This chapter draws on recent debates about geographies of responsibility and histories of connection to provide an analysis of the contemporary sugar industry. It draws on a series of life history interviews with sugar producers at various points along the supply chain to demonstrate how these geographies of responsibility operate at a variety of scales where what may seem morally justified at one scale can look quite different when analysed at another scale. The chapter makes a similar argument about histories of connection and disconnection, where the interviewees have recourse to particular forms of historical argument to establish some kinds of connection while denying others. The chapter concludes by advancing a relational understanding of the connections between geographical scales and historical temporalities, aiming to produce a more nuanced understanding of the moral geographies and histories of sugar.

A History of Sugar Production in Britain and Europe

Sugar cane is generally understood to have originated in the South Pacific, and was first harvested for its flavour-enhancing properties more than 5,000 years ago.

Shipments of large quantities of sugar to Europe began in the fourteenth century, and the West Indies soon became the world's main sugar-producing region. The first experiments in refining sugar from sugar beet took place in Europe in the eighteenth century.[14] A domestic (European) sugar beet industry was established during the Napoleonic Wars to reduce France's dependency on overseas producers in times of uncertain supply. By the end of the nineteenth century, the technical process of beet refining had been so improved that beet sugar was indistinguishable from cane sugar. By 1914, almost 11 million tonnes of sugar, comprising 45 per cent of world production, was produced from sugar beet, with almost 80 per cent of the refined and unrefined sugar imported into Britain coming from beet.

In Britain, the National Sugar Beet Association was founded in 1909 to help the British sugar beet industry. However, it was the threat to food supplies in the First World War that gave the impetus to state support for domestic production. Although a *laissez-faire* approach to the agricultural industry dominated during the 1920s, sugar was the one exception to this rule. The Sugar Industry (Subsidy) Act of 1925 provided new enterprises with direct subsidies from the Exchequer for ten years, reducing the risks for investors in sugar beet factories. By 1928, eighteen factories were in operation, thirteen of which were in the east of England. The interventionist approach continued following the Sugar Industry (Reorganisation) Act of 1936, which established the British Sugar Corporation (BCS) and an independent Sugar Commission to oversee the development of the sector.

Sugar beet production expanded markedly in Britain during the Second World War as part of the 'Dig for Victory' campaign to boost domestic food production. Production of sugar beet continued to grow under the postwar framework for British agricultural policy, which sought to protect the industry and encourage expansion and improvements in productivity, reaching its peak in 1980. Britain remained a major importer of sugar, although domestic self-sufficiency rose from about 33 per cent in 1970 to 57 per cent in 1987.[15] Before the Second World War, about 2.2 million tonnes of raw sugar were imported from colonies, with imports falling to around 1 million tonnes in the 1980s.

During the negotiations prior to the UK joining the European Common Market in 1973, the arrangements for imports of raw sugar to supply UK-based sugar refineries proved a significant issue. Along with the arrangements for financing the Common Market, accommodating the UK's former system of imperial preference in sugar supplies within the Common Agricultural Policy proved one of the main challenges for negotiators to overcome.[16] The UK had operated a preferential import regime in favour of the sugar-exporting Commonwealth countries (especially Fiji, Guyana, Jamaica, Mauritius and Swaziland). On accession this became a European Community responsibility, and a new preferential import system was established under the Lomé Convention, signed in 1975. The Convention allowed the admission into the Common Market of 1.3 million tonnes of cane sugar each year at a price linked to the support price paid to the Community's own sugar beet farmers.[17]

The Common Agricultural Policy's Sugar Regime was established in 1968. Its main purpose was to guarantee prices to producers and to protect the internal market for sugar within Europe. Import levies protected domestic producers from external competition and guaranteed prices were financed by higher prices for sugar paid for by consumers. Surplus production was dumped on the world market and production was controlled through a system of production quotas. Sugar therefore operated as a highly protected and regulated sector within the Common Agricultural Policy, and the British position within Europe was particularly distinctive because of the significance of imported raw sugar from cane-producing countries. Of the raw cane imported for processing in the EU, almost two-thirds comes to the UK for processing by Tate & Lyle.[18]

The Common Agricultural Policy came under increasing pressure for reform during the 1980s, primarily as a consequence of the budgetary costs of high levels of production support at a time of surplus production, but also because of an increasingly effective environmental critique of the policy. The first set of wide-ranging reforms, which crossed the various individual commodity regimes, was agreed in 1992, followed by further extensive reform in 1999 and 2003. However, the sugar regime within the CAP remained relatively unreformed throughout this period (1992–2003) of almost perpetual CAP reform.

Following the last significant reform of the CAP, agreed in 2003, the CAP's Sugar Regime came under increasing scrutiny. This was a result of several factors. First, international trade negotiations through the World Trade Organization (WTO) led to growing international pressure to eliminate export subsidies and reduce import tariffs. Indeed, a WTO appeal panel ruling in April 2005 on complaints brought by Australia, Brazil and Thailand affirmed that the Sugar Regime left the EU in breach on international export rules. Second, a unilateral trade agreement called the 'Everything But Arms' agreement made provision to eliminate duty and quota from all products except arms and ammunition from forty-nine Less Developed Countries (LDCs) with effect from 2001, but with a transitional phase-in of the trade liberalization for three sensitive commodities – sugar, rice and bananas. Under the Agreement, after 2009, restrictions on LDC sugar imports to the EU would be lifted, seriously threatening the functioning of the European sugar market. Finally, internal political pressures within the EU left the sugar regime exposed. It looked increasingly anachronistic in an age of liberalization and reform, and was widely believed to have detrimental impacts upon consumers, competition and efficiency.[19]

In September 2003, the European Commission produced an assessment of the options for reform of the sugar regime.[20] The options were: to maintain the status quo by extending the current regime arrangements for a further period; to operate a system of fixed quotas but at a severely reduced level of activity; to maintain quotas for a period, but significantly reduce the level of price support and compensate farmers through direct payments via the new Single Farm Payment system under the post-2003 reformed CAP; or to more radically liberalize by abolishing domestic price support and ending production quotas. In June 2005 the Commission produced its recommendation for sugar reform, which included a 39 per cent cut in the guaranteed price paid to sugar growers, coupled with a 60 per cent compensation scheme to EU producers who decided to leave the market. When the UK took over the Presidency of the EU in July 2005 it made securing reform of the Sugar Regime in the Agriculture Council one of its main priorities. Sugar has therefore been a significant anomaly within European agricultural policy, the first commodity to receive government subsidy and the last sector to be reformed.

Connections and Responsibilities along the Supply Chain

The arguments that follow are based on the analysis of in-depth life history recordings conducted with people involved in cane or beet sugar supply chains in the UK.[21] The life history approach allows us to examine the changes that have taken place in the sugar industry within living memory. It provides access to the way these changes are remembered and expressed in the respondents' own words, and it seeks to locate the respondents' accounts in their biographical and wider social context. As the interview extracts demonstrate, the way these accounts are told (their narrative style) is as important as what is actually said (their narrative content), though this is often better conveyed by listening to the recordings than by reading the transcripts. We focus here on just a handful of the interviews that best illustrate our argument about geographies of responsibility and histories of connection.[22]

Our first example comes from the life history of Henry Cross (b.1938), a tenant farmer on the Sandringham estate in Norfolk. Mr Cross describes sugar beet as 'a good safe crop to grow', 'a very sort of safe, fairly profitable, steady crop'[23] because of the way the market is regulated and prices guaranteed: 'you knew your market, you knew the price and if you could harvest it, you knew, depending upon what the sugar percentage was, you'd get your money… It was all very organized and safe.' He describes sugar beet as 'a cornerstone of farming in Norfolk', where a good acreage of beet meant that you were 'fairly safe' financially.[24] British Sugar supplies the seed and contracts and buys the crop in what Mr Cross describes as 'a total monopoly'.[25] Nonetheless, Henry Cross foresaw major changes ahead for sugar beet production in East Anglia as a result of the EU reforms described above. These changes were likely to lead to 'a sort of rationalisation of the sugar industry', causing 'quite a shake out' for East Anglian beet farmers.[26]

At a key point in the interview, Mr Cross told a story about how the safety and reliability of the current arrangements had been challenged by a clergyman who accused him of destroying the economy of the West Indies:

> He [the clergyman] said, "what do you grow?" And [I said] "I grow sugar beet and wheat and potato and barley" and … he said, "You do realise that … you sugar beet growers are destroying the economy of the West Indies" … 'Cos his brother was ambassador of

Barbados or something or other anyhow. And he sort of was ahead of the game … and he said, "Wouldn't it be far better if you, you lot all stopped growing sugar beet and the people who are coming over here looking for jobs, could have jobs where they are?"[27]

The clergyman challenged Henry Cross's uneasy moral position by advancing an argument about the connections between Britain and the Caribbean, and more specifically between Barbados and East Anglia, where the dynamics of agricultural production were, in the clergyman's eyes at least, connected to the politics of immigration ('the people who are coming over here'). Mr Cross recalls how he didn't really have an answer to the clergyman's question, but how it had made him think differently about Britain's membership of the European Union:

> I hadn't really got an answer to it, but I could see and that sort of rather alerted me to this and of course at the same time there was with the joining of the Common Market and all that sort of thing. They started to look at the sugar regime and it's been criticised I think quite a lot. Not entirely unfairly by the way, it's sort of manipulated sugar. But I'm afraid I've sort of just said, "We … you know, they keep wanting us to grow sugar beet and if we don't grow it, the French will", so we'll carry on growing it and it's been a profitable crop but the way the sort of the EEC has handled sugar I think is questionable.[28]

Here, then, Henry Cross accepts that the EU has 'manipulated' sugar production and that the current sugar regime may not be fair. But rather than attempting to justify the morality of growing sugar beet in general, he justifies his own involvement in the industry by reference to the national scale ('if we don't grow it, the French will').

At another point in the interview, Mr Cross cites a historical justification for maintaining the status quo ('the farmers fed us through the war'), though he admits that farmers were then, as now, mostly motivated by profit: 'I wouldn't claim any sort of fine motives for it':

> I mean farmers are realistic and they will do whatever you … if anybody, the government or a merchant says, "This'll make you money", they'll go for it, and like I should think anybody else would in any other industry. Because at the end of the day, you've got to try and keep yourself profitable [laughs]. That's not a very moral tone but it's a realistic one and, you know, I mean, I think that is, I'm sure the way they looked at it, that it was a good crop to grow and let's grow it.[29]

In this extract, Henry Cross accepts that farmers are 'realistic' and will grow whatever makes a profit. Accepting that this isn't a very 'moral' position, he justifies his 'realism' by saying that farming is no different from any other industry. Faced with a 'good crop' where current levels of subsidy guarantee a profitable price, farmers will simply follow the logic of the market.

A second interview raises similar arguments about geographies of responsibility and histories of connection. Mark Taylor (b.1934, pseudonym) is a second-generation beet farmer from Nottinghamshire. Mr Taylor recalls being visited by a young female journalist who compared his situation with that of farmers in the Third World. His sense of injustice is almost tangible:

> I mean, she came to my farm one day to interview me. And she sat in the field of sugar, we sat in a field of sugar beet – she was wanting to photograph things – and she said – and it was a damn good field of sugar beet – and she said, it was almost as if she'd rehearsed it, she said: "Well Mark Taylor, we're here in your field of sugar beet and I want to ask you, why are you growing this crop, why are you growing this crop and losing money when there are people in the Third World who can grow a lot more sugar cane than you, but they can't get the market and so therefore they can't make a good living out of it. Why are you growing it?" And there's me thinking, quite pleased with this crop of sugar beet, it's a very big crop, it was one of the best crops I've ever grown and I was quite proud of it. So I was a bit deflated I must say.[30]

When asked how he answered the journalist's question, he replied:

> Well, you're talking apples and oranges, aren't you? You know, I have to live with ... my wife has to shop with her husband or whoever, her partner, and we live in a sort of highly regulated, highly paid society. The object of the Common Agricultural Policy – and maybe they've got it wrong, I don't know – but the object was to lift European farmers out of peasantry, which they were soon after the war, and give them the same standard of living as people in the towns and cities. That was the original object of it ... but I think I'm entitled to a price that allows me to grow a crop and make a modest profit so that my wife too can feed my kids same as anybody else. Now you might say well, and so why can't the Mozambique farmer have the same thing, and I agree, why can't he? And you know I don't understand why he can't.[31]

In this extract Mark Taylor is forced into a justificatory position having been confronted by a set of connections with which he clearly feels uncomfortable. Where he sees a fine harvest, reflecting his good husbandry of the crop, the journalist sees evidence of global inequality and injustice. For Mr Taylor, these two worldviews are incommensurable ('apples and oranges'). The journalist wants 'straight answers' to her questions, having manoeuvred Mr Taylor into a defensive position. His response is to refuse the simple logic of her questioning, insisting that the world is a more complex place, characterized by a series of ethical dilemmas. While, in the previous extracts, Henry Cross attempted to explain his position with reference to the national scale and to the even more abstract level of the market, Mark Taylor refers to his family, to the highly regulated nature of the British economy, to the common aspirations of European farmers and to the rights of Third World producers, including farmers in Mozambique.

Later in the same interview, Mark Taylor reasserts a sense of ethical complexity, objecting to what he calls the 'emotive language' of charities like Oxfam who accuse sugar farmers of 'scams' and 'dumping':

Then suddenly, out of the blue, we get another report, using the same emotive language – "dumping" and "scam" and all that. I mean, I'm not scamming anybody, but I have to live where I live and I have to, in the society I live in, and I have to abide by the rules that Tony Blair and Michael Howard and Ted Heath and all the politicians before them adopted for me. You know, we joined the EU and they all said it was a good thing to do this, and we didn't, I didn't push to join the EU or to, in order to receive three times the world price for sugar. I just grow, do the job well, hope the products will allow me to make a profit and plant again for next year. So when somebody who has never grown a sugar beet and never done anything other than political mouthing all his life starts saying that I'm a scammer and a dumper and a rotten so-and-so, I ought to be put out of business, I take it pretty badly I'll tell you. You don't know how that grates, you really don't.[32]

Again, there is a sense of personal indignation at the injustice of accusations that come 'out of the blue' and from 'somebody who has never grown sugar beet and never done anything other than political mouthing all his life'.[33] Mark Taylor defends his position by referring to his geographical context ('I have to live where I live' and 'I didn't push to join the EU').

Mark Taylor also attempts to construct a historical justification of his role in the British sugar industry, arguing that farmers have made a long-term commitment to a particular crop and that they are vulnerable to sudden changes in government policy:

I mean, I guess the market has always regulated what farmers do, but when a farmer chooses to do something, it's long term, not short term. You can't switch off milk production or stop growing in the middle of the term. Nor can you, when you've decided on a course of action, modified by the market that there is at the time that causes you to make the decision, you … it's not easy, once you've sort of stocked up and tooled up to grow that crop, made the investment, to just change.[34]

While British farmers have regularly switched crops as the regulatory regime has changed, there is some truth in Mr Taylor's argument about technological investment as an obstacle to rapid change and the environmental consequences of switching rapidly from a long-established pattern of crop rotation:

For me, growing sugar is part of the rotation on my farm. It's so essential that I have this break in the rotation. I grow cereals, I grow oilseeds, I grow sugar beet and I've formed a rotation that is balanced, it is good, it's good in every way from, it's good from an environmental point of view, it's good that it breaks the monogamous [sic]crop routine up, it breaks disease cycles, both pests and sort of plant diseases as well and it's desperately important. My whole life, my farming has been based on this rotation … I have my own drill, have my own sprayer. I have my own inter-row cultivators, cleaner loaders and mechanical loaders as well, so you know, there's a lot of money invested, even for me and I call myself a fairly small, small-to-medium, grower, lot of money invested ... which, as I say, for a politician, it matters not a jot. They make decisions without taking into account that the disaster for me on my farm would be the destruction of a rotation that I've cultivated and worked at for all my life and, you know, at the stroke of a pen it could disappear.[35]

Whether or not one believes the kind of ecological argument that Mr Taylor advances, in terms of 'a rotation that I've cultivated and worked at for all my life', there is a clear argument here about different time-scales: the long-term investment of a farmer in machinery and know-how versus the shorter time-scale of political expediency, which threatens to undermine these investments 'at the stroke of a pen'.

Several other respondents refer to historical arguments as a way of explaining current policies and practices, exonerating themselves from blame by insisting that they are simply working within a framework that has been set by others. So, for example, Charles Cockburn (b.1947, pseudonym), a sugar beet area manager from Norfolk, refers back to the First World War in his account of British Sugar's attempt to control sugar price fluctuations.

British Sugar was actually formed in 1935. There'd been some, a start around about the First World War and a lot of those enterprises kind of failed. Sugar traditionally has been very much at the whims of the world market and you get sometimes like, you go through Depression, you got a low price for actual raw sugar. But in 1935 the kind of Government said, well we can't go on like this, there was about, there was two major groups of factories I believe and one or two others and they all pulled them together and started to rationalize, there was an agreement to subsidize sugar production, from the point – I think that they could see the war coming – from the point of securing the sugar, you know sugar production in the country. So it was about 1935 that that really all came together. Before then you had been selling to individual companies.[36]

In another part of the same interview, Mr Cockburn refers to the very restricted scale of personal (bodily) responsibility in discussing the culinary and nutritional properties of sugar:

Sugar is a marvellous commodity because, you know, we've always tried to replace it with sweeteners and things, but nobody's ever come up with the same taste. It's a preservative, it's what they call a bulking agent. In other words, like if you're going to make a sponge cake and you didn't put sugar in it and you put a sweetener in it, you wouldn't get such a deep sponge cake. So it's got lots of added benefits other than just being a sweetener. I mean to say, there's nothing wrong with sugar, it's a matter of a balanced life.[37]

In this extract, Mr Cockburn seems to be arguing that sugar is not a health risk if eaten as part of a 'balanced' lifestyle. Sugar is a 'marvellous commodity', with 'lots of added benefits' that is not harmful in and of itself. This is very similar to the industry's defence that sugar is only unhealthy when eaten together with other fatty foods. So, for example, a senior industry figure argued that 'there's no link whatever' between sugar consumption and heart disease or cancer or diabetes: 'if you're talking about sugar by itself, there's quite a lot of evidence that actually sugar keeps you thin, not fat, because a fair amount of sugar intake actually kills the appetite. Sugar satiates; salt and fats don't.' This same (anonymous) respondent did, however, admit that the greater proportion of sugar is consumed alongside fat, a combination that he conceded was 'not perfect'.

Historical justifications are also advanced by those involved in the logistics of the sugar beet industry, in purchasing decisions and political lobbying. Here, though, the argument is usually couched in terms of the morality of the market, often considered at a more 'global' level than the more 'local' level at which the beet farmers quoted above are inclined to talk. Here, for example, is an argument about the way the EU is currently distancing itself from the African, Caribbean and Pacific producers, with the blame placed squarely on the prevailing market forces:

> [The ACP countries]look to the British government ... I think the question was about who was going to speak for them in Europe. And the answer is, they're really worried because they don't, they see the EU distancing themselves now from the historic links. We're speaking entirely ... when we say we don't care where the sugar comes from, we do care at the moment because these are our partners, we've been in partnership with them. But at the end of the day, if the EU said, you've got a liberalised market, we'll buy on the world market as cheaply as we can. It's this question of which market are we in.[38]

This is a classic case of the morality of the market, where sugar importing companies are concerned about their source of supply but only as a form of temporary partnership, where the terms of trade are set by external bodies such as the EU. In a 'liberalized' market such loyalties would dissolve and sugar importers would 'buy on the world market as cheaply as we can'.

The moral logic that underpins this geographical selectivity is complex. On the one hand, places are recognized as distinct, with unequal resources and differential access to world markets. The same interviewee continues:

> I don't believe in looking at things on a very broad brush global basis. You've got to look at each country. It's like people, they're all individuals with their individual history, their own problems, their problem parents, their problem siblings. Some people have some things going for them, the same as countries, and I think you've got to look at things individually and there are people, there are countries that could benefit from being in sugar and they ought to be given an opportunity. And I know this is a difficult one because it was very much the argument of Oxfam which is, small is beautiful. And it's not an argument we would wish to get into, or I would want to get into, on European

farming, but there is something to be said for it if you're looking around the world and at some sort of fragile countries with peculiar circumstances, you've got to look at them individually. I think, and I shouldn't say this, but I think some of the big money in Brazil, the likes of Brazil, they're not small companies, they're big agro-industrial private companies, very rich companies.[39]

The argument in this extract moves rapidly from the 'individual history' of different countries, some of whom 'could benefit from being in sugar', to a different argument that suggests that some developing countries, such as Brazil, may not be as 'fragile' as they are sometimes represented, with their economies dominated by 'very rich' agro-industrial companies.

Finally, the responsibilities of sugar-importing companies are described principally in terms of the rights of their shareholders and customers, with much less reference to any wider responsibilities where, even in the case of nationalized industries, the company 'can't go in and dictate to governments'. Consider how this argument is applied to the implementation of an ethical trading policy in countries like Swaziland or Zimbabwe:

I mean, we know there's no really bad practice. I mean the basic things we're concerned about are things like child labour. On the other hand, even Clare Short [Secretary of State for International Development from 1997 to 2003] – and we often quote this to our customers – even the Government, the most left-wing of ministers who you'd think would be against child labour. You know, she had a big sort of statement and it was on a website, she deplored it, condemned it and quite rightly, but pointed out that in some cases, it is better than starving. And that the way to deal with it is not to apply sanctions to someone who is using child labour, that's a symptom, go and deal with the root of the problem. What is causing people to have to use child labour? And deal with the problem, not the symptom. And it's a difficult one, because if you look at what happened to Gap and various other [companies], and Nike and one or two other big profile cases, whereby the brand has suffered immense damage because of issues of conditions of labour. So, we're now doing something about this. We're going ahead with care and very slowly because we can't dictate from the outside, we're not in a position to do it. But what we've got to do is work with them. I mean, for example the one area which is controversial and I warned them, I warned our people that there were some very difficult ones. For example there has been an international focus on Swaziland's arrangements for the free association of labour. We can't get involved in issues like this. What we want to continue to do is receive our sugar from Swaziland and let those who can deal with these issues which is in the international political arena, that's where they should be dealt with. So we're going into this area now, but it's very difficult … I remember when the company first of all introduced ethical trading, I buy sugar from Sudan, and I said will you tell me what I'm meant to do about female circumcision? I buy sugar from Fiji, what am I meant to do when Fiji operates outside its constitution, is kicked out of the Commonwealth and it's condemned internationally? … You've got to have an ethical trading policy now. But in our case, it's very, very difficult.[40]

The moral argument here is extremely complex, comparing the exploitation of child labour with the stark alternative of starvation. Ethical issues are weighed up in terms of potential damage to the brand (where firms like Gap and Nike are seen to have 'suffered immense damage'). Meanwhile, the ethical issues of supporting repressive governments that deny the right to free association of labour or who practice female circumcision are left to 'those who can deal with these issues'.

Towards a Relational View of Time, Space and Moral Responsibility

How then are we to make sense of these various arguments about geographies of responsibility and histories of connection? We propose to address these issues in terms of a relational understanding of the politics of place, space and scale. While this approach does not provide a blueprint for resolving the complex moral issues outlined above, it does suggest potentially new ways of thinking about the very unequal relationships that characterize the contemporary sugar industry and new ways of thinking about the potential connections that might be forged across space and time.

In the extracts above, we have seen how our respondents advance moral arguments and justifications in terms of scale (both temporal and spatial). Some processes are said to occur at a scale that is simply beyond the individual's ability to control (whether reflecting decisions taken in Brussels or practices whose histories stretch back to the Second World War or beyond). British sugar farmers clearly feel that they are vulnerable to political decisions that are taken on much shorter time-scales than their own (measured in terms of growing cycles, crop rotations, investments in technology or less tangible notions of inter-generational knowledge and experience). Similarly, sugar-importing companies claim to be powerless to intervene in the internal affairs of foreign governments (even in the case of nationalized industries); yet they have been extremely active in lobbying for favourable change to the EU sugar regime. It has often been argued that capitalist industries have the ability to 'jump scales' in order to benefit from accumulation opportunities in different places and to avoid the dangers of becoming excessively place-bound.[41] Several of the interviewees quoted above illustrate the benefits of jumping scales. Mark Taylor, for example, talked about the allegiances that have been forged between the National Farmers' Union, British Sugar and Tate & Lyle in articulating a common position with respect to the changing EU sugar regime. In other cases, sugar producers claim to be the victim of decisions taken elsewhere, as when Mark Taylor talks about his livelihood being put at risk at the stroke of a politician's pen. Many of the arguments rehearsed above see scale as a series of successive layers, moving outwards from the individual body through the nation to the globe. Thinking relationally about the *connections between scales* may offer an alternative to conventional thinking about the politics of space and place.

In her recent work, Doreen Massey has criticized those who argue that 'space' is abstract and that 'place' is real.[42] This distinction is often employed in arguments about globalization, where local places are pitted against one another and subject to the abstract forces of globalization. In these arguments, 'the global' is seen as active and 'the local' as passive, with globalization always understood as having been produced elsewhere, ungrounded in any specific locality.[43] Massey argues strongly against such conceptions of space and place, suggesting that we should approach the global *through the local*, recognizing the existence of many different globalizations, depending on the particular locality from which the global is viewed. Such a relational view of space might help us understand the dilemma of our East Anglian farmer, proudly standing in his field of sugar beet, and grappling with his sense of moral responsibility for distant strangers in Mozambique. A relational view of space and place would insist on the impossibility of separating the farmer in his field in East Anglia from the politics of EU sugar reform or of disentangling the economics of sugar production in the Third World from the politics of public health in Britain. So, for example, when the clergyman accused Henry Cross of being responsible for the impoverishment of West Indian cane farmers or the journalist accused Mark Taylor of responsibility for the plight of farmers in Mozambique, a relational view of space, place and scale might offer a different way of understanding these issues from the stark alternatives with which our respondents were faced. A relational way of thinking might also help us address the current inequalities that characterize the global sugar industry without changes in one place (the ACP countries, for example) adversely affecting those located elsewhere (such as UK sugar beet farmers). To do so requires us to understand how responsibilities are stretched across scales and over time in exactly the way that Massey describes.

A relational way of thinking sees places in terms of networks, flows and connectivities rather than as discrete entities operating in isolation at different spatial scales. Thinking relationally about space, place and scale involves new ways of approaching questions of political responsibility. Massey draws on the work of the feminist philosophers Moira Gatens and Genevieve Lloyd, who argue that 'We are responsible for the past not because of what we as individuals have done, but because of what we are.'[44] But while Gatens and Lloyd are interested in present-day responsibility for historical events, Massey employs the same way of thinking about our geographical responsibilities. Just as the past inheres in the present, Massey argues, so are distant places implicated in our sense of the 'here and now' leading to what she calls a politics of connectivity:[45]

> If the identities of places are indeed the product of relations which spread beyond them (if we think space/place in terms of flows and (dis)connectivities rather than in terms only of territories), then what should be the political relationship to those wider geographies of connection?[46]

What, then, are the practical implications of these rather abstract ideas? Massey's approach suggests a radically different understanding of the moral geographies of distance and connection than are at play in current government thinking about food and farming in the UK. For example, though the Curry Commission report on the future of food and farming – written in the wake of the recent Foot and Mouth epidemic – is couched in terms of 're-connection' and 'sustainability', its emphasis is on re-connecting farmers, retailers and consumers along the supply chain on the basis that greater cooperation among the various players is in the national (economic) interest.[47] Similarly, the Government's White Paper on *Modern Markets, Confident Consumers* is focused on providing individual consumers with the knowledge and information they need to make informed decisions about what to purchase on the basis that their decisions will, in aggregate, shape the market.[48] Massey's vision suggests a totally different way of approaching these issues. Relational thinking might not help individual farmers like Mark Taylor or Henry Cross to answer their critics; but it might provide a more productive way of thinking about the inter-connections between places and across time, once it is acknowledged that our political responsibilities are stretched out across space and time. Moralities that have their own logic at one scale (standing in a field of sugar beet in East Anglia) look very different when seen from another scale (as the journalist and clergyman referred to above sought to demonstrate). Rather than pitting one locality against another (whether it be in Britain or the Caribbean, East Anglia or Mozambique), a relational approach would seek to transcend 'the local'. Relational thinking refuses to see 'the local' as always the victim of global forces that originate elsewhere. Instead, it would take seriously the proposition that 'the global' and 'the local' are mutually constituted and that local places have agency within globalized systems of production.[49] Rather than abrogating responsibility for forces that are beyond our control, Massey argues, we need instead to analyse the specific forms of power that apply in each particular place and the specific locations from which 'global' forces derive their power.[50]

What might this mean in practice for our analysis of the British sugar industry? We suggest three specific points by way of conclusion. First, there is merit in making more transparent some of the complexities involved in the current EU sugar regime and the ongoing process of reform. The present system of tariffs, quotas and subsidies is highly complex, and can lead to obfuscation of the very real political and economic issues at stake. So, for example, Oxfam's campaigning stance in the run-up to the recent reforms of the EU sugar regime was criticized from within the sugar industry for failing to understand the wider ramifications of the proposed changes. The complexity of the current arrangements was such that Oxfam's original stance may actually have worked against the interests of some former British and French colonies that benefited from the existing arrangements.

Secondly, we would argue that health issues are currently disconnected from wider discussions about the politics of sugar production and that there are distinct benefits to be gained in terms of public health from reconnection. This issue was raised at the recent Environment, Food and Rural Affairs sub-committee meeting on the reform of the sugar regime. The Oxfam representative was asked why he was advocating that less developed countries should move into sugar production at a time when the more developed countries in the West were facing up to the health implications of excess sugar consumption. The Oxfam representative replied that 'we are development NGOs and we lobby for development concerns. We have taken on board the health concerns ... [but]our remit puts us as having to represent the interests of developing countries'.[51]

Finally, we would argue that there are potential benefits to the industry itself from reconnecting the politics of sugar production and consumption. Companies like Tate & Lyle and British Sugar will need to become much more astute in terms of customer relations, marketing and advertising as sugar subsidies reduce and as consumers become more aware of the kind of connections that have been described in this chapter (whether in terms of public health, global inequalities or political regulation). Besides its intellectual appeal, a relational view of space and place may actually have commercial benefits for the industry as well as for campaigning groups and the public health agenda.

This chapter has provided a case study of the moral geographies associated with the globalization of a single commodity. The production of sugar on a global scale clearly has a long history, dating back to the Napoleonic Wars in the case of the domestic production of sugar beet in Britain and earlier in relation to the production of sugar cane in Britain's former Caribbean colonies. Complex webs of connection across space, place and scale have developed, through the global expansion of businesses like Tate & Lyle and the regulatory regime developed by the EU and other transnational agencies. Drawing on our life history interviews with sugar producers at various points along the supply chain, we have demonstrated that these connections have moral as well as political and economic dimensions. We have also argued that approaching these questions through a relational understanding of space, place and scale provides a valuable perspective on the moral complexities involved in contemporary debates about globalization.

Notes

1. S. Mintz, *Sweetness and Power: The Place of Sugar in Modern History* (London, 1985), p. xxiv.
2. Mintz, *Sweetness and Power*, pp. xv–xvi.
3. S. Hall, 'Old and New Identities, Old and New Ethnicities', in A. D. King (ed.), *Culture, Globalization and the World-System* (London, 1991), pp. 327–42. The

global consumption of tea, coffee and other beverages is discussed by Clarence-Smith (this volume, Chapter 2).

4. For a discussion of the academic roots of the 'commodity chain' metaphor and an analysis of its contemporary mobilization in British food politics and policy, see P. Jackson, N. Ward and P. Russell, 'Mobilising the Commodity Chain Concept in the Politics of Food and Farming', *Journal of Rural Studies* 22 (2006): 129–41.

5. The project on which this chapter draws was funded by the ESRC-AHRC *Cultures of Consumption* programme (award no. RES-143-25-0026). It was a collaborative project, undertaken by the authors in association with Dr Rob Perks (National Life Stories, The British Library) and with research assistance from Dr Polly Russell. The wider project involves a comparison of the geographical imaginaries of two specific commodities (chicken and sugar). Thanks to Frank Trentmann and Alexander Nützenadel for their comments on a previous draft of this chapter and to Paul Kratoska, who served as discussant for the paper at the Food and Globalization conference in Cambridge.

6. P. Jackson, 'Commercial Cultures: Transcending the Cultural and the Economic', *Progress in Human Geography* 26 (2002): 3–18. See also P. Jackson, M. Lowe, D. Miller and F. Mort (eds), *Commercial Cultures: Economies, Practices, Spaces* (Oxford, 2000).

7. On the concept of 'moral geographies', see D. M. Smith, *Moral Geographies: Ethics in a World of Difference* (Edinburgh, 2000). For an introduction to the politics of 'caring at distance', see J. Silk, 'Caring at a Distance', *Ethics, Place and Environment* 1 (1998): 165–82. For a critique of these ideas, see C. Barnett, P. Cloke, N. Clarke and A. Malpass, 'Consuming Ethics: Articulating the Subjects and Spaces of Ethical Consumption', *Antipode* 37 (2005): 23–45 and Trentmann (this volume, Chapter 14).

8. Jenny Linford interviewed by Polly Russell 14 December 2005 C821/38/14 Transcript p. 41.

9. Anonymous industry informant interviewed by Polly Russell 7 April 2004 C821/***/01.

10. See, for example, the special issue of *New Internationalist* on 'The Sugar Trap' (December 2003).

11. The EU sugar regime was reformed in December 2005. The reforms included a 39 per cent cut in the guaranteed price to EU producers (phased in over four years), accompanied by substantial compensation payments to farmers and a restructuring fund to enable firms to shift to other forms of production.

12. J. Yudkin, *Pure, White and Deadly: The Problem of Sugar* (London, 1972). By contrast, the whiteness of sugar has been credited with connotations of purity and esteem. See, for example, S. Mintz, *Tasting Food, Tasting Freedom* (Boston, 1996), p. 89.

13. See, for example, *The Great EU Sugar Scam* (Oxfam Briefing Paper 27, 2002); K. Watkins and P. Fowler, *Rigged Rules and Double Standards: Trade, Globalisation and the Fight against Poverty* (Oxfam Campaign Reports, 2003); and *An End to EU Sugar Dumping?* (Oxfam Briefing Note, August 2004).

14. S. O'Connell, *Sugar: The Grass that Changed the World* (London: 2004), pp. 108–9.

15. H. Marks and D. Britton (eds), *A Hundred Years of British Food and Farming: A Statistical Survey* (London, 1989), p. 47.

16. B. Pimlott, *Harold Wilson* (London, 1992), pp. 432–4; S. George, *An Awkward Partner: Britain in the European Community* (Oxford, 1994, 2nd edition), pp. 51–2.

17. R. Fennell, *The Common Agricultural Policy: Continuity and Change* (Oxford, 1997), pp. 373–4.

18. AgraEurope, 2 December 2005, p. 5. On the history of Tate & Lyle, see P. Chalmin, *The Making of a Sugar Giant: Tate & Lyle 1859–1989* (London, 1990).

19. Court of Auditors, 'Special Report No 20/2000 Concerning the Management of the Common Organisation of the Market for Sugar', *Official Journal of the European Communities* 2001/C 50/01.

20. Commission of the European Communities, *Reform of the European Union's Sugar Policy: Summary of Impact Assessment Work*, Commission Staff Working Paper (Brussels, 2003).

21. For an introduction to life history interviewing, see P. Thompson, *The Voice of the Past: Oral History* (Oxford, 1978) and R. Perks and A. Thompson (eds), *An Oral History Reader* (London, 2nd edition, 2006).

22. The full set of interviews (subject to the interviewees' consent) is available via The British Library online catalogue, accessible at http://www.bl.uk/collections/sound-archive/nlsc.html#food.

23. Henry Cross, interviewed by Polly Russell, 8 December 2003, C821/117/02 Transcript, p. 59.

24. Henry Cross, C821/117/04 Transcript, p. 92.

25. This monopolistic arrangement is criticized by charities like Oxfam, who argue that words such as 'efficiency' and 'competitiveness' have no place in discussions about the sugar sector. According to Kevin Watkins (Head of Research at Oxfam), 'there isn't a market – one company has the entire UK beet market', while the government protects against imports, facilitates exports and oversees a monopoly through the operation of the quota system (C821/159/01 Transcript, p. 11).

26. Henry Cross, C821/117/05 Transcript, p. 168.

27. Henry Cross, C821/117/02 Transcript, p. 67.

28. Henry Cross, Transcript, p. 67.

29. Henry Cross, Transcript, p. 68.

30. Mark Taylor (pseudonym), interviewed by Polly Russell, 21 April 2004, C821/**/04.
31. Ibid.
32. Mark Taylor, C821/**/03.
33. Ibid.
34. Mark Taylor, C821/**/01.
35. Mark Taylor, C821/**/02.
36. Charles Cockburn (pseudonym), interviewed by Polly Russell, 15 March 2004, C821/**/01.
37. Charles Cockburn, C821/**/04.
38. Anonymous industry informant, interviewed by Polly Russell, 4 May 2004, C821/**/07.
39. Anonymous industry informant, C821/***/08.
40. Anonymous industry informant, 28 July 2004, C821/***/10.
41. On the politics of scale, see N. Smith, 'Homeless/Global: Scaling Places', in J. Bird, B. Curtis, T. Putnam, G. Roberston and L. Tickner (eds), *Mapping the Futures: Local Cultures, Global Change* (London, 1993), pp. 87–119.
42. D. Massey, 'Geographies of Responsibility', *Geografiska Annaler* 86B (2004): 5–18.
43. Massey, 'Geographies of Responsibility', p. 14.
44. M. Gatens and G. Lloyd, *Collective Imaginings: Spinoza, Past and Present* (London, 1999), p. 81.
45. Massey, 'Geographies of Responsibility', p. 17.
46. Massey, 'Geographies of Responsibility', p. 11.
47. 'Re-connection' is the pervading motif of the Curry Commission's report on *Food and Farming: A Sustainable Future?* (London, 2002).
48. *Modern Markets, Confident Consumers* (DTI, 1999).
49. Compare Kevin Watkins' argument for Oxfam that 'globalization is neither inherently good or bad, it depends on how you organize it' (K. Watkins and P. Fowler, *Rigged Rules and Double Standards: Trade, Globalisation and the Fight against Poverty* (Oxfam Campaign Reports, 2003), p. 24).
50. Massey, 'Geographies of Responsibility', p. 14.
51. Oral evidence presented to the Environment, Food and Rural Affairs Sub-Committee on the Reform of the Sugar Regime (26 April 2004), Q84.

-14-

Before Fair Trade

Empire, Free Trade and the Moral Economies of Food in the Modern World

Frank Trentmann

Can moral communities be created and sustained across distance? Globalization has disrupted space and time, making us aware of the porous nature of place and identity. The international trade in food in particular has given physical and symbolic expression to 'caring at a distance', in debates about the lengthening of the food chain and the sympathy of consumers for distant producers, and vice versa. Within this broad set of questions, 'Fair Trade' has emerged as a test case of the changing moralities of space.

This chapter takes this renewed interest in the spatial ethics of consumption as a starting-point to explore more generally the changing moral imaginaries that have come with the lengthening of the food chain in the modern period. In the last decade, geographers have performed a moral turn just as historians have entered a 'spatial' turn, but these developments have more often resulted in divergence than in a shared conversation, in spite of the many potentially shared research questions and approaches. Geographers have inquired into the social justice of geographical differences and the moral construction of communities without proximity. Yet while the literature on Fair Trade has engaged with contemporary ethics and theory, it has side-stepped the historical genealogies of such consumption practices.[1] Historians, meanwhile, have traced the creation of maps and territoriality, and of the rise of geopolitics, but here the focus has been more on how societies were fenced in, mentally and geopolitically, and less on the norms and practices that opened up connections across space.[2] Transnational histories have been concerned with finance, institutions, and technologies, rather than ethics. Moral philosophers, by contrast, have rigorously debated our commitments to distant others, but, outside feminist inquiries into caring and philosophical interventions on the issue of famine,[3] this tends towards abstract reasoning, divorced from past values and practices.

My aim in this chapter is to explore the changing moral geography of trade and consumption over time by bringing these moral, spatial, and historical considerations together. Whether the globalization of the food system and the advancing distance between consumers and producers undermines reciprocity or facilitates new moral connections is not a new question. Its history is as long as the history of globalization itself. Already in seventeenth-century Holland about one-third of people's food came from afar.[4] Food became part of a fully integrated global economy in the late nineteenth century; by 1913 food made up 27 per cent of world exports.[5] Observers at the time wondered about the implications of this stretching of the food chain for feelings of care between producers and consumers; curiously, they worried as much about producers' caring for distant consumers as the other way around.

Where it has been addressed at all, the history of caring consumers has been written in a progressive mode. The current phenomena of Fair Trade and boycotts of sweated goods can be placed in a line stretching back to anti-slavery boycotts, cooperative movements, and buyers' leagues campaigning for better working conditions.[6] The point of this essay is not to distract from these precursors, but to argue that a simple progressive narrative ignores alternative and ambivalent moralities at play in the modern world. This has included an imperial project of caring for distant producers as well as Free Trade and progressive projects of international distributive justice. The roots of this blindness, I argue, can be traced to an intellectual tradition that has seen modern trade and consumption as opposed to an older customary form of 'moral economy'. Talk of contemporary 'remoralization' or of ethical consumerism as a 'new' terrain of politics presumes that earlier modern societies were somehow less morally equipped. Yet consumers and social movements have throughout modern history played an integral role in the creation of global markets and imperial systems. In the earlier wave of globalization a century ago, radical and liberal consumers in Britain rallied to the defence of Free Trade. After the First World War, conservative housewives began a mass crusade for Empire Fair Trade. I hope that greater attention to these ambivalent moralities will be of use to those reflecting on consumption as a way of caring for distant others today.

Precursors: Ethical Praxis and Imperial Consumers

Fair Trade began with a network of 'alternative trade organizations' in Western Europe and the United States in the 1960s and 1970s and then took off internationally in the 1980s and 1990s. The Fair Trade model encompasses a range of practices that seek to replace exploitative with beneficial terms of exchange between Southern producers and Northern consumers. The certification of 'Fair Trade' products offering producers a 'fair price' has spread from coffee and bananas to tea, sugar, chocolate, orange juice and beyond. Between 2002 and 2003 alone, global sales of Fair Trade products increased, from US$600 million to US$895 million. Currently the Fair Trade network is benefiting over 800,000 farmers in 500 producer groups in fifty-eight countries.[7] While its economic impact remains small – in 2002 Fair Trade products made up a mere 0.1 per cent of the US$3.6 trillion of goods exchanged in the world – Fair Trade has established itself across the North as a transnational social movement, with shops, festivals, campaigns, and national and international organizations.

Geographers studying Fair Trade have seen it as a new form of cosmopolitan ethics responding to the increasingly stretched relationship between consumers and producers. From an instrument of exploitation, trade is transformed into a vehicle of global solidarity. '[F]air trade represents the founding of a nascent international moral economy.' It is seen as 'promoting a "critical consumer culture" which challenges the individualistic, competitive and ethically impoverished culture of capitalism'.[8] Others have commented on the 'growth of ethical consumption as a new terrain of political action'.[9]

The precise workings of Fair Trade for producers and consumers are, of course, a subject of debate. Fair Trade may have improved the lives of many producers. But these new connections between Northern consumers and Southern producers have been constructed through uneven cultural representations. Fair Trade involves the cultural 'embedding' of consumers in the lives of distant farmers, at times exoticizing Southern producers.[10] Reconciling the commercial and ethical side of Fair Trade has never been easy. The language of the 'critical consumer' caring about distant others may be campaign language rather than an identity in practice.[11] Arguably, too, the mediating role of money and the physical distance between consumer and producer limit its potential as a caring practice. While buying a Fair Trade coffee may be a sign of 'caring for', it fails several other criteria identified by theorists of caring, including the physical work of 'care-giving' and a deep knowledge of a recipient's situation.[12] Finally, it could be asked whether Fair Trade is able to redress the significant inequalities of 'good fortune' that exist in an unequal world. It may simply reinforce the ability to care amongst more fortunate consumers in the North while failing to overcome unequal life-chances in the South.

These are important questions; but here I am concerned with widening the historical frame in which this discussion is conducted. Fair Trade emerged from a longer genealogy of morally motivated consumer politics and practices. The use of purchasing or boycotting to benefit one's community goes back to the American Revolution, and even to ancient times. It would be wrong, however, to see moral consumerism as the preserve of anti-imperialist movements. Here I want to start by retrieving two more recent precursors that shaped that moral landscape in the 1920s–1940s: buying for Empire campaigns and the movements for a 'just' world food plan. They complicate the conventional chronology where 'caring at a distance' is instinctively located in the 'stretching out' of communities and the increase of global exchanges in the 1980s–1990s, and follows on an age of affluence. Caring for distant others with one's purse is not the preserve of affluent post-modern shoppers, nor the novel outcome of the current age of globalization.

In Britain, many grandparents of today's ethical consumers would have been familiar with the idea of expressing care for distant producers via campaigns to 'Buy Empire Goods'. Formally, Britain was a Free Trade nation from the 1840s to

1931.[13] But the years after the First World War saw a growing movement to promote empire goods. An Empire Marketing Board was established in 1925. As important as this government-sponsored propaganda were efforts within civil society. In 1922 the British Women's Patriotic League first conceived of an Empire Shopping Week to celebrate Empire Day (24 May). The enormous Empire Exhibit in Wembley in 1924–5 mixed empire product exhibits with the thrills of an amusement park – 'bigger and more exciting than Coney Island and all the amusements sections of previous British exhibitions put together'.[14] In the Palace of Industry, the housewife could learn 'the right methods of thawing frozen meat from New Zealand, of soaking Australian dried fruits to make delicious summer dishes, and with many other interesting hints that will encourage her to introduce Empire dishes and Empire food into her own domestic programme'.[15] An estimated 30 million people saw the 'miniature Empire' at Wembley.

Figure 14.1 Two Women at an Empire Produce Stall in Driffield, Yorkshire. *Source: Home and Politics*, January 1925, p. 1. Reprinted with permission of the British Library.

The hub of this Conservative imperial consumerism was the Women's Unionist Organization, which reached one million members by 1928.[16] They organized empire cake competitions, canvassed shopkeepers to stock and label empire goods, and offered 'surprise Empire boxes' – the 5s. box included peaches, currants, tea and rice, as well as honey, salmon, spaghetti, sugar, pineapple slices, raisins, and prunes.[17] In association with the Empire Marketing Board and local retailers, they organized shop-window displays of Empire Goods. In 1930, in the midst of the world depression, over 200 Empire Shopping Weeks took place across Britain; there were also events in Canada and Jamaica. Empire processions, pageants, dinners, exhibits, lantern lectures and travelling cinema vans advertised the lusciousness of Australian sultanas and New Zealand honey. Posters by the Empire Marketing Board were sent to 25,000 schools. The campaign percolated through an expanding leisure and communication culture. Football fans at the 1927 Wembley Cup Final faced an enormous banner exhorting them to Buy British Empire goods. An estimated 12 million people encountered Buy British films in 1,000 cinemas.[18] But imperial consumerism also drew on the homemade cultural effort of suburban conservatism and women's clubs. One enterprising Conservative woman, Miss L. V. Sutton of Finchley in North London, even dressed up in a costume made of imperial products, not quite, perhaps, equal to matching the seductive charms of Carmen Miranda, but still enough to win her three first prizes.[19]

In Oxford, Empire Day in 1927 was celebrated with stalls for different Dominions that personalized products and makers in ways that anticipate what later would be called 'emotional branding'. As with the campaign in general, White farmers and their products from the Dominions were central. Canada's stall displayed bread, flour, grain; Australia's, tinned food as well as dried fruit. Kenya had a coffee-making demonstration 'and sample cups of coffee were much appreciated'.[20] But native products were displayed, too. From India there was brass and copper ware as well as foods, from Africa, native handwork, beads and trinkets. Here were precursors to the Traidcraft shops and FairTrade coffee that would spring up half a century later.

These mainly middle-class and upper-class Conservative housewives did not, of course, follow a universalist conception of beneficence. Yet, if they did not care equally about all distant strangers, they certainly envisaged an ethical connection linking metropolitan consumers with White producers in the Dominions of Australia, New Zealand and South Africa. As a non-contiguous geographic structure, the British empire did not fit territorial conceptions of community – Carl Schmitt, the German theorist of geopolitics and critic of liberal democracy, saw Britain as 'unmoored', 'turning from a piece of land into a ship or even a fish'.[21] This is what distinguished the Empire buying campaign from earlier nationalist product campaigns, whether in the American colonies in the mid-eighteenth century or in early twentieth-century China. The Buy Empire campaign bridged the furthest spatial, economic, and emotional distances of the global food system at the time.

Figure 14.2 Miss L. V. Sutton as 'Empire Products'.
Source: Home and Politics, August 1926, p. 16.
Reprinted with permission of the British Library.

Imperial consumerism explicitly appealed to some of the same values that philosophers associate with the ethics of care – 'sensitivity, responsiveness, and taking responsibility'.[22] Much more than in Fair Trade campaigns today, the 'Buy Empire Goods' movement looked to housewives as primary consumers and extended the relational ethics of maternal caring for children and home first to compatriots in Britain, and then beyond to distant members of the imperial family. Mrs Hudson Lyall, a member of the London County Council, explained why women should support the protection of British industry and preference for imperial goods: 'Because just as women realize that their own families have first claim on them, so we apply the same reasoning to our Country, and are prepared to protect the labour of our fellow-countrymen when need arises.' This duty to protect and practise reciprocity stretched to the distant Dominions. Like a mother putting her family before herself, consumers of empire products would express imperial care. 'True' Conservative housewives were not selfish, but understood the need to reciprocate, explained Anne Chamberlain, the wife of Neville, the future Prime Minister, in 1924. '[E]very white person in South Africa', for example, bought £3 5*s*. 11*d*. worth of British goods, but people in the United States only 10*s*. 9*d*. 'Are we to take all and give nothing? Surely not. The idea of Empire service makes a more certain appeal to women than the selfish bluntness of a question that asks, "What has the Empire done for *me*?"'.[23]

In the long run, Conservatives hoped, increasing imperial production would also lower prices; but the main argument, not dissimilar from that of Fair Trade today, was that value went beyond market price, to include welfare, solidarity, and public health. Dominion farmers 'need our practical help in purchasing fruits which they grow as a means of livelihood. We need these products of their labour for our health and well-being'.[24] As consumers, housewives became 'Empire builders'.[25]

The promotion of Empire goods wove together cleanliness, race, and standards of production. Empire fruit was grown and packed by 'competent and clean people', advocates stressed; Australian irrigation settlements were models of 'purity and cleanliness'.[26] A Merchandise Marks Act was passed in 1926 to distinguish British and imperial products from foreign rivals. In exposés consumers learnt of the 'sweet, clean and carefully packed dried fruits of Australia and South Africa' in contrast to the 'dirty' sultanas from Turkey, where 'bare-footed workers ... tramped freely over the fruit': 'This brown man was very dirty. His feet had certainly not been washed for a long period.'[27]

The connections between this imperial culture and current global food systems and cultures of consumption may be more significant than is often recognized. The export of baby vegetables from sub-Saharan Africa since the 1980s is a case in point. Here Northern retailers have imposed ethical and hygienic standards on producers that recent scholars have described as a 'neocolonial civilizing mission': ethical trade speaks to the growing food anxieties of affluent consumers, carrying echoes of earlier colonial crusades for Christian cleanliness.[28]

My point is not that there is a direct line between this kind of racial stereotyping and the ethical consumerism of more recent years – although the exoticizing of Southern farmers should not be underestimated. Yet, as a genre, the Buy Empire Goods campaign occupies an intermediary stage towards Fair Trade, representing to consumers the conditions of distant farmers, making visible social and cultural values (such as hygiene), and certifying origins and setting standards that seek to bridge the distance between consumers and producers. Moral consumerism, then, was not just a tool of anti-imperial struggles, like Gandhi's well-known campaigns, but could serve imperialist projects.

The imperial ethics of consumerism raise some difficult issues for a historical evaluation of Fair Trade as well as for the moral philosophical inquiry into caring at a distance more generally. Here I can only raise two points.

First, caring relationships can involve multiple social and cultural roles, and broader or narrower circles of inclusion or universality. The relational connection can draw on a sense of being a parent, consumer, producer, patriot, and so forth, or a mix of these. Consumerist campaigns, like those of Buy Empire Goods in the interwar years or Fair Trade more recently, are not pure, neutral vessels, but mobilize political traditions and value-systems that favour certain identities and relationships. For Imperial housewives a sense of reciprocity was always framed by familialism. It was not just that it was fair to buy the products of Dominion farmers, since they bought British goods (on that count British consumers should also have bought from other major foreign trading partners). They were family, and their welfare needed to be protected. Imperial consumerism here shows parallels with Fair Trade, which, in spite of its name, is strictly speaking also concerned with questions of justice and welfare rather than fairness in terms of reciprocity. Fair Trade may have broadened the scope of caring for others, beyond Empire and race, and included considerations of human rights. At the same time, it has also narrowed other identities. The caring in Fair Trade envisages a Northern consumer and a Southern producer. But people in the South are also consumers. And, likewise, there are few people in the North (rich rentiers or welfare recipients excepted) who are not also producers or their dependants. In this sense, Fair Trade may replicate and internationalize the uneven, hierarchical politics of early consumer leagues in the United States and Europe that introduced 'white labels' in the fight against sweating a century ago. These leagues similarly mobilized an exclusive idea of the 'consumer', urging middle-class 'consumers' to favour certain shops and products to improve the lot of lower-class 'producers'.[29] Caring is not a relationship between equals, as feminist theorists have pointed out.

Second, Empire is a reminder that, historically, caring for distant others is not limited to caring for strangers. In the debate over whether obligation diminishes with distance many philosophers proceed via concentric circles. Those closest to us, like family and friends, occupy the innermost circle normally seen to generate the strongest sentiment. Next come compatriots. Then the outlying circles contain distant strangers. Even those who argue against 'the compatriot principle' – the idea that our obligations to compatriots are necessarily stronger than to non-compatriots – tend to collapse compatriots with proximity and strangers with distance.[30] But to begin with a conception of a 'compatriot/non-compatriot border' may be unhelpful in the context of global modernity, with regard not only to transnational networks today but also to empires in the past. Partiality can be a special concern for those emotionally close but geographically distant from us, as well as for those geographically close to us. We may want to consider a more reciprocal spatial model that can take account of the back-and-forth between imperial metropole and colonial peripheries across vast distances – diasporas and other transnational communities would be other examples.

Towards Global Distributive Justice

The ethics of trade and consumption did not follow a unilinear path from local to national/imperial to global connections. Rather, national and imperial visions stood in tension and dialogue with other international traditions of distributive justice. In Britain, the two main rivals were an older tradition of Free Trade and an emergent progressive vision of trade coordination that sought to balance social welfare within states with the needs of the world community. While Free Trade was steadily losing ground in the inter-war years, a new vision was gaining support in the labour and cooperative movements and amongst progressives and international civil servants. Plans for international food coordination culminated in the Food and Agriculture Organization during the Second World War. Proposals for a World Food Board were cut short by the Cold War, but they nonetheless revealed a new conception of global obligations. Sections of Northern consumers, especially in the cooperative movement, began to see consumers and producers as linked together in one shared system. Hunger ceased to be a foreign country. Food security and social justice at home required global action.

The new internationalist vision wove together social democracy, nutrition, trade stabilization, and global citizenship. In Britain, the First World War blew apart what had been the dominant alliance between civil society, liberal and progressive politics, and unregulated Free Trade. Organized consumer movements, like the four-million-strong cooperatives, emerged from the war disillusioned with unregulated trade, demanding the control of basic foodstuffs. Across Europe, labour and social democratic parties increasingly looked to the state to guarantee basic food at stable prices.[31]

Fluctuating food prices sharpened awareness of the interdependence between consumers and producers. They created cycles of profiteering and uncertainty, threatened social peace and economic balance, and fuelled a protectionist 'beggar-thy-neighbour' climate. Malnutrition in Europe co-existed with overproduction and the destruction of food overseas. Only international action to help distant producers combined with domestic steps to help malnourished consumers could give everyone enough of the kinds of food needed for healthy development. As the League of Nations report on *The Relation of Nutrition to Health, Agriculture, and Economic Policy* emphasized in 1937, nutritional policy had to be directed at increasing both consumption and production.[32]

The Second World War provided an institutional opening for this symbiotic view of consumers and producers. Two years after the Allies promised 'freedom from want' in their Atlantic Charter, the Hot Springs conference in May/June 1943 proposed international action to boost world agricultural production and consumption. The Food and Agriculture Organization (FAO) was never given the chance to fulfil its founding mission to eradicate world hunger. Key food producers like the Soviet

Union and Argentina were absent. And proposals for a world food board were sabotaged by an alliance of powerful states and empires (the USA and Britain) and producer interests.

Yet underneath this policy failure, it is possible to trace an expanding global conception of distributive justice. For groups like the cooperatives, the war broadened the sense of global interdependence. In films like 'World of Plenty' (1943), Allied propaganda connected an earlier maternalist vision of the virtuous circle between healthy mothers and babies and strong soldiers and citizens to a vision of distributing food from one part of the world to another according to need. The end of the Second World War saw increasingly vocal opposition to rationing and controls, especially from conservative housewives, but also from sections of the working class.[33] At the same time it also showed strong support for a world food policy amongst cooperative and labour women. A higher standard of living in Britain, in this view, depended on more 'conscious cooperation between the rich nations and the poor'. Consuming nations had to stop exploiting cheap colonial labour. Food-producing nations had to stop taking advantage of shortages, but they also should not 'be victimised by unreasonably low prices in times of abundance'.[34]

Persistent malnutrition in Western Europe created a sense of the equivalence of the problems across the globe. To give all people in the world a healthy diet, the Women's Cooperative Guild told its members in 1948, world production needed to be increased significantly above pre-war levels, by 100 per cent in milk, 163 per cent in fruit and vegetables, 80 per cent in pulses, and 46 per cent in meat. Britons, too, needed to consume 57 per cent more milk and 70 per cent more fruit and vegetables than before the war. World food policy was a problem for everyone. Even as the global food supply was rising in the 1950s, the early World Food Surveys by the FAO for the first time put a number to the underfed.[35] By the mid-1950s hunger and deprivation were presented by British cooperators as a normal condition of humanity, not an exceptional problem of underdevelopment outside the West.[36]

This marked a seismic mental shift. British responses to the Indian famine of 1876–8, for example, had overwhelmingly seen 'scarcity' as an Eastern problem. If there was some philanthropy, there was little sense of a shared responsibility, let alone of a shared food system. Cooperative 'speaker notes' and study circle materials for the 1940s and 1950s show the jump to a more global ethics. As the cooperatives' notes on the FAO put it in 1955:

> Fifty years ago would anyone have *thought* about a WORLD food problem? When famine struck India, or the potato blight struck Ireland, other people heard of *India's* or *Ireland's* food problem. They were sympathetic and sent what help they could. But they didn't think about a *world* food problem that the WORLD should do something about solving.[37]

The sense of a shared problem, then, was already being formulated a generation before the 'world food crisis' of 1972–5.[38]

This mid-twentieth century evolution of global sympathy and distributive justice did not develop in isolation from Empire, however. International plans for food security ran directly into a wall of opposition where international agencies threatened existing imperial power. In the Bengal famine, where millions starved to death in 1943–4, the British government refused assistance from the United Nations Relief and Rehabilitation Administration (UNRRA). Not surprisingly, colonial nationalists saw a double moral standard at work in Allied ideals of 'Freedom from Want'. But the Empire also supplied stepping stones towards the new internationalist vision. Advocates of trade coordination, like E. M. H. Lloyd, had worked at the Empire Marketing Board. In food and trade policy, as in trusteeship and the use of an international police force, there were connections between international governance and Empire.[39]

The growing sense of mutual obligations came with a turn to global civil society. FAO emphasized the role of cooperatives for mutual aid, knowledge, and democratic development. It forged contacts with the International Cooperative Alliance and the All-India Cooperative Union. It promoted the transnational exchange of local knowledge. Latin Americans showed Ethiopians how to produce more coffee, Chinese experts gave advice to Afghans on their silk industry. Leading officials in the FAO's Rural Welfare Division stressed the importance of a 'social approach' to economic problems, and of building up social capital rather than relying on technology or capital investment.[40]

For social movements, too, global food policy was a project of democratic renewal. For the British cooperative movement, which reached its peak in the 1940s with over eight million members, the Food and Agriculture Organization promised to widen the scope of civil society by sidestepping centralized nation-states. FAO seemed a global self-help cooperative formed by 71 governments to increase consumption, distribution and production. 'The very idea of a democratic world order', the *Co-operative News* reflected in 1943, 'implies that the ordinary citizen, who is often scarcely equal to mastering local or national affairs, will have to understand the workings of great international structures.' Only in the cooperative movement would they find the universal principles 'which can link in one continuous line of thought the local with the global ... enabl[ing] the peoples to dominate the vast administrative and economic machines on which their lives and livelihood depend'.[41]

Free Trade

Progressive support for a world food policy and conservative campaigns for 'Buy Empire Goods' can be seen as two rival projects for bridging distance and reconnecting consumers and producers. Their rising fortunes reflected the rapid decline of an older moral vision of international exchange and reciprocity, that of Free Trade. In the course of the 1920s–1930s that older vision was driven from the centre of democratic culture which, in Britain, it had occupied for much of the modern period. Such has been the historic rupture with Free Trade that most social movements and commentators today find it impossible even to think of ethics, civil society, and Free Trade in the same frame. Much of the case for Fair Trade derives its strength from the suspicion that Free Trade is a selfish creed of multinationals, an idea of economists and not of the people. This antithesis ignores the ambivalent moral geography of modernity.

Freedom of trade was never without its critics in the modern period; but in parts of the Western world, especially in Britain, it was something akin to a national ideology. A century ago, it commanded support from leading figures in the working-class, radical, feminist and peace movements, as well as from sections of trade and finance. From the Repeal of the Corn Laws in 1846 to the popular defence of the 'cheap loaf' in the early twentieth century, Free Trade was supported for offering cheap food to the people, as well as for strengthening Britain's export industries and financial services. But to contemporaries it was about much more than economics. Free Trade was a source of ethics, civilization, and human progress. For many, the very 'purity and intensity of public spirit' depended on it, as the young Bertrand Russell put it: he felt 'inclined to cut my throat' if tariffs won.[42] Free Trade was firmly tied to the Christian ethics of the Golden Rule, which has been seen as the moral basis of reciprocity. A manual worker, for example, rallied to the defence of Free Trade in the Edwardian period because tariffs were 'an immoral policy' that 'substitutes "Do unto others as *they do unto you*," for the Golden Rule, "Do unto others *as ye would* they SHOULD do unto you"'.[43] As radicals tirelessly pointed out, Free Trade favoured non-discrimination within a society as well as between societies. Under free trade, unlike protectionism, groups did not enjoy privileges such as tariffs or subsidies, which were seen as the source of oligarchy, social anarchy, and imperialism. Internationally, it would promote good will by not discriminating in favour of one country at the expense of another. Support for Free Trade and the critique of militarism were two sides of the same coin for most radicals, ethicists, and Quakers.[44]

Radical feminists, like those in the Women's Cooperative Guild, still excluded from the national vote and from the male-dominated world of the Cooperative Congress, looked to Free Trade as a guardian of civil society and a step towards full citizenship. In Britain, but also in Belgium and Chile, organized workers saw an affinity between Free Trade and social welfare reforms. Consumer groups felt that Free Trade would strengthen the other-regarding mentality of 'citizen consumers', who would think about the impact of their consumption on producers, creating a virtuous circle of higher taste, higher quality, better working conditions and greater well-being.

This is not to suggest that the world operated according to these ideals. The historical reality was full of contradictions. Free Trade did not eliminate poverty, nor did it necessarily protect consumers. Cobden's ideal of peaceful, interdependent civil societies was premised on a hierarchical view of the world, with some countries developing as commercial, others as more agricultural societies. Free Trade, too, attracted support from imperialists. Robert Cecil, the son of the Conservative Prime Minister, Salisbury, and one of the founding fathers of the League of Nations, saw Free Trade as vital to Britain's imperial mission, because it kept money out of imperial relations and fostered trust. Yet, for all its blind spots, Free Trade was for many about an emotional engagement with those in need, precisely what recent moral philosophers have reclaimed as a vital part of caring practices.[45]

In recent debates, commerce and care are frequently located in a gendered divide between public and private spheres. In this view, modernity produces a split

Figure 14.3 A prize-winning Free Trade poster, 1904. *Source*: Robert Morley, National Liberal Club (1905)

between a public, male-dominated world of trade and justice, on the one side, and a female private world that becomes the domain of caring on the other. Food riots in eighteenth-century France and early twentieth-century America have received considerable attention as moments where a 'maternal terrain' of food provisioning and caring spilled over into the public arena.[46] Here it is market failure or the pressure of an expanding market system that threatens mothers' role as carers. Moral economy responds to the challenge of a market-driven political economy.

But this was not the only direction in which morality flowed in the modern world. In global food systems, consumers have also been able to envisage a quite different relationship between public and private ethics. Before the First World War, it was Free Trade and open markets that represented a maternalist ethic of caring. In millions of leaflets and posters, Free Traders defended open markets as saving mothers and their children from starvation. The maternal iconography later associated with social democracy was developed in popular political economy. Free Trade recognized housewives as consumers, part of a public interest, as well as mothers tending to the private sphere. Instead of undermining an ethic of care, an open market appeared as its conduit, connecting civic and private worlds of reciprocity and justice.

Moral Economies

In their respective 'moral turns', Western consumers and academics tend to draw on shared views of the essentially amoral, instrumentalist nature of modernity. In human geography and moral philosophy the recent concern with 'remoralizing' the economy often proceeds from an assumption that modernity saw the unfolding of capitalism at the expense of empathy and social solidarity.[47] After Adam Smith, one social theorist has argued, there was a 'moral devaluation of economic practice'.[48] Some philosophers of caring look to government to 'foster caring connections between persons and [to place]limits on markets that undermine them'.[49] As far as I have been able to see, there is little awareness that for large chunks of modernity people, goods and services have been mobile, and that many men and women looked to commercial exchange as a vehicle of civil society.

Part of the dilemma arises from a stark dichotomy between customary morals and modern markets. The portrayal of a 'moral economy' that became associated with pre-modern societies continues to find echoes in appeals to 'remoralize' global trade today. For some, Fair Trade promises a 'new moral economy'.[50] Irrespective of the vast differences between the global commercialized food system of the early twenty-first century and the eighteenth-century world of customary tradition and relatively closed communities pictured in E. P. Thompson's immensely influential portrayal of pre-industrial food riots, 'moral economy' has remained a powerful framework for discussions of fairness, justice and solidarity.[51] 'Modern' society is pictured as a demoralizing system, in which commerce, individualism, and instrumental action replace custom, sympathy, and reciprocity. For all his insistence on the historical specificity of eighteenth-century English food riots, Thompson's case study also expressed broader ideas about the essence of commercial modernity and the 'impersonal', inauthentic and corrupting force of consumerism. To Thompson there were 'universal' aspects both to the moral vision of the fair price and to the 'confrontations of the market' in pre-industrial societies.[52] Political economy had unleashed a universal process of demoralization, replacing social bonds and reciprocity with 'impersonal', self-regarding, and ultimately immoral consumerism. Post-industrial ethical consumerism appears to restore a moral dimension lost in the transition from pre-industrial to industrial society. There are echoes here of Karl Polanyi's *The Great Transformation* (1957), which inspired social historians and social scientists, with its action–reaction model of an expanding a-social system of liberal markets calling forth a response from social movements and social protection.[53]

These grand contrasts have proved as problematic for peasant societies as for commercial ones. Against the narrative of a single universal transition from peasant to modern society, anthropologists have stressed the role of religion, colonial rule, and values in different contexts. In 1930s Burma and Vietnam, for example, colonial governments lacked legitimacy and peasants rebelled when the world demand for rice dropped. In Siam, by contrast, there were no uprisings, partly because the moral legitimacy of the constitutional monarchy was stronger. Instead of shared customary views of obligation, revisionists have pointed to ethnic and ecological divisions. Nor are 'traditional' societies free of power or profit-motives. Peasants, like those in twentieth-century Bengal, have been characterized as '*both* moral econ-omizers and rational maximisers'.[54] On the other hand, cash and caring also exist in a symbiotic relationship in modern life, as in childcare and parenting.[55] Markets do not automatically erase morals.

Evaluations of what commerce does to caring often work with implicit assumptions about some greater ability to care for those geographically close to us. History is full of cases that raise doubts about such general contrasts. Food protests in nineteenth- and early twentieth-century Germany, for example, may have invoked a customary language of the 'fair price', but were also sites in which housewives attacked Jewish neighbours, pregnant women or soldiers' wives – little practised empathy there for compatriots during the First World War.[56] Nor did pre-industrial 'moral economy' necessarily show a lot of empathy for distant others. The rural blockades in 1795 England, for example, were a direct threat to the industrial populations of the Midlands, which depended on long-distance food. In twentieth-century Bengal, heads of families responded to famine by abandoning their dependants and selling their children for cash. To what degree the victims acquiesced in these responses has been debated,[57] but there can be little doubt that moral economies operate with different degrees of sympathy in different contexts. Scarcity does not automatically trigger a caring instinct or preserve social solidarities, any more than affluence automatically leads to indifference.

It is important to recognize the moral dimensions of sympathy, reciprocity, and social justice that 'political economy' carried forward into the modern period. The eighteenth century was not a turning point from a moral economy to a demoralized science of commerce. Adam Smith drew on the Augustinian theologian Pierre Nicole as well as on Pufendorf and Aristotelian notions of virtue. For Nicole, commercial sociability was a divine plan to push people towards closer cooperation. Reciprocity and interdependence in international exchange, in other words, had their origin in a conception of man as vulnerable and sinful, not as an all-knowing, autonomous or 'reflexive' consumer, as popular notions would have it today. For Smith, commercial man's morality was artificial; but it nonetheless helped build social bonds and dependence between people across unprecedented distance.

Growing awareness of social distance in the eighteenth century undermined the more organic belief in civic virtue as a guide to moral action that had characterized republican thought. Morality and politics became divorced. Trade and travel simultaneously loosened a sense of natural sympathy and mutual dependence between those nearby and raised the question of how trust and human feeling could be sustained across long distances. Smith doubted it was possible for an individual to relate to the entire world, but at the same time he identified new sources of concern connecting distant others. On its own, sympathy favoured those closest to us, Smith argued – it was our sense of propriety, of being considered proper by others, that drove moral sympathy. How then was it possible to show concern for people far away? Smith developed two answers, one looking to reason, the other to commerce. It was 'not the soft power of humanity ... that feeble spark of benevolence' that was capable of countering the 'strongest impulses of self-love', as Smith put it in the *Theory of Moral Sentiments*, as he pondered how a European might respond to the news of China's being swallowed up by an earthquake. 'It is reason, principle, conscience' – the qualities of the 'impartial spectator' – that steered people's responses.[58] Reason was complemented by commercial sociability and trust. Commerce built trust between distant others out of a shared self-interest in a fair deal and mutually respected codes of behaviour. Commercial sociability now went beyond both the more immediate, proximate bonds of love and friendship stressed by Hutcheson and the society of fear imagined earlier by Hobbes.[59]

Like the 'moral economy' school in the 1960s and 1970s, the recent focus on remoralizing trade tends to imagine modern history as the substitution of one social system (tradition) by another (modernity). The shift from moral economy to demoralized political economy appears as part of a larger transition from closeknit, cooperative communities to more open, fluid, and impersonal commercial societies, or from *Gemeinschaft* to *Gesellschaft*.[60] Such a sequential model of historical systems, however, is fraught with problems. In fact, for Ferdinand Tönnies, who originally developed the concepts in the 1880s, *Gemeinschaft* and *Gesellschaft*, and the different norms and practices they involved, were locked in tension across time, not isolated in successive historical eras.[61] More recently, Deirdre McCloskey has argued that we should credit modern capitalism for improving ethics, creating new virtues, peace, and refinement.[62]

A sequential view of social systems also distracts from the evolution of political economy into a variety of social and political projects. Political economy was not static. In the hands of Condorcet and Thomas Paine in the 1790s, Smith's model of free commerce became connected to an embryonic social democratic programme of greater social equality and civic inclusion.[63] This programme was defeated by the reaction generated by the French Revolution. Still, moral and social dimensions remained integral to liberal political economy as it developed in the nineteenth century. For many devout early Victorian evangelicals, Free Trade was acting out a divine plan.[64] To fail to support it amounted to moral failure; indeed, it might postpone the Millennium. For Alfred Marshall, the single most influential person for the professional development of economics, ethics was part of economics.[65]

These moral values were not just the stuff of high-minded writers, but percolated through popular movements. The popular support for Free Trade mentioned above showed that ideas of freedom of commerce and international reciprocity could be combined with ideas of civil society, social justice, and maternal nurture. Moralities of consumption are always specific to time and cultural context, and are mediated by other existing moralities and power. The early-nineteenth-century boycotts of slave-grown sugar, for example, were not a Fair Trade prototype. Many critics of slavery supported the expansion of imperial authority in other spheres. Caring for distant others, through missionary activism, an attack on indigenous practices, or the boycott of goods, was steeped in hierarchies of race and gender.[66] The women who boycotted slave products did so through a gendered set of values that placed women above and outside the marketplace and emphasized the corrupting potentialities of goods.[67] Gendered hierarchies were essential to the propensity to feel empathy, a good example of the mix of inequality and conflict that runs through the history of caring.

Conclusion

In the original turn to 'moral economy', E. P. Thompson criticized the 'condescension of posterity' towards the eighteenth-century artisan. Now, over three decades later, we are running the risk, not of condescension, but of indifference to the moral imaginaries of the past. Discussions of 'caring at a distance' and Fair Trade are mostly conducted in a historical vacuum. If the initial appeal of 'moral economy' in the social sciences was to rescue the food riot and 'the poor' from crass economic reductionism, the danger now is that the lived moral practices of modern commercial societies are becoming all but forgotten outside the historical community.

In this chapter I have tried to steer the discussion away from a simple contrast between rival systems, and between action (soulless capitalism) and reaction (ethical consumers), to suggest that current norms and practices of ethical consumerism are part of a longer genealogy. Fair Trade has emerged from the soil of historically changing moral landscapes. These have included not only the anti-slavery and cooperative movements, but also ideas of Empire and Free Trade and progressive ideas of global social justice. The ideas and practices of the men and women who shaped this ethical field deserve recognition. To conduct the debate about 'Fair Trade' in bipolar terms of markets versus morals is problematic. It fails to see that globalizing commerce and consumption have been moralized throughout modernity, and it is blind to more complex forms of moral reflection about trade and sympathy. As recent work on responses to suffering at a distance in our own media-saturated society suggests, such older languages of morality and 'the spectator' are far from obsolete.[68]

The ambivalence of the moral geographies of trade and global food systems raises broader questions of agency, authenticity, and material culture. Thinking in terms of a divide between 'moral economy' and 'political economy' triggers a whole series of contrasts between community and commerce, authentic worker and inauthentic consumer, slow food and fast food, and so forth. Many of the anxieties about consumption can be traced back to European and American debates about the corrosive effects of luxury and spending on private morals and public life in the eighteenth and nineteenth centuries; indeed, some can be traced to ancient Greece.[69] But the lives people have led in the modern world do not fit these tight ideal-typical containers. Across the world there have been many cycles of commodification and decommodification, fast food and slow food, public engagement and private withdrawal.[70] Ethnographic studies have shown that shoppers also care about their families.[71] We should neither presume that material goods erode caring, nor ignore the possibility that some people in developing societies may care more about goods than about relatives or friends. In the real world, most people take part in a multitude of slow and proximate, middle-range, and fast and distant food systems. These have historical trajectories that reach back to earlier phases of globalization in the seventeenth and eighteenth centuries. The moralities of these food systems have been as ambivalent as their material dynamics. Fair Trade needs to be viewed as their historical result, not just as a new moral beginning. Consumers played as important a role in the construction of an integrated global food system as large-scale agro-industries.

A historically sensitive inquiry into the genealogies of Fair Trade suggested here complicates a simple progressive narrative. Caring at a distance does not grow in a linear fashion, nor is it the recent discovery of heroic affluent consumers. Students of developing societies have observed the 'shrinkage of the circle of moral expectations and attributions' that occurs during times of scarcity and famine.[72] Similarly, we may want to ask about the extension of a circle of sympathy and reciprocity at different moments in the modern period. These extensions have not always taken the same shape or direction. Some are wider than others, but equally the trend is not all in the same direction. Recent movements like Fair Trade have involved a narrowing of certain social identities and relationships as well as a geographic widening. The point, then, is not that the commercial world lacks morals and hence needs to be remoralized. It is precisely because modern commerce has generated far-reaching powerful morals that it deserves our attention if we want to understand the potential and limits of caring at a distance today.

Acknowledgements

Earlier versions of this chapter were presented at the workshops on 'Food and Globalization' at the Netherlands Institute of Advanced Studies and at Cambridge, England. For a longer discussion, see *Environment and Planning D* (2007). I am grateful to participants for discussion, as well as to Heather Chappells, Jim Livesey, Sara Ruddick, William Ruddick, Vanessa Taylor, and Nigel Thrift. This work has been assisted by research grant L143341003 from the Economic and Social Research Council and the Arts and Humanities Research Council (Cultures of Consumption programme), which is gratefully acknowledged.

Notes

1. D. M. Smith, *Moral Geographies: Ethics in a World of Difference* (Edinburgh, 2000); P. Cloke, 'Deliver Us From Evil? Prospects for Living Ethically and Acting Politically in Human Geography', *Progress in Human Geography* 26(5) (2002): 587–604.
2. C. S. Maier, 'Consigning the Twentieth Century to History: Alternative Narratives for the Modern Era', *American Historical Review* 105(3) (2000): 807–31; J. Osterhammel, 'Die Wiederkehr des Raumes: Geopolitik, Geohistorie und historische Geographie', *Neue Politische Literatur* 43 (1998): 374–97.
3. J. C. Tronto, *Moral Boundaries: A Political Argument for an Ethic of Care* (New York, 1993); P. Singer, 'Famine, Affluence, and Morality', *Philosophy and Public Affairs* 1 (1974): 229–43; O. O'Neill, *Faces of Hunger: An Essay on Poverty, Justice and Development.* (London, 1986); V. Held, *The Ethics of Care: Personal, Political, and Global* (Oxford, 2006).
4. J. de Vries, *The Dutch Rural Economy in the Golden Age, 1500–1700* (New Haven, CT, 1974).

5. K. O' Rourke, '*Long-Distance Trade: Long-Distance Trade between 1750 and 1914*', in J. Mokyr (ed.), *Oxford Encyclopaedia of Economic History* (Oxford, 2003), Vol. 3, pp. 365–70.

6. C. Sussman, *Consuming Anxieties: Consumer Protest, Gender and British Slavery, 1713–1833* (Stanford, CA, 2000); E. Furlough and C. Strikwerda (eds), *Consumers Against Capitalism? Consumer Cooperation in Europe, North America, and Japan, 1840–1990* (Lanham, MD, and Oxford, 1999); and M. Micheletti, 'The Moral Force of Consumption and Capitalism: Anti-Slavery and Anti-Sweatshop', in K. Soper and F. Trentmann (eds), *Citizenship and Consumption* (Basingstoke, 2007), Chapter 8.

7. See www.fairtrade.org.uk, 6 March 2006; www.globalexchange.org/campaigns/fairtrade/, 27 March 2006; A. Nicholls and C. Opal (eds), *Fair Trade: Market-driven Ethical Consumption* (London, 2005).

8. G. Fridell, 'Fair Trade and the International Moral Economy: Within and Against the Market', in T. Shallcross and J. Robinson (eds), *Global Citizenship and Environmental Justice* (Amsterdam/New York, 2006), p. 86.

9. C. Barnett, P. Cloke, N. Clarke and A. Malpass, 'Consuming Ethics: Articulating the Subjects and Spaces of Ethical Consumption', *Antipode* 37(1) (2005): 23–45, cited at p. 41.

10. R. L. Bryant and M. K. Goodman, 'Consuming Narratives: The Political Ecology of Alternative Consumption', *Transactions of the Institute of British Geographers* 29(3) (2004): 344–66.

11. See R. Sassatelli, 'Virtue, Responsibility and Consumer Choice: Framing Critical Consumerism', in J. Brewer and F. Trentmann (eds), *Consuming Cultures, Global Perspectives* (Oxford, 2006), pp. 219–50.

12. Tronto, *Moral Boundaries*, pp. 104–7.

13. F. Trentmann, *Free Trade Nation: Commerce, Consumption and Civil Society in Modern Britain* (Oxford, 2008); S. Constantine, '"Bringing the Empire Alive": The Empire Marketing Board and Imperial Propaganda, 1926–33', in J. M. MacKenzie (ed.), *Imperialism and Popular Culture* (1986), pp. 192–231.

14. *Home and Politics*, May 1924, p. 10.

15. *Home and Politics*, May 1925, p. 14.

16. M. Pugh, *Women and the Women's Movement in Britain, 1914–1999* (Houndmills, 2000), p. 125.

17. *Home and Politics*, October 1924, p. 23.

18. Constantine, 'Empire Marketing Board,' p. 210.

19. *Home and Politics*, August 1926, p. 16.

20. *Home and Politics*, July 1927, p. 84.

21. Cited in Osterhammel, 'Wiederkehr des Raumes', p. 381, my translation.

22. Held, *Ethics of Care*, p. 119.

23. *Home and Politics*, August 1924, pp. 7f. Emphasis in original.

24. *Home and Politics*, June 1925, p. 2.

25. *Home and Politics*, December 1924, p. 8.
26. *Home and Politics*, December 1924, p. 15.
27. *Home and Politics*, June 1925, p. 4.
28. S. Freidberg, 'Cleaning up down South: Supermarkets, Ethical Trade and African Horticulture', *Social and Cultural Geography* 4(1) (2003): 27–44, at p. 35; T. Burke, *Lifebuoy Men, Lux Women: Commodification, Consumption, and Cleanliness in Modern Zimbabwe* (1996).
29. K. K. Sklar, 'The Consumers' White Label Campaign of the National Consumers' League, 1898–1918', in S. Strasser, C. McGovern and M. Judt (eds), *Getting and Spending: European and American Consumer Societies in the Twentieth Century* (Cambridge, 1998); M.-E. Chessel, 'Women and the Ethics of Consumption in France at the Turn of the Twentieth Century,' in F. Trentmann (ed.), *The Making of the Consumer: Knowledge, Power and Identity in the Modern World* (Oxford and New York, 2006), pp. 81–98.
30. G. Brock, 'Does Obligation Diminish with Distance?', *Ethics, Place and Environment* 8(1) (2005): 3–20, cited at p. 3. Peter Singer's expanding circle of moral concern, however, is driven by diminishing prejudice (rather than increasing empathy).
31. C. Nonn, 'Vom Konsumentenprotest zum Konsens', in H. Berghoff (ed.), *Konsumpolitik: Die Regulierung des Privaten Verbrauchs im 20. Jahrhundert* (Göttingen, 1999), pp. 23–45; F. Trentmann, 'Bread, Milk and Democracy: Consumption and Citizenship in Twentieth-Century Britain', in M. Daunton and M. Hilton (eds), *The Politics of Consumption: Material Culture in Europe and America* (Oxford, New York, 2001), pp. 129–63.
32. *Final Report of the Mixed Committee of the League of Nations on The Relation of Nutrition to Health, Agriculture and Economic Policy* (Geneva, 1937), p. 34.
33. I. Zweiniger-Bargielowska, *Austerity in Britain: Rationing, Controls, and Consumption, 1939–1955* (Oxford, 2000).
34. J. Bailey, *Co-Operators in Politics* (Manchester, 1950), p. 14.
35. D. Grigg, 'The Historiography of Hunger: Changing Views on the World Food Problem', *Transactions of the Institution of British Geographers* 6 (1981): 279–92.
36. F. Trentmann, 'Coping with Shortage', in F. Trentmann and F. Just (eds), *Food and Conflict in Europe in the Age of the Two World Wars* (Basingstoke, 2006), pp. 13–48.
37. University of Hull Archives, Cooperative Notes for Speakers, FAO 55/3/1806, topic 1 (1). Emphasis in original.
38. C. Gerlach, 'Die Welternährungskrise 1972–1975', *Geschichte und Gesellschaft* 31 (2005): 546–85.
39. K. Grant, P. Levine, and F. Trentmann (eds), *Beyond Sovereignty: Britain, Empire, and Transnationalism, c.1880–1950* (Basingstoke, 2006).

40. FAO Archive (Rome), RG39.0.D1, 'The Work of the FAO in the Development of Cooperatives', 4 April 1950. FAO, *Report of Technical Meeting on Cooperatives in Asia and the Far East* (November 1949). FAO Archive (Rome), RG 39 A. 2514 and 2611, H. Belshaw to the Director General of the FAO, Noriss Dodd, 4 June 1949 and 17June 1949; RG 39 1 A1, H. Belshaw to the Director General of FAO, Dr. Cardon, 29 July 1954.

41. *Co-operative News*, 18 September 1943.

42. Russell to Lucy Donnelly, 29 July 1903, in C. Moorehead, *Bertrand Russell: A Life* (London, 1992), p. 141.

43. W. Glazier in J. Cobden Unwin (ed.), *The Hungry Forties* (1904), p. 212 (emphasis in original).

44. F. Trentmann, 'National Identity and Consumer Politics: Free Trade and Tariff Reform', in P. K. O'Brien and D. Winch (eds), *The Political Economy of British Historical Experience, 1688–1914* (Oxford, 2002), pp. 215–42.

45. P. Singer, *Practical Ethics* (Cambridge, 1979).

46. O. Hufton, 'Women in Revolution 1789–1796', *Past and Present* 53 (1971), pp. 90–108; D. Frank, 'Housewives, Socialists and the Politics of Food: The 1917 New York Cost-of-Living Protests', *Feminist Studies* 11(2) (1985): 255–85; T. Kaplan, 'Female Consciousness and Collective Action: The Case of Barcelona, 1910–1918', *Signs: Journal of Women in Culture and Society* 7(3) (1982): 545–66.

47. Smith, *Moral Geographies*, pp.108 f.

48. A. Sayer, 'Moral Economy and Political Economy,' *Studies in Political Economy* 61 (2000): 79–104.

49. Held, *Ethics of Care*, p.119.

50. Fridell, 'Fair Trade and the International Moral Economy', p. 4.

51. E. P. Thompson, 'The Moral Economy of the English Crowd in the Eighteenth Century', *Past and Present* 50 (1971): 76–136; E. P. Thompson, 'The Moral Economy Reviewed', in his *Customs in Common* (London, 1991), pp. 259–351; J. Scott, *The Moral Economy of the Peasant: Rebellion and Subsistence in Southeast Asia* (New Haven, CT, 1977); J. Bohstedt, 'The Moral Economy and the Discipline of Historical Context', *Journal of Social History* 26(2) (1992): 265; M. Gailus, 'Food Riots in Germany in the Late 1840s', *Past and Present* (45) (1994): 157.

52. Thompson, 'Moral Economy', pp. 134f.

53. Karl Polanyi, *The Great Transformation: The Political and Economic Origins of Our Time* (New York, 1944); cf. M. Bevir and F. Trentmann (eds), *Markets in Historical Contexts: Ideas and Politics in the Modern World* (Cambridge, 2004).

54. P. R. Greenough, 'Indulgence and Abundance as Asian Peasant Values: A Bengali Case in Point', *Journal of Asian Studies* 42(4) (1983): 831–50, cited at p. 833.

55. V. A. Zelizer, *The Purchase of Intimacy* (Princeton, NJ, 2005).
56. Gailus, 'Food Riots'; B. J. Davis, *Home Fires Burning: Food, Politics, and Everyday Life in World War I Berlin* (Chapel Hill, NC, 2000); M. H. Geyer, 'Teuerungsprotest, Konsumentenpolitik und soziale Gerechtigkeit während der Inflation: München 1920–1923', *Archiv für Sozialgeschichte* XXX (1990): 181–215.
57. Greenough, 'Indulgence and Abundance as Asian Peasant Values: A Bengali Case in Point'.
58. Adam Smith, *Theory of Moral Sentiments* (London, 1759), III. 3. 4 and 3. 5; Tronto, *Moral Boundaries*, pp. 45–50.
59. I. Hont, *Jealousy of Trade: International Competition and the Nation-State in Historical Perspective* (Cambridge, MA, 2005)
60. E.g., Smith, *Moral Geographies*, p. 33.
61. J. Harris, 'Tönnies on "community" and "civil society"', in M. Bevir and F. Trentmann (eds), *Markets in Contexts* (Cambridge, 2004), pp. 129–44.
62. D. N. McCloskey, *The Bourgeois Virtues: Ethics for an Age of Commerce* (Chicago, IL, 2006).
63. E. Rothschild, *Economic Sentiments: Adam Smith, Condorcet, and the Enlightenment* (Cambridge, MA, and London, 2002); G. Stedman Jones, *An End to Poverty?* (London, 2004).
64. B. Hilton, *The Age of Atonement: The Influence of Evangelicalism on Social and Economic Thought, 1795–1865* (Oxford, 1988).
65. H. Pearson, 'Economics and Altruism at the Fin de Siècle', in M. Daunton and F. Trentmann (eds), *Worlds of Political Economy: Knowledge and Power in the Nineteenth and Twentieth Centuries* (Basingstoke and New York, 2004), pp. 24–46.
66. K. Grant, *A Civilised Savagery: Britain and the New Slaveries in Africa, 1884–1926* (New York, 2005); C. Hall, *Civilising Subjects: Metropole and Colony in the English Imagination, 1830–1867* (Oxford, 2002); A. Porter, 'Trusteeship, Anti-Slavery, and Humanitarianism', in A. Porter, *The Oxford History of the British Empire: The Nineteenth Century* (Oxford and New York, 1999), pp. 198–221.
67. K. Davies, 'A Moral Purchase: Femininity, Commerce and Abolition, 1788–1792', in E. Eger and C. Grant (eds), *Women, Writing and the Public Sphere: 1700–1830* (Cambridge, 2000), pp. 133–59; Sussman, *Consuming Anxieties*.
68. L. Boltanski, *Distant Suffering: Morality, Media and Politics* (Cambridge, 1999).
69. J. Davidson, *Courtesans and Fishcakes: The Consuming Passions of Classical Athens* (New York, 1999); M. Berg and H. Clifford (eds), *Consumers and Luxury: Consumer Culture in Europe 1650–1850* (Manchester, 1999); M. Hilton, 'The Legacy of Luxury: Moralities of Consumption Since the Eighteenth Century', *Journal of Consumer Culture* 4(1) (2004): 101–23; D. Horowitz, *The Morality*

of Spending: Attitudes Towards the Consumer Society in America, 1875–1940 (Chicago, 1992).

70. R. Wilk, *Fast Food/Slow Food: The Cultural Economy of the Global Food System* (Lanham, MD, 2006).

71. D. Miller, *The Dialectics of Shopping* (Chicago, 2001).

72. A. Appadurai, 'How Moral Is South Asia's Economy?: A Review Article', *Journal of Asian Studies* 43(3) (1984): 481ff.

Index

Lightning Source UK Ltd.
Milton Keynes UK
171509UK00001B/19/P